The
Vegetarian
Cook's Bible

Pat Crocker

Robert
ROSE

For complete cataloguing information, see page 373.

Disclaimers
The Vegetarian Cook's Bible is intended to provide information about the preparation and use of
whole foods and whole food ingredients. It is not intended as a substitute for professional medical
care. The publisher and authors do not represent or warrant that the use of recipes or other information
contained in this book will necessarily aid in the prevention or treatment of any disease or condition,
and specifically disclaim any liability, loss of risk, personal or otherwise, incurred as a consequence,
directly or indirectly, of the use and application of any of the contents of this book. Readers must assume
sole responsibility for any diet, lifestyle and/or treatment program that they choose to follow. If you have
questions regarding the impact of diet on health, you should speak to a health-care professional.

The recipes in this book have been carefully tested by our kitchen and our tasters. To the best of our
knowledge, they are safe and nutritious for ordinary use and users. For those people with food or other
allergies, or who have special food requirements or health issues, please read the suggested contents of
each recipe carefully and determine whether or not they may create a problem for you. All recipes are
used at the risk of the consumer.

We cannot be responsible for any hazards, loss or damage that may occur as a result of any recipe use.

For those with special needs, allergies, requirements or health problems, in the event of any doubt,
please contact your medical adviser prior to the use of any recipe.

Design and Production: PageWave Graphics Inc.
Editor: Carol Sherman
Recipe Editor: Jennifer MacKenzie
Contributor: Paulina Zettel
Proofreader: Sarah Silva
Indexer: Gillian Watts
Photography: Colin Erricson and Mark T. Shapiro
Food Styling: Kate Bush
Prop Styling: Charlene Erricson
Illustrations: Kveta

Cover image: Tomatoes Stuffed with Basil and Shiitake Mushrooms (see recipe, page 265)

We acknowledge the financial support of the Government of Canada through the Book Publishing
Industry Development Program (BPIDP) for our publishing activities.

Published by Robert Rose Inc.
120 Eglinton Avenue East, Suite 800, Toronto, Ontario, Canada M4P 1E2
Tel: (416) 322-6552 Fax: (416) 322-6936

Printed in Canada
    2 3 4 5 6 7 8 9 TCP 15 14 13 12 11 10 09 08

Contents

To Gary McLaughlin
for his humor and patience
and for helping me see the world
through the eyes of an artist.

Acknowledgments

Thanks go to naturopathic doctors Anthony Godfrey and Don Crosby, who both gave me their time and thoughts on how people can use food to stay healthy. Paulina Zettel did a superb job writing the Healthy Body Systems section. My editor Carol Sherman is fun and obviously enjoys the creative process of building cookbooks. She knows how to keep me and about one hundred other things on track, and does so with wit, humor and sincere talent. Thanks Carol for keeping the process sane and professional. Jennifer MacKenzie's attention to detail has been much appreciated as the recipes underwent her most capable scrutiny and testing. Sally Keefe-Cohen takes care of the business end of the creative process for me, balancing sensitivity and professional acumen.

The recipes for this book are a result of a beautiful journey of collaboration. My friends and family stepped up and tasted, commented and shared insights. Thanks to all for joining my vegetarian odyssey. Rita Salmon, chair, The Herb Society of America Baton Rouge Unit, shared her recipe for Almond Spread with me while we were touring a garden near Columbus Indiana in the summer of 2006. Like a recipe angel, John Monaghan saw what needed to be done and turned his capable head and hands to testing, tasting and tweaking. His steadfast and gentle nature helped when the going got tough. Thanks also to Yosuke Iwase for searching out food markets across the globe in order to bring me wasabi and miso from Japan, coffee from São Paulo and fine British cheddar cheese.

Writing a book of this size took a huge chunk out of my life and in the process I missed seeing the faces or hearing the voices of people I love to be with. I thought a lot about the following people as I withdrew and immersed myself in the work.

KC Compton, editor-in-chief of *The Herb Companion* and *Herbs for Health* magazines and Julia Woodford, publisher of *Vitality* magazine for giving me the space I needed to get the job done. Susan Belsinger and Tina Marie Wilcox, the garden imps, for Women-Spirit Listening. Claudia Wisdom-Good for offering me a world perspective. Chuck Voigt for reminding me to "gut it out and give us what we want." My daughter Shannon McLaughlin, because you are never far from my heart. Laurie Dearie-Bruce and Krista Dearie, because you joined me in the kitchen when you were small, and now we still share our lives through food. Lori and Dave Schaeffer for sharing their love of books, food and hard work.

Foreword

You can change the world one meal at a time.

That's what the David Suzuki Foundation has learned from our research. There are many actions individuals can take to protect nature, but it turns out, it begins with making better choices in our daily routine.

The kitchen is a great place to make positive changes in our lives. Making better food choices can do much to lighten the load on nature. Then by sharing with family and friends around your dinner table, the reasons why you are making these choices can lead to a ripple effect that will provide a better future for our children and the planet.

The average meal travels about 1,500 miles (2,400 km) from the field to your table. While this is an impressive feat, it's also a dangerous one. All that food transport results in emissions that are changing our climate and the quality of life in our cities. By choosing locally produced food, you'll be supporting farmers in your community as well as enjoying seasonal variation in your meals. There's also evidence that locally produced food is healthier, as well.

Vegetarian meals are also an important way of conserving energy, land and water. They also taste great! You'll find tasty recipes throughout *The Vegetarian Cook's Bible* that are easy to make, healthy for you and better for the environment. Who knew protecting nature could be so easy and so delicious?

Ann Rowan
Director, Sustainability Program,
David Suzuki Foundation
www.davidsuzuki.org

September 2006

Introduction

More than anything else, our way of eating dictates our ability to resist disease and enjoy good health. Studies on the traditional diets of Asians, Mediterranean people, Pima Indians in Arizona, and other aboriginal societies all confirm that their rates of modern diseases are significantly lower as long as they maintain their traditional diet, which typically includes a wide range of plants and is low in red meats and fats.

It is well known now that as stress increases in our lives, our immunity decreases. An even more disturbing fact is that as our lives become more pressured, our ways of nourishing ourselves usually become more reliant upon fast, unnatural foods — foods that offer no help in building up our immune responses. In fact, as life gets more complicated, we often suffer a double whammy — high stress and poor nutrition — and consequently, a downward spiral into poor health.

This book speaks to balance and harmony — the attitudes and practices that keep humans whole in body, spirit and mind. And it is no coincidence that many of the recipes have an Asian flavor because with its focus on the whole body in general, and the immune system in particular, the Oriental approach to food and health is a practical, non-invasive way of prevention through the yin-yang principle. Indeed, the Chinese Emperor Shen Nung (circa 2300 BC), believed to be responsible for the yin-yang theory, advocated the use of food, plants and herbs as medicine.

There are many different philosophies that support a vegetarian diet, but for me, the most convincing reason to eat more plant food in place of animal foods and saturated fats is simply that it is healthful. Science has shown that beta-carotene, vitamins C and E, phytonutrients, fiber and minerals all play important roles in preventing disease and all are found in abundance in a wide variety of plant food. On the other hand, those substances shown to aggravate disease — saturated fat, cholesterol, excess protein and excess sodium — all abound in animal foods.

This book is proof that a vegetarian diet is rich, varied and delicious. Cooking with the rainbow of natural, whole foods opens up more choices and combinations than the meat-potato-vegetable staples of an animal-based approach. It allows for a seasonal, less expensive pantry of ingredients and a spontaneous and simple way of preparing them.

A table covered with wholesome food, surrounded by faces we love is one of the threads that weave magic into the fabric of our lives. We eat to nourish our cells and we share meals with family and friends to nourish our lives. By taking an interest in the way our food is grown and processed and in the way it is handled and prepared, served and enjoyed, we take back responsibility for not only our nourishment and health, but also that of the planet. And that alone is a powerful act.

Use this book to learn how to eat cruciferous vegetables and protect against colon cancer. Try my personal favorite, Warm Mushrooms with Goat Cheese, and read about the research that shows how shiitake mushrooms bolster the immune system. Taste the difference fresh chopped garlic and ginger make to dips and sauces while lowering cholesterol and fighting infections.

You can start preventing health problems with your next trip for groceries. Using recipes from this book, you can increase plant-based whole food in every meal and truly find personal balance and harmony in food choices. Start now to decrease animal-based and refined food in your diet and see if you can feel the difference in your body and mind. I'm sure you will agree with me: it all makes delicious sense.

Eat well — Be well, Pat Crocker
www.riversongherbals.com

Healthy Body Systems

Healthy Living

Today, the big killers in Western societies are the cancers, cardiovascular disease, diabetes and hypertension, most of which are preventable by diet. Immunity and obesity play a role in either reducing or elevating disease, and they in turn are both affected by the foods we eat.

Doctors, scientists, naturopaths, nutritionists and medical herbalists all agree: to be healthy and prevent disease, a healthy lifestyle is essential. Following these guidelines will maintain and help restore good health:

Guidelines to Good Health

- Limit alcohol consumption — post-menopausal women who drink less than one drink per day can decrease the risk of dying of breast cancer by up to 30%
- Exercise — moderate daily physical activity can lower cancer risk, boost the immune system, help prevent obesity, decrease estrogen and insulin growth factor (IGF), improve overall health and emotional well-being
- Do not smoke — smoking is related to one-third of all cancers and 80% of all lung cancer
- Eat well — a healthy diet is the best defense against disease.

Guidelines to Eating Well

- Eat a minimum of five servings of fruit and vegetables every day
- Focus on the most colorful fruit and vegetables, such as red peppers, dark greens, oranges, carrots, apricots, blueberries
- Choose whole grains over processed grains and white flours

- Limit refined carbohydrates, such as pastries, sweetened cereals, soft drinks, candy, salty snacks
- Cook with olive or organic canola oil
- Avoid trans-fats found in many margarines, baked and convenience products
- Limit intake of saturated fats and cholesterol found in meats and dairy products
- Add avocados, natural nuts, seeds, cold water fish (cod, sardines, salmon) to the diet
- Control portion sizes

The body may be characterized by seven major systems: Cardiovascular (the heart and its components); Digestive (stomach, pancreas, bowels); Endocrine (glands and hormones); Immune (protective cells); Musculoskeletal (muscles, bones, joints, connective tissue); Nervous (the brain, spinal cord and nerves); and Respiratory (nose, trachea, bronchial tubes, lungs). Each system has a role to play in keeping the body disease-free. And each system responds positively to specific whole foods.

In the following pages, you will find information on each system including its importance to our health, what kinds of problems we develop when the systems break down, and the diet and lifestyle changes we need to make to keep each system working at top capacity. As you read about each system, check the corresponding table listing "Best foods" and how they affect the system. Use the "Top 10 Best Bets" to focus action that will bring the problems you may be experiencing back into a healthy balance. As you do so, you will see in some cases, fish is included as a Best Bet. This is because some body systems (for example, cardiovascular) require omega-3 fatty acids for disease prevention and cold water fish are the best sources.

As always, check with a health-care specialist if you are experiencing health problems.

Cardiovascular System

Healthy Cardiovascular System

The cardiovascular system consists of the heart, the blood, the arteries and veins. The heart is a muscular organ responsible for pumping oxygenated blood that has just come from the lungs, and for delivering it via the arteries to all body tissues and organs. The body's tissues and organs depend on this oxygen and other nutrients to function. The heart is also responsible for bringing de-oxygenated blood back from the body via the veins to the heart so this blood can be sent to the lungs to get more oxygen.

Cardiovascular Disease

Atherosclerosis, high cholesterol, high blood pressure

Cardiovascular disease — or heart disease, as it is most commonly called — is an illness that pertains to the heart and the blood vessels. Atherosclerosis is the most common precursor to heart disease.

Atherosclerosis occurs when fatty deposits build up on the inside of the arteries, restricting blood flow to the organs supplied by the arteries. If this narrowing and decreased blood flow happens in the coronary arteries, the arteries that supply the heart muscle itself, coronary heart disease occurs. Coronary heart disease has few signs or symptoms, until the arteries become severely occluded, resulting in tissue death and a heart attack.

With repeated heart attacks, the heart becomes weakened and the few areas that are still functioning are left to do most of the work. This inefficiency creates a backup of blood in the heart, lungs and other tissues. This is called congestive heart failure, and can result in difficult breathing even at rest and eventually heart failure and death.

Atherosclerosis also affects other organs and tissues, such as the brain and the legs and feet. If the occlusion happens in the brain, an area of the brain tissue dies and a stroke results. If the legs and feet are restricted of blood and oxygen, we get diminished peripheral circulation, pain with walking and even swelling and ulcerations of the legs.

For years, high cholesterol has been named as the culprit for the presence of fatty deposits inside of the arteries. But in fact, it is the presence of oxidized cholesterol in the bloodstream that can turn the fatty deposits in the arteries into harder plaques and eventually occlusion. This is why antioxidants in our foods are so important. It is also important to note that there are different types of cholesterol. LDL or low-density lipoprotein, is the "bad" cholesterol, the one that gets oxidized and causes the damage. On the other hand, HDL or high-density lipoprotein, is the "good" cholesterol and protects against heart disease.

Another important risk factor for heart disease is a high level of homocysteine. Homocysteine seems to reduce the integrity of the artery walls, as well as cause direct damage to the arteries. Vitamins B_6 (pyridoxine), B_{12} and folic acid help break down homocysteine in the body and keep levels low.

High blood pressure can damage the inside of the artery walls, starting the plaque build-up process and leading to heart disease. It is also much harder work for the heart to pump blood through a system with higher pressure, leading to heart disease and stroke.

Many risk factors contribute to high blood pressure, high levels of oxidized LDL cholesterol and atherosclerosis. The good news is that most of these risk factors can be controlled with diet, exercise and lifestyle modifications.

Optimizing Cardiovascular Function

To protect the cardiovascular system from disease, we need to maintain a healthy body weight, eat an antioxidant-plentiful diet, educate ourselves on the types of fats we should and should not consume, exercise regularly and learn how to cope with stress.

Increase antioxidant-rich foods

Antioxidants are responsible for preventing oxidation of LDL cholesterol inside of the arterial walls. This makes it essential for preventing heart disease, as it stalls the blockage of the arteries and allows oxygenated blood to be delivered to the organs. Vitamin C is especially important because it prevents the formation of free radicals, which damage the arterial walls, but it also helps heal the damaged areas before the plaque formation process begins. Numerous studies have shown antioxidants such as vitamin E, selenium and coenzyme Q10 to be efficient in both prevention and treatment of heart disease.

Best foods

- Polyphenols: extra virgin olive oil
- Bioflavonoids (quercetin): strawberries, onions, apples, green and black tea
- Vitamin C: oranges, strawberries, kiwifruit, red bell peppers, sweet potatoes, broccoli, kale
- Vitamin E: wheat germ, almonds, sunflower seeds, cooked organic soybeans
- Selenium: Brazil nuts, garlic, cooked barley, brown rice, oatmeal, tofu
- Coenzyme Q10: soy oil, mackerel, sardines, peanuts

Increase intake of whole foods that are high in soluble and insoluble fibers

Fruits and legumes are high in soluble fiber, vegetables and whole grains are high in insoluble fiber, and most foods have a combination of both. Soluble fiber, which forms a gel-like compound when dissolved in water, helps eliminate excess cholesterol by binding the cholesterol in the bowels and getting it ready for elimination. Oats in particular contain beta-glucans, which bind cholesterol, and have a significant impact on preventing heart disease. Insoluble fiber, which do not dissolve in water, aid in lowering cholesterol by forming bulk in the stool, and helping to move the bowels.

Best foods

- Legumes (beans, such as black, kidney, lima, pinto, navy, white) and lentils, chickpeas, split peas
- Rolled oats (large flake whole oats/not quick-cooking or instant varieties) and oat bran
- Fruits (apples, oranges, pears), fruit pectin
- Ground flaxseeds

Increase unsaturated fats in your diet

Foods high in unsaturated fatty acids are an important part of a heart healthy diet. Research studies have shown that gamma-linolenic acid (GLA), an omega-6 fatty acid found in evening primrose oil, can decrease LDL levels and increase HDL levels, reducing the risk for atherosclerosis. GLA has also proven to decrease blood pressure levels.

Please note that along with increasing unsaturated fats in your diet, you should also avoid saturated fats (found in animal products such as meats and dairy products) and trans fats (which occur from the hydrogenation process of oils for some margarines and fast foods to make them more stable and increase shelf life). Research shows that trans fats elevate LDL cholesterol and reduce HDL cholesterol

Best foods
• Extra virgin olive oil, evening primrose oil, nuts and seeds, flaxseed oil, fresh fish

Learn stress management techniques and keep stress levels low

When people are under stress, they form more free radicals, which cause more LDL cholesterol oxidation. Stress also stimulates the release of adrenaline, which can create more clots and increase the thickness of the blood. Clots are the start of plaque formation and increase the risk of atherosclerosis. They can also get lodged and lead to a heart attack or stroke. Daily relaxation techniques and learning some stress coping mechanisms can protect against heart disease.

It has also been found that with deep breathing, the body eliminates more sodium than with shallow breathing. This means that deep-breathing techniques can help reduce blood pressure levels by having an effect on water retention.

Best techniques
• Daily relaxation techniques, deep-breathing, rest, hobbies

Exercise regularly and maintain a healthy weight

Exercising regularly helps maintain a healthy body weight, lowers stress and anxiety, and lowers blood pressure levels — all essential components of a heart disease prevention program. Exercise also helps decrease LDL levels and elevate HDL cholesterol levels in the blood, protecting against heart disease. Aim for at least 20 minutes, three times a week. Before starting on a new exercise routine, consult your physician.

Best exercises
• Yoga, brisk walking, swimming, bicycling, dancing

Top 10 Best Bets for Heart Health

❶ Broiled or baked fish: Fish oils contain omega-3 fatty acids that help prevent heart disease and stroke. Studies have shown that there is a difference in health benefits between different types of cooking methods for fish. For example, broiled or oven-baked fish lower the risk of stroke, while fried fish or fish burgers increase the risk of stroke.

❷ Garlic: Garlic contains thioallyls, including allicin, which help platelet aggregation and blood pressure, decreasing the risk for heart disease and stroke.

❸ Soy foods and other beans: Soy isoflavones, the active constituents in soy foods, help protect the cardiovascular system. Soy foods can significantly lower LDL cholesterol levels by decreasing cholesterol and absorption of bile acid from the gastrointestinal tract, but they also decrease the oxidative damage to LDL with their strong free-radical scavenging potential. Look for organic, non-genetically modified soy.

❹ Pomegranate: This delicious and fun-to-eat fruit is important due to its benefits on the cardiovascular system. Pomegranate juice has been shown to reduce the oxidation of LDL cholesterol, protect the arteries from becoming thicker and reduce the development of atherosclerosis. Even though the mechanism of the pomegranate's action is not completely understood, the strong antioxidant potential from its polyphenol compounds may be partly responsible for the benefits.

❺ Extra virgin olive oil: Olive oil is an essential part of the Mediterranean diet, which has been shown to reduce blood pressure and improve lipid profiles, even compared to a lower-fat diet. Olive oil is also a source of antioxidant and anti-inflammatory polyphenols and is high in monounsaturated fats.

❻ Whole oats and oat bran: Whole oats and oat bran are an easy and inexpensive way to achieve a healthy heart. Oats contain beta-glucan, a soluble fiber that binds cholesterol in the bowels and prevents it from being reabsorbed into the bloodstream.

❼ Celery: Celery contains a compound called 3-n-butyl phthalide, which benefits the cardiovascular system. Four ribs of celery per day can help to reduce blood pressure levels.

❽ Apples: Apples are rich in pectin, a soluble fiber that is effective in lowering cholesterol levels, as well as an antioxidant against the oxidation of LDL.

Apples are also rich in the bioflavonoid quercetin, a multipurpose nutrient that contributes to heart health. Quercetin acts as an antioxidant by scavenging free radicals to inhibit LDL damage inside the arteries, and also by regenerating the levels of vitamin E. Quercetin has anti-inflammatory and antihistaminic properties that help control inflammation and allergic reactions anywhere in the body.

❾ Asparagus and leafy greens: Asparagus and leafy green vegetables are high in folate, essential for the lowering of homocysteine levels. High homocysteine levels are an independent risk factor for cardiovascular disease and stroke. Keep in mind that vitamins B_6 and B_{12} are also important factors for controlling the levels of homocysteine in the blood, and that vitamin B_{12}, which is found mostly in animal products, is hard to find in a vegetarian diet.

❿ Tea and cocoa: Tea and cocoa are good providers of bioflavonoids. Studies show that drinking an average of 3 cups (750 mL) of brewed black tea per day can have a long-term positive effect on the cardiovascular system. Similarly, when consumed in moderation, flavonoid-rich chocolate or cocoa can be a component of a heart-healthy diet.

Foods that Protect the Heart

Best Foods that Protect the Heart	Cardiovascular System Benefits	Comments
FRUITS		
Citus: • Kiwifruit • Oranges • Strawberries • Mandarins • Pomegranate • Lemons • Grapefruit	Rich in vitamin C and bioflavonoids, which are antioxidants. Contain pectins. Kiwifruit also contains vitamin E, a powerful antioxidant. Strawberries contain quercetin, a bioflavonoid.	Kiwifruit has proven to be one of the most nutrient-dense fruits. Caution: Grapefruit juice can interfere with some medications.
• Apples	Pectin in apples clean up and bind cholesterol in the intestines, preventing it from being absorbed into the bloodstream. Also high in quercetin.	Studies show that pectin, the soluble fiber found in apple peel, is comparable in results to cholesterol-lowering drugs.
Orange/Yellow: • Apricots • Mangoes	Contain carotenoids and vitamin C, which are antioxidants. Apricots and mangoes are rich in potassium, which helps control blood pressure.	Choose firm and bright orange-colored apricots.
• Bananas	High in potassium, which helps keep blood pressure in check.	
Blue/Purple: • Blueberries and other berries • Purple grapes • Plums	Contain anthocyanins, which destroy free radicals. Also high in pectin and vitamin C.	Frozen berries carry all the heart-health benefits that fresh berries do.
VEGETABLES		
Red Nightshades: • Tomatoes • Red bell peppers	Rich in lycopene, a potent antioxidant. High in vitamin C and beta-carotene.	Lycopene is fat-soluble and must be eaten with a fat in order to be absorbed. Lycopene is also found in processed tomato products, such as tomato juice, ketchup and pizza sauce.
Orange/Yellow: • Carrots • Yams • Sweet potatoes • Pumpkin and other winter squashes	Contain carotenoids, which make LDL cholesterol less susceptible to oxidation.	
Green: • Spinach • Swiss chard • Asparagus • Dandelion greens • Other dark leafy greens	Contain folic acid, essential for lowering homocysteine levels. Contain magnesium, calcium and potassium, which help control blood pressure. Asparagus is high in folate, which helps reduce homocysteine levels.	1 cup (250 mL) of leafy vegetables is equal to one serving.

Best Foods that Protect the Heart	Cardiovascular System Benefits	Comments
VEGETABLES (cont.)		
Cruciferous Family: • Broccoli • Cabbage • Cauliflower	Broccoli contains large amounts of vitamin C and beta-carotene, both powerful antioxidants. All contain folic acid and potassium.	
• Celery	Contains 3-n-butyl phthalide and high amounts of potassium to help with lowering blood pressure.	4 ribs of celery per day can help reduce blood pressure levels.
Allium Family: • Garlic • Onions • Chives	Allicin in garlic lowers blood pressure and reduces blood clotting. Yellow or red onions are high in quercetin.	Released during crushing, allicin gives garlic its characteristic smell. Eat garlic raw and cooked.
LEGUMES		
• Beans • Organic soybeans • Lentils • Peas • Chickpeas	Legumes are a source of soluble fiber that can help eliminate excess cholesterol through the bowels. Rich in flavonoids, which prevent LDL oxidation and damage to the artery lining.	For soy foods, see page 101. 1 cup (250 mL) of cooked soybeans contains 25% of recommended daily fiber and 1 oz (30 g) of protein. Soy products contain phytoestrogens, which may act like weak estrogens in the body. Consult with your naturopathic doctor or nutritionist before consuming large amounts of soy.
WHOLE GRAINS		
• Whole oats and oat bran • Brown rice • Pot barley • Whole ancient grains: spelt, kamut, amaranth	Beta-glucans in oats bind cholesterol molecules in the bowel for elimination. They can lower LDL levels without lowering HDL levels.	Whole grains, such as whole oats and brown rice, contain more fiber than processed flours, pasta, crackers and breads.
NUTS AND SEEDS		
Nuts: • Almonds • Brazil nuts • Walnuts	Nuts contain monounsaturated fats, vitamin E and fiber. They help decrease LDL while leaving HDL unchanged. Brazil nuts, high in selenium, are antioxidant.	Buy raw or dry-roasted nuts and seeds. Choose an unsalted variety; salt can increase blood pressure.
Seeds: • Flaxseeds • Sesame seeds • Sunflower seeds • Pumpkin seeds	Flaxseeds are high in omega-3 oils, fiber and calcium, and help decrease LDL cholesterol, platelet stickiness and blood pressure. Sesame seeds are an excellent source of vitamin E.	Flaxseeds must be ground to maximize absorption and digestion. Once ground, they go rancid quickly, especially if not refrigerated. Best to purchase small quantities of whole flaxseeds, store in the refrigerator and grind fresh just before using.

Best Foods that Protect the Heart	Cardiovascular System Benefits	Comments
FATS AND OILS		
Cold-pressed oils: • Extra virgin olive oil • Grapeseed oil • Flaxseed oil • Avocados	Olive oil, grapeseed oil and avocados contain heart-healthy monounsaturated fats. Grapeseed oil contains significant amounts of vitamin E and, unlike many fats, increases HDL levels.	Look for cold-pressed, less refined oils that are packaged in dark glass containers. Keep oils in the refrigerator to keep them from going rancid.
Fish: • Salmon • Mackerel • Albacore tuna • Sardines • Herring	Best source of omega-3 oils. Contain high amounts of vitamin B_{12}, which is usually lacking in a vegetarian diet, as well as high amounts of calcium (in bones).	Eat at least 2 servings of fish, fresh or canned, per week to cut your risk of heart attacks and stroke.
HERBS AND SPICES		
• Cayenne • Ginger • Garlic	Cayenne stimulates blood flow and strengthens the heart beat and metabolic rate. Ginger can lower cholesterol and decrease stickiness of platelets.	
OTHER		
• Beer • Chocolate • Coffee • Black tea • Wine	Black tea and red wine contain quercetin. Beer is rich in bioflavonoids from the fermented grains. Phenols in dark chocolate and red wine are antioxidant.	Caution: Caffeine and alcohol consumption can increase blood pressure levels. Consume in moderation. Not recommended during pregnancy and lactation.

Digestive System

Healthy Digestive System

The digestive system is responsible for mixing the food we eat and breaking it down into smaller molecules that our body can absorb and use. Digestion starts at the mouth with chewing and breaking carbohydrate molecules down with the aid of enzymes found in saliva. Food then travels down the esophagus into the stomach, where hydrochloric acid, also known as HCl, and digestive enzymes break down proteins and allow for the absorption of some substances. Most digestion and absorption of nutrients take place in the small intestine, with the help of the liver and gall bladder, which provide bile, and the pancreas, which provides digestive enzymes. Food molecules, such as monosaccharides (carbohydrate units), amino acids (protein units) and fatty acids, as well as vitamins, minerals and water are absorbed into the bloodstream and lymphatic system, while indigestible foods (mostly fiber) continue down to the large intestine and eventually get eliminated.

The entire digestive system is lined with mucous membranes. Mucous membranes act as a barrier and are responsible for mucous secretions that aid in the digestive process. A smooth muscle layer also exists in the entire digestive tract and is responsible for mixing and breaking food down, as well as propelling food downwards through the digestive tract.

Digestive Problems

Heartburn, constipation, inflammatory bowel disease, colon cancer

Heartburn is one of the most common digestive complaints. It can be a symptom of gastric reflux, a hiatal hernia or a gastric or duodenal ulcer. Determining the cause of heartburn is important, as these conditions can be easily treated, but can become serious if not attended to.

Another common indicator of suboptimal digestive function is constipation. Constipation occurs when bowel movements are infrequent or difficult, causing bloating, headaches or hemorrhoids, to name a few symptoms. Constipation can be caused by a lack of fiber or water in the diet, stress, or perhaps disease.

Constipation can be an indicator of other digestive system diseases. For example, constipation alternating with diarrhea can be one of the symptoms of irritable bowel syndrome (IBS). Other symptoms of IBS include abdominal pain and cramps, excess gas and bloating. IBS can be caused by sensitivity to foods and is often associated with emotional stress — and it can be extremely disabling.

Inflammatory bowel disease (IBD) includes two conditions with chronic inflammation of the bowels: Crohn's disease and ulcerative colitis. In these conditions, inflammation of the bowel can result in such symptoms as diarrhea, bleeding, cramping and a feeling of urgency. The cause of these conditions is not known. Consult a physician if you are suffering from any of the above symptoms.

The digestive system is also susceptible to cancer. Colon cancer is the second most common form of cancer, and one that can be easily prevented with a healthy lifestyle and regular bowel movements. Colon cancer is treatable, but early detection and treatment are crucial. If you experience a change in bowel habits, blood in the stool, unexplained weight loss or fatigue, consult your physician.

Optimizing Digestive Function

To protect the digestive system from disease and allow for optimal digestive function, we need to maintain healthy mucous membranes, and to heal them when necessary; create and maintain a healthy intestinal flora; eat a diet rich in fiber and antioxidants; drink plenty of water; eat fresh foods, which are rich in digestive enzymes, instead of frozen or prepared foods; and eliminate foods that irritate the bowel or cause inflammation. As the digestive system is closely linked with the nervous system, daily routines and stress-management techniques are also beneficial for digestive function.

Eat foods that create and maintain a healthy lining of the digestive tract

The lining of the digestive tract is responsible for choosing what is absorbed into the body and what gets eliminated, so it must be intact. The digestive process breaks food down into smaller molecules that are checked by the immune system as they are absorbed. If digestion is poor and food is not broken down properly, or the mucous membranes become increasingly permeable ("leaky gut"), molecules pass through the barrier in a larger form, and the immune system recognizes them as foreign invaders. This hypersensitivity of the immune system can create a number of symptoms that can manifest in any part of the body.

You can maintain the health of the digestive tract's lining by promoting repair of intestinal cells, reestablishing a healthy bacterial flora and decreasing inflammation. Foods such as cabbage are high in glutamine, an amino acid that helps regenerate and repair the cells of the digestive tract. Probiotics — the healthy bacteria that populate the intestines — and fiber help maintain a healthy intestinal environment and crowd out toxic bacteria. Fish oils and quercetin from apples and onions help decrease the inflammatory response, minimize damage to the digestive lining and dampen food sensitivity reactions.

Best foods
- Fish oils, whole grains (brown rice, rye, spelt, quinoa, millet)
- Fruits (apples, blueberries, blackberries, grapes)
- Vegetables (cabbage, onions, red bell peppers)
- Legumes (beans, peas, lentils)

Eat foods that create and maintain a healthy bacterial environment in the intestines

Friendly bacteria in our intestines are an important part of a healthy digestive system. They are responsible for crowding out pathogens and maintaining a beneficial acid-base balance (a balanced pH in the digestive tract is created by many factors, one being the production of lactic acid by "friendly bacteria,") that helps prevent infection from bacteria, viruses, yeast and parasites. Friendly bacteria optimize digestion by producing digestive enzymes. They also make B vitamins and vitamin K and protect against food allergies by maintaining a healthy immune system in the digestive tract.

When we eat a diet that is rich in processed foods and chemicals or take antibiotics to treat infection, the population of healthy bacteria is reduced. We can increase this by supplementing with probiotics and by eating foods that contain prebiotics. Prebiotics are vegetable fibers or complex sugars, which the healthy bacteria depend on for survival. These carbohydrate compounds, including fructooligosaccharides (FOS) are found in foods, such as fruits, vegetables, whole grains and legumes.

Best foods
- Garlic, onions, asparagus, leeks, artichokes, natural yogurt

Eat a diet rich in fiber and increase water intake

Fiber is the part of plant food that goes through the digestive tract undigested. It is necessary to clean the digestive tract by collecting dead cells and debris, and also helps prevent cholesterol and excess hormones from being reabsorbed back into the bloodstream. In general, both soluble and insoluble fibers help with these functions. Insoluble fiber is necessary to form bulk and stimulate the muscles of the digestive tract to move the bowels. Soluble fiber acts as a food source for friendly bacteria in the intestinal tract. Together with proper intake of water, all these factors help maintain a healthy digestive tract and protect against digestive system diseases, such as constipation, hemorrhoids and colon cancer. In fact, insufficient fiber contributes to a large percentage of digestive disorders. Fiber can come from many foods, such as whole grains, fruits and vegetables, nuts and seeds, and beans and other legumes. Most processed foods and animal products are devoid of fiber.

Best foods
- Whole grains (brown rice, rye, oats, millet, buckwheat, quinoa, spelt, whole wheat)
- Fruits (apples, pears, oranges, berries, peaches, dates, fresh or dried figs, prunes)
- Vegetables (carrots, celery, leafy greens and cruciferous vegetables, such as cabbage, broccoli, cauliflower)
- Seeds (sesame seeds, sunflower seeds, pumpkin seeds, flaxseeds)
- Nuts (almonds, hazelnuts, walnuts)
- Legumes (beans, lentils, peas, chickpeas, organic soybeans)

Eat foods that promote digestion

Digestion depends on different substances to break foods down, prepare them for absorption and help the body to utilize them. For example, starting at the mouth, salivary glands produce saliva, which can initiate the digestion of carbohydrates. Then hydrochloric acid (HCI) in the stomach helps dissolve food particles and activates other enzymes. Similarly, in the small intestine, digestive enzymes produced by the pancreas and bile from the liver and gall bladder help emulsify fats, break down carbohydrates, proteins and fats, and get them ready for absorption. See Top 10 Best Bets for foods that stimulate the release of saliva and enhance the production of HCl and the release of digestive enzymes and bile into the digestive tract. Foods high in enzymes (bananas, papaya, mangoes, pineapple) along with a nutritionally dense diet, can ensure healthy body functions.

Best foods
- Cider vinegar, bitter foods (dandelion greens and other bitter greens), lemon juice, "live" (sprouted) foods, bananas, pineapple, papaya, unpasteurized honey, sauerkraut, natural yogurt

Practice stress-management techniques and regular bowel habits

Conditions, such as heartburn and irritable bowel syndrome (IBS) are closely linked with the nervous system. It is also helpful to establish a daily routine that includes a regular time for bowel elimination. This encourages daily bowel movements and decreases the incidence of constipation. Managing stress and following a daily routine can help maintain a healthy digestive system, increase the frequency of bowel movements and reduce the risk for colon cancer.

Best techniques
- Yoga, breathing exercises, daily bowel routine (in this case, an overall daily routine is helpful for stress management), regular bowel habits, counseling for emotional stress

Top 10 Best Bets for Digestive Health

❶ **Cabbage:** Cabbage is rich in glutamine, an amino acid used by the intestinal cells as their principal fuel source. Glutamine helps the cells repair and regenerate themselves and prevents undigested foods from passing through the intestinal lining. Cabbage is also used to make sauerkraut through the process of fermentation. Sauerkraut helps populate the intestinal micro flora and contains digestive enzymes.

❷ **Onions:** Onions are essential for digestive health. Onions are a source of quercetin, which helps decrease hypersensitivity in the intestines. This helps to protect the lining of the digestive system from irritation and protect the body from food sensitivities. Onions are also a source of fructooligosaccharides (FOS), a complex sugar that acts as a prebiotic and feeds the healthy bacteria in our digestive system.

❸ **Apples and apple cider vinegar:** Apples are high in pectin, a soluble fiber that absorbs 100 times its weight in water. Pectin from apples helps calm the intestinal tract during diarrhea and prevents constipation. Quercetin, a flavonoid found in apples, helps stabilize immune reactions and decrease inflammation and irritation of the digestive system.

Apple cider vinegar helps increase production of hydrochloric acid (HCl) in the stomach. HCl helps break food particles down and activates other enzymes to digest proteins. As part of the immune system, HCl helps kill food pathogens before they reach the rest of the digestive system.

❹ **Garlic:** Garlic is a source of FOS, which helps nourish the healthy bacteria in our digestive system and maintain an optimal environment in our intestines. Garlic is also a powerful antimicrobial that protects against parasites, yeast, viruses and bacteria that could be harmful to our health when they populate our digestive tract.

❺ **Fennel and caraway seeds:** Fennel and caraway seeds help stimulate digestion and appetite. In Asian countries, they are also commonly chewed after a meal to relieve bloating, flatulence and colic, and even to freshen the breath.

❻ **Peppermint:** Peppermint is one of the most effective digestive herbs. It helps relax the stomach and intestines when they suffer from cramping and spasms, and it helps relieve nausea. This also means that peppermint can relax the esophageal sphincter. When relaxed, the sphincter can open and food and stomach acids from the stomach can travel upward to the esophagus and cause symptoms of heartburn. If you suffer from gastric reflux, avoid peppermint.

❼ **Dandelion greens and other bitter greens:** Dandelion greens and other bitter greens are indispensable to optimize digestion. These bitter foods help stimulate the release of bile from the gall bladder and digestive enzymes from the pancreas, enhancing digestive function. The greens can be eaten in a salad to increase appetite before the main course of a meal.

❽ **Pineapple and papaya:** Pineapple and papaya contain bromelain and papain, digestive enzymes that can complement the enzymes already produced by the body. These enzymes help break foods down in the digestive tract and can decrease symptoms of food sensitivities, as well as reduce bloating and flatulence after a meal.

❾ **Brown rice:** Brown rice and other whole grains are a source of insoluble fiber. Insoluble fiber increases bulk in the stool and helps prevent constipation and protect against colon cancer. Brown rice is an ideal food for people who suffer from IBS, IBD or constipation, in part because, unlike wheat, rye and spelt, brown rice is a gluten-free grain that does not seem to cause intestinal irritation or allergic reactions in patients with gluten sensitivity. In addition, brown rice contains phytic acid, which seems to protect against colon cancer.

❿ **Beans and other legumes:** Beans and other legumes are an excellent source of soluble fiber. Soluble fiber is a food source for friendly bacteria in the intestines, which then produce short chain fatty acids. These fatty acids create an optimal pH balance in the digestive tract and protect the lining of the digestive tract against colon cancer.

Foods that Protect the Digestive System

Best Foods for Protecting the Digestive System	Digestive System Benefits	Comments
FRUITS		
Citrus: • Oranges • Mandarins • Lemons • Grapefruit • Kiwifruit • Strawberries	Contain pectin and other soluble fiber, which provide food for healthy intestinal bacteria and protect against constipation and other digestive diseases.	Lemon juice can increase the release of HCl, helping with protection against pathogens, break down of proteins and absorption of nutrients.
• Apricots • Peaches • Pears • Apples	Contain pectin and other soluble fiber that prevent constipation and colon cancer. Apples contain quercetin, which helps decrease irritability in the digestive tract.	Most fruits and vegetables contain a mixture of soluble and insoluble fibers.
• Fresh or dried figs • Prunes	Help increase bowel frequency and prevent bowel toxicity and colon cancer.	Prunes are high in fiber; prune juice is not. (Prune juice is a natural laxative, but it does not contain fiber and does not have all the other benefits of a high-fiber food like prunes.)
Tropical fruits: • Bananas • Pineapple • Papaya	These tropical fruits are loaded with natural digestive enzymes that enhance the break down of foods in the digestive tract.	Take digestive tropical fruit drinks one hour before a meal.
Berries: • Blueberries • Blackberries • Grapes	Berries contain flavonoids, which help maintain the health of the lining in the digestive tract.	
VEGETABLES		
Green: • Spinach • Swiss chard • Asparagus • Dandelion greens • Endive • Other dark leafy greens	Dandelion greens and other bitter greens help improve digestion by stimulating the release of bile and digestive enzymes.	Raw foods are more difficult to digest. Steaming, covered, or sautéing briskly can make foods easier to digest without much loss of nutritive value.
Cruciferous Family: • Broccoli • Cabbage • Sauerkraut • Cauliflower	Sauerkraut contains healthy intestinal bacteria and digestive enzymes. Cabbage contains glutamine — an energy source for intestinal cells — and helps prevent a "leaky gut."	Sauerkraut is made of finely sliced cabbage that is fermented by various lactic acid bacteria, including *Lactobacillus*.

Best Foods for Protecting the Digestive System	Digestive System Benefits	Comments
VEGETABLES (cont.)		
Allium Family: • Garlic • Onions	Garlic, onions and asparagus contain fructooligosaccharides (FOS) or prebiotics. Onions contain quercetin, which helps decrease intestinal irritability and immune system hypersensitivity.	Garlic is an important antimicrobial for all the systems and fights against bacteria, viruses, yeast and parasites.
LEGUMES		
• Beans • Organic soybeans • Lentils • Peas • Chickpeas	Legumes are a source of soluble fiber, which feeds healthy intestinal bacteria.	Soaking beans for 8 hours before cooking makes them easier to digest.
WHOLE GRAINS		
• Oats (soluble fiber) • Brown rice • Pot Barley • Buckwheat • Quinoa • Whole wheat • Spelt • Rye	Whole grains are a source of insoluble fiber; they increase bulk and help prevent constipation. Contain phytic acid, which protects against colon cancer.	Whole grains containing gluten can be irritating to people with IBS, and cannot be tolerated by people with Crohn's disease.
NUTS AND SEEDS		
Nuts: • Almonds • Brazil nuts • Walnuts • Hazelnuts • Pine nuts	Nuts contain fiber. Brazil nuts are high in selenium, an antioxidant that helps protect against colon cancer.	
Seeds: • Flaxseeds • Sesame seeds • Sunflower seeds • Pumpkin seeds	Flaxseeds are high in omega-3 fatty acids, which help decrease inflammation, and lignins, an insoluble fiber that creates bulk for the stool and prevents constipation.	Lignins in flaxseeds also help maintain optimal levels of estrogen in the body. Flaxseeds must be freshly ground to avoid rancidity and maximize absorption and digestion.
FATS AND OILS		
Cold-pressed oils: • Extra virgin olive oil • Grapeseed oil • Flaxseed oil • Avocados	Oils are necessary for the absorption of fat-soluble vitamins A, E, D and K.	Adding a capsule of vitamin E into your oil container helps prevent oxidation and rancidity.
Fish: • Salmon • Mackerel • Albacore tuna • Sardines • Herring	Best source of omega-3 fatty acids, which have anti-inflammatory properties. Contain high amounts of vitamin B_{12}, which is usually lacking in a vegetarian diet.	Vitamin B_{12} is absorbed in the colon, not in the small intestine like most other vitamins and minerals.

Best Foods for Protecting the Digestive System	Digestive System Benefits	Comments
HERBS AND SPICES		
• Cayenne • Ginger • Turmeric • Cumin • Coriander (dried or fresh Cilantro) • Fennel • Peppermint • Caraway seeds	These herbs and spices enhance digestion, help flush toxins out of the body and help improve absorption and assimilation of nutrients. Ginger can stimulate digestion.	Eat or make tea with ginger. Take a slice of fresh ginger 30 to 60 minutes before a meal for optimal digestion. Peppermint can relax the esophageal sphincter and stimulate symptoms of acid reflux.

A Note about Food Combining

One short-term method of relieving indigestion, flatulence, fatigue, food allergies and, in some cases, inflammatory bowel and peptic ulcer, is to follow a discipline of eating certain foods in a set order. This order is as follows:

Fruits Alone

Fruits require the least time and energy for the body to digest and because of this it is recommended that fruit be eaten before a meal or at least two hours after a meal. Fruits are best taken alone at breakfast or as small, between-meal snacks.

Proteins with Non-starchy Vegetables

Protein foods (fish, eggs, nuts, seeds, dairy products, soy products) take the longest and use up the most of the body's effort to digest. When fruit or starchy vegetables are eaten before or with proteins, they break down and ferment long before the proteins are digested. This causes the digestive problems listed earlier. It is best to eat protein foods with non-starchy vegetables (leafy greens, asparagus, broccoli, cabbage, celery, cucumber, onion, sweet bell peppers, sea vegetables, tomatoes, zucchini).

Whole Grains with Non-starchy Vegetables

Whole grains and non-starchy vegetables are complex carbohydrates that break down at about the same rate, providing the body with a slow and steady supply of starches and sugars for fuel. If eaten together, they are best without fruit or protein.

Starchy Vegetables, Legumes and Refined Grains in Small Amounts, Alone

Squash, legumes, pasta, refined grains, beets, parsnips, carrots, sweet potatoes and pumpkin are starchy carbohydrate foods that break down faster than protein foods and other carbohydrates but not as quickly as fruits. It is recommended that starchy carbohydrates be eaten in small amounts, away from other foods.

Endocrine System

Healthy Endocrine System

The endocrine system consists of endocrine glands and the hormones produced by these glands, which work together to serve as one of the body's main control systems. Hormones are chemicals that carry messages through the blood. To do this, hormones travel from the endocrine glands in which they are produced to the target cells where they will perform their function. For example, the thyroid gland produces and secretes thyroid hormones (thyroxine or T4, and triiodothyronine or T3), which control the body's metabolic rate. The adrenal glands, located on top of the kidneys, secrete a number of hormones, including cortisol, which is released in response to stress and can help balance the immune system. Epinephrine, also known as adrenaline, and norepinephrine are also released in response to stress and can have an effect similar to that of sympathetic nerves (the "fight or flight" response).

Some organs have a function in more than one body system. For example, the pancreas, which secretes digestive enzymes as part of the digestive system, also performs an endocrine function by releasing the insulin and glucagon responsible for balancing blood sugar.

The reproductive organs are also part of the endocrine system. In females, the ovaries manage the functioning, growth and development of the female reproductive system, including the breasts, via hormones such as estrogen and progesterone. In males, the testes produce testosterone, which is responsible for the functioning, growth and development of the male reproductive system.

The hypothalamus in the brain and the pituitary gland just below it control many of these glands through hormones they secrete. Hormonal feedback can signal to these glands to produce more or less hormones that help keep the body's functions in balance.

Many other glands and organs are part of the endocrine system and no doubt many others remain to be discovered.

Endocrine Disorders

Hormone imbalance, hyperthyroidism, hypothyroidism, diabetes

Most endocrine disorders occur when too much or too little of a hormone is produced by an endocrine gland, when the target cell exerts a reduced response, or in some cases, when our body cannot properly eliminate excess hormones.

Hyperthyroidism is a condition where the thyroid gland secretes too much of the thyroid hormone, creating symptoms of an increased metabolic rate. On the other hand, in hypothyroidism, there is too little of the active thyroid hormone, giving rise to such symptoms as fatigue, weight gain, cold intolerance and other signs of low metabolic function. Hypothyroidism can be caused by mineral deficiencies, as minerals are essential to produce and activate the thyroid hormone, or by a destruction of thyroid cells due to inflammatory disease.

Adrenal glands produce cortisol, which has potent anti-inflammatory and immunosuppressive properties important for normal immune responses. However, under constant stress, cortisol is overproduced and the body's immune system can be suppressed, leading to an increased risk of infections. Also, as part of the blood glucose-regulating system, increased cortisol and epinephrine production due to chronic stress can lead to higher blood glucose and insulin levels and subsequent weight gain.

In Type 1 diabetes, the pancreas does not produce enough insulin, whereas in Type 2 diabetes, the target cells resist insulin. In both cases, glucose cannot enter the cells and there is an elevation of blood sugar levels that can lead to serious complications. For people with diabetes, diet is critically important to help restore insulin sensitivity, control blood sugar levels and prevent complications.

In the reproductive system, an excess of estrogen that is unbalanced by progesterone can be linked with many female disorders, such as menstrual difficulties, endometriosis, fibrocystic breasts, infertility and breast cancer. Estrogen and progesterone balance is affected by many factors, including the use of oral contraceptives and hormone replacement therapy, diet and chemicals in food and the environment. In males, testosterone is released from the testes and converted into the hormone dihydrotestosterone (DHT), which stimulates the synthesis and growth of prostate cells. High levels of DHT can cause benign prostatic hyperplasia or prostate cancer.

What makes the endocrine system so complex is that most times hormones act in concert with one another to produce their physiologic effects, and the improper function of one can deeply affect the function of others.

Optimizing Endocrine Function

Eat a diet rich in complex carbohydrates

The glycemic index (GI) is a dietary guide that ranks foods based on how they affect blood sugar levels. It is often used by people with diabetes to help them choose foods that do not increase blood sugar levels rapidly. Foods with a high GI rating increase blood sugar levels at a fast rate, which an individual with too little insulin (Type 1 diabetes) or insulin-resistant cells (Type 2 diabetes) may not be able to tolerate. In general, simple carbohydrates, found in foods such as pasta, breads and crackers made with refined flours, as well as in soft drinks and candy, have a high GI. Foods that contain complex carbohydrates, fat and proteins have a low GI and will slow the absorption of sugar into

the bloodstream. The GI should be utilized with other tools, as it does not take into consideration the fat content or the type of fat a food contains.

In particular, the fiber contained in complex carbohydrates is capable of slowing down the digestion and absorption of blood sugar and increasing insulin sensitivity, therefore giving it a low score on the GI scale. Water-soluble fiber is the most beneficial type for blood sugar control. Fruits and legumes are the best sources of water-soluble fiber. Soluble and insoluble fibers also encourage regular bowel movements, which helps eliminate excess estrogen from the body and prevent an estrogen/progesterone imbalance and breast cancer.

Best foods
- Whole grains (oats, brown rice, barley, quinoa, spelt, kamut, whole wheat)
- Legumes (beans, soybeans, chickpeas, lentils)
- Fruits (pears, apples, oranges, plums)
- All vegetables except white potatoes and parsnips
- Nuts and seeds (almonds, cashews, walnuts, sesame seeds, sunflower seeds, pumpkin seeds, ground flaxseeds)

Eat a diet rich in essential fatty acids

Essential fatty acids are precursors to all hormones and therefore, constitute an indispensable part of a diet that promotes a healthy endocrine system.

Omega-3 fatty acids are part of cell membranes, where insulin receptors are located. Insulin receptors become more responsive to insulin when there are more omega-3 fatty acids in the cell membrane. Therefore, omega-3 fatty acids can help prevent insulin resistance and diabetes.

Best foods
- Fish oils (wild salmon, mackerel, albacore tuna, sardines, herring), flaxseed oil, soy oil, hempseed oil, canola oil, walnuts

Eat foods rich in minerals

Minerals are important in every aspect of endocrine function. For example, iodine is a component of thyroid hormones T4 and T3, and it must be obtained from the diet. T4 and some T3 are produced and released by the thyroid gland and travel to tissues where these hormones act in the body. Within the cell, T4 is converted to T3, the most active form. This conversion depends on the minerals zinc, copper and selenium.

Chromium, vanadium, manganese and zinc are essential for regulating blood sugar, either by increasing the production of insulin, by increasing the target cell's sensitivity to insulin or by acting on enzyme systems of glucose metabolism. That is why these minerals are important in the prevention of diabetes.

Minerals such as selenium and manganese are antioxidants, prevent damage to the cell's DNA and decrease the risk of cancer.

Best foods

- Zinc: black-eyed peas, pumpkin seeds, tofu, wheat germ
- Copper: nuts, legumes, potatoes, vegetables, cereal grains (oats and wheat)
- Selenium: Brazil nuts, yeast, whole grains
- Chromium: brewer's yeast, grains, some beers
- Vanadium: cereal grains, parsley, mushrooms, corn, soy foods
- Manganese: nuts, wheat germ, wheat bran, leafy green vegetables, beet tops, pineapple, seeds
- Iodine: iodized salt, sea vegetables (kelp), vegetables grown in iodine-rich soil

Learn ways of coping with stress

When a person suffers from stress, cortisol and adrenaline are released from the adrenal glands. These adrenal hormones can then trigger the pancreas to release glucagon, which is responsible for increasing blood sugar levels when the body demands more sugar to be available as an energy source. This usually happens when a person has not eaten in a while or in stress situations ("fight or flight" response) by a process called glycolysis, where stored glycogen is broken down into glucose molecules and released into the blood stream. This response is ideal during a state of crisis, but can be detrimental to the endocrine system over a long period. It is important to keep in mind that sugar and caffeine tend to stimulate the adrenal glands and it is best to consume these products in moderation, especially at times of high stress.

Techniques that induce a relaxation response and prevent the release of excess stress hormones from the adrenal glands can be beneficial.

Best methods

- Daily routine, meditation, prayer, breathing exercises, physical exercise, counseling

Exercise

The benefits of exercise for the endocrine system cannot be overstated. Exercise can decrease insulin resistance, and it increases the concentration of chromium in the tissues, helping the body maintain normal blood sugar levels. Exercise can help increase metabolic rate, energy and endurance, and for many people it helps achieve a proper body weight. Maintaining an ideal body weight is an important factor for prevention of diabetes. Exercise can help stimulate blood and lymphatic circulation, essential for the transport of hormones and elimination of excess hormones. Exercise also reduces secretions of stress hormones from the adrenal glands in response to psychological stress.

Best exercises

- Weight lifting, brisk walking, jogging, bicycling, swimming, dancing, yoga, racquet sports (such as tennis), team sports

Top 10 Best Bets for Endocrine Health

❶ **Cruciferous vegetables:** Cruciferous vegetables, such as broccoli, cauliflower, kale, Brussels sprouts and bok choy contain a phytochemical called indole-3-carbinol, which induces the break down of estrogen into its harmless metabolites, decreasing the risk for breast cancer.

❷ **Sea vegetables:** Sea vegetables, such as nori, arame, kelp, dulse and kombu, contain iodine, an essential mineral that is needed for the production of thyroid hormones. As part of thyroid hormones, iodine helps increase metabolism and reduce the risk of symptoms of hypothyroidism.

❸ **Pumpkin seeds:** Pumpkin seeds are high in zinc, a mineral essential for the normal function of the male reproductive system. Zinc is associated with proper testosterone levels, sperm production and sperm motility. Maintaining adequate levels of zinc may help prevent male infertility. Eat a handful of raw pumpkin seeds daily.

❹ **Stevia:** Stevia is an extract from the plant *Stevia rebaudiana*. The extract has 200 times the sweetness of sugar and contains no calories. It is a safe alternative for people with diabetes, as it does not raise blood sugar levels and has glucose-lowering properties. Stevia extract can be used to sweeten foods and drinks. (See also Herbs, page 103)

❺ **Soy foods:** Soybeans contain phytoestrogens, chemicals that are plant-based and similar in structure to estrogen. Although the research is conflicting and inconclusive, the phytoestrogens found in soy (genistein and daidzein), act like weak estrogens and may help block estrogen's cancer promoting effect. Soybeans and soy foods should only be consumed if they are organic and non-genetically modified.

❻ **Onions and garlic:** Onions and garlic have blood sugar-regulating properties. They contain sulfur, which aids in liver detoxification and elimination of excess hormones. Garlic is also high in selenium, a potent antioxidant that can help prevent cancer.

❼ **Ground flaxseeds:** Ground flaxseeds are a source of omega-3 fatty acids and phytoestrogens. Lignins, the phytoestrogens found in flaxseeds, stand out in their ability to regulate the menstrual cycle in women. They have been shown to be mildly estrogenic or anti-estrogenic, depending on the body's need to balance hormones.

❽ **Brewer's yeast:** Brewer's yeast is the dried, powdered form of the *Saccharomyces cerevisiae* fungus used in the brewing process. It is the highest source of chromium, a mineral that works in conjunction with insulin to promote the uptake of glucose by the target cells. For this reason, chromium is essential for blood sugar regulation and diabetes prevention.

❾ **Citrus fruits:** Citrus fruits are a rich source of vitamin C. Vitamin C is stored in high concentration in the adrenal glands and helps in the production of adrenal hormones. In addition, vitamin C increases insulin's response to sugar, thus helping lower blood sugar levels. Vitamin C is also an antioxidant that can help prevent breast and prostate cancer.

❿ **Spinach:** Spinach is one of the best sources of alpha-lipoic acid, a vitamin-like nutrient that is very important for glucose metabolism and prevention of diabetes. Alpha-lipoic acid is also an antioxidant that helps prevent free-radical damage and decreases the risk of cancer. Spinach is also a source of many minerals that can be beneficial for endocrine function.

Foods that Protect the Endocrine System

Best Foods for Protecting the Endocrine System	Endocrine System Benefits	Comments
FRUITS		
Citrus: • Oranges • Mandarins • Lemons • Grapefruit • Kiwifruit • Strawberries	Contain soluble fiber, which helps control blood sugar levels. Contain vitamin C and bioflavonoids, antioxidants that can help reduce the risk of cancer. Vitamin C in particular is essential for the production of stress hormones by the adrenal glands.	Fructose, the natural sugar found in fruits, is first absorbed in the digestive tract and then has to be converted into glucose, so it does not increase blood sugar levels as rapidly as other simple sugars obtained from the diet.
• Apricots • Peaches • Pears • Apples	Contain pectin and other soluble fiber, the most beneficial type of fiber for the control of blood sugar levels.	Most fruits and vegetables contain a mixture of soluble and insoluble fibers and can slow down the absorption of sugar.
Berries and grapes: • Blueberries • Blackberries • Raspberries • Grapes	Berries and grapes are a rich source of bioflavonoids. These are antioxidants and help prevent breast and prostate cancer.	Bioflavonoids help the body use vitamin C. They are found in highest concentration in the skin or peel of fruits and vegetables.
VEGETABLES		
Green: • Spinach • Swiss chard • Dandelion greens	Rich in many minerals needed for optimal endocrine function, including iodine, selenium and manganese. Spinach is a source of alpha-lipoic acid, an important nutrient for glucose metabolism.	
Red Nightshades: • Bell peppers • Tomatoes	Tomatoes are the best source of lycopene, a strong antioxidant that helps protect cells against damage and plays an important role in cancer prevention.	Lycopene is a carotene that gives tomatoes their deep red color.
Cruciferous Family: • Broccoli • Cabbage • Sauerkraut • Cauliflower • Kale • Bok choy	Cruciferous vegetables contain indole-3-carbinol, a chemical that helps break down estrogen into its harmless metabolites.	Cooking destroys indoles, so eat these foods raw or lightly steamed.
Sea Vegetables: • Nori • Arame • Kelp • Dulse • Kombu	Contain minerals, including iodine, calcium and iron. Iodine is needed for the production of thyroid hormones.	Caution: Do not consume sea vegetables if you have a hyperthyroid condition. Also, hijiki may contain high levels of inorganic arsenic, a carcinogen, and food safety agencies in many countries, including Canada and Britain, have cautioned against its consumption.

Best Foods for Protecting the Endocrine System	Endocrine System Benefits	Comments
VEGETABLES (cont.)		
Allium Family: • Garlic • Onions	Garlic and onions can help regulate blood sugar levels.	
LEGUMES		
• Beans (kidney, adzuki, mung) • Lentils • Peas (black-eyed) • Chickpeas	Legumes are a source of soluble fiber, which helps eliminate excess estrogen through the bowels. Black-eyed peas and tofu are rich sources of zinc, essential for endocrine system function.	Consult with your naturopathic doctor or nutritionist before consuming large amounts of soy.
WHOLE GRAINS		
• Whole oats • Brown rice • Pot Barley • Buckwheat • Quinoa • Whole wheat • Spelt • Rye	Barley is the grain with the lowest glycemic index (GI) rating, which means it is highly efficient at slowing the rate at which sugar is absorbed into the blood stream.	Whole grains score lower in the GI scale in comparison to refined carbohydrates.
NUTS AND SEEDS		
Nuts: • Almonds • Brazil nuts • Walnuts • Hazelnuts • Pine nuts	Nuts contain fiber, which helps control blood sugar levels. Nuts are high in minerals, such as zinc and manganese essential for the functioning of the endocrine system.	Try natural nut butters without added hydrogenated oils, sugar or salt.
Seeds: • Flaxseeds • Sesame seeds • Sunflower seeds • Pumpkin seeds	Seeds are high in fiber and unsaturated fats, which help control blood sugar levels. Sesame seeds are a source of iodine, a component of thyroid hormones. Pumpkin seeds are high in zinc, needed for all aspects of insulin metabolism and male reproductive system.	Try natural seed butters without added hydrogenated oils, sugar or salt.

Best Foods for Protecting the Endocrine System	Endocrine System Benefits	Comments
FATS AND OILS		
Cold-pressed oils: • Flaxseed oil • Soybean oil • Hempseed oil • Canola oil • Avocados	Flaxseed and hempseed oils are rich sources of omega-3 fatty acids, necessary for the production of all hormones.	Do not cook with flaxseed oil (or any of the oils listed at the left), but use them unheated, in small amounts with foods such as cooked vegetables, salads, beans, grains, or smoothies.
Fish: • Salmon • Mackerel • Albacore tuna • Sardines • Herring	Best source of omega-3 fatty acids, which help in prevention of diabetes and decrease inflammation.	Choose fresh wild fish, instead of farmed fish.
HERBS AND SPICES		
• Turmeric • Sage	Turmeric has antioxidant and antitumor activity, helping prevent against cancer. Sage balances endocrine glands.	Add turmeric to stir-fries, soups or curry dishes. Caution: Sage should not be consumed during pregnancy. Sage contains steroid-like factors and can encourage miscarriage.
• Brewer's yeast	Best source of chromium, a mineral that works closely with insulin and helps increase insulin sensitivity, reducing the risk of diabetes.	Do not confuse brewer's yeast with baking yeast or nutritional yeast.

Immune System

Healthy Immune System

The immune system consists of a complex collection of cells found throughout the body. These cells are responsible for protecting the body against infection, as well as for constant surveillance and destruction of the cancer cells.

The skin and mucous membranes, along with chemical substances like mucous, tears and stomach acid, are also an important part of the immune system, acting as front-line barriers that prevent foreign materials and pathogenic organisms from entering and harming the body.

When the immune system does not work optimally, we see an increased risk for infections and cancers, as well as the development of allergies and inflammatory disease.

Support and enhancement of the immune system through consumption of whole foods, proper intake of water, regular moderate exercise and mental relaxation can increase the body's resistance to colds, flus and cancers, and keep allergies and inflammation in check.

Immune System Disorders

Frequent and chronic infections, cancer, inflammation, allergies

Frequent and chronic infections may include anything from a common cold, flu, ear infections and urinary tract infections to more serious illnesses, such as herpes virus infections, bronchitis and pneumonia. Viruses, bacteria, fungi and parasites can all cause infections, especially when they do not meet adequate resistance from a weakened immune system.

Similarly, cancer risk increases when there is damage to a cell's DNA and the immune system's DNA repair or cancer surveillance systems are not functioning at an optimal level. DNA can be damaged by free radicals produced inside the body or by elements from the external environment, such as chemicals, radiation or viruses.

Another way the body defends itself is through inflammation. Inflammation is a normal immune system response responsible for destroying invaders or setting the stage for tissue repair. When the immune system is out of control, inflammation can become chronic and cause pain and damage body tissues.

Allergies are the body's exaggerated response to foreign invaders. This reaction is usually a manifestation of a leaky gut (an increase in permeability of the lining of the digestive tract, which allows undigested food particles to enter the bloodstream and be recognized as foreign invaders or antigens — see Digestive System, page 18), and/or excessive allergens overtaxing the immune system. Maintaining a whole foods diet can have a profound effect on the management of allergies.

Optimizing the Immune System

To optimize the functioning of the immune system, we need to choose foods that increase antioxidant levels, boost cellular immunity and enhance mucous membrane integrity, maintain proper levels of stomach acid and other body secretions, and stabilize immune reactions.

Eat five to nine servings of fruit and vegetables daily

Antioxidants in fruit and vegetables, nuts, seeds and whole grains act as a defense mechanism against free radicals by collecting the free electron that floats outside some oxygen-containing molecules. This action makes the molecule more stable and prevents it from damaging the cell's DNA. Beta-carotene, lycopene and other carotenoids, vitamin E, vitamin C, selenium and glutathione are some of the best antioxidants we can find in our foods. Many of these substances have antihistamine properties (vitamin C) and tumor destruction abilities (selenium). Studies also show that carotenoids can boost immune cells. Green tea is also an excellent antioxidant with antimicrobial properties.

Best foods

- Beta-carotene, lycopene and other carotenoids: carrots, tomatoes, red and orange bell peppers, sweet potatoes, pumpkin and other winter squashes, kale, spinach, apricots, mango
- Vitamin E: wheat germ, almonds, sunflower seeds, cooked organic soybeans
- Vitamin C: oranges, strawberries, kiwifruit, red bell peppers, sweet potatoes, broccoli, kale
- Selenium: Brazil nuts, garlic, barley, brown rice, oatmeal, tofu
- Glutathione: watermelon, avocados, cruciferous vegetables

Increase foods that are high in lean protein

The body uses amino acids, the building blocks of protein, to assemble immune cells and immunoglobulins responsible for fighting infections. These building blocks are also essential for skin and mucous membrane integrity and as biological enzymes. Enzymes are needed for chemical reactions in the body, including antioxidant and detoxification systems.

Best foods

- Legumes (beans, peas, lentils, organic soybeans)
- Nuts and seeds (ground flaxseed, sesame seeds, sunflower seeds, almonds, cashews)
- Fresh fish

In particular, soy foods, which are rich in protein, are also high in phytoestrogens, plant derived estrogens that may protect against some cancers by blocking estrogen's cancer-promoting effect. (See Caution, page 101.)

Best foods

- Organically, non-genetically modified soybeans, tofu, soy milk

Increase unsaturated fats in your diet

Reducing trans-fats and saturated fats can boost immune function because these fats appear to impair the immune system. Omega-3 and omega-6 polyunsaturated fatty acids are anti-inflammatory (omega-3) and help protect against cancer. They also help with the absorption of fat-soluble vitamins, such as vitamins A and E. Phytosterols, or plant-based oils, also help reduce inflammation. Of particular benefit are sterols and sterolins, which can be found in abundance in nuts and seeds.

Best foods

- Avocados, olives and extra virgin olive oil, nuts and seeds (especially flaxseeds and flaxseed oil), fresh fatty fish (salmon, halibut, sardines)

Learn stress-management techniques and keep stress levels low

When our body is exposed to constant high levels of stress, our adrenal glands produce higher levels of the hormone cortisol. Cortisol is the body's natural corticosteroid, which in normal amounts helps keep allergies and inflammation under control. At high levels, however, cortisol is an immune suppressant, causing the body to have a reduced ability to fight infections.

Best techniques

- Regular moderate exercise, daily relaxation techniques, deep breathing, daily routine, rest

Top 10 Best Bets for Immune Health

❶ Soy foods: High in protein, complex carbohydrates and phytonutrients, organic, non-genetically modified soy products are a favorite food for disease prevention. Although the research is conflicting and inconclusive, the soy phytoestrogens, genistein and daidzein may protect women against some forms of cancer by blocking estrogen receptors. Some studies show that a diet rich in phytoestrogens may also reduce the risk of prostate cancer in men. Look for organic, non-genetically modified soybeans and soy foods. (See Caution, page 101)

❷ Cruciferous vegetables: Broccoli, cauliflower, cabbage, Brussels sprouts, kale and collard greens are part of the cruciferous, or Brassica family. These are a favorite because they provide a wide range of nutrients, including indoles. Indole-3-carbinol has the ability to convert a harmful estrogen molecule into its non-harmful metabolites, thereby protecting against some forms of cancer.

❸ Flaxseed oil: Flaxseed oil is an excellent choice because it is one of the few sources rich in omega-3 polyunsaturated fatty acids. Polyunsaturated fatty acids from flaxseed oil are converted to EPA (eicosapentaenoic acid), the active molecule also found in fish oils, which acts to inhibit the inflammatory cascade. Studies show that using flaxseed oil in foods reduces the substances that contribute to inflammation. So, add flaxseed oil to salads and soups or blend a small amount in smoothies in the morning. Remember not to heat flaxseed oil, and keep it refrigerated in a dark bottle to prevent rancidity.

❹ Shiitake mushrooms: Time and time again, shiitake mushrooms have been reported to have cancer-preventing properties. Mycochemicals, the active constituents in shiitake mushrooms, may stop the growth of tumors by suggesting a programmed death to the individual cancer cells.

❺ Tomatoes: Lycopene, found abundantly in tomatoes, plays a crucial role as an antioxidant in our bodies, providing protection against some forms of cancer (including lung and prostate) and boosting the immune system. Lycopene is also found in tomato juice and pizza sauce. In fact, processed and cooked tomato products contain a more bioavailable form of lycopene than do raw tomatoes.

❻ Avocados: This simply delicious fruit — among the most studied and documented foods — proves to be one of the best in providing symptom relief for patients with osteoarthritis. Avocados are high in the antioxidant glutathione and rich in monounsaturated fats.

❼ Brown rice: Rice is a staple of the diet in Asia, where the incidence of breast and colon cancer is below that of the Western world. Rice can offer protection against cancer, including breast and colon cancers, when eaten unprocessed instead of in its white form. Brown rice is also extraordinary in that it has low allergenic potential when compared to other grains. This makes it less of a burden for our immune system, which is overtaxed by many other allergens and pollutants.

❽ Blueberries: Blueberries are a rich source of anthocyanins, which destroy free radicals in the body. In fact, studies put blueberries at the top of the list of best antioxidant foods, especially on the basis of typical serving sizes.

❾ Green tea: Polyphenols in green tea have significant antioxidant, anti-inflammatory and antimicrobial properties. Even with moderate consumption (2 cups/500 mL per day), green tea has the ability to protect against oxidative damage of the DNA in the cells, lowering the risk of cancer.

⑩ **Pumpkin seeds:** Pumpkin seeds are high in zinc, a mineral that boosts immunity, protects against free radicals and is needed for wound repair. Zinc helps prevent recurrent infections, and reduce the duration of cold symptoms. Pumpkin seed oil can also be used to destroy parasites in the intestinal tract.

Foods that Enhance the Immune System

Best Foods for Enhancing Immune System	Immune System Benefits	Comments
FRUITS		
Citrus: • Oranges • Mandarin • Lemons • Grapefruit	Rich in vitamin C and bioflavonoids, which are antioxidants and protect against cancer.	Whole fruit is best; otherwise, use freshly squeezed juices. Caution: Grapefruit juice can interfere with some medications.
Orange/Yellow: • Mangoes • Apricots • Peaches	Contain carotenoids and vitamin C, which are antioxidants. Enhance immune system function.	Choose locally grown fruits when possible.
Blue/Purple: • Blueberries and other berries • Purple grapes • Plums	Contain anthocyanins, which destroy free radicals.	Blueberry season runs from May though September; otherwise, choose frozen ones to use in your cooking.
VEGETABLES		
Red Nightshades: • Tomatoes • Red bell peppers	Rich in the antioxidant lycopene. High in beta-carotene, which has immune cell-boosting properties.	Lycopene is fat-soluble and must be eaten with a fat in order to be absorbed.
Orange/Yellow: • Carrots • Yams • Sweet potatoes • Pumpkin and other winter squashes	Contain carotenoids rich in antioxidants and support the immune system.	Eat carrots lightly steamed for better nutrient absorption.
Green: • Spinach • Swiss chard • Asparagus • Dandelion greens • Other dark leafy greens	Contain folic acid, essential for healthy cell reproduction and genetic material (DNA) replication.	1 cup (250 mL) of leafy vegetables is 1 serving.
Cruciferous Family: • Broccoli • Cauliflower • Brussels sprouts • Cabbage • Kale • Collard greens	Contain glutathione, a powerful antioxidant. Contain indoles, which eliminate excess estrogens and carcinogens, helping in cancer prevention.	Eat raw or lightly steamed.

Best Foods for Enhancing Immune System	Immune System Benefits	Comments
VEGETABLES (cont.)		
Allium Family: • Garlic • Onions and chives	Contain allyl sulfides, which destroy cancer cells and support immune function. Contain antimicrobial properties.	Use garlic and onions daily in your cooking, raw or cooked.
Mushrooms: • Shiitake • Maitake • Enoki	Powerful immune-boosting and antiviral properties.	Enjoy them in soups and salads. Can be found dried. Rehydrate them in boiling water and keep the soaking liquid for a rich and nutritious soup.
LEGUMES		
• Beans • Organic soybeans • Lentils • Peas • Chickpeas	Beans are high in protein, soluble fiber and complex carbohydrates. Soybeans contain phytoestrogens, plant-derived estrogens that may protect against some cancers.	Soy products include tofu, tempeh, organic soybeans and soymilk. Use dried peas and beans in soups, salads and dips. Must be soaked before cooking.
WHOLE GRAINS		
• Brown rice • Whole oats • Barley	Whole grains are important for their B vitamin content. Many contain high amounts of the antioxidant selenium. Brown rice seems to be less allergenic than other grains.	Choose whole grains rather than refined products and flours. The hull, removed during processing, contains most of the nutrients.
NUTS AND SEEDS		
Nuts and nut butters: • Brazil nuts • Almonds • Walnuts	High in protein, fiber and unsaturated fats needed for healthy immune function.	Nut and nut butters add protein to salads, snacks and soups. Nuts are an incomplete source of protein; complete the protein by eating with a grain.
Seeds and seed butters: • Sunflower seeds • Pumpkin seeds • Sesame seeds • Flaxseeds	Contain essential fatty acids (EFAs), needed for healthy immune function. Flaxseeds contain omega-3 fats, which have anti-inflammatory properties. Pumpkin seeds are high in zinc, essential for boosting cellular immunity and thymus gland development.	Eat the seeds whole or freshly ground daily. Try seed butters. Flaxseeds must be ground.

Best Foods for Enhancing Immune System	Immune System Benefits	Comments
FATS AND OILS		
Cold-pressed oils: • Extra virgin olive oil • Flaxseed oil	Flaxseed oil contains omega-3 essential fatty acids (EFAs), which have anti-inflammatory properties.	Look for cold-pressed, less refined oils that are packaged in dark glass containers. Keep oils in the refrigerator to keep them from going rancid.
Fish: • Salmon • Mackerel • Albacore tuna • Sardines • Herring	Contain omega-3 essential fatty acids (EFAs), which have anti-inflammatory properties.	These fish are the highest in EFAs. Consume 2 to 3 times per week and choose wild instead of farmed fish.
HERBS AND SPICES		
• Fennel • Ginger • Turmeric • Rosemary • Thyme • Sage	Most herbs are antioxidant. Turmeric has anti-inflammatory properties. Thyme has 75 identified antioxidants.	Use fresh or dried in cooking on a regular basis
OTHER		
• Beer • Coffee • Tea • Wine	Rich in bioflavonoids. Green tea is a rich source of the catechin epigallocatechin gallate (EGCG) that seems to offer antigen-fighting abilities.	Consume in moderation. Not recommended during pregnancy and lactation. Limit coffee to one cup per day and substitute green tea for the other times when coffee might be consumed.

Musculoskeletal System

Healthy Musculoskeletal System

Muscles, bones, joints and connective tissue make up the musculoskeletal system, responsible for the movement of the human body and its individual parts. The musculoskeletal system also gives structure to the body and physically protects the internal organs.

Nutrition is very important in the management of this system. For example, muscle contraction and relaxation depend on minerals like calcium and magnesium to perform movements and maintain an upright posture and balance. Bones also need minerals to maintain their density and withstand the pulling forces created by the muscles and the impact of accidents and falls.

Another important part of the musculoskeletal system is the joints, such as the hip, knees and elbows. Within the joints, the ends of the bones are covered with cartilage and are surrounded by synovial fluid, a lubricating fluid, which allows smooth and frictionless motion where two bones meet.

Musculoskeletal Disorders

Arthritis, osteoporosis, low back pain, muscle spasms and cramps, sprains and strains

Muscle cramping and spasms can occur with dehydration and if minerals such as calcium, sodium, potassium and magnesium are not in the proper balance. This can cause simple cramping of the calf muscle or can aggravate existing conditions, such as low back pain. Low back pain can also be due to misalignment of the spine or other parts of the skeleton, nerve impingement, injury and chronic inflammation.

Inflammation also occurs during arthritis. There are many types of arthritis, some with more inflammation than others. For example, osteoarthritis, the most common type, is characterized by wear and tear at the joints, wearing down of the joint cartilage, and causing changes in the bone. Although minimal, osteoarthritis consists of some inflammation at the joint and in surrounding tissues. Symptoms can be stiffness and pain at the joint and eventually restricted joint function. On the other hand, rheumatoid arthritis is an autoimmune condition characterized by chronic inflammation that can affect the joints as well as other areas of the body. Rheumatoid arthritis can give symptoms of inflammation at the joint, such as pain, redness, swelling and eventually deformity, but also generalized symptoms of fatigue, weakness and low-grade fever. Regardless of the cause and the differing symptoms and location, nutrition is essential to repair and build cartilage and decrease inflammation.

Unlike arthritis, osteoporosis is mostly symptom-free, which is why people at increased risk must get regular bone-density checks. In osteoporosis, the bone density is diminished and the bones become brittle and susceptible to fractures. The density of the bone depends on many nutrients, such as calcium, magnesium and zinc, for the strength to withstand trauma, perform movement and provide support.

Optimizing Musculoskeletal Function

To maintain the musculoskeletal system in top shape, we need to eat foods that are high in vitamins and minerals, foods that help us maintain a balanced acid-base environment, and foods that deal with inflammation. Of course, regular exercise is just as important as eating well.

Eat foods that are high in minerals

Foods such as leafy green vegetables, nuts and seeds, legumes and grains are loaded with minerals that are essential for the functioning of the muscles, the building of bones and the maintenance of healthy joints. For example, calcium and magnesium are essential for muscle contraction and relaxation. Calcium, magnesium, zinc and many trace minerals, such as boron, manganese and copper, are needed to build strong bones and prevent the risk of fractures with osteoporosis.

Best foods
- Calcium: leafy green vegetables, broccoli, almonds, canned fish bones (sardines, salmon), tofu, soymilk, corn tortillas
- Magnesium: nuts and seeds, grains, beans, dark green vegetables
- Zinc: pumpkin seeds, black-eyed peas, tofu, wheat germ
- Boron: raisins, prunes, almonds
- Manganese: nuts and seeds, wheat, leafy green vegetables, beet tops, pineapple
- Copper: nuts, legumes, cereals, potatoes

Eat foods that are high in vitamins

Many vitamins essential for lowering the risk of osteoporosis can be found in foods, such as leafy green vegetables, cruciferous vegetables and fish. For example, vitamin D, which is converted to its active form by the ultraviolet rays of the sun, helps increase the absorption of the calcium that is important for keeping bones strong.

Vitamin K helps mineralize bone during bone formation. Increasing the levels of vitamin K can decrease the risk of osteoporosis. This is easily achieved by increasing the consumption of leafy green vegetables.

B vitamins, especially vitamins B_6 (pyridoxine), B_{12} and folate, are needed to decrease homocysteine levels in the blood. High levels of homocysteine are detrimental in cardiovascular disease, as well as increasing the risk of osteoporosis by interfering with bone formation.

Best foods
- Vitamin D: sunlight, cod liver oil
- Vitamin K: leafy green vegetables (kale, collard greens, beet greens, parsley, broccoli, spinach)
- B vitamins: B_6: chickpeas, halibut
- B_{12}: fish, leafy green vegetables, grains

Eat foods that alkalinize the diet

When we eat a diet rich in fruits and vegetables, especially leafy greens, the body's acid-base (or pH) balance is at normal levels and calcium remains in the bones. On the other hand, when we eat a diet high in protein, refined sugars and soft drinks, as is common in our society, the pH of the body decreases and becomes too acidic. To buffer this high acidity, calcium from the bones is leached into the bloodstream, decreasing the density of the bone and increasing risk of osteoporosis and bone fractures.

Refined sugars, a high-protein diet and soft drinks (high in phosphates) can also increase the excretion of calcium in the urine.

Best foods
- String green beans, bananas, dandelion greens, grapes, fresh or dried figs, prunes, raisins, Swiss chard
- Also almonds, asparagus, avocados, beets, carrots, cranberries, kale, pomegranate, raspberries, spinach

Eat foods that decrease inflammation

Whole foods are especially important for the musculoskeletal system, which deals with trauma such as sprains and strains; and cases of chronic inflammation, such as arthritis. Fish oils are high in omega-3 fatty acids, which redirect the inflammation cascade and ease such symptoms as pain, swelling and stiffness.

Best foods
- Fish (salmon, mackerel, albacore tuna, sardines, herring), ground flaxseed and flaxseed oil, hemp seeds and hemp seed oil

Participate in a regular exercise routine

When a bone is exposed to repetitive physical stresses, its mass will increase over time. An increase in bone mass makes the bone stronger and less susceptible to fracture. Weight-bearing exercises, such as when the bones make contact with the ground while supporting body weight or when the muscles pull on the bone to make a movement, are an excellent way to place physical stress on bones. For example, walking is considered a weight-bearing exercise as compared to swimming. Swimming is still a good form of cardiovascular exercise, but it does not entail supporting the body's weight against the forces of gravity and contact with the ground. Lifting light weights is another safe way to increase bone density and decrease the risk of osteoporosis.

Exercise is also excellent for maintaining a healthy body weight. And it helps reduce pain and stiffness, increase circulation, and keep muscles toned to support the joints and prevent injuries.

Best exercises

- Brisk walking, weight training, yoga, jogging, swimming

Top 10 Best Bets for Musculoskeletal Health

❶ Almonds: Almonds are high in calcium and, like other nuts, high in magnesium. These minerals are important for contraction and relaxation of muscle and mineralization of bone. Almonds are a great all-round nutritious snack that is high in protein and monounsaturated fats.

❷ Tofu: Tofu has been the staple food of Asian cultures. It is made from curdled soy milk, the milky liquid extracted from cooked and ground soybeans. Tofu is an excellent source of high-quality protein, calcium (check the label first to see if calcium was added as a coagulant), iron and zinc. With its high mineral content, tofu is a great food to prevent against loss of bone mass and risk of fractures with osteoporosis.

Tofu, like all other soybean products, contains phytoestrogens (isoflavones), plant-based estrogens that may help to prevent osteoporosis, especially in post-menopausal women. Whenever possible, choose calcium sulfate (over magnesium sulfate) as the coagulating additive in tofu.

❸ Cruciferous vegetables: Broccoli, cabbage, cauliflower, Brussels sprouts and especially kale are very high in an easily absorbed form of calcium. Calcium, along with other minerals, is essential for maintaining high-bone density, helping decrease the risk of osteoporosis. Calcium is also essential for muscle contraction and nerve conduction.

Cruciferous vegetables are also high in vitamin C, which protects the joints against free-radical damage created during inflammation and helps stop the progression of arthritis by repairing and building new cartilage in the joints.

❹ Leafy greens: Vitamin K, found in leafy green vegetables, such as collard greens, Swiss chard, dandelion greens and beet greens, helps bind calcium to the bone matrix and reduce the excretion of calcium in the urine. Leafy green vegetables are also high in calcium and folic acid. Leafy greens are also beneficial because they create an alkaline environment in the body and prevent calcium extraction from the bones, thus protecting the body from osteoporosis.

❺ Fish oils: There is growing evidence that omega-3 fats are beneficial in the prevention and treatment of arthritis. Omega-3 fatty acids, found in fish and flaxseed oil, have anti-inflammatory properties. Fish oils in particular contain the fatty acids in their final form and help control inflammation, while fatty acids from flaxseed oil must be converted in the body before they can perform their anti-inflammatory function.

❻ Turmeric: Turmeric can halt the enzyme that produces inflammation and inhibits the break down of cortisone in the body, which makes turmeric a great anti-inflammatory. Cortisone, the body's own anti-inflammatory steroid, helps reduce inflammation. Through these means, turmeric can help decrease the symptoms of arthritis and prevent further damage to the cartilage in the joints.

❼ Ginger: Ginger is anti-inflammatory in two ways. One way it decreases inflammation is by inhibiting the enzymes that promote inflammation. This helps terminate the inflammation cascade and prevent swelling and pain. Ginger also helps make white blood cells more stable so they release fewer inflammation mediators. This means that ginger can help diminish the destruction of cartilage and reduce symptoms of arthritis.

❽ Citrus fruit: Citrus fruits, such as oranges, grapefruit, lemons, limes and mandarins, are alkalinizing to the body. Foods that alkalinize are beneficial in preventing osteoporosis because the body

no longer needs to take calcium from the bones to buffer acidity. Vitamin C from citrus fruits is also essential for building cartilage in the joints and other connective tissue. This can help with the progression of osteoarthritis and the repair of muscles, tendons and ligaments after surgery or injury. Vitamin C has anti-inflammatory, antihistaminic and antioxidant properties.

❾ Sunlight: Ultraviolet light from the sun converts 7-dehydrocholesterol in the skin into vitamin D_3. Vitamin D_3, which is converted to its more active forms in the liver and kidneys, stimulates the absorption of calcium through the digestive tract and the kidneys. This process is essential in the prevention of osteoporosis. People who live further away from the equator, have darker skin or use a sunscreen with SPF 8 or higher may need longer exposure to the sun to get the same benefits.

❿ Nuts and seeds: Nuts and seeds are an excellent source of magnesium, a mineral that is just as important for bone formation as is calcium, making it an essential nutrient for the prevention and treatment of osteoporosis. Magnesium from nuts and seeds is also essential for muscle relaxation, and can prevent muscle spasms and pain in such conditions as chronic low back pain.

Foods that Enhance the Musculoskeletal System

Best Foods for Enhancing Musculoskeletal System	Musculoskeletal System Benefits	Comments
FRUITS		
Citrus: • Oranges • Lemons • Limes • Grapefruit • Kiwifruit • Strawberries	Rich in antioxidants essential to prevent damage to inflamed joints. Citrus fruits alkalinize the body and inhibit the calcium loss from bones. Rich in vitamin C, which helps build and repair cartilage and connective tissue.	Choose oranges that do not look perfect and are not spongy in texture. Perfect-looking oranges likely have been treated with preservatives, pesticides and colorings. Spongy texture may indicate that the fruit is soft inside and either damaged or not fresh.
• Pineapple • Papaya • Mangoes • Apricots • Melons (cantaloupe, honeydew, watermelon)	Contain vitamin C, which helps build and repair cartilage in joints.	
Blue/Purple: • Blueberries and other berries • Purple grapes • Plums	Contain anthocyanins, which destroy free radicals and prevent further damage to the joints.	Choose blueberries that are dark blue, plump, firm, dry and free from stems and leaves.
VEGETABLES		
Nightshades: • Tomatoes • Potatoes • Peppers (bell peppers, hot peppers) • Eggplant	Contain vitamin C and carotenoids.	Avoiding nightshade vegetables, which contain solanine, may bring relief to some arthritis patients.
Leafy green vegetables: • Spinach • Swiss chard • Dandelion greens • Beet greens	Contain folate, which helps decrease homocysteine levels, a risk factor for osteoporosis. Leafy green vegetables help alkalinize the diet and keep calcium in the bones. Source of vitamin K for mineralization of bone.	Vitamin K is not available as a supplement. High doses can interfere with the effect of some pharmaceutical drugs.
Cruciferous Family: • Broccoli • Cauliflower • Brussels sprouts • Cabbage • Kale • Collard greens	High in calcium needed for muscle contraction and bone formation.	Collard greens have leaves that are relatively tough in texture. Cook for 8 to 10 minutes on medium heat. Use as a substitute for cabbage. Great for juicing.

Best Foods for Enhancing Musculoskeletal System	Musculoskeletal System Benefits	Comments
LEGUMES		
• Beans • Organic soybeans • Lentils • Peas • Chickpeas	Beans are high in magnesium for muscle relaxation and bone building. Soybeans contain phytoestrogens, which may help protect women against osteoporosis. Tofu is a great source of calcium, as this mineral is often added to help set the tofu.	Generally, soy milk is fortified with calcium and other minerals. Soft tofu is ideal for blending into smoothies, creamy soups and dressings. Consult with your naturopathic doctor or nutritionist before consuming large amounts of soy.
WHOLE GRAINS		
• Brown rice • Whole oats • Barley	Whole grains are important for their B vitamin content, which helps keep homocysteine levels low and decrease the risk of osteoporosis.	Choose whole grains rather than refined products and flours. The hull, removed during processing, contains most of the nutrients.
NUTS AND SEEDS		
Nuts and nut butters: • Brazil nuts • Almonds • Walnuts	Contain magnesium, essential for muscle relaxation; and preventing some forms of low back pain. Magnesium is also needed for making energy in the body.	Eat 10 raw almonds per day. Try almond butter.
Seeds and seed butters: • Sunflower seeds • Pumpkin seeds • Sesame seeds • Flaxseeds	Seeds are high in magnesium and zinc (pumpkin seeds), which are necessary for bone mineralization.	Eat the seeds whole or freshly ground daily. Try seed butters.
FATS AND OILS		
Cold-pressed oils: • Extra virgin olive oil • Flaxseed oil • Hemp seed oil • Canola oil	Flaxseed oil and hemp seed oil contain omega-3 essential fatty acids (EFAs), which have anti-inflammatory properties. Canola oil is a source of vitamin K, needed for bone formation.	Vitamin K is a fat-soluble vitamin that must be eaten with a source of fat in order to be absorbed. Vitamin K is also produced by the healthy bacteria in the intestines.
Fish: • Salmon • Mackerel • Albacore tuna • Sardines • Herring	Contain omega-3 essential fatty acids (EFAs), which have anti-inflammatory properties.	These fish are the highest in EFAs. Consume 2 to 3 times per week and choose wild instead of farmed fish.
HERBS AND SPICES		
• Ginger • Turmeric	Ginger is highly effective at decreasing pain and inflammation. Turmeric has anti-inflammatory properties.	One teaspoon (5 mL) of ground turmeric blended in a smoothie will help prevent post-exercise cramping.

Nervous System

Healthy Nervous System

The nervous system is a highly complex system made up of two main parts, the central and the peripheral nervous systems, which together allow us to respond to our internal and external environments. The central nervous system consists of the brain and the spinal cord, while the peripheral nervous system is made up of nerves (sensory and motor) and connects the central nervous system with other parts of the body.

The peripheral nervous system is responsible for receiving information, such as taste, sound or hormone levels, from the internal and external environments and for relaying that information to the central nervous system via peripheral sensory nerves. The spinal cord and brain integrate this information in the central nervous system and generate a response, which is then sent to other parts of the body via the peripheral motor nerves. For example, the peripheral sensory nerves might relay information about a song on the radio to the spinal cord and the brain. A response would then be sent through the peripheral motor nerves to make a movement to turn up the radio.

Of course, not all responses are conscious. The peripheral nervous system also consists of the autonomic nervous system, which controls internal organs and glands, such as the heart, or the thyroid gland, which is responsible for the body's metabolism. Through this system, consisting of sympathetic and parasympathetic responses, the body can maintain an internal balance and react to different stimuli based on the needed responses. For example, a sympathetic or "fight or flight" response is created when you are frightened or stressed. This response causes your heart rate to increase. In contrast, a parasympathetic response allows you to perform such functions as relaxing and digesting your food after a meal. These two parts of the autonomic nervous system act on the same organs and glands, but have opposing effects, helping maintain balance in the body.

Individual nerve cells (neurons) use neurotransmitters, chemicals that allow them to communicate with each other and with other cells in the body. For example, the neurotransmitter seratonin is involved in memory, emotions, wakefulness, sleep and temperature regulation. Acetylcholine allows for communication between the nervous system and the muscles to create a movement. An imbalance of neurotrasmitters can result in dysfunction in the nervous system, which is why neurotransmitters are often the target of pharmaceutical and recreational drugs.

Nervous System Disorders

Depression and seasonal affective disorder (SAD), memory loss and decreased cognitive function

Depression is a condition that occurs when there is an imbalance of neurotransmitters in the brain. It can be characterized by a loss of interest or pleasure in usual activities and a lack of energy. It can also affect appetite, with either a decrease or increase, and subsequent changes in body weight. Depression can be quite debilitating and can trigger feelings of worthlessness or even thoughts of death or suicide.

Seasonal affective disorder (SAD) is a form of depression that occurs with diminished exposure to sunlight in the winter months. This disorder may result in the general symptoms of depression, and also an increase in sleep, appetite and perhaps body weight.

Anxiety is a devastating psychiatric disorder that can consist of feelings of agitation, nervousness, fearfulness, irritability or shyness. Other symptoms may include heart palpitations, flushing of the face, sweating, shallow breathing or even fainting. Both anxiety and depression can be caused by psychological factors; a physical cause, such as trauma or illness; nutrient deficiencies; or the side effects of medications.

As a result of normal living and aging, the nervous system suffers from oxidation of its cells, improper nutrient status and a decrease in blood circulation. These and other factors can lead to a decline in neurotransmitter levels, a decrease in the number of connections between neurons and an actual decrease in brain size, leading to a decrease in cognitive function and memory loss.

Optimizing the Nervous System

To help maintain optimal nervous system functioning, you must eat whole foods that are rich in vitamins and minerals and that help maintain constant blood sugar levels. It's also important to engage in regular physical exercise, go outside to catch some sunlight and practice relaxation techniques.

Eat a diet rich in complex carbohydrates

The brain relies on a constant supply of glucose as its primary source of energy. Glucose is one of the building blocks of carbohydrates. However, there are a few other things to take into consideration. Carbohydrates can come in two forms — simple and complex. Simple carbohydrates, when broken down in the digestive tract, are absorbed rapidly into the bloodstream and can cause a quick rise in blood sugar. This rapid increase in blood sugar can lead to symptoms of hyperactivity or anxiety and is followed by a rapid decline or sugar "crash," which can give symptoms of fatigue, irritability or depression. Pasta, breads, crackers and cereals made of refined products, candy and soft drinks are examples of simple carbohydrates. These foods are also devoid of nutrients, such as vitamins and minerals.

On the other hand, complex carbohydrates contain fiber, which slows down the rate at which sugar is absorbed into the body, allowing for a more constant level of blood sugar that can help stabilize mood patterns. Complex carbohydrates are found in whole grains, beans and other legumes, fruits and vegetables, and nuts and seeds. Proteins and fats can also help slow down the absorption of sugar into the bloodstream.

It is also important to note that caffeine can affect blood sugar levels in a negative manner and can cause symptoms of hyperactivity, depression, fatigue, irritability, insomnia or anxiety.

Best foods
- Whole grains, legumes (beans, soybeans, chickpeas, lentils)
- All fruits and vegetables
- Nuts and seeds (almonds, cashews, walnuts, sesame seeds, sunflower seeds, pumpkin seeds)

Eat a diet rich in omega-3 fatty acids

The nervous system, including the brain, contains a high concentration of omega-3 fatty acids, which cannot be made in the body and must be obtained from the diet. Omega-3 fatty acids, such as those obtained from flaxseed oil and fish oils, are not only components of all cell membranes, including nerve cells (neurons), but they also help regulate nerve cell function and signal transmission. The brain and neurons are highly dependent on the quality of the fats from the diet, and this factor can impact behavior, mood and mental function.

Omega-3 fatty acids have also been proven to have some effect through their anti-inflammatory function, preventing the production of inflammatory mediators that might be linked with mood disorders.

Best foods
- Fish oils (salmon, mackerel, albacore tuna, sardines, herring), flaxseed oil, organic soy oil, hempseed oil, canola oil, walnuts

Eat a diet rich in B vitamins

B vitamins are essential for the functioning of the nervous system. For example, the brain needs vitamin B_1 (thiamin) to be able to use glucose as fuel. Without vitamin B_1, the brain cannot function properly and can lead to symptoms of anxiety, irritability, fatigue and depression. B_1 also inhibits an enzyme that breaks down neurotransmitters, thereby boosting their levels in the brain. Vitamins B_6 (pyridoxine), B_{12} and folic acid are absolutely essential for the manufacturing of mood-regulating neurotransmitters, such as melatonin, seratonin and dopamine, which may be why these vitamins seem to have antidepressant effects. Vitamin B_{12} is also involved in the production of the myelin sheath, the fatty covering of the neurons that helps protect them and speed up the conduction of nerve impulses.

Foods such as whole grains, legumes and fish are good sources of B vitamins. It is also interesting that refined carbohydrates and some prescription medications, including oral contraceptives and antidepressants, can deplete the body's levels of B vitamins. If you are taking prescription medications, check with your health professional to see what foods you should be eating to prevent deficiencies.

Best foods
- Vitamin B_1: whole wheat, sweet potatoes, peas, beans, fish, peanuts
- Vitamin B_6: potatoes, bananas, legumes (lentils, chickpeas) fish (halibut), whole grains (rice)
- Vitamin B_{12}: fish (and other animal products), spirulina (blue-green algae), seaweed
- Folate: lentils, pinto beans, rice, leafy green vegetables

Learn ways of coping with stress

The stress of everyday life or stress caused by a major life event can produce a sympathetic response known as a "fight or flight" response. The nervous system here works in conjunction with the endocrine system by signaling to the adrenal glands to release adrenalin and other stress-related hormones. These hormones can alter blood sugar levels and change moods accordingly. In fact, excess or ongoing stress, can create feelings of irritability, fatigue, insomnia, depression or anxiety.

Techniques that induce a relaxation response and switch the nervous system from sympathetic to parasympathetic mode help optimize your nervous system.

Best techniques
- Meditation, prayer, breathing exercise, physical exercises, counseling

Get plenty of exercise

Exercise is one the most powerful antidepressants available and has repeatedly proven to decrease feelings of anxiety, depression and fatigue. Exercise increases endorphins, neurotransmitters that give a sense of well-being and elevate mood. It can also help increase self-image, self-confidence, mental performance and happiness.

Physical activity can benefit the nervous system in many different ways. For example, group exercises or sports can help elevate mood by creating a feeling of belonging. Other exercises give you a chance to "play" and can also be an excellent channel to let out frustrations and anger. Exercise can make you feel productive if lawn mowing, vacuuming or other types of yard or housework make up part of your work-out routine. Similarly, activities such as hiking or cross-country skiing can take you outdoors, breathing fresh air and enjoying different scenes. Any of these forms of physical activity are a step toward achieving a balanced nervous system.

Best exercises
- Weight lifting, brisk walking, jogging, bicycling, swimming, dancing, yoga, lawn mowing, vacuuming, racquet sports (such as tennis), team sports

Top 10 Best Bets for Nervous System Health

❶ **Fish:** The human brain is more than 60% fat, the majority being omega 3-fatty acids, which cannot be made in the body and must be obtained from the diet. Fish oils are the best source of omega-3 fatty acids. These fatty acids are essential for regulating mood and emotions and preventing depression. Fish oils are also beneficial for attention and memory.

Fish oils are also an excellent source of B vitamins, including vitamin B_{12}, which can be hard to find in a vegetarian diet. B vitamins are necessary for neurotransmitter and myelin sheath production, nerve conduction and utilization of fuel by the brain.

❷ **Whole grains:** Among the most important nutrients for the proper functioning of the nervous system is the group of B vitamins. B vitamins can be found in whole grains, such as whole wheat, whole oats, barley and brown rice. B vitamins are responsible for the manufacture of neurotransmitters and the proper use of fuel by the brain.

Whole grains also help maintain stable moods and energy levels throughout the day by helping to control blood sugar levels.

❸ **Spirulina or blue-green algae:** Spirulina, or blue-green algae, is a microscopic plant that is found in some lakes. Spirulina is a rich source of protein, as it contains amino acids essential for neurotransmitter production. It also contains vitamins, minerals and essential fatty acids. Spirulina can provide small amounts of vitamin B_{12}, which helps produce red blood cells and myelin, helping to increase oxygen to the brain and the speed of nerve impulses.

❹ **Oats:** Oats are one of the best foods for nourishing the nervous system. They can be used specifically to prevent debility and exhaustion caused by anxiety and depression. Oats can help relax the nervous system in conditions, such as insomnia, anxiety and stress. Oats can also help with the symptoms of drug withdrawal, especially nicotine withdrawal in smoking cessation. Oats are a rich source of B vitamins and contain fiber, which can help control blood sugar levels.

❺ **Brewer's yeast:** Brewer's yeast is the dried, powdered *Saccharomyces cerevisiae* fungus used in the brewing process. Brewer's yeast is an extraordinary source of B vitamins, which help maintain a healthy nervous system. It is also the best source of chromium, a mineral that is essential for blood sugar regulation.

❻ **Blackstrap molasses:** Molasses is a by-product of the manufacture of sugar. Blackstrap molasses is mostly sugar, but unlike refined sugars, it contains significant amounts of vitamins and minerals. In particular, blackstrap molasses is a source of B vitamins, calcium, magnesium and iron. These nutrients help with the production of brain neurotransmitters and general nervous system functioning.

❼ **Chocolate:** Chocolate consumption has been linked with the release of seratonin in the brain, a neurotransmitter that is thought to produce feelings of pleasure. Caution: Chocolate contains small amounts of caffeine and most likely contains sugar, substances that can lead to blood sugar fluctuations and mood changes. Consume dark chocolate in moderation.

❽ **Exercise:** Exercise is a very important component of a healthy nervous system. Exercise helps increase the circulation of blood, oxygen and glucose to the brain, which can help sharpen your cognitive skills such as memory. It also helps increase self-confidence and self-image, and by stimulating the release of endorphins, it can elevate mood.

⑨ **Barley:** The glycemic index (GI) is an index that ranks foods on how they affect blood sugar levels. Barley is exceptional because it has the lowest GI rating of any grain. This means that when eating barley, blood sugar levels remain relatively constant and so does the supply of glucose to the brain. The low GI of this food means it can help prevent mood fluctuations that may occur with anxiety, depression, hyperactivity or premenstrual syndrome in women.

⑩ **Nuts and seeds:** Nuts and seeds are a source of protein that when broken down provide amino acids, the building blocks for neurotransmitters. B vitamins, also found in these foods, help with the production of these neurotransmitters and make glucose available to the brain for fuel. Nuts and seeds also contain fiber, which helps keep blood sugar levels constant. Magnesium, calcium, zinc and selenium, found in a variety of nuts and seeds, may help prevent neurological disorders.

Foods that Protect the Nervous System

Best Foods for Protecting the Nervous System	Nervous System Benefits	Comments
FRUITS		
Citrus: • Oranges • Mandarins • Lemons • Grapefruit • Kiwifruit • Strawberries	Contain fiber, which helps control blood sugar levels. Contain vitamin C and bioflavonoids, required to synthesize neurotransmitters and as antioxidants for the nervous system.	Fruit juice contains large amounts of fructose, a natural sugar, and it does not contain fiber. Fruit juice can raise blood sugar levels rapidly.
• Apricots • Peaches • Pears • Apples	Contain pectin and other soluble fiber that can help control blood sugar levels. Pears contain B vitamins, and can help optimize nervous system function.	Most fruits and vegetables contain a mixture of soluble and insoluble fibers and have the ability to slow down the absorption of sugar.
Berries and grapes: • Blueberries • Blackberries • Raspberries • Red grapes	Red grapes are a great source of B vitamins, and like berries are rich sources of bioflavonoids. These protect brain cells against oxidation, and some nervous system disorders.	
VEGETABLES		
Green: • Spinach • Swiss chard • Dandelion greens • Endive • Other dark leafy greens	Leafy green vegetables contain folate, essential for the manufacture of neurotransmitters and optimal function of the nervous system.	Lightly steam these vegetables to reduce nutrient loss and increase nutrient absorption.

Best Foods for Protecting the Nervous System	Nervous System Benefits	Comments
VEGETABLES (cont.)		
Cruciferous Family: • Broccoli • Cabbage • Sauerkraut • Cauliflower • Kale • Bok choy	Cruciferous vegetables contain large amounts of vitamin C, a powerful antioxidant that helps protect the nervous system and restore normal levels of neurotransmitters.	Note that oral contraceptives, antibiotics, stress, pregnancy, infection and surgery can increase the need for vitamin C.
LEGUMES		
• Beans (lima, navy, organic soybeans) • Lentils • Peas • Chickpeas	Legumes are a source of soluble fiber. Soybeans are a good source of vitamins B_1, B_3, B_5 and B_6, which help prevent anxiety and depression. Lima and navy beans contain folate.	Soaking beans for 8 hours and rinsing well before and after cooking makes them easier to digest.
WHOLE GRAINS		
• Whole oats • Brown rice • Pot Barley • Buckwheat • Quinoa • Whole wheat • Spelt • Rye	Barley is one of the best whole grains for controlling the rate at which glucose is absorbed into the bloodstream. All whole grains are a good source of B vitamins.	
NUTS AND SEEDS		
Nuts: • Almonds • Brazil nuts • Walnuts • Hazelnuts • Pine nuts	Nuts contain fiber, which helps control blood sugar levels and contain B vitamins. They also contain amino acids, the building blocks for mood-regulating neurotransmitters. Brazil nuts are high in selenium, which can elevate mood and decrease anxiety.	Magnesium, which is found in abundance in nuts, may help prevent depression and other neurological disorders.
Seeds: • Sesame seeds • Sunflower seeds • Pumpkin seeds	Seeds are high in fiber, and fats, which help control blood sugar levels. Contain amino acids, the building blocks for mood-regulating neurotransmitters.	Zinc found in pumpkin seeds may help prevent depression.

Best Foods for Protecting the Nervous System	Nervous System Benefits	Comments
FATS AND OILS		
Cold-pressed oils: • Flaxseed oil • Soy oil • Hempseed oil • Canola oil • Avocados	These oils are a source of omega-3 fatty acids, which are an essential component of the nervous system and necessary for its function. Avocados are a good source of B vitamins.	Other vegetable oils, such as sunflower and safflower oils, are higher in omega-6 fatty acids, another type of essential fatty acid that must be obtained from the diet. These vegetable oils contain little omega-3 fatty acids.
Fish: • Salmon • Mackerel • Albacore tuna • Sardines • Herring	Best source of omega-3 oils, which make up a large portion of the nervous system. Contain high amounts of B vitamins, including B_{12}, essential for nervous system function.	Small amounts of vitamin B_{12} can also be obtained from algae and seaweed.
OTHER		
• Blackstrap molasses	Contains B vitamins, essential for nervous system function. Also a source of magnesium, required for neurotransmitter production.	1 cup (250 ml) molasses can be used as a substitute for 1 cup (250 mL) liquid honey, $1/2$ cup (125 mL) brown sugar or 1 cup (250 mL) dark corn syrup or 1 cup (250 mL) pure maple syrup.
• Brewer's yeast	A good source of B vitamins, including B_1, B_3, B_5, B_6 and folate.	Do not confuse brewer's yeast with baking yeast or nutritional yeast.
• Spirulina (blue-green algae) Seaweed	A source of vitamin B_{12}, otherwise hard to find in a vegetarian diet. Essential for the manufacture of neurotransmitters and myelin sheath and for nerve conduction.	Hydrochloric acid (stomach acid) and intrinsic factor (a protein that binds vitamin B_{12}) are both produced by the stomach cells and aid its absorption in the large intestine.

Respiratory System

Healthy Respiratory System

The respiratory system is responsible for the exchange of oxygen and carbon dioxide between the external environment and the blood. The air that we breathe travels in through the nose, past the pharynx and larynx, down the trachea, into the bronchi and bronchioles and eventually reaches its destination, the lungs. In the lungs, the exchange of gases occurs in tiny air sacs called alveoli, where oxygen from the air enters the bloodstream and carbon dioxide from the bloodstream enters the air to be expelled. Through the actions of inspiration and expiration, the air flows in and out of the lungs providing all body cells with the fresh supply of oxygen essential to them for survival.

The respiratory system is also responsible for protecting the body against microbes, toxic chemicals and foreign matter. This is achieved with the help of cilia, tiny hair-like structures that sweep mucous and foreign materials out of the system. The cilia also work with the immune system to produce mucous and perform phagocytosis (engulfing pathogens and debris).

Respiratory System Disorders

Asthma and allergies, respiratory tract infections, lung cancer

Asthma is the most common illness associated with the respiratory system. It is an inflammatory condition of the lungs and airways in which swelling, smooth muscle contraction and excess mucous production create acute breathing difficulties. Someone who suffers from asthma might experience a feeling of tightness and constriction of the chest, with shortness of breath, wheezing and coughing. It is believed that asthma, like allergies, is a hypersensitivity disorder and therefore greatly linked to the immune system.

The respiratory system is the most susceptible to infection because it is directly exposed to the external environment. Therefore, respiratory infections, such as colds, sinusitis, bronchitis and pneumonia, also greatly depend on the immune system. Here, the immune system is responsible for protecting the respiratory system by producing mucous, attacking foreign invaders and developing a proper response to fight pathogens once they enter the body.

The respiratory system is also susceptible to cancer. Lung cancer is the most prevalent form of cancer today and can affect one or both lungs. Smoking is the biggest risk factor for lung cancer, so quitting smoking is a valuable method in its prevention. Other methods include eating a vitamin-rich diet, which can help reduce the risk of cancer, but there is also the chance that cancer will come back once treated.

Optimizing the Respiratory System

To protect the respiratory system from disease, we need to heal and moisten the mucous membranes, keep the cilia healthy and functioning well, strengthen and restore the balance of the immune system (see Immune System, page 32), and eliminate possible environmental triggers and foods that produce mucous and irritate the respiratory tract.

Eat foods that moisten the respiratory tract and thin excess mucous

Proper water intake helps keep the mucous membranes in the respiratory tract moist and capable of resisting infection. Water also helps thin mucous that builds up in your respiratory passageways and causes congestion. Vegetable broths and hot herbal teas can also be beneficial for maintaining hydration and clearing congestion. Warm drinks also help the cilia move to clear pathogens and foreign materials from the system.

Spices and flavoring agents, such as garlic, cayenne and horseradish, can also help get things moving by thinning mucous and stimulating the respiratory tract.

Humidifiers that moisten the air can help the respiratory system by preventing the mucous membranes from becoming dry and prone to infection, especially in the winter months.

On the same note, avoid foods and beverages that stimulate production of excess mucous (dairy products, sugar), dehydrate the body or irritate the respiratory passageways (alcohol, coffee).

Best foods
- Plenty of filtered water, hot herbal teas (peppermint, fennel, thyme), homemade vegetable broths

Eat a diet rich in antioxidants

In general antioxidants help prevent damage of the respiratory system by protecting against free radicals and boosting immune function. Antioxidants are also important in prevention of cancer.

Vitamin A helps maintain healthy mucous membranes in the mouth, nose, sinuses and lungs, as well as the cilia in the respiratory passageways. This helps protect the passageways from virus and bacteria. Vitamin A also helps boost the immune system.

Vitamin C has an antihistaminic effect that can benefit asthma and allergy sufferers. It also protects against infection, helps heal wounds and strengthens the adrenal glands, essential glands for fighting allergic reactions and inflammation.

Vitamin E helps maintain healthy mucous membranes and is a powerful antioxidant.

Quercetin, a bioflavonoid, has anti-inflammatory and antihistaminic properties.

Histamine is the substance that is released during an allergic reaction causing symptoms of itching and swelling. Quercetin can help with allergies, asthma and respiratory infections.

Best foods
- Beta-carotene (converted in the body into vitamin A): apricots, carrots, cantaloupe, pumpkin and other winter squashes
- Vitamin C: bell peppers, broccoli, cantaloupe, cauliflower, kale, kiwi, oranges, strawberries, sweet potatoes, tomatoes
- Vitamin E: almonds, hazelnuts, walnuts, sunflower seeds, vegetable oils
- Quercetin: apples, red and yellow onions, black tea, tomatoes

Eat foods that contain essential fatty acids

Asthma, allergies and respiratory infections are associated with inflammation of the respiratory tract. Foods that are high in omega-3 fatty acids, such as fish oils and flaxseed oil, have anti-inflammatory properties that can keep allergies and asthma in check. Essential fatty acids along with other unsaturated fats help keep mucous membranes healthy and resistant to infection.

Best foods
- Fresh fish (salmon, mackerel, albacore tuna, sardines, herring)
- Flaxseeds and flaxseed oil, borage oil, evening primrose oil

Breathe good-quality air and do breathing exercises

The quality of the air we breathe is directly related to the condition of the lining of the respiratory tract. If the air we breathe is polluted with pollens, dust, dander, mold, smoke, bacteria and viruses, it can cause chronic irritation and inflammation of our airways and lungs. If you live or work in a polluted environment, use air filters to purify the air.

Breathing exercises increase the amount of oxygen that enters our system and the amount of carbon dioxide that is eliminated via the lungs.

Best techniques
- Use air filters, vacuum and clean carpets frequently, check homes and basements for mold, dust frequently, practice abdominal breathing

Top 10 Best Bets for Respiratory Health

❶ Sprouted seeds and grains: According to traditional Chinese medicine, sprouted seeds and grains are alive and full of chi (life energy). These foods help strengthen the body's chi along with the lungs and respiratory system.

❷ Fish oils: Fish oils, high in omega-3 fatty acids, have anti-inflammatory properties that could help relieve asthmatic patients. Studies have shown that when asthma patients consume more fish oils, they are able to breathe more easily and use less medication.

❸ Garlic: The antibacterial properties of garlic have been tested and proven to be effective against the bacteria that cause pneumonia. Garlic can also be used to fight viruses and fungal infections that target the respiratory system.

❹ Pumpkin seeds: Studies have found that people who suffer from allergic asthma and other allergies have a deficiency of zinc. Pumpkin seeds are an excellent source of zinc, which may help reduce the incidence of allergies and asthma as well as boosting the immune system to protect against infection. Have a handful per day as a snack.

❺ Yellow and red onions: Yellow and red onions contain quercetin, a bioflavonoid that has antioxidant, anti-inflammatory and antihistaminic properties. Quercetin also seems to protect the lungs against viral infections, such as those caused by the flu virus, due to its antioxidant properties.

❻ Ginger: Ginger extracts have been shown to have antimicrobial activity against bacteria and viruses that cause respiratory infection. Ginger is also an antioxidant and has anti-inflammatory properties. Make a ginger tea by slicing and slightly bruising fresh gingerroot and adding the slices to boiling water. Continue to boil the water until it looks darker in color. Let it steep and enjoy with a bit of lemon.

❼ Almonds: Almonds are high in calcium, and like all other nuts, are a great source of magnesium. Calcium and magnesium are essential for muscle contraction and relaxation, even for the smooth muscle in the respiratory airways. Almonds also contain monounsaturated fats and are a good source of protein. Delicious and satisfying as a mid-afternoon snack.

❽ Berries: Berries contain anthocyanins, which destroy free radicals, and are high in vitamin C. Vitamin C is a natural antioxidant and anti-inflammatory. Vitamin C is also antihistaminic, as it makes mast cells (the cells that contain histamine) more stable during allergic reactions. Vitamin C in berries is essential in the prevention of allergies, asthma and inflammation and helps boost the immune system.

❾ Cruciferous vegetables: Broccoli, cauliflower, cabbage, Brussels sprouts and bok choy are part of the cruciferous family. They contain cancer-fighting chemicals and other minerals important for health. Cabbage, with its high glutamine content, is beneficial for the building and repair of mucous membranes, including the mucous membranes in the respiratory tract. This helps keep allergens, and pathogens from attacking the body.

⑩ **Thyme and Oregano:** Thyme has a high content of volatile oils that are powerful agents for fighting infections. Thyme can be used to sooth sore throats and calm irritating coughs by helping reduce spasm reactions. It is also used for bronchitis, whooping cough and asthma. It can be taken as a delicious and refreshing tea.

Oregano is a powerful antioxidant with potent antibacterial, antifungal and antiparasitic properties, which make it useful for treating swollen glands, asthma, cough, earache and viral infections. The essential oil is effective both internally and externally. Take oregano oil diluted in herbal tea or water.

Foods that Protect the Respiratory System

Best Foods for Protecting Respiratory System	Respiratory System Benefits	Comments
FRUITS		
Citrus: • Oranges • Mandarins • Lemons • Grapefruit • Kiwifruit • Strawberries	Rich in vitamin C and bioflavonoids, which are antioxidants. Vitamin C containing foods are anti-inflammatory and antihistaminic helping reduce allergic-type reactions including asthma and allergies.	Caution: Grapefruit juice can interfere with some medications. Strawberries are heavily sprayed; choose organic when possible.
Orange/Yellow: • Apricots • Mangoes • Cantaloupe	Contain carotenoids and vitamin C, which are antioxidants. Beta-carotene helps maintain healthy mucous membranes of the respiratory tract.	When buying cantaloupe, choose fruit that is thick, with a coarse surface and veins standing out. Avoid fruit with mold.
Blue/Purple: • Blueberries and other berries • Purple grapes • Plums	Contain anthocyanins, which destroy free radicals. Also high in pectin and vitamin C.	Choose well-colored, plump grapes that are firmly attached to their stems.
VEGETABLES		
Red Nightshades: • Tomatoes • Red bell peppers	Rich in the antioxidant lycopene. High in vitamin C and beta-carotene, which help keep mucous membranes intact and control allergic reactions.	Lycopene is fat-soluble and must be eaten with a fat in order to be absorbed.
Orange/Yellow: • Carrots • Yams • Sweet potatoes • Pumpkin and other winter squashes	Contain carotenoids, which maintain resistance in mucous membranes and cilia to protect against infections and foreign materials.	
Green: • Spinach • Swiss chard • Asparagus • Dandelion greens • Other dark leafy greens	Contain magnesium, which helps decrease bronchial reactivity and constriction in asthma sufferers.	1 cup (250 mL) of these leafy vegetables is equal to one serving.

Best Foods for Protecting Respiratory System	Respiratory System Benefits	Comments
VEGETABLES (cont.)		
Cruciferous Family: • Bok choy • Broccoli • Brussels sprouts • Cabbage • Cauliflower • Kale	Broccoli contains large amounts of vitamin C, beta-carotenes and calcium. Calcium is a mineral needed for smooth muscle relaxation of the respiratory tract.	Broccoli sprouts have high amounts of cancer fighting nutrients.
Allium Family: • Chives • Garlic • Onions	Yellow or red onions are high in quercetin, an antihistaminic compound that helps reduce allergy symptoms. Garlic has antimicrobial properties that help the body fight infections.	Allicin, which is released during crushing, gives garlic its characteristic smell. Research indicates that for optimum benefit, garlic should be crushed and allowed to sit for a few minutes before using. Eat garlic raw or cooked.
LEGUMES		
• Beans (lima, pinto, organic soy) • Lentils • Peas (black-eyed peas) • Chickpeas	A source of protein essential for building and repairing tissues and immune cells to fight infection. A source of zinc, essential for resisting infection and tissue repair.	
WHOLE GRAINS		
• Whole oats • Brown rice • Barley • Whole wheat • Quinoa • Millet	Grains are a source of selenium, a strong antioxidant that works along with vitamin E. High in B vitamins, including B_6, which nourishes the adrenal glands.	Brown rice, quinoa and millet are less allergenic, so choose these grains, especially when the body is fighting an infection to prevent excess mucous formation.
NUTS AND SEEDS		
Nuts: • Almonds • Walnuts • Brazil nuts • Hazel nuts • Pecans	Nuts contain monounsaturated fats, vitamin E and magnesium. Almonds are a good source of calcium. Magnesium and calcium help relax the smooth muscle of the respiratory airways.	Buy raw or dry-roasted nuts and seeds. Choose an unsalted variety.
Seeds: • Flaxseeds • Sesame seeds • Pumpkin seeds • Sunflower seeds	Flaxseeds are high in omega-3 oils, which are anti-inflammatory. Sesame and sunflower seeds are an excellent source of vitamin E, a fat-soluble antioxidant. Pumpkin seeds are high in zinc, essential for immune function.	Sunflower seeds, pumpkin seeds and sesame seeds are excellent mixed together and eaten as a snack. Make your own trail mix.

Best Foods for Protecting Respiratory System	Respiratory System Benefits	Comments
FATS AND OILS		
Cold-pressed oils: • Extra virgin olive oil • Flaxseed oil • Borage oil • Evening primrose oil • Avocados	Flaxseed, borage and evening primrose oil have been known to offset inflammation.	Do not use flaxseed oil for cooking. Use in salads, smoothies or over vegetables.
Fish: • Salmon • Mackerel • Albacore tuna • Sardines • Herring	Contain omega-3 fatty acids, which inhibit the inflammatory cascade in the body, including chronic inflammation in asthma.	
HERBS AND SPICES		
• Thyme • Peppermint • Ginger • Parsley • Oregano • Cumin • Mustard • Basil • Sage	Ginger is antiviral, antioxidant and anti-inflammatory. Peppermint stops coughs and releases congestion. Thyme helps clear the respiratory passageways and fight infection. Caution: Peppermint can relax the stomach sphincter and stimulate acid reflux.	
OTHER		
• Beer • Chocolate • Coffee • Tea • Wine	Tea and red wine contain quercetin. Beer is rich in bioflavonoids from the fermented grains. Phenols in dark chocolate and red wine are antioxidant.	Caution: Caffeine and alcohol can dehydrate and irritate the respiratory tract. Not recommended during pregnancy and lactation.

Whole Foods

Whole Foods for Health

There is no doubt about it. What you eat affects not only who you are and what you can accomplish, but also how you look and feel, including your overall health and vitality. Eating a variety of whole, fresh foods including fruit and vegetables is essential. As developed countries produce more and more refined and processed foods — foods like sugarcoated breakfast cereals, fat and chemical-laden, frozen and convenience foods and empty calorie snack foods — there is also an increase in "modern" diseases. According to the 1988 U.S. Surgeon General's Report on Nutrition and Health, dietary choices are a factor in two-thirds of all deaths from coronary heart disease, stroke, atherosclerosis, diabetes and some cancers.

Whole foods are our first line of defense against those diseases. Whole foods are those foods that are as close to their natural state as possible. They are full of the essential vitamins, minerals, proteins, enzymes, complex carbohydrates and phytonutrients that combine to keep us active, alert and free from disease. What follows is a comprehensive outline of whole foods — foods that contain the optimum healing compounds so vital for human health.

For many reasons, locally grown, organic whole foods are the best possible foods we can choose for our family. Most notably, children are most vulnerable to pesticides, fertilizers, ionizing radiation and growth hormones, but everyone deserves to enjoy food that is produced without these human and environmental hazards. Farmers who use renewable resources, along with soil and water conservation practices, produce organic food in order to preserve a healthy environment for future generations. Most organic farms sell food locally. Their consumers are their friends and neighbors. Organic living provides a practical and painless first step that everyone can take towards a healthier lifestyle and planet.

MESSAGE FROM THE SURGEON GENERAL

I am pleased to transmit to the Secretary of the Department of Health and Human Services this first Surgeon General's Report on Nutrition and Health. It was prepared under the auspices of the Department's Nutrition Policy Board, and its main conclusion is that over consumption of certain dietary components is now a major concern for Americans. While many food factors are involved, chief among them is the disproportionate consumption of foods high in fats, often at the expense of foods high in complex carbohydrates and fiber — such as vegetables, fruits, and whole grain products — that may be more conducive to health.

— C.Everett Koop, M.D., Sc.D., Surgeon General, U.S. Public Health Service

Fruits

Apples

Malus pumila

Actions: Tonic, digestive, diuretic, detoxifying, laxative, antiseptic, lower blood cholesterol, antirheumatic, liver stimulant.

Uses: Fresh apples help cleanse the system, lower blood cholesterol levels, keep blood sugar levels up, and aid digestion. The French use the peels in preparations for rheumatism and gout as well as in urinary tract remedies. Apples are useful components in cleansing fasts because their fiber helps eliminate toxins. Apples are good sources of vitamin A and also contain vitamins C, B$_2$ (riboflavin) and K. Apples are high in the phytonutrients, pectin and boron and are a good source of proanthocyanidins, which may contribute to maintenance of urinary tract and heart health.

Buying and Storing: Look for blemish-free apples with firm, crisp flesh and smooth, tight skin. Because of the widespread use of pesticides on apples, choose organic whenever possible or peel before using. Apple orchards produce seasonal gluts and since apples have excellent keeping qualities, local varieties may be available out of season. Keep in a cool dry and dark place (or the produce drawer of your refrigerator) for 1 month or more.

Culinary Use: Apples can be blended with most fruits and many vegetables. They add natural sweetness and lots of fiber and texture to both sweet and savory dishes. Not all sweet, crisp and delicious eating apple varieties are as good when cooked. Cox's Orange Pippin, Jonathan, Gravenstein or Baldwin apples are varieties that can be eaten raw and used as an ingredient in cooked dishes.

One apple, peeled and cored yields approximately 1 cup (250 mL) roughly chopped fruit. Homemade or commercially canned, unsweetened applesauce may be used in recipes as a natural sweetener.

Recipes:
- Apple and Cheddar Cheese Flan (page 353)
- Apple-Carrot Popovers (page 162)
- Apple-Cranberry Compote (page 351)
- Apple Fresh Smoothie (page 342)
- Apple-Spinach Pâté (page 137)
- Apricot-Apple Bars (page 365)
- Baked Apple Polenta Custard (page 168)
- Buckwheat Apple Pancakes (page 164)
- Fennel Celery and Apple Salad (page 184)
- Grated Beet and Apple Salad (page 181)
- Green Tomato and Apple Salsa (page 312)
- Harvest Salsa (page 313)
- Herbed Nut and Bean Patties (page 234)
- Hot Spiced Applesauce (page 317)
- Kasha Pudding with Apple and Raisins (page 167)
- Wakame Cabbage Salad (page 175)

Apricots

Prunus armeniaca

Actions: Antioxidant, anticancer.

Uses: Apricots are very high in beta-carotene, a precursor of vitamin A. Vitamin A may prevent the formation of plaque deposits in the arteries, thus preventing heart disease. Three small fresh apricots deliver 2,770 IU and ½ cup (125 mL) dried contains 8,175 IU of vitamin A. Also high in B$_2$ (riboflavin), potassium, boron, iron, magnesium and fiber, apricots have virtually no sodium or fat. Fresh or dried apricots are especially recommended for women because they are a good source of calcium and an excellent source of vitamin A. Apricots help normalize blood pressure, heart function and maintain normal body fluids.

Buying and Storing: Choose firm, fresh apricots that range from dark yellow to orange. Keep in a dry cool place for up to 1 week. Dried apricots have the highest protein content of all dried fruit. Buy naturally sun-dried, sulphur-free dried fruit whenever possible, and without exception, if given regularly to children. The sulphur dioxide gas used to fumigate dried fruit (to keep the bright colors) is poisonous and if taken in excess can cause severe alimentary problems and possibly genetic mutations.

Culinary Use: Leave the peel on fresh apricots if organic but do not use the seeds. Peel in the same way as peaches, by pouring boiling water over and allowing them to cool enough to slip the skins off. Lemon juice will prevent browning.

Dried apricots are an excellent source of natural sugar and are generally sweeter than fresh fruit so use them to reduce refined sugar in sauces and cooked fruit recipes. Substitute 2 dried apricot halves for each fresh apricot. Canned apricots in unsweetened juice may also be used in dessert recipes and smoothies.

Recipes:
• Apricot-Apple Bars (page 365)
• Brandied Fruit Custard (page 355)
• Broccoli Pesto Salad (page 191)
• B-Vitamin Smoothie (page 170)
• Fruit Spread (page 150)
• Mango Chutney (page 314)
• Peach-Rose Sauce (page 318)
• Poached Pears with Apricot-Ginger Sauce (page 349)
• Roasted Eggplant with Plums and Apricots (page 271)
• Roasted Fruit with Custard (page 169)
• Squash Tagine (page 249)
• Whole-Grain Granola (page 160)

Bananas

Musa cavendishii, syn. *M. chinensis*

Actions: Boost immunity, lower cholesterol, prevent ulcers, antibacterial.

Uses: Due to their ability to strengthen the surface cells of the stomach lining and protect against acids, bananas are recommended when ulcers (or the risk of ulcers) are present. High in potassium and vitamin B_6 (pyridoxine) bananas help prevent heart attack, stroke and other cardiovascular problems.

Buying and Storing: Look for ripe bananas that are soft to the touch, yellow from neck to bottom and that are only very slightly speckled. Store in a cool dry and dark place.

Culinary Use: Bananas are peeled and added to salads and desserts just before serving whenever possible. Brushing bananas with lemon juice will prevent browning. Over-ripe bananas (very darkly speckled, almost solid brown) may be used in quick breads, puddings and sauces. Plantains are larger and green, usually used for cooking baked goods or in Caribbean and African dishes.

To Freeze Bananas: For freezing, choose fully yellow bananas with no bruises or brown spots. Peel and cut each into four chunks and arrange on a baking sheet. Freeze in coldest part of the freezer for 30 minutes. Transfer to one large or several individual resealable freezer bags. Seal and store in freezer for up to 6 months. Four frozen chunks are equal to one whole fresh banana. Use frozen bananas in baked goods and smoothies.

Recipes:
• Breakfast Cocktail (page 170)
• B-Vitamin Smoothie (page 170)
• Peanut Butter and Banana Bread (page 165)
• Strawberry-Rhubarb Crêpes (Variation, page 348)
• Sweet Almond Spread (see Tips, page 152)

Blackberries

Rubus species

Actions: Antioxidant.

Uses: Blackberries are an excellent source of vitamin C and fiber. They have high levels of potassium, iron, calcium and manganese.

Buying and Storing: Choose plump berries with dark, glossy color and firm flesh. Fresh blackberries are best used immediately (if necessary, store for 1 day only in the refrigerator). Wash just before using.

Culinary Use: Use blackberries in all recipes that call for blueberries, raspberries or strawberries. Blackberries combine well with other berries, apples and peaches in pies, jams, puddings and soufflés.

Recipes:
• Buckwheat Apple Pancakes (Variation, page 164)
• Fresh Berry Mousse (page 346)
• Fruited Pesto Pasta (Variation, page 297)
• Gingered Summer Fruit (page 346)
• Raspberry Coulis (Variation, page 357)
• Roasted Fruit with Custard (page 169)
• Sweet Almond Spread (page 152)

Black Currants

Ribes nigrum

Actions: Antioxidant, antibacterial, boost immunity, promote healing, antidiarrheal, anticancer.

Uses: Black currant flesh is extremely high in vitamin C. Three ounces (90 grams) contain 200 mg of vitamin C. Black currant skins and the outer layers of their flesh contain anthocyanins, a flavonoid, proven to prevent the development of bacteria such as E. coli. Black currants (especially the seeds) are high in gamma linolenic acid (GLA), important for heart health and a number of body functions. Although red currants are not as common as black, they have similar properties.

Buying and Storing: Black (or red) currants are not widely available but are sometimes found in midsummer at farmers' markets. While not as fragile as blackberries or raspberries, fresh currants must be stored in the refrigerator and will keep up to 1 week. Wash just before using.

Culinary Use: Remove the tiny stems before cooking fresh black currants. Fresh currants are usually simmered in water until tender before being used in recipes. Dried currants are not generally the dried version of fresh currants, but tiny raisins from the small seedless grapes of Corinth. Soak dried currants in water before using in baked goods or compotes.

Recipes:
• Apple-Cranberry Compote (Variation, page 351)
• Buckwheat Apple Pancakes (Variation, page 164)
• Fresh Berry Mousse (page 346)
• Gingered Summer Fruit (page 346)
• Roasted Fruit with Custard (page 169)

Blueberries

Vaccinium species

Actions: Antidiarrheal, antioxidant, antibacterial, antiviral.

Uses: High concentrations of tannins are found in blueberries. Tannins kill bacteria and viruses and help prevent (or relieve) bladder infections. Anthocyanosides in blueberries protect blood vessels against cholesterol buildup. Anthocyanidins bolster

cellular antioxidant defenses and may contribute to maintenance of brain function. Blueberries are high in pectin, vitamin C, potassium and natural aspirin and add extra fiber to the diet.

To Prevent Bladder Infections: Add at least $\frac{1}{2}$ cup (125 mL) fresh or frozen blueberries to smoothies, cereals or salads and take daily for a minimum of 3 weeks.

Buying and Storing: A silvery bloom on blueberries indicates freshness. Choose plump, firm, dark blue berries with smooth skin. Pick over and discard split or soft berries. Blueberries are best used immediately but can be stored in the refrigerator for up to 3 days. Wash just before using.

Culinary Use: The flavor of blueberries can be tart, especially in wild varieties so combine with sweeter fruits (apples, apricots, bananas, pineapple) in order to avoid adding sugar to recipes. Frozen, canned or dried blueberries can be used when fresh are not available without sacrificing their medicinal qualities.

Recipes:
• Blueberry Sauce (page 317)
• Brandied Fruit Custard (Variation, page 355)
• Buckwheat Apple Pancakes (Variation, page 164)
• Fresh Berry Mousse (page 346)
• Fruited Pesto Pasta (Variation, page 297)
• Raspberry Coulis (Variation, page 357)
• Roasted Fruit with Custard (page 169)

Cantaloupe

See Melons

Cherries

Prunus species

Actions: Antibacterial, antioxidant, anticancer.

Uses: Cherries are high in ellagic acid, a potent anticancer agent. They are also high in vitamins C and A, biotin and potassium. Black cherry juice (from the Morello variety) protects against tooth decay unless sweetened. Cherries are a good source of anthocyanidins.

Buying and Storing: Choose sweet varieties and look for dark red, firm, plump, tight-skinned, glossy fruit with the stems attached. Whole ripe cherries are best used immediately but will keep in the refrigerator for up to 2 days.

Culinary Use: Wash, cut in half and remove stones. Sweet cherries such as the Bing variety range from pale yellow to deep purple-red and are juicy-sweet. The bitter, dark-skinned cherries are used mainly for jam that will be sweetened. When fresh cherries are not available, use pitted frozen, dried, or canned in recipes.

Recipes:
- Fresh Berry Mousse (page 346)
- Fruited Bread Pudding (page 354)
- Fruited Pesto Pasta (page 297)
- Gingered Summer Fruit (page 346)
- Green Tea Sauce (page 318)
- Roasted Fruit with Custard (page 169)
- Whole-Grain Granola (page 160)

Citrus Fruits

Citrus species
oranges, lemons, limes,
grapefruit, tangerines

Actions:
Antioxidant,
anticancer.

Uses: All citrus fruits are high in vitamin C and limonene, which is thought to inhibit breast cancer. Red grapefruit is high in cancer-fighting lycopene. Oranges are a good source of choline, which improves mental functioning. The combination of carotenoids, flavonoids, terpenes, limonoids and coumarins make citrus fruits a total cancer-fighting package.

Buying and Storing: Plump, juicy citrus fruits that are heavy for their size and yield slightly to pressure are best. Although citrus fruits will keep for at least a couple of weeks if kept moist in the refrigerator, they are best if used within a week. Look for organic citrus fruits because they are not injected with gas for transportation.

Culinary Use: Make fresh citrus juice with a citrus press or juicing machine. Lemon or lime juice adds a fresh, sharp-tasting edge that complements many vegetable dishes and tones down the cloying sweet taste of other fruits. One half of a lemon or lime yields about 3 tbsp (45 mL) of juice. Sauces and dressings use various citrus juices. Whole or sliced citrus fruit is used in salads, desserts and some main dish recipes.

Buy organic citrus fruit and wash the peel with food-safe soap if using the rind. Candied citrus peel is used in cakes, cookies and fruit compotes. Canned oranges or grapefruit and their juice may be used in most dishes such as sauces and compotes that call for those fruits.

Caution: Grapefruit juice can interfere with some medications.

Recipes:
- Citrus Cocktail (page 171)
- Fruit Explosion (page 171)
- Ginger-Citrus Sauce (page 231)
- Makrut Lime Leaf Sauce (page 316)
- Lemon Custard (page 359)
- Lemon Pesto (page 310)
- Mango Chutney (page 314)
- Moroccan Orange and Onion Salad (page 174)
- Orange Aid (page 171)
- Sunrise Supreme (page 172)

Cranberries

Vaccinium macrocarpum

Actions: Antibacterial, antiviral, antioxidant, anticancer.

Uses: The proanthocyanidins in cranberries make them extremely useful in urinary and bladder infections. Whole cranberries or juice work in the same way as elderberries to prevent the barbs on the bacteria from attaching to the cells of the bladder or urinary tract, rendering them ineffective in causing infection. Best used as a first step in preventing urinary tract and bladder infection, cranberry juice does not take the place of antibiotic drugs, which are more effective in eliminating bacteria once an infection has taken hold. High in vitamins C and A, iodine and calcium, cranberries also prevent kidney stones and deodorize the urine.

To Prevent Bladder Infections: Add at least $\frac{1}{2}$ cup (125 mL) cranberries to smoothie recipes or fruit salads and take every day for a minimum of 3 weeks.

Buying and Storing: Choose bright red, plump cranberries that bounce. Keep fresh cranberries in a cold, dark place or produce drawer of the refrigerator for 2 to 3 weeks. Cranberries may be frozen whole in a freezer bag. Wash just before using.

Culinary Use: Unless used in small quantities or combined with very sweet fruits, their tartness makes it appropriate to use fresh cranberries with honey, stevia or other sweeteners. Cook fresh cranberries in a small amount of water or juice before combining with other ingredients in recipes. Canned whole cranberries or cranberry sauce are high in sugar so dried, fresh or frozen cranberries are preferred.

Recipes:
- Apple-Cranberry Compote (page 351)
- Creamy Couscous with Quinoa and Cranberries (page 292)
- Grated Carrots with Dates and Walnuts (Variation, page 184)
- Fettuccine and Fiddleheads in Thyme Vinaigrette (page 298)
- Moroccan Orange and Onion Salad (Variation, page 174)
- Squash Tagine (page 249)
- Whole-Grain Granola (page 160)

Crenshaw Melon

See Melons

Dates

Phoenix dactylifera

Actions: Boost estrogen levels, laxative.

Uses: Dates are good sources of boron, which prevents calcium loss, so important in the fight against osteoporosis and weakening of bones. Dates contain vitamins A, B_1 (thiamin), B_2 (riboflavin), C and D and valuable mineral salts as well as fiber.

Buying and Storing: Dried dates are widely available and keep in a cool dark place for a couple of months. Fresh dates may be found in Middle Eastern markets when in season. Buy firm, plump, fresh dates with dark shiny skins. Fresh dates will keep for several days in the refrigerator.

Culinary Use: High in sugar (60% in fresh and 70% in dry), dates sweeten and add fiber to stews, tagines, salads, baked goods, puddings, grain dishes and desserts. Golden or dark brown in color, fresh dates are very different from dried and are becoming more and more common in upscale supermarkets. Use fresh dates in appetizer and salad recipes to show off their superior flavor and texture.

Recipes:
- Baked Apple Polenta Custard (page 168)
- Brandied Fruit Custard (page 355)
- Christmas Pudding (page 358)
- Date and Nut Bars (page 364)
- Grated Beet and Apple Salad (page 181)
- Grated Carrots with Dates and Walnuts (page 184)
- Kasha Pudding with Apple and Raisins (Variation, page 167)
- Spiced Root Vegetables (page 273)

Elderberries

Sambucus species

Actions: Increase perspiration, diuretic, laxative.

Uses: Elderberries support detoxification by promoting bowel movements, urination, sweating and mucus secretion. They are effective in combating viruses, such as those that cause colds and flu. Elderberries work in the same way as cranberries, by providing protection from the barbs that puncture the body's cell walls. Viruses slide off and are eliminated before they can enter the cells and cause damage.

Buying and Storing: Elderberries are still mainly harvested from the wild (although some are now grown commercially in the United States and Canada). They are usually available at farmers' markets from mid- to late summer. Look for plump, deep, purple-black berries with tight, shiny skin and firm flesh. Use immediately or if necessary, store for 1 day in the refrigerator. Wash just before using.

Culinary Use: Elderberries add a dark blue color to foods. Their taste can be sweet or slightly tart. Use fresh or frozen elderberries, or small amounts of elderberry syrup, or elderberry jam in puddings, sauces, dressings, salads, beverages and vegetable dishes. Elderberries may be used in place of blueberries or raspberries in recipes.

Recipes:
- Apple-Cranberry Compote (Variation, page 351)
- Buckwheat Apple Pancakes (Variation, page 164)
- Fresh Berry Mousse (page 346)
- Gingered Summer Fruit (page 346)
- Roasted Fruit with Custard (page 169)

Figs

Ficus carica

Actions: Antibacterial, anticancer, antiulcer, digestive, demulcent, laxative.

Uses: Figs contain benzaldehyde, a cancer-fighting agent. They are also high in potassium, B vitamins, calcium and magnesium, and are naturally sweet.

Buying and Storing: Dried figs are readily available in supermarkets throughout the year. In summer and early fall, some supermarkets and most Middle Eastern food markets carry fresh figs. There are over 700 varieties of figs and they range in color from green to purple or dark brown. Choose soft, plump fresh figs with thin skins that yield to a gentle touch. Fresh figs are delicate but keep in a cool dark place for several days.

Culinary Use: Fresh figs contain 12% sugar and are best eaten whole, with cheese or fruit. Cook with dried figs, which contain about 50% sugar. Dried figs are used to sweeten and thicken dressings, puddings and sauces. Figs can be substituted for apricots and dates in most recipes.

Recipes:
- Brandied Fruit Custard (page 355)
- Christmas Pudding (page 358)
- Date and Nut Bars (page 364)
- Grated Beet and Apple Salad (page 181)
- Mâche with Fruit, Nuts and Blue Cheese Dressing (page 182)

Gooseberries

Ribes grossularia

Actions: Protect skin and gums, laxative.

Uses: High in vitamin C, potassium and pectin, gooseberries are often added to jams to make them set.

Buying and Storing: Once found in many home gardens, gooseberries are now sometimes found at farmers' markets in early summer. Be sure to use dessert varieties (early ripening amber and yellow varieties) and look for plump, bright, almost transparent berries with tight, shiny skin and firm flesh. Use immediately or if necessary, store for 1 day in the refrigerator. Wash just before using.

Culinary Use: Refreshingly tart-sweet, gooseberries add depth to the sweet taste of seasonal berries and bananas. Red-skinned and green gooseberries are too tart to use raw and require sweetening when cooked.

Recipes:
- Apple-Cranberry Compote (Variation, page 351)
- Fresh Berry Mousse (page 346)
- Gingered Summer Fruit (page 346)

Grapefruit

See Citrus Fruits

Grapes

Vitis vinifera

Actions: Antioxidant, antiviral, anticancer.

Uses: Grapes contain large amounts of ellagic and caffeic acids, which deactivate carcinogens. Grapes are a good source of potassium. The flavonoids in grape juice protect the heart, and the resveratrol found in red wine and red grape juice has a protective effect on the cardiovascular system. Grapes are also high in boron, a substance that helps maintain estrogen levels and may be instrumental in preventing osteoporosis.

Buying and Storing: Organic grapes are preferred due to the high amounts of pesticides used on commercial crops. Look for bright color, firm flesh and unwrinkled skin. Wash grapes in food grade hydrogen peroxide or vinegar because they are heavily sprayed. Store in the produce drawer of refrigerator for 3 or 4 days.

Culinary Use: Grapes are sweet and their mild taste blends with most fruit in salads and desserts. Grapes are generally used raw but may be added to tagines and other cooked dishes that will not overpower their delicate flavor.

Raisins are dried grapes and are a good source of fiber, boron, calcium, phosphorus, iron, potassium and vitamin A. They add natural sweetness to recipes. Add $\frac{1}{4}$ cup (50 mL) to salads, baked goods and grain recipes. Golden sultanas are a very good cooking variety because they are light in color and plump. Use only sulphur-free raisins that have not been sprayed with mineral oils.

Recipes:
- Swiss Chard with Almond Butter Sauce (raisins) (page 190)
- Broccoli Pesto Salad (raisins) (page 191)
- Curried Sweet Potato Soup (raisins) (page 207)
- Kasha Pudding with Apple and Raisins (page 167)
- Mango Chutney (raisins) (page 314)
- Squash Tagine (raisins) (page 249)
- Sunrise Supreme (page 172)
- Whole-Grain Granola (raisins) (page 160)

Honeydew Melon

See Melons

Kiwifruits

Actinidia chinensis

Actions: Antioxidant, anticancer, aid digestion.

Uses: Kiwifruits are often used as part of a cleansing regimen or to aid digestion. They are high in vitamins C and E (one of few fruits that contain vitamin E) that both act as antioxidants, protecting cells from damage. Kiwifruits are also high in potassium and contain some calcium.

Buying and Storing: Choose ripe kiwifruit that yield to gentle pressure. Kiwifruit will ripen at room temperature in a brown paper bag after 2 or 3 days. Ripe kiwifruit keep for at least 1 week in the produce drawer of the refrigerator.

Culinary Use: Use fresh in salads, jams, cakes and desserts. They make an attractive garnish for cooked sweet or savory dishes.

Recipes:
- Fruited Pesto Pasta (Variation, page 297)
- Watercress, Raspberry and Avocado Salad (Variation, page 180)

Lemons

See Citrus Fruits

Limes

See Citrus Fruits

Mangoes

Mangifera indica

Actions: Antioxidant, anticancer.

Uses: High in vitamins A (there are 8,000 IU of beta-carotene in one mango) and C, potassium, B_3 (niacin) and fiber, mangoes help protect against cancer and atherosclerosis. They help the body fight infection and maintain bowel regularity.

Buying and Storing: Choose large, firm, yellow to yellow-red, unblemished fruit with flesh that gives slightly when gently squeezed. Store ripe fresh mangoes in the produce drawer of refrigerator for 3 or 4 days.

Culinary Use: Mangoes are fibrous with a sweet, banana-pineapple flavor. They combine well with peaches, apricots, nectarines and plums. Use fresh mangoes in salads, grain dishes, desserts and beverages.

Handle mangoes carefully because the peel contains a skin irritating sap. To separate the flesh from the fibrous seed, cut the fruit lengthwise on one side, close to the seed. Repeat on the other side of the seed. With the tip of a paring knife, separate the two halves from the seed. Using a large spoon, scoop the flesh out of the skin. Dried mangoes are available, but use them sparingly due to their extra sweetness and look for ones that are dried naturally (and not treated with sulphur).

Recipes:
- Breakfast Cocktail (page 170)
- Dandelion Salad (Variation, page 178)
- Fruited Bread Pudding (page 354)
- Mango Chutney (page 314)
- Moroccan Orange and Onion Salad (Variation, page 174)
- Watercress, Raspberry and Avocado Salad (Variation, page 180)

Melons

Cucumis melo
cantaloupe, honeydew, crenshaw, spanish, musk

Actions: Antioxidant, anticancer, anticoagulant (cantaloupe and honeydew).

Uses: Melons are a good source of vitamin A and contain vitamin C and calcium. Adenosine, the anticoagulant chemical found in cantaloupes and honeydews lessens the risk of heart attacks and strokes due to its ability to thin the blood.

Buying and Storing: Ripe melons are heavy and have a full, sweet perfume. Blemished, soft fruit should be avoided.

Culinary Use: The low caloric value along with their high water content and delicate sweet flavor make melons a good choice for desserts, smoothies and sweet or savory salads. Melons are often paired with savory spreads or fillings and served as appetizers.

Recipes:
- Dandelion Salad (Variation, page 178)
- Fruit Explosion (page 171)
- Orange Aid (page 171)
- Watercress, Raspberry and Avocado Salad (Variation, page 180)

Musk Melon

See Melons

Nectarines

Prunus persica var. *nectarina*

Actions: Antioxidant, anticancer.

Uses: Nectarines are a good source of vitamins A and C, and potassium. They are an original ancient fruit and not, as many people think, a cross between a peach and a plum.

Buying and Storing: Choose fruit that have some bright red areas and are smooth and tight without soft patches. Nectarines should be heavy (full of juice) and firm when pressed, giving way gently, but not hard.

Culinary Use: Nectarines are usually sweeter than peaches and can be used in place of peaches, plums and apricots in recipes. Peel in the same way as peaches, by pouring boiling water over and allowing them to cool enough to slip the skins off. Lemon juice will prevent browning.

Recipes:
- B-Vitamin Smoothie (page 170)
- Fruited Bread Pudding (page 354)
- Gingered Summer Fruit (page 346)
- Mango Chutney (page 314)
- Mojo Sauce (Variation, page 324)
- Orange Aid (page 171)
- Roasted Fruit with Custard (page 169)

Oranges

See Citrus Fruits

Papayas

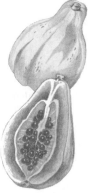

Carica papaya

Actions: Antioxidant, anticancer, aid digestion.

Uses: High in vitamins A, E and C, folate and potassium.

Buying and Storing: Choose large, firm, yellow, unblemished fruit with flesh that gives slightly when gently squeezed. Store in the produce drawer of refrigerator for 3 or 4 days.

Culinary Use: Papayas sweeten and blend well with other fruits in dressings, sauces and desserts. Use fresh papayas with breakfast grain dishes and in smoothies where they add a creamy texture. Dried papaya is usually treated with sulphur and is very sweet, so use sparingly.

Recipes:
- Breakfast Cocktail (page 170)
- Dandelion Salad (Variation, page 178)
- Fruited Bread Pudding (page 354)
- Moroccan Orange and Onion Salad (Variation, page 174)
- Watercress, Raspberry and Avocado Salad (Variation, page 180)

Peaches

Prunus persica

Actions: Antioxidant, anticancer.

Uses: Rich in vitamin A and potassium, peaches also contain boron, B$_3$ (niacin) and some iron and vitamin C. Peaches help protect against cancer, osteoporosis and heart disease. Their sugar content is low (about 9%).

Buying and Storing: Fruit that is full and heavy with fuzzy down and flesh that gives when lightly pressed is preferable. Store peaches in the produce drawer of the refrigerator for up to 4 days. Freestone varieties (such as Loring and Redhaven) are easier to pit than clingstone varieties.

Culinary Use: Use frozen or canned peaches packed in unsweetened juice when the fresh fruit is not in season. Peaches can replace nectarines, plums and apricots in recipes. They complement blackberries, blueberries and raspberries in salads and fruit desserts. Peel by pouring boiling water over and allowing them to cool enough to slip the skins off. Lemon juice will prevent browning. Dried peaches are added to compotes, chutneys and other long-simmering dessert dishes.

Recipes:
- B-Vitamin Smoothie (page 170)
- Brandied Fruit Custard (page 355)
- Fall Fruit en Papillote (page 352)
- Fruited Bread Pudding (page 354)
- Fruited Pesto Pasta (page 297)
- Gingered Summer Fruit (page 346)

- Harvest Salsa (page 313)
- Mojo Sauce (Variation, page 324)
- Peach Melba (page 350)
- Peach-Rose Sauce (page 318)
- Roasted Fruit with Custard (page 169)

Pears

Pyrus communis

Actions: Protect the colon.

Uses: Pears are a good source of fiber, which helps prevent constipation and ensures regularity and protects the colon. Pears' insoluble fiber binds to cancer-causing chemicals in the colon, preventing them from damaging the colon cells.

Perhaps one of the oldest cultivated fruit, pears are a good source of vitamin C, boron and potassium. Healthcare professionals often recommend pears because they are less likely to cause an adverse response. For this reason, they are one of the first fruits introduced to infants.

Buying and Storing: Shop for pears that are lightly firm, unblemished and sweetly "pear smelling." Often available before fully ripe, pears may be ripened in a brown paper bag for 1 to 3 days. Eat pears as soon as they ripen or store in the produce drawer of the refrigerator for up to 3 days.

Culinary Use: Use fresh, frozen or canned pears in sweet and savory dishes. Juicy varieties such as Bartlett, Comice, Seckel and Bosc are great for poached pear desserts. Pears soften in cooking faster than apples so add to stewed fruit compotes 5 to 10 minutes after the apples. Pears team nicely with plums and grapes in recipes.

Recipes:
- Fall Fruit en Papillote (page 352)
- Fruited Pesto Pasta (page 297)
- Mâche with Fruit, Nuts and Blue Cheese Dressing (page 182)
- Maple Pear and Portobello Mushroom Salad (page 195)
- Mojo Sauce (page 324)
- Poached Pears with Apricot-Ginger Sauce (page 349)
- Spiced Pear Salsa (page 312)

Pineapples

Ananas comosus

Actions: Aid digestion.

Uses: A 1-cup (250 mL) serving of pineapple delivers 128% of the body's daily requirement of manganese and they are a good source of potassium and vitamin C. Pineapples also contain vitamin B_1 (thiamin), copper, iron and vitamin B_6 (pyridoxine).

Buying and Storing: Choose large, firm fruits (heaviness in the ripe fruit indicates juiciness), with overall yellow color.

Culinary Use: Pineapples add a fresh sweet taste to smoothies, salads and dessert dishes. The sweetness of pineapples helps soften the tartness of cranberries, blueberries and gooseberries. Pineapple juice is very sweet. Frozen or canned pineapple packed in unsweetened juice may be used in recipes.

To Use Fresh Pineapple: Trim off the base and top leaves. Cut in half and use one half at a time. Slice one half into four wedges. Slice away and discard the skin from each wedge and remove and discard the woody core. One whole, fresh wedge yields about 1 cup (250 mL) chopped fresh pineapple.

Recipes:
- Apple-Cranberry Compote (Variation, page 351)
- B-Vitamin Smoothie (page 170)
- Peach Melba (Variation, page 350)

Plums

Prunus species

Actions: Antibacterial, antioxidant.

Uses: Plums contain vitamins A and C, a small amount of vitamin B_2 (riboflavin) and potassium. They have an exceptionally high content of unique phytonutrients called neochlorogenic and chlorogenic acids. These substances, found in both plums and prunes, are classified as phenols, and their function as antioxidants has been well documented.

Buying and Storing: Ripe plums are firm with no soft spots or splits. Look for bright, (yellow, black or red sweet plums), tight skin and heavy, sweet smelling fruit. Keep in the produce drawer of the refrigerator for up to 4 days.

Culinary Use: Wash and peel (if not organic) and remove pit. Dessert plums can be eaten fresh or added to fruit salads. Cooking plums may be stewed in a little water for 10 to 15 minutes or until soft. Canned and frozen plums may be substituted for fresh in some recipes.

For Umeboshi plums, see page 124.
Prunes are dried plums and are high in colon cancer-fighting pectin (and other insoluble fiber), low in sugar, and act as a natural laxative.
To treat constipation: Take 4 to 6 dried or stewed prunes up to three times a day for 1 or 2 days.

Recipes:
- Crustless Plum Pie (page 347)
- Fall Fruit en Papillote (page 352)
- Gingered Summer Fruit (page 346)
- Mojo Sauce (Variation, page 324)
- Prune Smoothie (page 172)
- Roasted Eggplant with Plums and Apricots (page 271)

Pomegranates

Punica granatum

Actions: Antidiarrheal, antifever, astringent.

Uses: Used in gargles and thought to reduce fevers, pomegranates are widely used in Indian medicines.

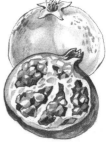

Buying and Storing: Choose firm, even-colored and heavy fruit. Keep in the produce drawer of the refrigerator for up to 4 days.

Culinary Use: The bright red, juicy seeds are eaten fresh and for Middle Eastern recipes are dried and pounded to a powder. Fresh pomegranate seeds are used in salads and as a garnish for dips and desserts and can be pressed for drinks. Crushed dried seeds are sprinkled on hummus and used in

Middle Eastern sweet dishes. Pomegranate molasses is available in specialty stores and may be used in place of honey in beverages, dressings, sauces, puddings and other desserts.

Recipe:
• Moroccan Orange and Onion Salad (page 174)

Raspberries

Rubus idaeus

Actions: Support the immune system.

Uses: Raspberries are rich in manganese and vitamin C (supplying over 50% of the daily recommended amounts of each). They contain folate, vitamin B_2 (riboflavin), magnesium, vitamin B_3 (niacin), potassium and copper. See also Red Raspberry leaf (page 118).

Buying and Storing: Buy or pick fresh raspberries in peak season and choose whole, plump berries with bright color. Sort and discard soft or broken berries. Use immediately or store in the produce drawer of refrigerator for 1 day. Wash just before using.

Culinary Use: Raspberries blend with other berries in desserts and salads and the taste is enhanced with a small amount of citrus juice. Substitute frozen, dried or canned raspberries for fresh. Up to $\frac{1}{4}$ cup (50 mL) raspberry jam may also be used in sauces and dressings.

Recipes:
• Brandied Fruit Custard (Variation, page 355)
• Fresh Berry Mousse (page 346)
• Fruited Bread Pudding (page 354)
• Fruit Explosion Smoothie (page 171)
• Green Tea Sauce (page 318)
• Raspberry Coulis (page 357)
• Raspberry Dressing (page 177)
• Raspberry Dressing #2 (page 180)
• Sunrise Supreme (page 172)
• Watercress, Raspberry and Avocado Salad (page 180)

Rhubarb

Rheum species

Actions: Laxative.

Uses: Actually a vegetable that is almost always used as a fruit, rhubarb is high in potassium and contains a fair amount of iron. The amount of calcium in 1 cup (250 mL) cooked rhubarb is twice that of milk.

Caution: Never use the leaves of rhubarb, which are toxic and inedible due to the high concentration of oxalic acid in them.

Buying and Storing: If a rhubarb patch is not available, farmers' markets may be the only source in spring. Choose thin, firm stalks with all or 90% red color. Rhubarb should snap when bent. Store in a cool dry place or the produce drawer of refrigerator for 1 or 2 days only.

Culinary Use: Cooking mellows the tart taste and softens the laxative effect. To cook fresh rhubarb: Place 1 cup (250 mL) chopped fresh rhubarb in a saucepan. Add 1 cup (250 mL) chopped apple and $\frac{1}{4}$ cup (50 mL) sugar or honey or 2 tsp (10 mL) stevia to sweeten. Cover with water or apple juice and simmer until soft. Frozen or canned rhubarb may also be used in recipes.

Recipes:
• Apple-Cranberry Compote (Variation, page 351)
• Fettuccine and Fiddleheads in Thyme Vinaigrette (page 298)
• Strawberry-Rhubarb Crêpes (page 348)

Spanish Melon

See Melons

Strawberries

Fragaria species

Actions: Antioxidant, antiviral, anticancer.

Uses: Effective against kidney stones, gout, rheumatism and arthritis, strawberries are also used in cleansing juices and as a mild tonic for the liver. Strawberries are high in the cancer fighting ellagic acid and vitamin C. They are also a good source of vitamin A and potassium and contain iron. Both the leaves and the fruit have been used medicinally. A tea from strawberry leaves is used for diarrhea and dysentery.

Buying and Storing: Pick your own or choose brightly colored, firm berries with hulls attached. They are best used immediately but may be stored for no more than a couple of days in the refrigerator. Wash just before using.

Caution: Strawberries are heavily sprayed; choose organic when possible.

Culinary Use: Strawberries add a sweet and powerful flavor to salads, desserts, sauces, dressings and drinks. They blend well with bananas and other berries and the taste is enhanced with a small amount of lemon or lime juice.

Recipes:
• Chilled Fruited Gazpacho (page 206)
• Fresh Berry Mousse (page 346)
• Fruit Explosion (page 171)
• Fruited Bread Pudding (page 354)
• Fruited Pesto Pasta (page 297)
• Orange Aid (page 171)
• Strawberry-Rhubarb Crêpes (page 348)
• Sunrise Supreme (page 172)

Tangerines

See Citrus Fruits

Watermelon

Citrullus vulgaris

Actions: Antibacterial, anticancer.

Uses: Watermelons contains vitamins C and A, iron and potassium. Their high water content makes them a refreshing summer ingredient.

Buying and Storing: A watermelon should be bright green with firm flesh (no blemishes or soft spots) and feel heavy for its size.

Culinary Use: Watermelon is a refreshing summer fruit that combines well with other fruits as a sweet thirst quencher. To use in salads and smoothies, cut in half lengthwise and use half at a time. Use a slice whole as a garnish or remove and discard rind and seeds, and chop the flesh. One slice (from half a watermelon) yields approximately 1 cup (250 mL) chopped fruit. Wrap tightly and keep cut watermelon in the refrigerator.

Recipe:
• Watermelon-Strawberry Splash (page 172)

Vegetables

Artichokes (Globe)

Cynara scolymus

Actions: Antioxidant, anticancer, heart protective.

Uses: Artichokes are high in flavanones, phytochemicals that offer protection against heart disease. They also contain phosphorus, iron, zinc and calcium.

Buying and Storing: Artichokes are the flower of a thistle plant and as such, have tough outer leaves and hairy, inedible centers or chokes. Choose bright green-purple artichokes with no signs of browning and tightly closed leaves.

Culinary Use: Fresh artichokes have a delicate flavor. Trim the thick stems and remove the tough outer leaves. Simmer in a saucepan half filled with boiling water for 30 to 40 minutes or until the outer leaves pull away easily. Cut in half and remove the hairy, inedible center. Serve fresh artichokes with any of the mayonnaise recipes (pages 306 and 307) for a starter dish. Canned artichoke hearts are usually marinated and are more flavorful than fresh. Artichoke hearts are used in salads, pasta and in baked legume and grain dishes.

Recipes:
- Artichokes in Italian Dressing (page 141)
- Artichoke and Mushroom Lasagna (page 245)
- Fall Vegetable Paella (Variation, page 238)
- Greek Soufflés (page 158)
- Mediterranean Bean Salad (page 186)

Asparagus

Asparagus officinalis

Actions: Antioxidant, anticancer, promotes healing, prevent cataracts, diuretic.

Uses: Asparagus is an excellent source of vitamin K (supplying over 100% of the Recommended Daily Amount) and folate, needed for the production of red blood cells and the release of energy from food. It is also a good source of vitamins C and A. It contains B vitamins, tryptophan, manganese, copper, protein, potassium, iron, zinc and some calcium.

Buying and Storing: Look for tight buds at the tips and smooth green stalks with some white at the very end. Fresh asparagus will snap at the point where the tender stalk meets the tougher end. Store stalks upright in $\frac{1}{2}$ inch (1 cm) of water in the refrigerator for up to 2 days.

Culinary Use: Wash grit from flower ends by soaking and swishing in cool water. Snap off and discard the tough stem bottoms. Roasting caramelizes the sugars and brings out the nutty, slightly smoky flavor of asparagus. Steam tender tips by standing whole stalks upright in a tall, narrow pot so that only the lower two-thirds of the stems are immersed in boiling water. Cover and gently simmer for 3 to 5 minutes. Frozen or canned asparagus may be substituted in recipes when fresh is not available.

Recipes:
- Asparagus with Spring Green Sauce (page 262)
- Asparagus Three-Cheese Burritos (page 229)
- Braised Greens with Citrus Dressing (page 260)
- Stir-Fried Vegetables and Bulgur (page 230)

Avocados

Persea americana

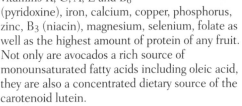

Actions: Antioxidant, anticancer, heart protective.

Uses: Avocados contain more potassium than many other fruits and vegetables (banana is just slightly higher). While high in essential fatty acids, they contain 17 vitamins and minerals including vitamins K, C, A, E and B_6 (pyridoxine), iron, calcium, copper, phosphorus, zinc, B_3 (niacin), magnesium, selenium, folate as well as the highest amount of protein of any fruit. Not only are avocados a rich source of monounsaturated fatty acids including oleic acid, they are also a concentrated dietary source of the carotenoid lutein.

Buying and Storing: Look for ripe, heavy avocados with dull dark green skin. When held in the hand, ripe avocados give gently. Don't press the flesh and avoid avocados with dents in the skin.

Ripen in a paper bag and store in the refrigerator for just over 1 week once ripe.

Culinary Use: One avocado added to salads adds a creamy texture and exceptional nutrients. Brush with lemon juice to keep avocado flesh from turning brown once peeled. Avocados thicken uncooked sauces, dips and smoothies (in much the same way as bananas) due to their lower water content. Up to 30% of the fruit's weight may be oil and for this reason, avocados should be used sparingly.

Recipes:
- Guacamole (page 148)
- Watercress, Raspberry and Avocado Salad (page 180)

Beans

Phaseolus vulgaris
fresh green runner, yellow wax runner, broad, flat, Italian, snap, string, green peas

Pisum sativum
snow peas

For Legumes (dried peas and beans), see page 85.

Actions: Help memory, antioxidant.

Uses: Green beans and peas are leguminous plants — the same botanically as dried beans and peas because they all produce their seeds in pods. However, fresh beans and peas have a lower nutrient level than dried legumes. A good source of choline, which improves mental functioning beans, beans and peas contain vitamin A and potassium along with some protein, iron, calcium and vitamins B and C. The amino acids in beans and peas make them a valuable food for vegetarians.

Buying and Storing: Buy fresh peas and beans with firm pods showing no signs of wilting. The bigger the size of the pea or bean inside the pod the older the vegetable. Fresh yellow or green beans are pliant but still snap when bent. Store unwashed fresh peas (in their pods) and beans in a vented plastic bag in the refrigerator for 2 or 3 days. Parboiled fresh beans and peas freeze well.

Culinary Use: Fresh, frozen, canned or cooked dried peas and beans (legumes) can all be used in recipes. Fresh summer beans are exceptional as a dish on their own or in salads or baked vegetable dishes and they complement grains.

Recipes:
- Braised Greens with Citrus Dressing (page 260)
- Green Beans Gado Gado (page 279)
- Fettuccine and Fiddleheads in Thyme Vinaigrette (Variation, page 298)
- Minestrone Soup (page 212)
- Stir-Fried Vegetables and Bulgur (page 230)
- Summer Vegetable and Millet Salad (page 187)
- Vegetarian Pie with Sweet Potato Topping (page 244)
- Vegetable Red Curry (page 222)

Beets

Beta vulgaris

Actions: Antibacterial, antioxidant, tonic, cleansing, laxative, fight colon cancer.

Uses: Beets (the roots of the beet plant) are high in folate, manganese, potassium and the enzyme betaine, which nourishes and strengthens the liver and gall bladder. With 8% chlorine, beets are cleansing for the liver, kidney and gall bladder. The pigment that gives beets their rich, purple-crimson color — betacyanin — is also a powerful cancer-fighting agent. Beets are also a good source of vitamin C, magnesium, tryptophan, iron, copper and phosphorus.

Buying and Storing: Bright glossy, crisp green beet tops or leaves indicate fresh beets. Buy firm, unblemished, small beets with greens intact, if possible. For storing, cut off the tops and treat as leafy greens. Store unwashed beets in a vented plastic bag in the refrigerator. Beets will keep for up to $1\frac{1}{2}$ weeks.

Culinary Use: Grate fresh, raw beets into salads. Roast, steam or boil fresh beets in water for a vegetable side dish. Use cooked canned or frozen beets when fresh are not available. For using beet tops as a leafy vegetable, see page 77.

Recipes:
- Autumn Harvest Salad (page 179)
- Beet and Feta Cheese Salad (page 185)
- Borscht (page 211)
- Grated Beet and Apple Salad (page 181)
- Summer Vegetable Casseroles (page 232)
- Vegetable Jewel Gingerbread (page 363)
- Warm Beet Salad (page 194)
- Warm Root Vegetable Salad (page 198)

Broccoli

Brassica oleracea var. *italica*

Actions: Antioxidant, anticancer, promotes healing, prevents cataracts.

Uses: Like other cruciferous vegetables, broccoli contains cancer-fighting indoles, glucosinolates and dithiolthiones. A 1-cup (250 mL) serving of broccoli packs over 200% of the body's daily requirement of vitamin C and over 190% of vitamin K. It is high in vitamin A and is one of only four vegetables with vitamin E. It has a fair amount of folate, manganese, tryptophan and potassium. Vitamin B_6 (pyridoxine), B_2 (riboflavin), phosphorus, magnesium, protein, omega-3 fatty acids, vitamin B_5, iron, calcium, vitamins B_1 (thiamin) and B_3 (niacin) and zinc are also present in broccoli. Purple sprouting broccoli is an excellent source of lignans, believed to help protect against hormone-related cancers and may help relieve symptoms associated with menopause.

Buying and Storing: Broccoli yellows as it ages. Deep green color and firm tight buds are a sign of freshness. Thin stalks are more tender than thick, woody stems that tend to be hollow. Store in a vented plastic bag in the produce drawer of the refrigerator for up to 3 days.

Culinary Use: Raw broccoli is eaten with dips and sauces. Fresh broccoli may be boiled, steamed or stir-fried. Cooked broccoli should retain some crunch and bright green color. Use frozen broccoli when fresh is not available.

Recipes:
• Barley and Vegetable Ragout (page 220)
• Broccoli Pesto Salad (page 191)
• Cheesy Broccoli Crêpes (page 156)
• Eight-Treasure Noodle Pot (page 300)
• Fall Vegetable Paella (page 238)
• Sesame Broccoli (page 276)
• Vegetable Oatmeal Crumble (page 254)
• Vegetable Pie with Sweet Potato Topping (page 244)
• Vegetables and Tempeh au Gratin (page 243)
• Whole-Grain Broccoli Stir-Fry (page 286)
• Whole-Grain and Vegetable Stuffing (page 263)

Brussels Sprouts

See Cabbage

Cabbage

Brassica oleracea var. *capitata*
green, red, Savoy, bok choy, Chinese, kohlrabi, Brussels sprouts

Actions: Immune building, antibacterial, anticancer, helps memory, antioxidant, promotes healing, prevents cataracts, detoxifying, diuretic, anti-inflammatory, tonic, antiseptic, restorative, prevents ulcers.

Uses: Cruciferous vegetables, of which cabbage is one, appear to lower our risk of cancer more effectively than any other vegetables or fruits. Cabbage is high in cancer-fighting endoles and a good source of choline, which improves mental functioning. It is also an excellent source of vitamins K and C. A very good remedy for anemia, cabbage has also been used as a nutritive tonic to restore strength in debility and convalescence. Of benefit to the liver, cabbage is also effective in preventing colon cancer and may help diabetics by reducing blood sugar. Cabbage juice is significant in preventing and healing ulcers. Cabbage contains manganese, vitamins B_1 (thiamin), B_2 (riboflavin), B_6 (pyridoxine), folate, omega-3 fatty acids, calcium, potassium, vitamin A, tryptophan, protein and magnesium.

Buying and Storing: Fresh cabbage has loose outer leaves around a firm center head. Older, stored cabbage does not have the outer wrapper leaves and tends to be paler in color. Cabbage will keep for up to 2 weeks in a vented plastic bag in the refrigerator. Wash and cut or slice just before using.

Culinary Use: Fresh cabbage is available year-round and is an excellent vegetable to have on hand at all times. It is an essential ingredient in vegetable stock. Steam, broil or stir-fry cabbage with other vegetables, legumes and grains or slice thin and serve raw in salads.

Recipes:
• Baked Onion, Leek and Cabbage Casserole (page 278)

- Braised Winter Vegetables (page 270)
- Brussels Sprouts with Walnuts and Blue Cheese (page 275)
- Curried Vegetable and Lentil Soup (page 216)
- Eight-Treasure Noodle Pot (page 300)
- Tomato-Thyme Soup (page 209)
- Vegetable Red Curry (Variation, page 222)
- Wakame Cabbage Salad (page 175)

Carrots

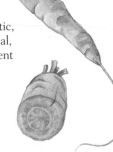

Daucus carota ssp. *sativus*

Actions: Antioxidant, anticancer, artery protecting, expectorant, antiseptic, diuretic, immune boosting, antibacterial, lower blood cholesterol, prevent constipation.

Uses: Carrots have a cleansing effect on the liver and digestive system, help counter the formation of kidney stones and relieve arthritis and gout. Their antioxidant properties from carotenoids (including beta-carotene) have been shown to cut cancer risk, protect against arterial and heart disease and lower blood cholesterol. Carrots enhance mental functioning, decrease the risk of cataracts and promote good vision. Carrots are extremely nutritious and rich in vitamins A (1 cup/250 mL supplies over 600% of our daily requirement), K and C. Potassium, some B vitamins, manganese and folate are also present.

Buying and Storing: The inedible green tops continue to draw nutrients out of the carrot so choose fresh carrots that are sold loose with the tops removed or remove and discard the tops immediately. Choose firm, well-shaped carrots with no cracks. The deeper the the carrot's color, the higher the concentration of carotene. If stored unwashed in a cold but moist place, carrots should not shrivel. Keep for up to 2 weeks in a vented plastic bag in the produce drawer of the refrigerator.

Culinary Use: Carrots are a versatile vegetable with natural sweetness that can be used in almost any vegetable recipe. Cooking frees up carotenes (precursors to vitamin A), the anticancer agents in carrots. Steam, roast, stir-fry or simmer carrots just until tender. Grated carrots are used raw in salads, grain and pasta dishes.

Recipes:
- Apple-Carrot Popovers (page 162)
- Autumn Harvest Salad (page 179)
- Barley and Vegetable Ragout (page 220)
- Breakfast Cocktail (page 170)
- Cheddar Cheese and Root Vegetable Soup (page 208)
- Grated Carrots with Dates and Walnuts (page 184)
- Roasted Vegetable and Tomato Ratatouille (page 217)
- Spiced Root Vegetables (page 273)
- Summer Vegetable and Millet Salad (page 187)
- Tomato-Thyme Soup (page 209)
- Vegetable Cakes (page 241)
- Vegetable Jewel Gingerbread (page 363)

Cauliflower

Brassica oleracea var. *botrytis*

Actions: Antioxidant, anticancer.

Uses: As are all cruciferous vegetables (cabbage, Brussels sprouts, broccoli, collard greens, kohlrabi), cauliflower is rich in endoles, the cancer preventing phytonutrients. Cauliflower is an excellent source of vitamin C. It is a good source of vitamin K, folate and vitamin B_6 (pyridoxine). Potassium and some protein and iron are also present.

Buying and Storing: Fresh cauliflower has dense, tightly packed florets and crisp, green leaves surround the head. Keep loosely covered in the refrigerator for no longer than 1 week.

Culinary Use: Wash and cut away outer leaves, save and use them as you would any leafy green vegetable. Cut the head into florets, discarding the woody core and stems. Use cauliflower raw in salads and appetizers with dips and sauces. Cauliflower is very good in soups, curries, stir-fries and chutneys. Steam or boil cauliflower or bake with other ingredients.

Recipes:
- Barley and Vegetable Ragout (page 220)
- Cauliflower and Wheat Berries (page 291)
- Fall Vegetable Paella (page 238)
- Golden Cauliflower with Split Peas (page 264)
- Spiced Cauliflower with Pasta (page 302)
- Vegetable Oatmeal Crumble (page 254)
- Whole-Grain and Vegetable Stuffing (page 263)

Celery

Apium graveolens var. *dulce* and *Celeriac Apium graveolens* var. *rapaceum*

Actions: Mild diuretic, anticancer.

Uses: Sometimes used as a treatment for high blood pressure (two to four stalks per day). The coumarins in celery help prevent free radicals from damaging cells, thus helping to prevent cell mutation, a pre-cancer condition. Coumarins also boost immune responses. The acetylenic compounds in celery have been found to stop the growth of tumorous cells. For the healing properties of celery seed, see page 106.

Buying and Storing: Fresh celery has some crisp green leaves and firm crisp ribs. Older stalks have had the leaves removed. Celery varieties range in color from very light to dark green and as the color darkens, the taste gets stronger. Store for up to 2 weeks in a vented plastic bag in the refrigerator.

Culinary Use: Use celery (stalks and leaves) when making salads, appetizers and vegetable cocktails to add a natural saltiness. Celery combines well with eggs, apples and walnuts. The light, almost white inner stalks are tender and serve well with dips. Pan-fry, include in stir-fries, braise or chop and include celery in baked dishes.

Celeriac is the root of a different variety of celery than the common table celery. It adds a stronger celery flavor to dishes. Scrub and cut celeriac into wedges. Peel the tough outer skin of celeriac and slice or chop. To prevent browning, drop the pieces into a bowl of water with a squeeze of lemon juice added. Steam, broil, stir-fry or cook celeriac au gratin with other vegetables.

Recipes:
- Barley and Vegetable Ragout (page 220)
- Cracked Wheat and Lima Bean Wrap (page 282)
- Fennel, Celery and Apple Salad (page 184)
- Jambalaya (page 219)
- Rainbow Chowder (page 224)
- Tomato-Thyme Soup (page 209)
- Whole-Grain and Vegetable Stuffing (page 263)
- Winter Cassoulet (page 221)

Celeriac

See Celery

Chile Peppers

Capsicum annuum

Actions: Stimulant, tonic, diaphoretic, stimulates blood flow to the skin, antiseptic, antibacterial, expectorant, prevents bronchitis, prevents emphysema, decongestant, blood thinner, carminative.

Uses: Chiles are hot peppers (including cayenne, jalapeño, ancho/poblano, habanero, serrano and pasilla to name only a few) that contain the active element capsaicin. They are high in vitamin A and contain some vitamin C, iron, magnesium, phosphorus and potassium. Chile peppers help people with bronchitis and related problems by irritating the bronchial tubes and sinuses by causing the secretion of a fluid that thins the constricting mucus and helps move it out of the body. Capsaicin also blocks the pain message from the brain making it an effective pain reliever. In addition, it also has clot-dissolving properties that make it useful if taken on a consistent basis. See also Cayenne Pepper (page 106).

Buying and Storing: Look for firm, crisp peppers with smooth skin and no blemishes. Store peppers in a paper bag in the produce drawer of the refrigerator for up to 4 days. Peppers freeze easily and may be added to sauces, soups and stews without thawing. Buy clean, fully dried chile peppers and store in a cool dry place.

Culinary Use: Wash and handle chile peppers carefully and wash hands thoroughly after handling because capsaicin will irritate skin and eyes. Remove the stem and inside pulp including seeds (seeds do not contain the fire). When first using chile peppers add half of the recommended amount to the recipe. Taste and add more, if desired.

Use fresh, reconstituted dried or canned chiles in recipes. Whisk in a drop of hot or jerk sauce or a quarter teaspoon (1 mL) of powdered cayenne to sauces, dips, dressings, soups or smoothies to substitute for fresh chiles.

Recipes:
- Artichokes in Italian Dressing (page 141)
- Cajun Black Spice (page 330)
- Ethiopian Hot Pepper Seasoning (page 332)
- Harissa (page 145)
- Open-Faced Samosas (page 140)
- Red Curry Spice (page 331)
- Yellow Curry Spice (page 331)

Collard Greens

See Leafy Greens

Corn

Zea mays

Actions: Anticancer, antiviral, raises estrogen level, neutralizes stomach acid, high fiber helps with kidney stones and water retention.

Uses: Corn is a good source of B_1 (thiamin) and B_6 (pyridoxine). Corn adds roughage to the diet.

Caution: Corn and corn products (cereals, corn chips or foods with cornstarch) may trigger food intolerances that lead to chronic conditions, including rheumatoid arthritis, headaches and irritable bowel syndrome.

Buying and Storing: Fresh corn is best if cooked within minutes of picking. When that is not possible, buy fresh corn that has been kept cold and use as soon as possible.

Culinary Use: Corn is sweet and blends with most vegetables. It is added to soups, risottos, egg dishes, salads, grains and baked vegetable dishes. Use leftover cooked fresh corn by slicing kernels off the cob with a sharp knife. Frozen or canned whole-kernel corn packed in water can be used when fresh is not available.

Recipes:
- Black-Eyed Pea Casserole (page 252)
- Cajun Blackened Potato and Mung Bean Salad (page 192)
- Corn and Rice Chowder (page 223)
- Rainbow Chowder (page 224)
- Summer Vegetable Casseroles (page 232)

Cucumbers

Cucumis sativus

Actions: Diuretic, anti-inflammatory.

Uses: The ascorbic and caffeic acids in cucumbers help soothe skin irritations and reduce swelling. Cucumbers are moderate sources of vitamins C and A, potassium, manganese and folate. They are high in water, making cucumbers refreshing vegetables for summer salads. Cucumbers contain sterols, which may help the heart by reducing cholesterol.

Buying and Storing: Choose bright shiny green-skinned, firm cucumbers. Avoid yellow spots (although this is a sign of ripeness the seeds will be bitter and the flesh too soft) and wax on the skin. Store in the produce drawer of the refrigerator for 4 to 5 days.

Culinary Use: Wash before using, peel (especially if skin has been waxed or if not organic), cut into cubes and leave seeds intact. Shred into salads and sauces. Use thinly sliced fresh cucumbers to replace greens in some salads.

Recipes:
- Chilled Fruited Gazpacho (page 206)
- Cucumber in Sake and Rice Vinegar Dressing (page 183)
- Herbed Feta Dip (page 144)
- Tzatziki (page 144)

Eggplant

Solanum melongena

Actions: Antibacterial, diuretic, may lower blood cholesterol, may prevent cancerous growths.

Uses: Now used topically to treat skin cancer, eggplant's terpenes may also work internally to deactivate steroidal hormones that promote certain cancers. A fair amount of potassium in eggplant normalizes blood pressure. They are a good source of folate, vitamin B_6 (pyridoxine) and vitamin C. Eggplant is low in fat and calories.

Buying and Storing: Choose small, heavy, deep purple eggplants with firm, smooth skin that have no scrapes, cuts or bruises. Use immediately or keep for 1 to 2 days in the produce drawer of the refrigerator.

Culinary Use: Wash before using, peel (if not organic), cut into cubes and leave seeds intact. Salting is not as important now because the varieties sold today are not as bitter, but it can prevent the absorption of oil in recipes where they are fried. The meaty texture and subtle, earthy flavor are what makes eggplant popular in vegetarian dishes. Eggplants are used in dips, appetizers and baked vegetable dishes such as moussaka, ratatouille and curries. Garlic, onions, tomato sauce and mozzarella cheese enhance eggplant in baked dishes.

Recipes:
- Baked Eggplant with Tomatoes and Mozzarella (page 256)
- Cheese-Stuffed Eggplant Rolls (page 138)
- Country Vegetable Pâté (page 159)
- Eggplant Manicotti with Spinach Pesto (page 236)
- Eggplant Salsa (page 311)
- Grilled Eggplant and Tomato Salad (page 197)
- Roasted Eggplant with Plums and Apricots (page 271)
- Roasted Eggplant with Walnut Sauce (page 259)
- Turkish-Stuffed Baked Eggplant (page 248)
- Winter Cassoulet (page 221)

Fennel

Foeniculum vulgare

Actions: Antioxidant, anti-inflammatory, anticancer. For the medicinal benefits of fennel seeds, see page 110.

Uses: A bulb-like vegetable similar to celery, but with a distinctly sweet anise taste, fennel is a good source of vitamin C. Fennel also contains potassium, manganese, folate, phosphorus and calcium.

Buying and Storing: Avoid bulbs with wilted or browning stalks or leaves. The bulb should be firm and white with a light green tinge. Remove leaves and keep for up to 1 week in the refrigerator.

Culinary Use: Use the leaves in recipes if they are still attached to the stalks. Use raw fennel with

vegetables for dipping or in a salad. Soups and stews and all baked vegetable dishes are enhanced by fennel. One-quarter fennel bulb measures about 1 cup (250 mL) when chopped.

Recipes:
- Fennel and Potatoes au Gratin (page 267)
- Fennel, Celery and Apple Salad (page 184)
- Turkish-Stuffed Baked Eggplant (page 248)
- Warm Beet Salad (page 194)
- Whole-Grain and Vegetable Stuffing (page 263)

Garlic

See Herbs

Kale

See Leafy Greens

Kohlrabi

See Cabbage

Leafy Greens

kale, Swiss chard, collard greens, mustard greens, turnip greens, lettuce

Actions: Antioxidant, anticancer.

Uses: Although the nutrient amounts change with each green, in general it can be said that leafy greens are excellent sources of vitamin A and chlorophyll, and good sources of vitamin C, with some calcium, iron, folic acid and potassium.

Buying and Storing: Buy bright green, crisp (not wilted) greens and store them unwashed in a vented plastic bag in a cold spot in the refrigerator. Leafy greens are very tender and will go limp and turn yellow (or brown) when not stored or handled properly. Store away from fruits and wash just before using.

Culinary Use: Remove tough spine and stem, and shred or chop leafy greens or tear the tender greens for salads. The stronger-tasting greens (kale, Swiss chard, collard, mustard, turnip) work well in hearty dishes like curries, legumes and spicy Indian and Moroccan dishes. Use the milder flavored greens in salads, with grains and as garnishes.

Recipes:
- Baked Wild Rice with Sorrel and Mustard Greens (page 283)
- Cannellini with Roasted Peppers and Shaved Parmesan (page 188)
- Dandelion Salad (page 178)
- Kale and Lentil Soup (Variation, page 214)
- Mâche with Fruit, Nuts and Blue Cheese Dressing (page 182)
- Mediterranean Red Pepper and Tomato Salad (page 176)
- Roasted Onion and Parsnip Gratin with Greens (page 277)
- Spring Green Sauce (page 328)
- Summer Flower Salad (page 177)
- Swiss Chard with Almond Butter Sauce (page 190)
- Udon Noodle Soup with Shiitakes and Bok Choy (page 215)
- Warm Mushrooms with Goat Cheese (page 189)

Leeks

Allium ampeloprasum

Actions: Expectorant, diuretic, relaxant, laxative, antiseptic, digestive, hypotensive.

Uses: Leeks are easily digested and often used in tonics, especially during convalescence from illness. They can be blended in toddies for relief from sore throats due to their warming, expectorant and stimulating qualities.
Leeks are good sources of folate and contain some vitamin C, B$_2$ (riboflavin), allicin, quercetin and magnesium.

Buying and Storing: Choose leeks with firm white bulbs with white roots still intact and crisp, bright green tops. Leeks with the base removed will deteriorate quickly. Unwashed and kept in a plastic bag in the refrigerator, leeks should last from 1 to 2 weeks.

Culinary Use: Trim white roots and outer dark green leaves, split and wash under running water to remove grit or soil trapped between the layers. Slice, chop or cut into chunks. Leeks may be used raw but mellow and soften when cooked. Savory tarts, casseroles, soups, stuffing, egg dishes, pasta and baked vegetable dishes make good use of the milder onion-like taste of leeks.

Recipes:
- Baked Onion, Leek and Cabbage Casserole (page 278)
- Baked Potatoes with Caramelized Onions and Leeks (page 269)
- Cheddar Cheese and Root Vegetable Soup (page 208)
- Hot Sweet Potato Salad (page 196)
- Leek and Mushroom Pilaf (page 285)
- Mushroom and Barley Soup (page 213)
- Potato and Leek Tart (page 154)
- Soba with Caramelized Onions, Leeks and Chives (page 296)
- Spring Green Sauce (page 328)
- Vegetable Frittata (page 155)
- Vegetables and Tempeh au Gratin (page 243)
- Whole-Grain and Vegetable Stuffing (page 263)

Lettuce

See Leafy Greens

Mushrooms

Actions: see Maitake and Shiitake, right.

Uses: Used and thought of as a vegetable, mushrooms are actually fungi living off other host organisms. Mushrooms reproduce by spores and have no roots, leaves, flowers or seeds, as do plants.

Buying and Storing: Look for mushrooms that are firm, plump and clean. Mushrooms should be free of any signs of softness, deterioration or mold. Common button mushrooms are widely available. Fresh mushroom varieties such as portobello, oyster, cremini, shiitake and maitake, and dried whole or cut mushrooms are available in Oriental markets, whole or natural food stores and some supermarkets. Store fresh mushrooms, loosely covered, in a paper bag for up to 5 days. Dried mushrooms keep for up to 6 months if stored in a cool dry place.

Caution: Always purchase mushrooms from reliable sources such as supermarkets and food markets. Many mushroom varieties are toxic and eating varieties from the wild may be fatal.

Raw mushrooms contain hydrazines, potentially toxic substances that are destroyed in cooking or drying. Do not eat fresh, raw mushrooms — always cook them.

Culinary Use: Clean mushrooms using a minimum amount of water or wipe with a clean, damp cloth. Cooking with shiitake and maitake mushrooms at least three times per week (more if possible) will contribute to overall immune and cardiovascular health and may lower your risk of cancer.

Whole, fresh mushrooms are roasted or grilled. Halved or chopped mushrooms are used in stews, broths and soups. Sliced mushrooms for rice (risotto) and grain dishes, stir-fries and roasted vegetable dishes. Shredded mushrooms complement cooked salads and sandwich fillings.

Dried mushrooms are added to soups and stews or reconstituted by soaking them in water or other liquids. Save the soaking water and use it in soups, stews, gravies and sauces or add to other cooking liquids in recipes.

Recipes:
• Almond and Herb-Stuffed Mushrooms (page 132)
• Artichoke and Mushroom Lasagna (page 246)
• Cantonese Noodles (page 250)
• Kale and Lentil Soup (page 214)
• Maple Pear and Portobello Mushroom Salad (page 195)
• Mushroom and Barley Soup (page 213)
• Mushroom Broth (page 203)
• Mushroom Sauce (page 321)
• Spelt and Vegetable Pilaf (page 289)
• Vegan Stroganoff (page 255)
• Vegetable Pie with Sweet Potato Topping (page 244)
• Warm Mushrooms with Goat Cheese (page 189)
• Whole-Grain and Vegetable Stuffing (page 263)
• Winter Cassoulet (page 221)

Maitake Mushroom

Grifola frondosa

Maitake means dancing mushroom in Japan because it is made up of many overlapping, fan-shaped fruit bodies that resemble butterflies dancing. In North America, maitake mushrooms are referred to as "hen of the woods" because they grow at the base of trees or stumps in big clusters resembling a hen's tail feathers.

Actions: Liver protective, lowers blood pressure, protect against breast and colorectal cancers, antioxidant.

Uses: In the late 1980s, Japanese scientists identified the maitake mushroom as being more potent than any mushroom previously studied. Maitake has remarkable tonic effects, especially on the immune system. It is used in the prevention of some cancers and may help protect against high blood pressure, constipation, diabetes and HIV.

Maitake's polysaccharide compound, known as beta 1,6 glucan (or D-fraction) is recognized by researchers as the most effective active agent stimulating cellular immune responses and inhibiting tumors.

Recipes:
• Cantonese Noodles (page 250)
• Hot and Sour Summer Soup (page 205)
• Mushroom-Almond Bisque (page 225)
• Mushroom and Barley Soup (page 213)
• Mushroom Broth (page 203)
• Roasted Peppers with Wild Rice and Walnuts (page 266)

Shiitake Mushroom

Lentinula edodes

Amber to brown, medium in size and traditional mushroom shaped. Shiitake have a flat, leathery cap, with a tough, woody stem.

Actions: Recognized as a symbol of longevity in Asia, shiitake mushrooms have long been used in traditional Chinese medicine. They have proven immune-boosting, antitumor, anticancer, antiviral, anti-AIDS, antibacterial, cholesterol lowering, hepato-protective and liver-protective properties.

Uses: A strengthened immune response due to the action of shiitake mushrooms means increased body resistance to bacterial, viral, fungal and parasitic infections. Shiitake is beneficial in soothing bronchial inflammation, regulating urinary incontinence, reducing chronic high cholesterol and inhibiting cancer metastasis. It is used to treat arthritis and chronic fatigue syndrome.

Lentinan in shiitake mushrooms has been shown to enhance immunity cells in clearing the body of tumor cells and in fighting HIV and hepatitis B viruses. Lentinan is one of three different anticancer drugs extracted from mushrooms approved by Japan's Health and Welfare Ministry. According to Dr. Moss, an expert in cancer treatment, incorporating fresh or dried shiitake into a diet rich in whole grains, vegetables and fruits is a low-cost cancer prevention strategy.

One 8 oz (250 g) serving yields 20% of the body's daily requirement of iron. Shiitake mushrooms are high in vitamin C, protein, dietary fiber and calcium.

Caution: Shiitake mushrooms contain uric acid forming purines and individuals with kidney problems or gout may wish to limit or avoid them.

Recipes:
• Cantonese Noodles (page 250)
• Country Vegetable Pâté (page 159)
• Hot and Sour Summer Soup (page 205)
• Leek and Mushroom Pilaf (page 285)
• Mushroom-Almond Bisque (page 225)
• Mushroom and Barley Soup (page 213)
• Mushroom Broth (page 203)
• Roasted Peppers with Wild Rice and Walnuts (page 266)
• Stir-Fried Vegetables and Bulgur (page 230)
• Tomatoes Stuffed with Basil and Shiitake Mushrooms (page 265)
• Udon Noodle Soup with Shiitakes and Bok Choy (page 215)
• Warm Mushrooms with Goat Cheese (page 189)

Mustard Greens

See Leafy Greens

Onions

Allium species

Actions: Antibacterial, anticancer, antioxidant, circulatory and digestive stimulant, antiseptic, lower cholesterol, hypotensive, hypoglycemic, diuretic, heart protective.

Uses: Onions help prevent thrombosis, reduce high blood pressure, lower blood sugar, prevent inflammatory responses and prohibit the growth of cancer cells. Shallots and yellow or red onions are the richest dietary source of quercetin, a potent antioxidant and cancer-inhibiting phytochemical. Onions are good sources of vitamin B_1 (thiamin), vitamin B_6 (pyridoxine) and vitamin C.

Buying and Storing: Choose onions that feel firm and have dry, tight skins. Avoid onions with woody centers in the neck and black powdery patches. If stored in a cool dry place with good air circulation, onions will keep for up to 1 month or more.

Culinary Use: Vidalia, red and Spanish onions are milder in flavor than yellow cooking onions. Shallots have a mild delicate flavor and are used whole in some dishes. Use onions raw in salads, sandwich fillings and for toppings. Include onions in stir-fries, salsas and other sauces, pasta, stuffing, baked vegetable dishes, soups and stews. They caramelize and sweeten when roasted.

Recipes:
• Baked Onion Leek and Cabbage Casserole (page 278)
• Baked Potatoes with Caramelized Onions and Leeks (page 269)
• Cheddar Cheese and Root Vegetable Soup (page 208)
• Country Vegetable Pâté (page 159)
• Moroccan Orange and Onion Salad (page 174)
• Potato and Leek Tart (page 154)
• Roasted Onion and Parsnip Gratin (page 277)
• Roasted Squash, Caramelized Onion and Garlic Soup (page 210)
• Scalloped Turnips with Potatoes and Onions (page 261)
• Soba with Caramelized Onions, Leeks and Chives (page 296)
• Tomato Pesto Udon (page 297)
• Vegetable Pie with Sweet Potato Topping (page 244)

Parsnips

Pastinaca sativa

Actions: Anti-inflammatory, anticancer.

Uses: Parsnips are best fresh, after frost has concentrated the carbohydrate into sugar, making them sweeter. They are a good source of vitamin C and E, as well as potassium with some protein, iron and calcium. Like other root vegetables, parsnips store well and are an excellent fresh winter vegetable.

Buying and Storing: Look for firm flesh with no shriveling, soft spots or cuts. Parsnips should snap when bent. Small thin parsnips with tops still intact are best (remove and discard the tops before storing). Keep in a vented plastic bag in the refrigerator for up to $1^{1}/_{2}$ weeks.

Culinary Use: Small, fresh parsnips are surprisingly sweet and roasting brings out the sugars even more. Parsnips add natural sweetness to baked goods, soups, sauces, stir-fries, baked vegetable dishes and jams. Pair older parsnips with apples and/or carrots for a more pleasant taste.

To cook parsnips, wash and peel if not organic, roughly chop, place in a small saucepan, cover with water and simmer until soft.

Recipes:
- Barley and Vegetable Ragout (page 220)
- Cheddar Cheese and Root Vegetable Soup (page 208)
- Curried Vegetable and Lentil Soup (page 216)
- Herbed-Glazed Parsnips (page 272)
- Herbed Vegetable Spread (page 150)
- Roasted Onion and Parsnip Gratin (page 277)
- Roasted Vegetable and Tomato Ratatouille (page 217)
- Spiced Root Vegetables (page 273)
- Vegetable Jewel Gingerbread (page 363)
- Vegetable Pie with Sweet Potato Topping (page 244)
- Warm Root Vegetable Salad (page 198)
- Whole-Grain and Vegetable Stuffing (page 263)

Peas

See Beans

Peppers

Capsicum annuum
green, red, yellow, orange and purple bell peppers

Actions: Antioxidant, anticancer, heart protective.

Uses: Red peppers are high in vitamins C and A (supplying over 100% of the Daily Recommended Amounts of each) and are good sources of vitamin B_6 (pyridoxine), with some manganese, folate and potassium.

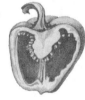

Buying and Storing: Look for firm, crisp peppers with smooth skin and no blemishes. Avoid waxed peppers because the wax can accelerate bacteria growth. Store peppers in a paper bag in the crisper drawer of the refrigerator for up to 4 days. Peppers freeze easily and may be added to soups and stews without thawing.

Culinary Use: Peppers are versatile vegetables, used raw in appetizers, salads and fillings. Mediterranean cooking relies on peppers for vegetable dishes. Orange, red and yellow varieties are sweeter in flavor than the green and purple types. For directions on roasting red peppers, see page 135.

Recipes:
- Basil and Roasted Pepper Quinoa (page 293)
- Cannellini with Roasted Peppers and Shaved Parmesan (page 188)
- Creamy Red Pepper Spread (page 149)
- Jambalaya (page 219)
- Mediterranean Red Pepper and Tomato Salad (page 176)
- Mediterranean Savory Bread Pudding (page 251)
- Red Pepper Sauce (page 224)
- Roasted Garlic and Red Pepper Pesto (page 309)
- Roasted Peppers with Wild Rice and Walnuts (page 266)
- Roasted Red Peppers (page 135)
- Roasted Squash and Red Pepper Salad (page 193)
- Roasted Vegetable and Tomato Ratatouille (page 217)

Potatoes

Solanum tuberosum
white, yellow, red, purple

Actions: Anticancer, heart protective.

Uses: Potatoes are high in potassium, which may help prevent high blood pressure and strokes. Potatoes are an excellent source of vitamin B_6 (pyridoxine) and are good sources of vitamins C and B_1 (thiamin), folate and fiber. They are a low fat, satisfying vegetable but cooking and garnishing methods determines how nutritious they are.

Buying and Storing: Select clean, smooth, well-shaped potatoes. Wrinkled skin, soft spots and bruises should be avoided. One medium potato weighs about 8 oz (250 g) and dices into about 1 cup (250 mL). If kept in a dry cool and frost-free place (cellar or porch), potatoes will last for 2 to 3 weeks. Keep covered with a brown paper or burlap bag because light causes potatoes to form chlorophyll and turn green. The green itself is not harmful but it is a sign that there is an increase in solanine, a glycoalkaloid that can cause allergic reactions and illness.

Culinary Use: Fresh potatoes are a versatile staple, cooked in gratins, soups, stews, and salads and baked vegetable dishes. They are mashed, boiled, roasted, sautéed, baked or deep-fried. Always use fresh potatoes.

Recipes:
• Braised Greens with Citrus Dressing (page 260)
• Cajun Blackened Potato and Mung Bean Salad (page 192)
• Cheddar Cheese and Root Vegetable Soup (page 208)
• Fennel and Potatoes au Gratin (page 267)
• Potato and Adzuki Latkes (page 242)
• Potato and Leek Tart (page 154)
• Scalloped Turnips with Potatoes and Onion (page 261)
• Vegetable Pie with Sweet Potato Topping (page 244)
• Vegetable Red Curry (page 222)

Pumpkin

See Squash

Rutabagas

Brassica napo brassica
See Turnips

Spinach

Spinacea oleracea

Actions: Anticancer, helps memory, antioxidant, promotes healing, prevents cataracts, anti-anemia.

Uses: A good source of choline, which improves mental functioning, and folic acid (a heart protector), spinach is one of only four vegetables high in vitamin E. It is also high in cancer-fighting lutein, as well as chlorophyll and vitamins C and A. Spinach is a good source of calcium, iron, protein and potassium.

Buying and Storing: Choose loose spinach instead of packaged whenever available. Look for broad, crisp leaves with deep green color and no signs of yellow, wilting or softness. Spinach keeps for up to 3 days in a vented plastic bag in the produce drawer of the refrigerator. Pick over and remove yellow or wilted leaves of pre-packaged spinach and rewrap in a vented plastic bag for storing.

Culinary Use: Wash fresh leaves well, remove tough spine and stem and shred or coarsely chop the leaves. Spinach is served raw in salads and appetizers. It may be added to soups, sauces, stuffing, risottos, vegetable dishes and pasta. To measure, tightly pack torn or chopped spinach into a dry measuring cup. Use frozen, or canned spinach when fresh is not available.

Recipes:
• Apple-Spinach Pâté (page 137)
• Cantonese Noodles (page 250)
• Dandelion Salad (page 178)
• Herbed Feta Dip (page 144)
• Medieval Green Sauce (Variation, 323)
• Spinach and Sea Vegetable Soup (page 204)
• Spinach Pesto Filling (page 237)
• Spinach Pie (page 284)
• Spring Green Sauce (page 328)
• Vegetable Frittata (page 155)
• Vegetable Oatmeal Crumble (page 254)

Squash

Cucurbita species
acorn, butternut, hubbard, pumpkin, turban

Actions: Antioxidant, anticancer.

Uses: A good winter vegetable, squash is high in vitamins A and C and potassium. Squash is also a good source of manganese, folate and omega-3 fatty acids.

Buying and Storing: Summer squash, such as zucchini, pattypan, cocozelle and the marrows, are small and tender with pliable skin and seeds. Winter squash, such as acorn, spaghetti, butternut, hubbard and pumpkin, have matured on the vine and their rind and seeds are tough and woody. Keep whole squash in a cold moist place or in the produce drawer of the refrigerator. Winter squash may keep as long as 1 month if stored properly. Cooked squash freezes well for use in recipes.

Culinary Use: Squash is often baked whole or split, seeded and baked. Acorn squash is often stuffed with a variety of savory fillings and baked.

Use squash in soups, stews, pasta sauces and some baked goods. To bake, wash and prick with a sharp knife. Arrange whole squash on a baking dish and bake at 375°F (190°C) for 40 to 45 minutes or until tender.

Recipes:
- Christmas Pudding (page 258)
- Pumpkin and Black Beans (page 280)
- Rainbow Chowder (page 224)
- Roasted Squash and Red Pepper Salad (page 193)
- Roasted Squash, Caramelized Onion and Garlic Soup (page 210)
- Squash Tagine (page 249)

Sweet Potatoes

Ipomoea batatas

Actions: Antioxidant, anticancer, heart protective.

Uses: Sweet potatoes are high in vitamin A (retinol), beta-carotene, vitamin C and fiber. They are a good source of copper and potassium and they also contain some calcium, iron, magnesium and zinc.

Buying and Storing: Select clean, smooth, well-shaped and firm sweet potatoes. Wrinkled skin, soft spots and bruises should be avoided. If kept in a cool dry and frost-free place (cellar or porch), sweet potatoes will last for up to 1 month.

Culinary Use: Although not related to the ordinary potato, sweet potatoes are often prepared in the same way with baking as the most common method. Mashed sweet potatoes make a good topping for baked vegetable dishes. One medium sweet potato weighs about 10 ounces (300 grams) and dices into about 1 cup (250 mL).

Recipes:
- Curried Sweet Potato Soup (page 207)
- Hot Sweet Potato Salad (page 196)
- Open-Faced Samosas (page 140)
- Potato and Leek Tart (page 154)
- Scalloped Turnips with Potatoes and Onion (page 261)
- Spelt and Vegetable Pilaf (page 289)
- Sweet Potato Crisps (page 133)
- Sweet Potato Pie with Ginger Crust (page 360)
- Vegetable Pie with Sweet Potato Topping (page 244)

Swiss Chard

See Leafy Greens

Tomatoes

Lycopersicon esculentum

Actions: Antioxidant, anticancer.

Uses: High in lycopene and glutathione, two powerful antioxidants, raw tomatoes reduce the risk of many cancers. Lycopene is also thought to help maintain mental and physical functioning and is absorbed by the body more efficiently when tomatoes are juiced. Tomatoes also contain glutamic acid that is converted in the human system to gamma-amino butyric acid (GABA), a calming agent, known to be effective for kidney hypertension. Drink tomato juice or smoothies made with tomatoes to relax after a stressful day. Tomatoes are also good sources of vitamins B_6 (pyrodoxine) and C.

Buying and Storing: Vine-ripened, heritage varieties have the best flavor. Tomatoes are best bought fresh only when in season (use canned or reconstituted dried at other times). Local tomatoes are not treated with ethylene gas to force reddening. Plump, heavy, firm skinned, bright red tomatoes keep for 2 to 3 days at room temperature. When almost over-ripe, store tomatoes in the refrigerator for 1 or 2 more days only.

Culinary Use: Raw fresh tomatoes are used in salads, sandwiches and as a side dish in the summertime. Fresh tomatoes are stuffed and eaten raw or baked. To remove the skin, cut a cross in the skin of each tomato using a paring knife. Place in a heatproof bowl and cover with boiling water. Leave for 30 seconds and drain. The skins will easily slip off. To remove the seeds, cut tomatoes in half and gently squeeze the seeds out. Use canned tomatoes in sauces, soups, stews and baked vegetable dishes.

Recipes:
- Baked Eggplant with Tomatoes and Mozzarella (page 256)
- Barbecue Sauce (page 320)
- Black Bean Chili (page 240)
- Green Tomato and Apple Salsa (page 312)
- Grilled Eggplant and Tomato Salad (page 197)

- Mediterranean Red Pepper and Tomato Salad (page 176)
- Roasted Vegetable and Tomato Ratatouille (page 217)
- Sun-Dried Tomato Pesto (page 309)
- Tomatoes and Goat Cheese with Pesto and Balsamic Vinegar (page 185)
- Tomato Sauce (page 319)
- Tomatoes Stuffed with Basil and Shiitake Mushrooms (page 265)
- Tomato-Thyme Soup (page 209)

- Spinach and Sea Vegetable Soup (page 204)
- Tomato-Thyme Soup (page 209)
- Vegetable Cakes (page 241)
- Vegetable Pie with Sweet Potato Topping (page 244)
- Warm Root Vegetable Salad (page 198)
- Whole-Grain and Vegetable Stuffing (page 263)

Turnips

Brassica rapa

Actions: Tonic, decongestant, antibacterial, anticancer, diuretic.

Uses: Turnips have a beneficial effect on the urinary system. They purify the blood and aid in the elimination of toxins. For this reason, they make a good addition to recipes. Both the root and the green tops are high in glucosinolates, which are thought to block the development of cancer. Good sources of calcium, iron and protein, small fresh tender turnips are available in the spring and sometimes in the fall.

Buying and Storing: Small, firm turnips with dark green leaves showing no signs of wilting or yellow are best. Rutabagas (similar to turnips but a different species in the cabbage family) may be waxed to hold in their moisture and are generally a lot bigger than the young fresh turnip. Turnips keep for up to 1 week in a vented plastic bag in the refrigerator. Rutabagas will keep longer.

Culinary Use: Fresh turnips can be hot and peppery in taste. They may be steamed, boiled or shredded and added raw to salads. Treat young turnips as you would parsnips — add to soups, stews and baked vegetable dishes. For using the green leafy turnip tops, see Leafy Greens.

Recipes:
- Autumn Harvest Salad (page 179)
- Braised Winter Vegetables (page 270)
- Cheddar Cheese and Root Vegetable Soup (page 208)
- Hot and Sour Summer Soup (page 205)
- Scalloped Turnips with Potatoes and Onion (page 261)

Watercress

Rorippa nasturtium-aquaticum

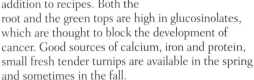

Actions: Antioxidant, diuretic, anticancer, tonic, antibiotic, cleansing.

Uses: High in fiber and vitamin C, and a good source of vitamin A. Purchase from farmers' markets in spring. Watercress grows wild around streams and wet areas, but be careful not to harvest in areas where fields drain directly into streams.

Buying and Storing: Pick watercress just before using. If purchasing, choose bright green, crisp sprigs with leaves intact. Sort through and remove any yellow or wilted stems. Watercress is fragile and should be used immediately or wrapped in a towel in the produce drawer of the refrigerator for 1 or 2 days.

Culinary Use: Watercress adds a hot and peppery bite to salads and baked dishes. Use watercress to replace spinach, parsley or other greens in sauces, soups, fillings and egg dishes.

Recipes:
- Dandelion Salad (Variations, page 178)
- Herbed Feta Dip (Variation, page 144)
- Mâche with Fruit, Nuts and Blue Cheese Dressing (Variation, page 182)
- Tzatziki (Variation, page 144)
- Watercress, Raspberry and Avocado Salad (page 180)

Wild Greens

dandelion leaves, mustard, sorrel, turnip, wild garlic mustard, wild leeks or ramps

See Leafy Greens

Zucchini

Cucurbita pepo
Italian, yellow straightneck,
yellow crookneck

Actions: Antioxidant.

Uses: A good source of vitamins A and C, folate, potassium and B_3 (niacin), zucchini is mild tasting and blends well with stronger vegetables.

Buying and Storing: Although zucchini grows quite large, the smaller fruit are tender and less woody. Look for soft thin skin with no cuts or bruises and stem end intact.

Culinary Use: The fresh flowers may be stuffed and baked. Zucchini are eaten raw in salads, often mixed with carrot. They are steamed, stir-fried or added to soups, sauces, stews and baked vegetable dishes.

Recipes:
• Baked Vegetable Falafel (page 134)
• Black-Eyed Pea Casserole (page 252)
• Country Vegetable Pâté (page 159)
• Curried Vegetable and Lentil Soup (page 216)
• Fall Vegetable Paella (page 238)
• Greek Soufflés (page 158)
• Minestrone Soup (page 212)
• Roasted Vegetable and Tomato Ratatouille (page 217)
• Summer Vegetable and Millet Salad (page 187)
• Summer Vegetable Casseroles (page 232)
• Vegetable Red Curry (page 222)
• Whole-Grain and Vegetable Stuffing (page 263)

Legumes

Definition: Leguminous plants include 10,000 plant species. Peas and beans, along with clover, alfalfa, wisteria and lupines all produce their seeds in pods. The term "legume" is applied to the plant, the pods or the seeds. "Pulse" is a common term in Asia that means fresh or dry edible leguminous seeds. The words "pulse" and "legume" may be interchanged. Dal is a Middle Eastern term applied to lentils, mung beans and split peas. The word dal also refers to a puréed dish made from lentils, mung beans or split peas.

Actions/Uses: The high levels of fiber in legumes work to lower cholesterol in the body and prevent blood sugar levels from rising too rapidly after a meal. This makes legumes a good choice for individuals with diabetes, insulin resistance or hypoglycemia.

Legumes help to control weight by retaining water in the digestive tract, giving the feeling of fullness. Legumes flush fats rather than allowing the body to store them. The oils in legumes are rich in linoleic and linolenic acids, two of the three essential fatty acids, which help the immune system. The fiber in legumes is a valuable tool for preventing colon cancer.

The amino acids (protein) in beans and peas make them a valuable food for vegetarians. Legumes are low in the amino acid methionine and high in lysine. Cereals are high in methionine and low in lysine. When legumes are combined with cereals in a dish (for example Red Beans and Rice), the combined amino acids make up complete, high-quality protein, an important issue for vegetarians.

A 1-cup (250 mL) serving of most legumes delivers 100% or more of the Recommended Daily Amounts of molybdenum, a trace mineral responsible for detoxifying damaging sulfites in the body.

Legumes are high in most B vitamins — 1 cup/250 mL cooked beans yields 40% of the daily requirement of B_1 (thiamin) and B_6 (pyridoxine). A good source of iron and choline, which improves mental functioning, legumes also contain vitamin A and potassium as well as calcium and vitamin C.

Buying and Storing: Whole or natural food stores and ethnic (Middle Eastern, Indian, Caribbean) stores carry a wide selection of legumes both prepackaged and in bulk. Look for clean dried peas and beans with no signs of wrinkling or mildew. Dried legumes will keep for a very long time if kept in a clean glass container away from heat and light.

Culinary Use: Grain and legume dishes are especially important for vegetarians who benefit from the complete proteins formed when grains and legumes are combined. Lentils and split peas may be added to soups and stews without soaking but all other legumes must be soaked to soften and rehydrate them. Soaking reduces the cooking time by half. Cooked canned peas, beans and lentils are an excellent and easy way to use legumes when time does not permit soaking and cooking the dried beans. When using canned legumes, if the recipe calls for them to be drained, reserve the liquid and use it in soups and stock recipes because it retains many of the water-soluble nutrients.

To Soak Legumes: Place washed beans in a large saucepan and cover with 2 inches (5 cm) of water. Bring to a boil over high heat. Reduce heat and gently simmer for 2 minutes. Leave the pan on the element and turn off the heat. Let stand 1 hour or overnight. Discard the soaking water and rinse the beans. Legumes have now been rehydrated and are ready to cook.

To Cook Legumes: Place soaked, drained, rinsed beans in a large saucepan. Cover with 2 inches (5 cm) of fresh water. Cover the pan and bring to a boil. Reduce heat and simmer for 45 minutes to 2 hours (cooking times differ for the varieties), or cook until tender. Add salt or other seasonings after legumes have been cooked because if added before, salt toughens the beans.

Adzuki Beans

Phaseolus angularis

Native of Asia, the small, oval, dark red adzuki beans grow on bushes rather than vines, as do most legumes. They are eaten fresh, dried or sprouted and ground into flour. The taste is mild, slightly nutty. Adzuki beans have a thick skin and take up to 2 hours to cook.

Recipes:
• Potato and Adzuki Latkes (page 242)

Black Beans

Phaseolus vulgaris

Large, shiny black, kidney-shaped beans from South America, black beans are a staple in South and Central American and Caribbean dishes. In traditional dishes, they are boiled and fried and often paired with rice for complete protein. The taste is earthy, with overtones of mushroom. Cook black beans for 1 hour.

Recipes:
• Black Bean Chili (page 240)
• Black Bean Quesadillas (page 136)

• Black Bean and Roasted Garlic Spread (page 147)
• Pumpkin and Black Beans (page 280)
• Red Beans and Rice (Variation, page 274)
• Whole-Grain and Vegetable Stuffing (page 263)

Black-Eyed Peas

Vigna unguiculata

Originating in China, black-eyed peas traveled the Silk Route to Arabia and from there to Africa. Slaves carried them to America where they became an important part of "soul food" dishes. Kidney-shaped and smooth, with thin skin, black-eyed peas are cream-colored with a definite black or brown spot or eye. They are smooth and buttery in texture and the taste is subtle. Black-eyed peas may be cooked in soups or stews without soaking. Check for doneness after 30 minutes and do not overcook, which will cause them to loose their texture. Substitute black-eyed peas for flageolets in any recipe.

Recipes:
• Black Bean Chili (Variation, page 240)
• Black Bean Quesadillas (Variation, page 136)
• Black Bean and Roasted Garlic Spread (Variation, page 147)
• Black-Eyed Pea Casserole (page 252)
• Pumpkin and Black Beans (Variation, page 280)

Cannellini Beans

Phaseolus vulgaris

See also Haricot Beans

Cannellini beans are a member of the haricot bean family and are used extensively in Italian cooking. Cannellini beans are white, oval and medium size. Their tough skin means that cannellini beans will take 1 to 1½ hours to soften. Their texture is smooth and buttery and the taste is subtle, making them a good bean for soups and spreads.

Recipes:
• Black Bean and Roasted Garlic Spread (Variation, page 147)
• Herbed Vegetable Spread (page 150)
• Hummus (Variation, page 146)
• Mediterranean Bean Salad (page 186)
• Three-Bean Enchiladas (page 239)
• Whole-Grain and Vegetable Stuffing (page 263)

Chickpeas

Cicer arietinum

(also known as Garbanzo)

The Roman word, arietinum means "like a ram." Arietinum is an apt name for chickpeas because they resemble a ram's head with horns curling around the sides. Large, round tan-colored, chickpeas are nutty in flavor and firm in texture. Chickpeas require up to $1\frac{1}{2}$ hours to cook. They are very versatile, used in salads, soups, stews, sauces, spreads and dips.

Recipes:
- Baked Vegetable Falafel (page 134)
- Black Bean Chili (page 240)
- Dandelion Salad (Variation, page 178)
- Fruit Spread (page 150)
- Herbed Nut and Bean Patties (page 234)
- Herbed Vegetable Spread (page 150)
- Hummus (page 146)
- Mediterranean Red Pepper and Tomato Salad (Variation, page 176)
- Three-Bean Enchiladas (page 239)
- Whole-Grain and Vegetable Stuffing (page 263)

Fava Beans

Vicia faba

(also known as broad beans)

Used in European soups and stews since before medieval times, the fava bean has been an important staple throughout history. Fava beans are large, light brown or taupe in color with wrinkled skin and a strong, earthy flavor. They are usually tender after 1 hour of cooking. Fava beans can overwhelm some dishes and are at their best in hearty soups and stews.

Recipes:
- Black Bean Quesadillas (page 136)
- Baked Vegetable Falafel (page 134)
- Cajun Blackened Potato and Mung Bean Salad (Variation, page 192)

Flageolets

Phaseolus vulgaris

See also Haricot Beans

Popular in French and Mediterranean dishes, flageolets are immature kidney beans, picked before they ripen and considered a delicacy. Smaller than mature kidney beans, flageolets are pale green, tender and very mild tasting. Salads are the best way to feature the subtle taste and texture of flageolets.

Recipes:
- Cajun Blackened Potato and Mung Bean Salad (Variation, page 192)
- Dandelion Salad (Variation, page 178)
- Mediterranean Red Pepper and Tomato Salad (Variation, page 176)

Haricot Beans

Phaseolus vulgaris

The Haricot family of beans includes cannellini beans, great Northern beans, white kidney, navy beans, flageolets and small whites. They are the mature (except in the case of flageolets), dried white, small round or oval seeds of the green bean (string bean), known as *haricot vert* in France. These beans are common beans, easily found in most supermarkets and in dried soup packets. Haricot beans take about 1 hour to cook but stand up to long, slow simmering. They are the beans used in the fabulous French cassoulet and the popular Boston Baked Bean dish that originated in the city still known as Beantown.

Recipes:
- Mediterranean Bean Salad (page 186)
- Three-Bean Enchiladas (page 239)
- Whole-Grain and Vegetable Stuffing (page 263)

Red Kidney Beans

Phaseolus vulgaris

Native to Mexico, red kidney beans (sometimes called kidney) are now used throughout the world in ethnic dishes such as Chile con Carne and Three-Bean Salad. Also known as red beans, they have evolved into many different varieties. Kidney-shaped and usually deep red in color, kidney beans also come in brown, black and white varieties. The texture is mealy and the taste is rich and unique. Check for doneness after 1 hour of simmering because red kidney beans will start to loose their texture if cooked too long.

Recipes:
- Black Bean Chili (page 240)
- Black Bean Quesadillas (Variation, page 136)
- Potato and Adzuki Latkes (page 242)
- Red Beans and Rice (page 274)
- Whole-Grain and Vegetable Stuffing (page 263)

Lentils

Lens esculenta and *L. culinaris*

Dating from about 8000 BC, lentils are believed to be the first legumes to be cultivated. They originated in Asia and spread to India and the Middle East and are still very popular in dishes from those areas where they play an important role in providing protein to the diet.

Lentils range in color from a tan and gray-brown, to dark brown, green, red, yellow and blue. They are small flat disks that can be very small ($1/8$ inch/0.25 cm) or larger ($1/4$ inch/0.5 cm). Lentils do not need to be presoaked and cook in 10 to 15 minutes. They should not be overcooked because they will loose their texture and turn to mush. Lentils are used in soups, baked vegetable dishes, stews and purées.

Recipes:
- Amaranth Chili (page 295)
- Cajun Blackened Potato and Mung Bean Salad (page 192)
- Curried Vegetable and Lentil Soup (page 216)
- Dandelion Salad (Variation, page 178)
- Kale and Lentil Soup (page 214)
- Mediterranean Bean Salad (page 186)
- Mediterranean Red Pepper and Tomato Salad (Variation, page 176)
- Nut and Lentil Wraps (page 228)
- Sea Vegetable Chowder (page 226)

Lima Beans

Phaseolus lunatus

There are two main species of lima bean, the large lima from Central America and the smaller variety originating in Mexico. The name actually comes from the capital city of Peru. American Indians used lima beans as part of their three sisters dishes. Corn and squash were the other sisters. They have traveled around the world and are now the most important bean in Africa.

Lima beans are flat, white to pale green seeds with a mealy texture when cooked. Cook lima beans for 1 to $1\frac{1}{2}$ hours. They are available fresh, dried, canned and frozen and can be added to soups and stews and baked grain and vegetable dishes.

Recipes:
- Corn and Rice Chowder (page 223)
- Cracked Wheat and Lima Bean Wrap (page 282)
- Dandelion Salad (Variation, page 178)

- Mediterranean Red Pepper and Tomato Salad (Variation, page 176)
- Potato and Adzuki Latkes (page 242)

Mung Beans

Vigna radiata

Mung beans are sold with or without their husk. They can be whole or split. Native to India, they are known as *moong dal*. Mung beans are the variety of legume that the Chinese sprout (they are five times richer in vitamins A and B and contain vitamins C and B_{12} when sprouted). Each of the many varieties of mung beans are small, round and most often yellow inside a dull green skin. There are brown and black varieties but the green or yellow (when hulled) mung beans are the most common. Cook mung beans for less than 1 hour or add directly to soups and other dishes that will simmer for at least that long.

Recipes:
- Cajun Blackened Potato and Mung Bean Salad (page 192)
- Dandelion Salad (Variation/sprouts) (page 178)
- Fennel, Celery and Apple Salad (Variation/sprouts) (page 184)
- Golden Cauliflower with Split Peas (Variation, page 264)

Peas

Pisum sativum

Peas originated in the Middle East and spread to China, the Mediterranean, India and Europe. A staple in Greece, Rome and ultimately Great Britain, peas were the perfect food to grow in earlier times because they would keep all winter. Small, round, bright green when fresh, dried peas are usually split. Dried split peas are green or yellow. Use fresh, dried, canned or frozen peas. Fresh peas have a fresh, sweet taste. All dried split peas cook quickly without soaking and have a deeper, richer flavor than their fresh counterparts.

Recipes:
- Golden Cauliflower with Split Peas (page 264)
- Nut and Lentil Wraps (page 228)

Soybeans

Glycine max

See Soy Foods (page 101)

Whole and Ancient Grains

Definition: Cereal grains are part of the grass family of plants. Whole grains have not been refined and stripped of their outer bran and inner germ. Whole grains supply complex carbohydrates and nutrients to the body because the whole seed package with its three major sections and their nutrients is intact.

Ancient is a term that is often used to describe grains (spelt, kamut) and herb seeds (quinoa, amaranth, teff) that have survived thousands of years without hybridization or significant genetic modification. They are much the same now as when prehistoric man gathered them. Ancient grains have largely been introduced to the Western world within the last half of the twentieth century and enjoy limited availability.

The outer layer, called bran, protects the life force and nourishment of all grains. Bran contains fiber, some minerals and protein. It is always removed when grains are refined. The largest part of grain is the endosperm, which provides a storehouse of food in the form of carbohydrate intended for the growing seed. The third, perhaps most important section of whole grains, the germ, is the life-spark of the grain. It is a rich source of protein, antioxidant vitamin E, phytate, iron, zinc and magnesium.

Actions/Uses: Whole grains supply fiber, which helps prevent against colon cancer. They are rich in phytoestrogens that halt the early stages of breast cancer and protect against cancer of the large intestine. The vitamin E in grains has an antioxidant effect. Whole grains protect against heart disease, fight obesity and lower blood sugar levels. Whole grains supply selenium, potassium and magnesium to the body. Each grain or seed listed below has its own nutrient quota.

Buying and Storing: Whole or natural food stores carry a wide selection of whole and ancient grains both packaged and in bulk. Purchase small quantities of ground grain and a wide variety of whole grains. Use them often, and store in glass containers below 65°F (18°C) or in the refrigerator.

Flavor: The presence of the outer bran makes whole grains chewier and more flavorful. A nutty flavor is evident, yet each grain species has its own characteristic flavor.

Culinary Use: Whole grains are sprouted, toasted, used with dried fruit as a breakfast cereal or casserole topping, cooked and added as an ingredient in baked products, soups, salads and stir-fries and baked with custard and fruit for desserts.

To Wash Whole Grains: Place whole grains in a sieve and swish in cool water. Whole grains benefit from presoaking for up to several hours before cooking. Whole grains double their bulk when cooked.

To Cook Whole-Grain Berries: Measure berries into a medium-size pot. Cover with twice the amount of water, place over medium-high heat and bring to a boil. Cover pot with a lid, turn heat off and set aside overnight or for a minimum of 2 to 3 hours. Most of the liquid will be absorbed. Test to see if the grain is tender. If not, add enough water to cover and simmer until tender (whole grains retain a chewy texture and never get soft like processed grain). Drain and store in a tightly covered glass jar in the refrigerator until ready to use. Cooked whole grains keep 2 to 3 days in the refrigerator.

Amaranth

Amaranthus cruentus

The only seed to provide humans with the most effective balance of protein matched only by milk, amaranth plays an important role in dairy-reduced diets. Lysine is higher in amaranth than any other complex carbohydrate. The ancient Aztecs revered amaranth as a "wonder food" not knowing that science would show it to be lean and high in vitamins and minerals and calcium.

Forms Available: Whole seed, flour and sometimes mixed with other grains in whole-grain blends.

Recipes:
• Amaranth Chile (page 295)
• Cracked Wheat and Lima Bean Wrap (page 282)
• Stir-Fried Vegetables and Bulgur (Variation, page 230)

Barley

Hordeum vulgare

Barley is one of the oldest domesticated crops. The gummy fiber in barley is thought to be what is responsible for its ability to reduce high serum cholesterol levels in the body. Barley is a source of potassium, magnesium and B$_3$ (niacin).

Forms Available: Pot barley is the preferred form because it is milled just enough to remove the inedible hull. Scotch barley is coarsely ground hulled barley and has as many of the nutrients as pot barley. Not really a whole food, pot barley is whiter than pot barley because more of the hull and bran layers are stripped along with much of the protein, fiber, vitamins and minerals. Rolled barley is pot barley that has been sliced, steamed, and rolled into flakes.

Recipes:
- Barley and Vegetable Ragout (page 220)
- Green Barley Water (page 341)
- Mushroom and Barley Soup (page 213)

Buckwheat

Fagopyrum esculentum

Buckwheat is not related to wheat, but is a plant in the same family as rhubarb. Buckwheat is an excellent source of antioxidants and it increases the quality of protein in the diet because it is higher in the amino acid, lysine.

Forms Available: Whole kernel, white hulled buckwheat (called groats), kasha (hulled, crushed and toasted white buckwheat), flour and noodles (called soba).

Recipes:
- Apricot-Apple Bars (page 365)
- Buckwheat Apple Pancakes (page 164)
- Fudge Bars (page 366)
- Kasha Pudding with Apple and Raisins (page 167)
- Soba with Caramelized Onions, Leeks and Chives (page 296)
- Spicy Soba Noodles (page 299)

Bran

Bran is the outer layer of grains and contains fiber, protein and other nutrients. The easiest way to cook with bran is to buy whole grains with the bran still attached. Bran may be purchased at most supermarkets and whole or natural food stores. Store bran in the refrigerator and use it to add fiber and nutrients to most recipes or to enrich milled flour. Use 1 to 2 tbsp (15 to 25 mL) in baked goods, toppings, stir-fries, legume and vegetable dishes.

Forms Available: Oat, wheat and rye bran is available in flakes or buds.

Recipes:
- Apple-Carrot Popovers (page 162)
- Whole-Grain Granola (page 160)

Corn

Zea mays

Commonly called maize, corn is the only widely used grain that is native to the Western hemisphere. It has been proven that corn was grown and used some 80,000 years ago.

Forms Available: Whole corn kernels (see Corn, page 76) are dried and ground into other products. Corn flour is ground from a variety of corn with a soft starch that makes it easy to grind. Hard shell flint corn is ground to a coarse meal called polenta — very deep yellow-orange polenta is highest in beta-carotene. The Algonquin Indians discovered that soaking fresh corn with wood ashes until the kernels burst out of their skins and drying and grinding the inner corn kernels produces hominy and grits. Hominy and grits are not exactly whole foods, but they do deliver fiber and some protein and are usually combined with eggs, vegetables, cheese or legumes for balanced dishes. Cornmeal, polenta, hominy or grits that are processed by the old, traditional stone-ground method retain more of the bran and germ.

Recipes:
- Baked Apple Polenta Custard (page 168)
- Black-Eyed Pea Casserole (page 252)
- Cajun Blackened Potato and Mung Bean Salad (page 192)
- Corn and Rice Chowder with Parsley Persillade (page 223)
- Rainbow Chowder (page 224)
- Summer Vegetable Casseroles (page 232)

Kamut

Triticum polonicum

A non-hybrid form of wheat originating in the Fertile Crescent between Egypt and the Tigris-Euphrates region, kamut is truly an ancient grain. It is a good source of calcium, magnesium, phosphorus and potassium and supplies 12% of the body's daily protein requirements. Kamut is a much larger grain than wheat, with a mild, sweet, buttery and nutty flavor. Substitute kamut for wheat or spelt in any recipe.

Forms Available: Whole kernel and flour.

Recipes:
- Kamut with Sautéed Summer Vegetables (page 288)
- Whole-Grain and Vegetable Stuffing (page 263)
- Whole-Grain Broccoli Stir-Fry (page 286)

Millet

Panicum miliaceum

Native to Africa and Asia, millet is the round yellow seed of an annual grass. Millet is not a true cereal but related to sorghum, a type of millet. A good source of protein, millet is an excellent source of the B vitamins, magnesium, zinc, copper and iron. Combine millet in vegetarian dishes with a good source of Vitamin C such as carrots, oranges or broccoli.

Forms Available: Whole seed often mixed with other grains in whole-grain blends.

Recipes:
- Stir-Fried Vegetables and Bulgur (Variation, page 230)
- Summer Vegetables and Millet Salad (page 187)

Oats

Avena sativa

Oats are higher in protein and essential fatty acids than other cereals because when hulled, the bran and germ remain intact with the groat. Oats are an excellent source of B vitamins and minerals.

Forms Available: Steel-cut oats contain the bran and germ while Scotch-cut (also known as Irish oats) are ground with stones and may be missing some nutrients. Steamed oat groats are sliced and rolled to make rolled oats. Whole rolled oats (also known as old-fashioned oats) are higher in nutrients than quick-cooking oats and the even thinner instant oats, which are partially cooked and may cook faster but are not considered whole foods.

Recipes:
- Apricot Granola Biscuits (page 161)
- Savory Oatmeal Topping (page 253)
- Scottish Oatcakes (page 163)
- Whole-Grain Granola (page 160)

Quinoa

Chenopodium quinoa

Actually an herb seed, quinoa is protein rich and extremely high in calcium (1 cup/250 mL of cooked quinoa equals the amount of calcium found in 1 quart/liter of milk). Gluten-free and easily digested, quinoa is classed as an ancient grain.

Rinse thoroughly before using to remove the bitter saponin coating.

Forms Available: Whole seed.

Recipes:
- Basil and Roasted Pepper Quinoa (page 293)
- Creamy Couscous with Quinoa and Cranberries (page 292)

Rice

Oryza sativa var.

A cereal originating in Asia, rice has been a staple there since about 5000 BC. Brown rice, or rice with the bran intact, is rich in B vitamins, protein, magnesium and fiber and that is why it is considered whole. Eat rice with a fruit or vegetable high in vitamin C.

Forms Available: More than 25 varieties of rice are available — basmati, Wehani, black and red rice are a few — and most can be purchased in the following forms: brown (missing only the hull and the most nutritious); polished white rice, which lacks the protein and other nutrients in brown rice; parboiled rice is steamed white rice; quick-cooking or instant brown rice has been partially cooked and slit to make it cook faster; brown rice farina (stone-ground brown rice); and rice flour, which is usually made by grinding white rice. See also Wild Rice (page 92).

Recipes:
- Cajun Dirty Rice and Tempeh (page 301)
- Country Vegetable Pâté (page 159)
- Eight-Treasure Noodle Pot (page 300)
- Fall Vegetable Paella (page 238)
- Jambalaya (page 219)
- Lemon Cloud Rice Pudding (page 356)
- Lemon Risotto (page 290)
- Red Beans and Rice (page 274)
- Tomatoes Stuffed with Shiitake Mushrooms (page 265)
- Whole-Grain and Vegetable Stuffing (page 263)

Rye

Secale cereale

Rye originated in Southwest Asia and is similar in nutrients to wheat but with more of the lysine amino acid. When rye is crossed with wheat, the hybrid triticale is the result.

Forms Available: Whole kernel called rye berries, rolled, cracked and flour.

Recipe:
• Gingerbread (page 166)

Spelt

Triticum aestivum spelta

One of the original natural grains known to man, spelt was grown in Europe more than 9,000 years ago. It contains more protein, fats and crude fiber than wheat, and is high in mucopolysaccharides. Spelt is usually organically grown because it is hardier, resistant to pests and diseases and therefore, doesn't require fertilizers, pesticides or insecticides.

Caution: Spelt may be tolerated by people with wheat allergies, but should be avoided by people with celiac disease or gluten intolerance.

Forms Available: Whole kernel called spelt berries, rolled spelt or flakes and flour.

Recipes:
• Apple-Carrot Popovers (page 162)
• Apricot Granola Biscuits (page 161)
• Buckwheat Apple Pancakes (page 164)
• Spelt and Vegetable Pilaf (page 289)
• Whole-Grain Broccoli Stir-Fry (page 286)
• Whole-Grain and Vegetable Stuffing (page 263)
• Whole-Grain Granola (page 160)

Teff (or Tef)

Eragrostis abyssinica

Grown by Ethiopians for centuries, teff means "lost" in reference to the tiny seeds that are hard to harvest. Now available in limited supply in the West, teff is a good wheat substitute for some dishes because it does not contain gluten. However, the lack of gluten means that teff will not hold the structure for baked products. The seed is so small it cannot be refined so all the nutrients are intact.

Forms Available: Whole grains.

Recipes:
• Apricot-Apple Bars (page 365)
• Fudge Bars (page 366)
• Gingerbread (page 166)
• Vegetable Jewel Gingerbread (page 363)

Wheat

Triticum aestivum

Wheat may have been one of the first cultivated plants 11,000 years ago. There are two main types of wheat — hard (with a higher protein and gluten content) and soft. The berry contains both insoluble and soluble fiber, vitamins, minerals, protein, carbohydrates and phytochemicals. Eating whole wheat with legumes and seeds helps to enrich the incomplete proteins in vegetarian dishes.

Forms Available: Whole kernels called wheat berries are the most nutritious form. Bulgur is wheat that has been steamed, dried and crushed. Couscous is a processed flour product made from cracked wheat that cooks faster than berries but does not have their nutrients. Farina (a fine cracked wheat), rolled wheat or flakes, whole and crushed germ and bran (see page 90) are the other semi-whole wheat forms. Whole unbleached flour is preferred to refined white wheat flour and udon noodles are more nutrient-rich than pasta made from refined white flour. Seitan is a high-protein food made from the gluten in wheat flour (see page 124) and for wheat grass in Cereal Grasses (see page 125).

Recipes:
• Amaranth Chili (Variation, page 295)
• Apple-Carrot Popovers (page 162)
• Cantonese Noodles (page 250)
• Cauliflower and Wheat Berries (page 291)
• Cracked Wheat and Lima Bean Wrap (page 282)
• Gingerbread (page 166)
• Peanut Butter and Banana Bread (page 165)
• Stir-Fried Vegetables and Bulgur with Ginger Citrus Sauce (Variation, page 230)
• Tabbouleh (page 297)
• Tomato Pesto Udon (page 297)
• Vegan Stroganoff (page 255)
• Whole-Grain Broccoli Stir-Fry (page 286)

Wild Rice

Zizania palustris

Wild rice is not rice at all, but is an aquatic grain harvested from the brown and green reeds of a long-stemmed annual plant that grows primarily in the shallow waters of northern Ontario, Manitoba and Minnesota. It is a sacred plant, central to the Ojibwe religion and the foundation of their belief system. At the same time, it was a staple food, one that can be stored for years against times of famine. The taste of wild rice is nutty and pleasant and the texture is chewy. Wild rice has more protein than wheat and brown or white rice, less fat than corn and is high in B_1 (thiamin), B_2 (riboflavin), B_3 (niacin) and potassium. Substitute wild rice for brown rice in recipes. Use cooked wild rice in soups, salads, breads and cakes and as a breakfast cereal.

Forms Available: Whole grain and mixed with other rice varieties in gourmet blends.

Recipes:
- Baked Wild Rice with Sorrel and Mustard Greens (page 283)
- Corn and Rice Chowder (page 223)
- Fall Vegetable Paella (page 238)
- Jambalaya (page 219)
- Roasted Peppers with Wild Rice and Walnuts (page 266)
- Whole-Grain and Vegetable Stuffing (page 263)

Nuts and Seeds

Definition: The term nut describes any seed or fruit of a plant that has an edible kernel and is found in a hard shell. Seeds are found in the fruit of plants or growing on the stalk after the flower dies. Both nuts and seeds are the embryo of the plant — its way of reproducing new life. Unless they are salted, spiced or treated with additives, preservatives or dyes, most raw or dry-roasted nuts are considered whole foods.

Actions/Uses: Because they contain all that is necessary for a plant's new life, nuts and seeds are extremely nutritious, supplying protein, vitamin E and fiber along with essential minerals. Five human epidemiological studies found that nut consumption is linked to a lower risk for heart disease. This is likely due to their monounsaturated fats and the antioxidant action of the vitamin E found in most nuts.

   Most nuts (with the exception of coconut and pine nuts) contain linoleic acid and alpha-linolenic acid. These essential fatty acids are associated with decreased risk of tumor formation and heart disease and are also essential for healthy skin, hair, glands, mucus membranes, nerves and arteries. Although their fat is polyunsaturated or monounsaturated, which may actually help decrease blood cholesterol levels, nuts and seeds should be used regularly but in moderation.

Buying and Storing: Whole or natural food stores carry a wide selection of whole raw nuts and seeds that are available packaged and in bulk. Unshelled nuts will keep in a cool place for up to 6 months. Purchase small quantities of shelled whole nuts in the fall when they are harvested and store in a cool place or the refrigerator for up to 2 months. Due to their high oil content, chopped nuts will go rancid quickly and should be stored in the refrigerator for up to 6 weeks.

Flavor: Each nut and seed has its own characteristic flavor and texture. Roasting accentuates and intensifies the "nutty" flavor of nuts and seeds.

Culinary Use: Nuts and seeds are best eaten raw (or lightly toasted). They can be used whole or chopped as snacks, in salads, casseroles, stuffing, cereals and baked goods, as a topping for baked vegetable and fruit dishes, as well as in grain and lentil dishes. Whole shelled nuts may retain their skins, which do not need to be removed unless the taste is just too bitter.

To Blanch Nuts: To remove the skins from almonds, pistachios and walnuts, cover with boiling water, let cool and rub or pinch the skins off. Dry on absorbent towels. To blanch hazelnuts: Place in a single layer in a baking pan in a 350°F (180°C) oven for about 15 minutes or until the skins dry and rub off easily.

To Toast Nuts or Seeds: Preheat the oven to 375°F (190°C). Spread nuts or seeds evenly in one layer on an ungreased baking sheet and bake for 3 minutes. Using a metal lifter, turn the nuts/seeds over and toast for 1 to 3 minutes more, watching closely. Nuts/seeds are done when they color slightly. Remove from the oven and let cool before using. Seeds take much less time to toast than nuts. Store toasted nuts in an airtight container in a cool, dry place for up to 1 week.

Almonds

Prunus amygdalus

Of the two types of almonds — bitter and sweet — only the sweet is edible in the raw state. The poisonous prussic acid in bitter almonds is removed by heating. Bitter almonds are used mainly in the production of almond oil and almond essence and are not readily available to consumers. Jordan and Valencia varieties of sweet almonds from Spain and Portugal are widely available. The flat, medium-size Californian almonds are used mostly for processing but may be available to home cooks in North America.

One-quarter cup (50 mL) of almonds supplies the body with 45% of its daily requirements of manganese and vitamin E. Almonds are high in protein, potassium, magnesium and phosphorus and they have the highest calcium content of all nuts.

Forms Available: Whole unshelled, whole shelled with skin, whole shelled and blanched, blanched halves, blanched slivers, flaked, roasted, chopped and ground (almond meal). Marzipan is a confectionary paste made from ground almonds, sugar and egg whites often used as an icing base for fruitcakes.

Recipes:
- Almond and Herb-Stuffed Mushrooms (page 132)
- Almond Butter Sauce (page 190)
- Almond Pie Crust (page 353)
- Basic Almond Spread (page 151)
- Grated Beet and Apple Salad (page 181)
- Mediterranean Pesto (page 310)
- Mushroom-Almond Bisque (page 225)
- Mushroom Sauce (page 321)
- Parsley Persillade (page 223)
- Sea Vegetable Chowder (page 226)
- Spicy Almond Spread (page 152)
- Spinach Pie (page 284)
- Sweet Almond Spread (page 152)
- Tangy Almond Spread (page 151)
- Whole-Grain Broccoli Stir-Fry (page 286)
- Whole-Grain Granola (page 160)

Brazil Nuts

Bertholettia excelsa

Native to the tropical regions of Brazil, Venezuela and Bolivia, Brazil nuts are rich and sweet tasting. The meat is found inside a coconut-like shell that is larger than most nuts. The taste lends itself to sweet dishes but Brazil nuts may also be used in savory dishes where nuts are called for. Brazil nuts are the best source of selenium, a trace mineral that reduces the risk of cancer and arthritis. They are also high in protein and exceptionally high in potassium, manganese and phosphorus. They are a good source of calcium and sodium, with small amounts of B vitamins.

Forms Available: Whole unshelled, whole shelled with skin, whole shelled and blanched, chopped and roasted.

Recipes:
- Almond and Herb-Stuffed Mushrooms (Variation, page 132)
- Country Vegetable Pâté (Variation, page 159)
- Creamy Couscous with Quinoa and Cranberries (Variation, page 292)
- Date and Nut Bars (Variation, page 364)
- Fennel, Celery and Apple Salad (page 184)
- Herbed Nut and Bean Patties (page 234)
- Savory Oatmeal Topping (page 253)
- Whole-Grain and Vegetable Stuffing (page 263)

Cashews

Anacardium occidentale

Originating in Brazil, cashews now grow in many other tropical areas. Cashews are attached to the outside of pear-shaped fruits (called cashew apples) that grow on small evergreen trees. Often eaten as a snack, the buttery taste of cashews also complements grain and baked vegetable dishes, stuffing and salads. Cashew nuts contain some protein but have high oil content. Cashews are high in copper and have significant amounts of magnesium, tryptophan and phosphorus and they are the only nuts that contain a small amount of vitamin C.

Forms Available: All forms of cashews come shelled. They are available whole raw or roasted, in halves, pieces and chopped, and salted.

Recipes:
- Almond Butter Sauce (Variation, page 190)
- Autumn Harvest Salad (page 179)
- Buckwheat Apple Pancakes (Variation, page 164)
- Creamy Couscous with Quinoa and Cranberries (page 292)
- Fall Fruit en Papillote (page 352)
- Fennel, Celery and Apple Salad (page 184)
- Herbed Nut and Bean Patties (page 234)
- Peanut Butter and Banana Bread (page 165)
- Savory Oatmeal Topping (page 253)
- Sea Vegetable Chowder (page 226)

- Spicy Soba Noodles (page 299)
- Whole-Grain and Vegetable Stuffing (page 263)

Chestnuts

Castanea sativa

Sweet chestnuts grow on wild trees in Britain, Europe and North America and are cultivated in Italy, France and Spain. Raw chestnuts do not keep long before the flesh deteriorates and so are usually cooked before they are sold. If fresh, chestnuts should be bought in the shell and cooked or used right away. They can be boiled, steamed, roasted or stewed. Chestnuts are low in oils and high in carbohydrates. They are high in potassium, are good sources of calcium, magnesium and phosphorus and have small amounts of the B vitamins.

Forms Available: Cooked whole, usually peeled, dried and ground or canned chestnut purée.

Note: The water chestnut is unrelated to chestnuts. Water chestnuts are the edible fruit from an herbaceous water plant.

Recipes:
- Autumn Harvest Salad (page 179)
- Buckwheat Apple Pancakes (Variation, page 164)
- Country Vegetable Paté (Variation, page 159)
- Date and Nut Bars (Variation, page 364)
- Fennel, Celery and Apple Salad (page 184)
- Herbed Nut and Bean Patties (page 234)
- Mâche with Fruit, Nuts and Blue Cheese (page 182)
- Savory Oatmeal Topping (page 253)
- Whole-Grain and Vegetable Stuffing (page 263)
- Whole-Grain Granola (Variation, page 160)

Coconuts

Cocos nucifera

The coconut, largest of all nuts, is the fruit of the coconut palm that grows on tropical islands. Coconuts may be eaten fresh along with their milk or the flesh is dried and usually sweetened. Coconuts are rich in potassium and have significant amounts of phosphorus and magnesium. They are a good source of protein. Both the coconut flesh and milk are used in curries, toppings, fruit dishes, sauces, rice dishes and desserts and baked goods.

Forms Available: Whole (fresh) in the shell and dried, grated, shredded, flaked or desiccated. Canned coconut milk and coconut oil are also available.

Recipes:
- Apricot Granola Biscuits (page 161)
- Creamy Couscous with Quinoa and Cranberries (page 292)
- Gado Gado Sauce (page 276)
- Makrut Lime Leaf Sauce (page 316)
- Peach Melba (page 350)
- Red Pepper Sauce (milk) (page 224)
- Savory Oatmeal Topping (page 253)
- Sea Vegetable Chowder (milk) (page 226)
- Whole-Grain and Vegetable Stuffing (page 263)

Flaxseeds

Linum usitatissimum

Flaxseed oil is the best vegetable source of essential omega-3 fatty acids, which help lubricate the joints and prevent absorption of toxins by stimulating digestion. They contain 30% of the body's daily requirement of manganese and are high in dietary fiber. Flaxseeds also contain magnesium, folate, copper, phosphorus and vitamin B_6 (pyridoxine).

Flaxseeds must be ground for the body to absorb and benefit from the oils. Once ground, the seeds deteriorate rapidly. It is best to buy in small amounts and store whole, ground seeds and flaxseed oil in the refrigerator.

Forms Available: Whole, ground and flax meal. Flaxseed oil is also available.

Recipes:
- Fennel, Celery and Apple Salad (page 184)
- Herbed Nut and Bean Patties (page 234)
- Savory Oatmeal Topping (page 253)
- Vegetable Cakes (page 241)
- Whole-Grain and Vegetable Stuffing (page 263)
- Whole-Grain Granola (page 160)

Peanuts

Arachis hypogaea

Widely available and most extensively used, peanuts are an important food staple in some areas, a snack in others. Peanuts are actually legumes encased in a dry, fibrous pod. High in manganese and protein and containing tryptophan, vitamin B_3 (niacin), folate and copper, peanuts also have significant amounts of vitamin E.

Caution: Many individuals experience an allergic reaction when exposed to peanuts and peanut products. Peanuts that have been deep-fried, battered, candied or combined with additives, dyes, fats or sugars have no place in a whole foods diet.

Forms Available: Whole unshelled, shelled raw with skin, shelled and blanched, roasted and salted. Also available chopped.

Recipes:
• Almond Butter Sauce (Variation, page 190)
• Cocktail Peanut Sauce (page 326)
• Fennel, Celery and Apple Salad (page 184)
• Ginger-Citrus Sauce (page 231)
• Green Beans Gado Gado (page 279)
• Herbed Nut and Bean Patties (page 234)
• Parsley Persillade (page 223)
• Peanut Butter and Banana Bread (page 165)
• Savory Oatmeal Topping (page 253)
• Whole-Grain and Vegetable Stuffing (page 263)

Pecans

Carya pecan

Native to North America, pecans are sweetly pleasant tasting. Grafting techniques developed thin-shelled varieties in the 19th century. This was crucial to their widespread use. Pecans lend texture and interest to salads, fruit dishes, baked vegetables and grains and can replace most nuts in recipes. They are well used in sweets, pies and fruitcakes. Pecans are high in protein with significant amounts of B vitamins. They have some iron, calcium, potassium and phosphorus.

Forms Available: Whole unshelled, shelled raw with skin, shelled blanched and roasted whole, halves and chopped.

Recipes:
• Baked Apple Polenta Custard (page 168)
• Buckwheat Apple Pancakes (page 164)
• Country Vegetable Paté (page 159)
• Date and Nut Bars (page 364)
• Fall Fruit en Papillote (page 352)
• Fennel, Celery and Apple Salad (page 184)
• Gado Gado Sauce (page 276)
• Herbed Nut and Bean Patties (page 234)
• Pecan Topping (page 360)
• Roasted Peppers with Wild Rice and Walnuts (Variation, page 266)
• Savory Oatmeal Topping (page 253)
• Whole-Grain and Vegetable Stuffing (page 263)

Pine Nuts

Pinus pinea

Pine nuts are the edible seed of just over a dozen varieties of pine tree. Pine nuts are probably the most expensive of all the edible nuts. They are small, creamy-colored and buttery in texture. Their oil-rich flesh is what contributes to their taste and texture. High in protein and carbohydrate, they are also good sources of B vitamins. Keep pine nuts in the refrigerator for up to 1 month.

Forms Available: Except when purchased directly from harvesters, pine nuts always come shelled and are usually whole. They may be raw or roasted and salted.

Recipes:
• Basil Pesto (page 308)
• Coriander Pesto (page 308)
• Fennel, Celery and Apple Salad (page 184)
• Grated Beet and Apple Salad (Variation, page 181)
• Grated Carrot with Dates and Walnuts (page 184)
• Herbed Nut and Bean Patties (page 234)
• Lemon Pesto (Variation, page 310)
• Roasted Garlic and Red Pepper Pesto (page 309)
• Savory Oatmeal Topping (page 253)
• Spinach Pie (Variation, page 284)
• Sun-Dried Tomato Pesto (page 309)
• Whole-Grain and Vegetable Stuffing (page 263)

Pistachio Nuts

Pistacia vera

Small, green pistachio nuts are native to the Middle East, where they are a symbol of happiness. Pistachio nuts have a soft texture and mild flavor which makes them versatile in cooking. They are used in salads and as a topping for vegetables, grains and legume dishes. Pistachio nuts are also used in sweet dishes and confections.

Forms Available: Whole unshelled raw and salted, shelled raw and salted. Pistachio nuts may be dyed, however, the natural form is preferred.

Recipes:
• Baked Apple Polenta Custard (Variation, page 168)
• Fennel, Celery and Apple Salad (page 184)
• Herbed Nut and Bean Patties (page 234)
• Lemon Pesto (page 310)
• Mediterranean Red Pepper and Tomato Salad (page 176)

• Savory Oatmeal Topping (page 253)
• Whole-Grain and Vegetable Stuffing (page 263)

Pumpkin Seeds

The pumpkin's small, flat green seeds are used to treat and prevent parasites as well as to nourish and restore the prostate gland. They are high in manganese, magnesium, phosphorus and tryptophan and contain iron, copper, vitamin K, zinc and essential fatty acids. According to nutritionist and naturopathic physician Dr. Paavo Airola, pumpkin seeds contain pacifarin, an antibiotic resistance factor that increases man's natural resistance to disease.

Forms Available: Whole unshelled raw, unsalted and salted, shelled raw, unsalted and salted or toasted and salted.

Recipes:
• Autumn Harvest Salad (page 179)
• Baked Wild Rice with Sorrel and Mustard Greens (page 283)
• Creamy Couscous with Quinoa and Cranberries (Variation, page 292)
• Fennel, Celery and Apple Salad (page 184)
• Grated Carrot with Dates and Walnuts (page 184)
• Herbed Nut and Bean Patties (page 234)
• Pumpkin Seed Spread (page 149)
• Savory Oatmeal Topping (page 253)
• Spinach Pesto Filling (page 237)
• Wakame Cabbage Salad (page 175)
• Whole-Grain and Vegetable Stuffing (page 263)
• Whole-Grain Granola (page 160)

Sesame Seeds

Sesamum indicum

Tiny, cream-colored and almond-shaped, sesame seeds are widely available. They originate from Africa where they are called *benne*. Sesame seeds are high in copper and manganese and are a good source of protein. They work well with legumes or whole grains. They have high levels of tryptophan, calcium, magnesium and iron and some phosphorus, zinc and vitamin B_1 (thiamin). Sesame seeds and sesame oil lend a nutty taste to breads, fruit or vegetable dishes, grains and beans.

   Tahini is a thick paste made from ground sesame seeds. It is used in dips, spreads and falafel dishes. Halva is a sweet sesame cake made with honey or cane sugar.

Forms Available: Whole with hulls, raw, hulled and polished, hulled and roasted. Sesame seed oil is available raw and toasted. Tahini paste is available in Middle Eastern stores and some whole or natural food stores.

Recipes:
• Autumn Harvest Salad (page 179)
• Cauliflower and Wheat Berries in Sesame Sauce (page 291)
• Fennel, Celery and Apple Salad (page 184)
• Mediterranean Red Pepper and Tomato Salad (page 176)
• Mushroom-Almond Bisque (page 225)
• Savory Oatmeal Topping (page 256)
• Sesame Broccoli (page 276)
• Sesame Dressing (page 291)
• Spicy Soba Noodles (page 299)
• Sweet Potato Pie (page 360)
• Whole-Grain and Vegetable Stuffing (page 263)
• Whole-Grain Granola (page 160)

Sunflower Seeds

Helianthus annuus

Sunflowers most probably originated in Mexico. The long, flat, gray or black-striped seeds are cultivated for oil as well as for eating. One-quarter cup (50 mL) of sunflower seeds supply 90% of the body's daily requirement of vitamin E and almost 55% of vitamin B_1 (thiamin). Sunflower seeds are high in protein, manganese, magnesium, copper, tryotophan and selenium. They also contain significant amounts of phosphorus, vitamin B_5 (pantothenic), folate and potassium. They may be used to replace the more expensive pine nuts in pesto recipes and salads. Sunflower oil is polyunsaturated and has a light, nutty taste making it a popular salad oil.

Forms Available: Whole and raw with hulls, hulled raw, roasted and salted.

Recipes:
• Apple-Spinach Pâté (Variation, page 137)
• Baked Apple Polenta Custard (Variation, page 168)
• Baked Wild Rice with Sorrel and Mustard Greens (page 283)
• Basil Pesto (page 308)
• Fennel, Celery and Apple Salad (page 184)
• Herbed Nut and Bean Patties (page 234)
• Savory Oatmeal Topping (page 253)
• Spinach Pesto Filling (page 237)

- Spinach Pie (Variation, page 284)
- Wakame Cabbage Salad (page 175)
- Whole-Grain and Vegetable Stuffing (page 263)
- Whole-Grain Granola (page 160)

Walnuts

Juglans regia (English) or *J. nigra* (black)

There are two main varieties of walnut, the English (or Persian) walnut, and the Black walnut (native to North America). Walnuts are widely available and used often in a wide variety of dishes, both savory and sweet. Walnuts are high in oil, protein, potassium and phosphorus. They contain some vitamin B_6 (pyridoxine), and folic acid, which is not found in other nuts. Eaten as a snack or used in stuffing, salads, cakes, vegetable and grain dishes, $1/4$ cup (50 mL) supplies 90% of the body's requirement of omega-3 fatty acids and 40% of

manganese. They also contain copper and tryptophan.

Forms Available: Whole unshelled raw, whole shelled raw, halves, pieces, chopped and ground. Walnut oil is available.

Recipes:
- Apple-Spinach Paté (page 137)
- Brussels Sprouts with Walnuts and Blue Cheese (page 275)
- Buckwheat Apple Pancakes (page 164)
- Fennel, Celery and Apple Salad (page 184)
- Grated Carrot with Dates and Walnuts (page 184)
- Herbed Nut and Bean Patties (page 234)
- Roasted Peppers with Wild Rice and Walnuts (page 266)
- Savory Oatmeal Topping (page 253)
- Walnut Sauce (page 325)
- Whole-Grain and Vegetable Stuffing (page 263)
- Whole-Grain Granola (page 160)

Sea Vegetables

Definition: Often called seaweeds or sea herbs, sea vegetables are edible, wild plants that grow abundantly in the oceans. They are primitive plants with blades for leaves, stipes for stems and holdfasts for roots. Sea vegetables have been honored by cultures of the Far East and harvested by seaside communities around the world for food, salt, medicine and fertilizer for many thousands of years.

Actions/Uses: Sea vegetables are rich in minerals and trace elements, particularly iodine, calcium, potassium and iron. They contain small amounts of protein, but their protein includes essential amino acids, unlike most plants that only contain incomplete amino acids. They have a significant amount of vitamin A, B, C and D, including vitamin B_{12}, which is only found in three other plant foods (alfalfa, comfrey and fermented soybean products). Most sea vegetables have anticancer properties.

Caution: Do not consume sea vegetables if you have a hyperthyroid condition.

Buying and Storing: Whole or natural food stores carry a selection of packaged dried sea vegetables. Some supermarkets offer a few dried and prepackaged sea vegetables for sale. Store unopened dried sea vegetables indefinitely and once opened, keep in an airtight container for up to 3 months.

Culinary Use: Most dried sea vegetables require a quick rehydration by soaking in cool water for 10 to 15 minutes. Shredded dried sea vegetables, such as arame, wakame and hijiki, may be added to soups, broths, sauces and stews without soaking but will need to simmer for 20 to 30 minutes to cook and may require slightly more liquid depending on the dish. Finely chopped or powdered dried sea vegetables are almost always used with other herbs as a salt substitute.

Arame

Eisenia bicyclis

Arame appears as short, thin, curled strands. It is dark yellow-brown when growing, black when dried. Arame grows off Japan's northern and southern coasts. It is soft with a slightly resistant texture and sweet, delicate flavor.

Actions/Uses: Alleviates high blood pressure and builds strong bones and teeth. Arame is one of the richest sources of iodine and is highly concentrated in iron and calcium.

Culinary Use: Add to curries, salads, soups, stews, and tomato sauce and baked vegetable and grain dishes. Soak in water for 3 to 5 minutes, then cook as directed in recipe or add to long-simmering soups and stews directly.

Recipes:
- Jambalaya (page 219)
- Sea Gumbo (page 218)
- Sea Vegetable Chowder (page 226)
- Spinach and Sea Vegetable Soup (page 204)
- Wakame Cabbage Salad (Variation, page 175)

Agar (or Agar-Agar)

See Whole Food Ingredients (page 125)

Dulse

Palmaria palmata

Dulse has large, dark red fronds. Found off North Atlantic waters, it has a chewy texture that is salty and nutlike.

Actions/Uses: Prevents scurvy, induces sweating, is a remedy for seasickness and treats symptoms of the herpes virus. Dulse is exceptionally concentrated in iodine, which is important to the thyroid gland. It is rich in manganese, which activates the enzyme system. Dulse is a good source of phosphorus, B vitamins, vitamins E and C, bromine, potassium, magnesium, sulfur, calcium, sodium, radium, boron, rubidium, manganese, titanium and other trace elements.

Culinary Use: Use dulse in the same way as spinach — chopped, in stuffing, relishes, salad dressings, grain and vegetable bakes. Toast and eat dulse as a snack. It thickens gravies and sauces. Soak in water for 20 minutes, then cook as directed in recipe, or add to long-simmering soups and stews directly.

Recipes:
- Country Vegetable Pâté (page 159)
- Sea Gumbo (page 218)

Hijiki

Hizikia fusiforme

Brown when fresh and black when dried, hijiki has short, thin, curled strands. It is harvested off the northern and southern coasts of Japan, Korea and China. The sweet, delicate flavor and crisp texture of hijiki make it very popular in vegetarian dishes.

Actions/Uses: Diuretic, resolves heat-induced phlegm, helps remove toxins, benefits thyroid, helps normalize blood sugar levels, aids weight loss, soothes nerves, supports hormone functions, builds bones and teeth. Hijiki is an excellent source of calcium, iron and iodine, and is abundant in vitamin B_2 (riboflavin) and B_3 (niacin).

Caution: Canadian, Hong Kong, UK and New Zealand government food safety agencies advise consumers to avoid consumption of hijiki seaweed. Test results have indicated that levels of inorganic arsenic were significantly higher in hijiki than in other types of seaweed. Inorganic arsenic, which can occur naturally in some foods, is known to add to the risk of people developing cancer.

Culinary Use: Hijiki adds interest and texture to salads and rice dishes, soups, stews, stuffing and stir-fries. Soak in water for 15 to 20 minutes, then cook as directed in recipe, or add to long-simmering soups and stews directly.

Kelp

Pleurophycus gardneri

Kelp's broad light brown to light olive-brown leaf-like fronds are found off the Pacific coast of North America. The fresh or dried frond has a delicate, mild taste when cooked. Kelp is usually available in granular, powdered or tablet form. However, the dried and shredded or long strips may be available in whole or natural food stores.

Actions/Uses: Antibacterial, antiviral (herpes), may lower blood pressure and cholesterol, high in calcium, phosphorus and iodine.

Culinary Use: Wrap fresh kelp fronds (if you can find them) around rice or other fillings, or steam, chop and add to stir-fries, salads or stuffing. Use the dried whole or strips of kelp in the same way as fresh but rehydrate first. Sprinkle the powder or granules into soups, stews, salads and stir-fries, or mix with dry ingredients in breads, pancakes and muffins. Granular kelp is added to most vegetable and grain dishes, sauces, gravy, dips and spreads. No soaking is needed if the granular or powdered forms are used but rehydrate if using dried whole or strips.

Recipes:
- Jambalaya (page 219)
- Sea Vegetable Chowder (page 226)

Kombu

Laminaria japonica

Fresh kombu (called sashimi) is a long, thick, dark green frond. Most often kombu is sold dried whole or in strips or shredded. Used for centuries, kombu is found mainly off the coastal waters of China, Korea and Japan, where it's cultivated. Kombu's taste is sweet and yet robust.

Actions/Uses: Rich in protein, calcium, iodine, magnesium, iron and folate.

Caution: Kombu contains significant amounts of glutamic acid, a forerunner of monosodium glutamate (MSG) and so should be used in small quantities.

Culinary Use: Kombu is used to flavor soups, broths, sauces and stews. The Japanese make a soup broth called Dashi using kombu. Kombu is removed and discarded before the soup is served. Soak dried kombu for 10 minutes and simmer for 15 to 20 minutes to soften it.

Recipes:
• Red Beans and Rice (page 272)

Nori

Porphyra tenera

Both coasts of North America and the middle and lower tidal zones of Europe's seacoasts grow nori. Called "laver" in Britain, nori is bright pink when young, turning to dark purple as the plant ages. To get a consistent size and thickness that works for rolling rice, the leaves are pressed into thin sheets. Nori tastes like mild, salty corn. The sheets are often toasted before being used in sushi or other dishes.

Actions/Uses: Antibacterial, diuretic, treats painful urination, goiter, edema, high blood pressure, beriberi, appears to heal ulcers, is high in protein and rich in vitamins A, C, B_1 (thiamin), B_3 (niacin) and phosphorus.

Culinary Use: Use green, black or toasted nori sheets to wrap vegetables and rice for sushi. Chopped or crumbled, nori adds interest and texture to salads, stir-fries and vegetable dishes. Toast nori sheets lightly over a low flame or element on high until black and crisp.

Recipes:
• Cantonese Noodles (page 250)
• Vegetable Sushi (page 142)

Wakame

Undaria pinnatifida

The thin black fronds of the wild wakame grow in Japan's northern seas. Wakame has a softly resistant texture and a strong, sweet flavor.

Actions/Uses: Boosts immune functioning, promotes healthy hair and skin. Wakame is used in Japanese tradition to purify mother's blood after childbirth. It is rich in calcium, B_3 (niacin) and B_1 (thiamin).

Culinary Use: Chop whole fresh wakame and use as any leafy green vegetable in soups, stews, salads, sandwiches, vegetable and stir-fry dishes. The shredded dried wakame strips may be added to most vegetarian dishes. Soak dried wakame in water for 5 minutes, drain and simmer for 45 minutes.

Recipes:
• Jambalaya (page 219)
• Sea Vegetable Chowder (page 226)
• Spinach and Sea Vegetable Soup (page 204)
• Wakame Cabbage Salad (page 175)

Soy Foods

Definition: Soybeans are legumes that are generally classed as oilseeds. They are native to China where they have been cultivated for 13,000 years although they no longer resemble their wild progenitors. Their smooth texture and bland taste make soybeans adaptable to processing into other forms. Foods made from soybeans are called "soy foods."

Soybeans

Glycine max

Actions/Uses: Soybeans are the only known vegetable source of complete protein, meaning they contain all of the essential amino acids in the appropriate proportions essential for the growth and maintenance of body cells. In addition to being an excellent source of fiber, the fat in soybeans (34%) is polyunsaturated, lower than animal fat in calories and rich in linolenic fatty acids.

Caution: A large percentage of soybeans grown today are genetically modified and are produced using high amounts of pesticides. Fresh soybeans contain enzyme inhibitors that block protein digestion and may cause serious gastric distress and organ damage. The inhibitors are not present in such high amounts in the fermented bean products of tofu, tempeh or soy sauce. The high amounts of phytic acid in soybeans and soy foods may block the uptake of essential minerals and cause deficiencies. Isoflavones, once thought to minimize cell damage from free radicals, block the damaging effects of hormonal or synthetic estrogens, and inhibit tumor cell growth, may in fact, be toxic.

Soybeans and soy foods contain goitrogens, naturally occurring substances in certain foods that can interfere with the functioning of the thyroid gland. Individuals with already existing and untreated thyroid problems may want to avoid soy foods.

Textured vegetable protein (TVP) made from soybeans is produced using chemicals and harmful techniques and is not considered a whole food.

Excessive soy intake should be avoided during pregnancy and soy-based baby formulas should not be used.

Forms Available: Dried organic soybeans are available in whole or natural food stores.

Buying and Storing: Keep dried soybeans as you would other legumes in a dry, dark and cool place for up to 1 year. Processed soybeans in the forms of tofu and tempeh are available in most supermarkets. Follow package directions for storing these foods. Canned soybeans are sometimes available along with other canned legumes.

Culinary Use: Use fresh or dried whole organic soybeans infrequently in cooking and add fermented soy products (tofu, tempeh, tamari and soy sauce) on an occasional basis only. Soak and cook dried soybeans as you would other dried legumes. Fresh, canned or frozen beans are added to soups, stews and baked vegetable dishes.

Whole dried soybeans must be rehydrated in the same way that other legumes are soaked, then cooked.

To Soak: Place washed beans in a large saucepan and cover with 2 inches (5 cm) water. Bring to a boil over high heat. Reduce heat and simmer for 2 minutes. Leave the pan on the element and turn off the heat. Let stand for 1 hour or overnight. Discard soaking water and rinse beans. Soybeans have now been rehydrated and are ready to cook. Never use salt or other seasonings at the soaking stage.

To Cook: Place soaked, drained and rinsed beans in a large saucepan and cover with 2 inches (5 cm) fresh water. Cover pan and bring to boil over high heat. Reduce heat and simmer for about 3 hours or until tender. Using a pressure cooker reduces the soaking and cooking time significantly (check manufacturer's instructions).

Using cooked canned soybeans is a convenient way to use these legumes without any significant loss of nutrients.

Recipes:
• Spicy Soba Noodles (page 299)

Edamame

Edamame is the Japanese name for fresh green soybeans in the pod. They can be cooked and eaten as a green vegetable. The beans are round, smooth and green with firm, unbruised pods.

Forms Available: Edamame is usually frozen but the fresh can be found in some urban supermarkets as well as in whole or natural food stores and Asian markets.

Caution: It is wise to eat small amounts of fresh soybeans and not often (see Caution, left).

Recipes:
• Spicy Soba Noodles (page 299)

Miso

See Whole Food Ingredients (page 123).

Natto

See Whole Food Ingredients (page 123).

Soy Milk

Soy milk is made from ground soybeans that are mixed with water to form a milk-like liquid. Soy milk is an excellent source of protein, B vitamins and iron, and if fortified, provides adequate calcium. It has low levels of saturated fat and no cholesterol.

Caution: Use moderate amounts in cooking and do not consume large amounts on a daily basis (see Caution, page 101).

Forms Available: Non-flavored, called natural or original, or with flavors added.

Recipes:
- Baked Apple Polenta Custard (page 168)
- Baked Onion, Leek and Cabbage Casserole (page 278)
- Black-Eyed Pea Casserole (page 252)
- Buckwheat Apple Pancakes (page 164)
- B-Vitamin Smoothie (page 170)
- Cheesy Broccoli Crêpes (page 156)
- Chocolate Pudding (page 357)
- Corn and Rice Chowder with Parsley Persillade (page 223)
- Fresh Berry Mousse (page 346)
- Gingerbread with Hot Spiced Applesauce (page 166)
- Greek Soufflés (page 158)
- Kasha Pudding with Apple and Raisins (page 167)
- Mushroom-Almond Bisque (page 225)
- Peanut Butter and Banana Bread (page 165)
- Roasted Fruit with Custard (page 169)
- Rosemary Custard (page 361)
- Scalloped Turnips with Potatoes and Onion (page 261)
- Vegetable Frittata (page 155)

Soy Sauce

See Whole Food Ingredients (Tamari Sauce, page 124).

Tamari Sauce

See Whole Food Ingredients (page 124).

Tempeh

Pronounced tem-PAY, this soy food is mild and meaty-tasting. The firm white cake is made from fermenting cooked soybeans. Tempeh gives a chewy texture to vegetarian dishes and is a good substitute for ground beef in pasta sauce or chili. It can be fried, baked, broiled, grilled or simmered with vegetables in other dishes.

Forms Available: Usually frozen in a solid cake form.

Recipes:
- Cajun Dirty Rice and Tempeh (page 301)
- Gingered Tempeh in Barbecue Sauce (page 235)
- Vegetables and Tempeh au Gratin (page 243)

Tofu

Also called bean curd or soy cheese, tofu is one of the most versatile of all the soy foods. Tofu is a custard-like product made from heating soymilk with either calcium sulfate (the preferred method) or magnesium sulfate and pressing the curds into "cakes." Tofu can be frozen (the color turns yellow and the texture is more chewy), marinated, stir-fried, used as cottage cheese, as sandwich spreads, or mixed with salads, soups and pastas.

Forms Available: Tofu can be purchased as silky, soft and firm, with the harder forms having more water pressed from them.

Recipes:
- Black Bean Chili (page 240)
- Cantonese Noodles (page 250)
- Creamy Red Pepper Spread (page 149)
- Rosemary Custard (page 361)
- Summer Soup Garnish (page 205)
- Tofu Mayonnaise (page 306)

Herbs

Definition: Herbs are defined as plants whose parts are used to enhance our lives. Strictly speaking, an herb (pronounced *herb* or *erb*) is a plant that is used for culinary, medicinal, cosmetic or ornamental purposes. That definition is broad enough to encompass some trees, spices and flowers that we otherwise might not think of as herbs.

Actions/Uses: The vitamins, minerals and phytochemicals found in herbs can make a significant contribution to our health through diet. Generally, most herbs are antioxidant and the green parts supply chlorophyll, which enhances the body's ability to produce hemoglobin and thus, to increase the delivery of oxygen to cells. (See the individual herbs for their specific actions.)

Caution: Avoid medicinal doses of all herbs while pregnant unless following advice by a medical herbalist or midwife.

Buying and Storing: As with fruits and vegetables, the whole fresh herb is the best form to use in cooking. Grow your own or look for fresh organic herbs in supermarkets and farmers' markets. Store fresh herbs rolled in a damp tea towel in the produce drawer of the refrigerator.

For teas, beverages and medicinal applications, dried herbs are used. Dry fresh herbs for use over the winter or purchase small quantities of organic dried herbs from a farm or whole or natural food stores. Replace all dried herbs after 8 to 10 months. Use dark-colored glass or ceramic containers with tight-fitting lids to store herbs individually. Label and date and keep in a cool, dark place for no longer than 1 year.

Culinary Use: Herbs are used in both savory and sweet dishes. They enliven and are an integral part of vegetarian recipes. When a smooth texture is desired in sauces, beverages or dressings, it is advantageous to make an herb tea. Strain off the herbs and use the infused liquid to flavor the dish. The recipes in this book call for the use of fresh herbs except where dried are indicated. (See the individual herbs for the specific flavors and combinations that they complement.)

To substitute dried herbs in recipes: Use one-half to one-third less dried herbs than the quantity of fresh called for in the recipe. Crush or grind the dried herb to a powder then add to the recipe.

To Make Herbal Infusion (Tea or Tissane): Bring 1 cup (250 mL) of pure or filtered water to a boil. Measure 1 tsp (5 mL) dried herb into a teapot. Pour boiled water over top. Place a lid on the teapot and a cork in the spout (to prevent steam from escaping). Steep the tea for 10 to 15 minutes. Let the infusion cool before adding to recipes. Strain and discard solids. For convenience, make 1 to 2 cups (250 to 500 mL) medicinal tea and store in a covered jar in refrigerator for use throughout the day.

To Dry Herbs: Most herbs dry well, except for parsley, chives and basil, which are better frozen. To dry well, herbs require a warm, dry, dark atmosphere where air circulates freely, such as an attic, dark corner of a room, basement or a barn.

For long-stemmed herbs (mints, yarrow, sage), gather in small bunches, tie the stems and hang upside down in a warm, dry, dark place. Paper bags may be used to catch the falling bits and to keep the light away. For leaves on short stems (thyme) and flowers (calendula, violets and all others), strip leaves off the stems and the petals off the center of the flower (or dry the flower head whole). Scatter leaves or petals in a single layer on a nylon net or screen. The faster the plant parts dry, the more color and fragrance they will retain. Scrub roots, cut into $1/2$-inch (1 cm) pieces, and place in one layer on a drying rack, screen or suspended fabric to dry. Leave in pieces for longer storage. Grind small amounts to a powder just before using. Bottle and store in dark-colored bottles in a cool, dark place.

Alfalfa

Medicago sativa

A hardy perennial that is easily grown in most parts of North America.

Parts Used: Leaves, flowers and sprouted seeds.

Actions: Tonic, nutritive, lower blood cholesterol, anti-anemia.

Uses: Alfalfa is a cell nutritive and overall tonic for the body. It promotes strong teeth, bones and connective tissue. Alfalfa is one of the best sources of chlorophyll, which has the ability to stimulate new skin growth, heal wounds and burns, diminish the symptoms of arthritis, gout and rheumatism, lower cholesterol levels, reduce inflammation and improve the body's resistance to cancer.

The mature tops and seeds are high in amino acids and chlorophyll, as well as minerals such as calcium, magnesium, phosphorus and potassium and vitamins K, B and P, which the body uses to repair and build musculoskeletal system structures and tissues.

Sprouted seeds have an enhanced concentration of vitamins. Alfalfa shoots (per 100 g) have 3,410 I.U. of beta-carotene and 162 mg of vitamin C.

Caution: Alfalfa seeds and sprouts are rich in the amino acid canavanine, which can contribute to inflammation in rheumatoid arthritis, systemic lupus erythematosus and other rheumatoid and inflammatory conditions. Alfalfa leaf is NOT a source of canavanine and can be used in inflammatory and rheumatic conditions.

Availability: Whole or cut dried leaf is available in whole or natural food stores. Sprouted seeds are readily available.

Culinary Use: Alfalfa has a light, grassy taste to the fresh flowers and leaves and a stronger, also grassy taste to the dried aerial parts. Add fresh or dried whole sprigs to soups and stews during the last hour of cooking, then remove. Fresh leaves are perfect in salads, rice and vegetable dishes. Use a generous handful of fresh or dried alfalfa in vegetable stock. Add the chopped fresh leaf to soups and stews during the last 10 minutes of cooking.

Fresh flowers and sprouts work well in salads, stir-fries and sandwiches. Add them when juicing vegetables and include alfalfa tea with liquids in breads.

Astragalus

Astragalus membranaceus

Astragalus is a hardy, shrub-like perennial native to eastern Asia but grown in temperate regions including Canada and the United States.

Parts Used: Root.

Actions: Immune stimulant, antimicrobial, heart tonic, diuretic, promotes tissue regeneration.

Uses: Used throughout the Orient as a tonic, astragalus is a safe and powerful immune system stimulator for virtually every phase of immune system activity. It also has been shown to alleviate the adverse effects of steroids and chemotherapy on the immune system and can be used during traditional cancer treatment.

Availability: While more and more North American herb farms are growing this exceptional medicinal herb, the most reliable sources for the dried, sliced root are Oriental herb stores centered in large urban areas. However, whole or natural food stores do carry cut or powdered astragalus and the tincture form.

Culinary Use: The mild, slightly sweet, earthy taste of astragalus is so subtle it can be used in soups and vegetable stocks without detection. Add one or two pieces of the dried root to soups or vegetable stock or grind and include in root beverages and seasoning blends. Astragalus tincture may be added to smoothies and soups just before serving.

Basil

Oscimum basilicum

A bushy annual with large, waxy, deep green leaves and small tubular flowers that grow in long spikes.

Parts Used: Leaves and flowering tops.

Actions: Antispasmodic, soothing digestive, antibacterial, antidepressant, adrenal stimulant.

Uses: To relieve indigestion, nervous tension, stress and tension headaches.

Availability: Fresh sprigs are sold in season at farmers' markets and supermarkets. Dried, cut and sifted leaves are available in whole or natural food stores.

Culinary Use: Slightly nutmeg and clove with citrus undertones, each variety has a variation of the spicy basil taste. Use about three to six large fresh basil leaves for baked vegetable, legume and grain dishes. Wash, pat dry and strip leaves from stem (discard stem) and roughly chop leaves or cut in chiffonade (see Tips, page 179).

Burdock

Arctium lappa

A hardy biennial that produces fruiting heads covered with hooked burrs that catch on clothing and the fur of animals. Grows wild extensively in North America.

Parts Used: Root, stalk, leaves and seeds.

Actions: Leaves are a mild laxative, diuretic. The root is also a mild laxative, antirheumatic, antibiotic, promotes sweating, diuretic, cleansing, stimulating efficient removal of waste production, a skin and blood cleanser. Burdock also stimulates urine flow. Root and seeds are a soothing demulcent and tonic. They soothe kidneys and relieve lymphatics. The seeds prevent fever, are anti-inflammatory, antibacterial and reduce blood sugar levels.

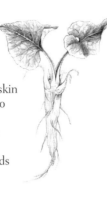

Uses: Leaves may be used in the same way as roots although they are less effective. Burdock root is a cleansing, eliminative remedy. It helps to remove toxins causing skin problems (including eczema, acne, rashes, boils), digestive sluggishness or arthritic pains. It supports the liver, lymphatic glands and digestive system. Burdock seeds relieve lymphatics, are a soothing demulcent tonic, and soothe the kidneys.

For every 1 cup (250 mL) of boiled burdock root, there is 61 mg calcium, 450 mg potassium and 116 mg phosphorus.

Availability: Fresh root is available seasonally at Asian food markets. Due to its extensive growth habit in rural and urban waste areas, burdock can be easily foraged. Dig roots from the wild in the fall. Scrub and chop, then dry for storage. Cut dried leaves and root and tinctures are available in whole or natural food stores.

Culinary Use: Fresh burdock leaves have a taste similar to spinach or Swiss chard. Roots are nutty and pleasant tasting when cooked. Use fresh burdock leaves as you would spinach and other leafy greens. In the summer, use the large fresh leaves to wrap vegetables, fish and meat for grilling. In the spring, use the tender young sprouts and smaller leaves in salads and soups or cooked as a vegetable. The fresh leaf stalks may be peeled and roasted or boiled. They are a delicate vegetable, much like asparagus when cooked.

Use fresh burdock roots and stalks in soups instead of potatoes, roast or grill them as a vegetable, grate and mix with potatoes for latkes. Roasted, dried burdock roots are a good coffee substitute.

Use fresh or dry burdock seeds in tea blends or as seasonings, in the same way you would use sesame seeds.

Calendula

Calendula officinalis

A prolific annual (easily grown from seed) with bright yellow to orange marigold-like flowers, calendula's common name is pot marigold.

Parts Used: Petals.

Actions: Astringent, antiseptic, antifungal, anti-inflammatory, heals wounds, menstrual regulator, stimulates bile production.

Uses: Calendula acts as an aid to digestion and as a general tonic. It is taken to ease menopausal problems, period pain, gastritis, peptic ulcers, gall bladder problems, indigestion, and fungal infections.

Availability: Calendula is widely used in gardens and in vegetable gardens. Whole dried flower heads are available in whole or natural food stores.

Culinary Use: Formerly used to color cheese, calendula adds a soft, flecked yellow color to baked products, rice and sauces. Calendula petals have a delicate floral taste and smell. The flavor and aroma strengthens upon drying, but is still overpowered by other robust ingredients in food. Use calendula as a substitute for saffron and as a natural food coloring. Use fresh petals chopped in salads, soups, stews, rice, egg dishes, custards and puddings. The fresh or dried petals add color as a garnish for all main or dessert dishes, cakes, breads and muffins. They are also used for color in non-alcoholic punches and frozen ices.

Cardamom

Elettaria cardamomum

Originally from Indian rainforests, cardamom is a rhizomatous perennial with large lanceolate leaves. For centuries it has been exported to Europe mainly for its fragrance. When coaxed into blooming, the flowers are white with a dark pink-striped lip.

Parts Used: Seeds.

Actions: Antispasmodic, carminative, digestive stimulant, expectorant.

Uses: Cardamom is a pungent herb with stimulating, tonic effects that work best on the digestive system. It relaxes spasms, stimulates appetite and relieves flatulence.

Availability: The whole dried (white or green) pods are preferred because they keep up to 1 year. Whole pods are available at Asian, Indian or Middle Eastern markets. Hulled seeds are widely available in supermarkets and whole or natural food stores. As with all hulled seeds, buy in small quantities and use frequently.

Culinary Use: Used ground or as whole seeds, the lemon and floral taste of cardamom is slightly similar to nutmeg with camphor and smoky notes. Toasting cardamom brings out its complex flavors. It is used in sweet and savory dishes and in many spice blends and some teas. Cardamom is especially good in custards, puddings, with apples and pears, and in rice pilafs. Cardamom combines well with coffee, chiles, coriander, cumin, ginger, pepper, saffron, basil and yogurt.

Cayenne Pepper

Capsicum annum and *Capsicum frutescens*

A tropical perennial, grown as an annual in temperate zones. (See also Chile Peppers, page 75)

Parts Used: Fruit

Actions: Stimulant, tonic, carminative, induces perspiration, rubefacient, antiseptic, antibacterial.

Uses: Cayenne stimulates blood circulation, purifies the blood, promotes fluid elimination and sweat, and is most often used as a stimulating nerve tonic. Over-the-counter creams and ointments containing the active capsaicin extract are applied externally and are often effective in relieving the pain of osteoarthritis and rheumatoid arthritis, shingles infection, as well as the burning pain in the toes, feet, and legs of diabetic neuropathy and fibromyalgia. The capsaicin in cayenne works by blocking a protein that normally relays pain messages from nerve endings to the brain.

Cayenne supplies 7.8 mg calcium, 0.4 mg iron, 8 mg magnesium, 15.5 mg phosphorus, 107 mg potassium, 4 mg vitamin C and a whopping 2,205 I.U. vitamin A for every 1 tbsp (15 mL).

Caution: Cayenne has an irritating property that heals unbroken inflammations by bringing the blood to the surface when applied externally. Use on unbroken skin or it will irritate and not be as effective. Natural practitioners often advise that capsaicin should not be used internally in cases of chronic inflammation of the intestinal tract, such as in irritable bowel syndrome, ulcerative colitis and Crohn's disease.

Availability: Fresh, whole chile peppers are available in some ethnic markets, supermarkets and whole or natural food stores. Dried whole chiles and powdered cayenne pepper are widely available.

Culinary Use: To enjoy the health benefits of the hot and biting cayenne, start with small doses. Experts say that virtually everybody can gradually build up a tolerance to the hot taste and learn to love it. Milk, yogurt and ice cream soothe the tongue. Cayenne pepper is the principal ingredient of hot pepper sauce.

Use chopped fresh chiles in tomato sauces, soups and stews, and preserved in chili sauce and in raw or cooked salsas. Roasted, peeled and chopped fresh chiles are excellent in sauces, especially barbecue sauces. Dried, whole chiles complement soups, soup stocks, and may be crushed as a garnish for salads, cooked dishes and blended in teas.

Dried powdered cayenne pepper serves as a garnish for main dish meals and in spice blends and rubs for roasted or grilled vegetables.

Celery Seeds

Apium graveolens

The celery plant is a biennial with a bulbous root and thick, fleshy grooved stems. The leaves are pinnately divided. Small gray-brown seeds follow umbels of tiny green-white flowers. Medicinal celery seeds are collected from wild celery.

Parts Used: Seeds (for medicinal purposes). For Celery stalk, see page 75.

Actions: Anti-inflammatory, antioxidant, carminative, reduce blood pressure, sedative, urinary antiseptic.

Uses: Aromatic, tonic, relieve muscle spasms and are used to treat gout, inflammation of the urinary tract, cystitis, osteoarthritis and rheumatoid arthritis.

Caution: Do not use seeds in pregnancy.

Availability: Dried seeds should be purchased from herbalists or whole or natural food stores. The dried seeds found in supermarkets do not have the medicinal value because they are not gathered from the wild plant.

Culinary Use: Medicinal celery seeds have a mild celery taste and can be used in the same ways as other seeds such as sesame or poppy. Crush and add to ingredients in seasonings, soups, baked vegetables, legumes and grain dishes, and use in blended drinks.

Chamomile

See German Chamomile

Cinnamon

Cinnamomum zeylanicum

Cinnamon is the dried, smooth inner bark of an evergreen tree indigenous to Sri Lanka and cultivated in hot, wet tropical regions of Mexico, India, Brazil, East and West Indies and Indian Ocean islands.

Parts Used: Bark.

Actions: Carminative, diaphoretic, astringent, stimulant, antimicrobial.

Uses: Cinnamon is a warming carminative used to promote digestion and relieve nausea, vomiting and diarrhea. It is used for upset stomach and irritable bowel syndrome. Recent research has shown that cinnamon helps the body use insulin more efficiently.

Availability: Most of the cinnamon available in supermarkets is *Cinnamomum cassia*, a harder, darker and slightly more bitter-tasting variety of cinnamon. True cinnamon, *C. zeylanicum*, is softer, paler and sweeter in taste. Dried, rolled sticks, called quills may be sold in 2- to 18-inch (5 to 45 cm) lengths in specialty food stores and whole or natural food stores. The ground cinnamon and cinnamon powder widely available is *C. cassia*.

Culinary Use: Fragrant and warm with tones of clove and citrus, cinnamon's sweetly spicy flavor blends well with apples, chile pepper and chocolate. Cinnamon is one of the spices in Garam Masala Spice Blend (see page 333), an Indian seasoning used for savory dishes, rice and curries. Cinnamon is usually used as a carminative with other herbs and spices. It may be used freely to flavor other herbal teas.

Whole quills are used to flavor syrups, sauces, custards, drinks and other liquids. The woody sticks are usually removed after imparting flavor. Crushed sticks are toasted and added to herbal spice and tea blends.

Sweet milk, cream and rice puddings and desserts take advantage of powdered cinnamon and it is widely used in cakes and biscuits, pastries, doughnuts and sweet fritters. Ground cinnamon is mixed with brown or white sugar and sprinkled on porridge, cereal, coffee and toast. Apple crisp, apple pie and pickled dishes are traditional foods that use cinnamon for a dominant flavor.

Cloves

Syzygium aromaticus

Once exotic and only for royalty, cloves are the pink, unopened flower buds of an evergreen tree native to Indonesia, now grown in Zanzibar, Madagascar, West Indies, Brazil, India and Sri Lanka.

Parts Used: Dried buds.

Actions: Antioxidant, anesthetic, antiseptic, anti-inflammatory, anodyne, antispasmodic, carminative, stimulant, prevents vomiting, antihistamine, warming.

Uses: Used for asthma, bronchitis, nausea, vomiting, flatulence, diarrhea and hypothermia. Some studies indicate that cloves may have anticoagulant properties and stimulate the production of enzymes that fight cancer. Clove oil, which is 60 to 90% eugenol, is the active ingredient in some mouthwashes, toothpastes, soaps, insect repellents, perfumes, foods, various veterinary medications and many over-the-counter toothache medications.

Availability: Whole, dried buds and powder widely available.

Culinary Use: Cloves are fragrantly pungent and hot with strong camphor that can leave numbness on the tongue. Their unique flavor is used in spiced or mulled wines, liqueurs, pickles, vegetable stock, sauces and other liquids and studded in fruit and baked goods.

Ground cloves are added to sweet and savory sauces and glazes, fruit dishes, curries, rice, soups and stews, mincemeat, traditional fruit puddings, cakes and stewed fruit dishes. Cloves complement apples, pears, figs and eggplant and they blend well with coriander, cumin, nutmeg, allspice and mace.

Coriander Seeds

Coriandrum sativum

A hardy annual with slender, erect, branched stems that bear pinnate, parsley-like aromatic leaves. Small, flat umbels of tiny white to pale mauve flowers yield round green berries (seeds) that ripen to a brownish yellow.

Parts Used: Seeds.

Actions: Soothing digestive, stimulates appetite, improves digestion and absorption.

Uses: Digestive problems, flatulence.

Availability: Whole dried seeds are readily available in whole or natural food stores and Indian markets. Ground seeds are common at supermarkets.

Culinary Use: Not at all similar in taste to the green leaves (cilantro) that grow on the same plant, coriander seeds are warm, sweet and mild with citrus and floral notes. Coriander seeds are used in most curry seasonings and they are often added to coffee and dessert dishes. Sweet-and-sour dishes and pickles make use of coriander's sweet floral flavors. Coriander complements mushrooms, onions, cinnamon, fennel, nutmeg, plums, apples and pears.

Cumin Seeds

Cuminum cyminum

Cumin seeds are taken from a slender annual plant with dark green leaves that is found wild from the Mediterranean to the Sudan and central Asia. Bristly, oval seeds follow umbels of tiny white or pink flowers.

Parts Used: Seeds.

Actions: Stimulant, soothing digestive, antispasmodic, diuretic, increase milk in breastfeeding.

Uses: Indigestion, flatulence.

Availability: Whole dried seeds are readily available in whole or natural food stores and Indian markets. Usually supermarkets only carry the ground seeds.

Culinary Use: Toasting the seeds in a dry skillet brings out a nutty sweetness to the seeds that, without toasting are pungent, sharp and bitter with earthy spice. Cumin seeds are combined with coriander, cardamom, allspice and anise in spice blends. They are one of the main spice flavors in chili con carne.

Dandelion

Taraxacum officinalis

A low-growing, common, hardy and herbaceous perennial, dandelion develops from a long, thick, dark brown taproot with white and milky flesh. One brilliant yellow round flower head sits atop a smooth, hollow stem. Oblong, bright green, deeply toothed leaves grow in a basal rosette directly from the root.

Parts Used: Roots, stems, leaves and flowers.

Actions: Dandelion leaves are diuretic and a tonic for the liver and digestive system. The root is a liver tonic, promotes bile flow, diuretic, mildly laxative and antirheumatic.

Dandelion is highest in lecithin (29,700 ppm) of any of the plant sources. Lecithin is important for cell membrane protection and replacement, reducing cholesterol, converting fat into energy, prevention of strokes and heart attacks and is used in treating Alzheimer's disease.

Uses: Leaves are used specifically to support the kidney. The root works to support the liver. Dandelion is used for gall bladder, kidney and bladder ailments. It is used for liver ailments, including hepatitis and jaundice to promote the liver's processing of toxins for elimination. It also provides important nutrients for storage or release into the system. It's used in skin problems and rheumatism and increases the flow of urine. As a diuretic, dandelion is important for its high potassium content since many other diuretics deplete the body's supply of potassium. Related disorders of digestion, such as dyspepsia, have also been shown to benefit from the ingestion of dandelion.

Dandelion is high in inulin, a form of carbohydrate easily assimilated by diabetics and hence is a potential source of nutritional support for diabetics. It is one of the best food sources of vitamin A (8,400 I.U. beta-carotene per 100 g). The greens yield 187 mg calcium, 66 mg phosphorous, 3 mg iron, 397 mg potassium and 35 mg vitamin C per 100 grams.

Availability: The whole plant is easily foraged spring through fall. Fresh leaves are found in some supermarkets, farmers' markets and whole or natural food stores. The chopped, dried leaf is available in whole or natural food stores.

Culinary Use: Dandelion leaves are tart, bitter and somewhat lemon-like in taste. The fresh root is similar to parsnip but not as strong and the roasted, dried root has a nutty, earthy flavor. Treat the fresh, peeled root in the same way as any root vegetable. Chop and use the fresh root to make a decoction for spring tonic or grate it into salads to help the transition from winter to spring. The dried root is excellent in teas, broths, soups, sauces, stews or any other long-simmering dish. Roasted roots are used as a coffee substitute, often blended with roasted chicory and/or burdock roots.

The fresh, young spring leaves are used as a salad staple or steamed, braised or sautéed as greens, with pasta, in soups and stocks.

Dandelion flower has traditionally been used to flavor wine. The fresh or dried leaves add color to sauces, butter, dips and cheese mixtures. They may be added to baked products, rice dishes or chopped in salads, soups, egg dishes, custards and puddings. Dandelion flowers make a healthy substitute for saffron and may be used as a garnish for all main or dessert dishes, in cakes, breads and muffins. The unopened buds are steamed or sautéed with vegetables. Dried leaves and flowers are combined with other herbs, such as nettles, burdock and yellow dock, to make herb beer or a healing tea blend.

Dill Seeds

Anethum graveolens

Dill is a tall top-heavy, annual plant with a long hollow stem growing out of a spindly taproot. Terminal flowers appear in a wide, flat umbel with numerous yellow flowers. Branches along the stem support feathery blue-green leaflets.

Parts Used: Seeds.

Actions: Soothing digestive, antispasmodic, increase milk in breastfeeding.

Uses: Flatulence, infant's colic, bad breath.

Availability: Dill is easy to grow. Harvest seeds in late summer, early fall. Dried seeds are readily available in whole or natural food stores and supermarkets.

Culinary Use: Dill seeds combine well with potatoes, rye, squash and sweet potatoes, cabbage, onion and vinegar, lending a warm, pleasantly anise and citrus flavor. Salad dressings, sauces and some seasonings use dill seeds.

Echinacea

Echinacea angustifolia or *E. purpurea*

The bright purple petals surrounding a brown cone make echinacea a top choice for perennial beds. A hardy perennial native to North America, its common name is purple coneflower.

Parts Used: Root, leaves and flowers with the root being the most potent.

Actions: Immune stimulating, anti-inflammatory, antibiotic, antimicrobial, antiseptic, analgesic, antiallergenic, lymphatic tonic.

Uses: Studies have shown that echinacea works best at the first sign of cold or flu, taken in 4 to 6 doses daily for not more than 10 days. It has interferon-like actions, helping to prevent and control viral infections. It hastens the healing of tissue and also fights viruses and candida. Echinacea root is more potent than the leaves.

Availability: Dried root, dried stems and leaves are available whole or cut in whole or natural food stores. Echinacea is also available in tincture and tablet form.

Culinary Use: The root is sweet and pleasantly aromatic while the flowers and stems are faintly aromatic. Using echinacea in cooking may aid in general well being and help head off minor illnesses if taken in a soup for 2 or 3 days following bouts of stress or excessive fatigue. Echinacea root combines well with garlic for fighting colds and flu.

Petals and leaves enliven salads, vegetable

dishes and stir-fries, as garnish. Dried petals are used in seasonings.

Whole, fresh or dried echinacea root is added to long-simmering soups and stews. Fresh roots are grated into salads, vegetable and grain dishes. Ground root is dried and combined with other spices or added to sauces, dips, puddings and desserts.

Dried echinacea leaves, petals and finely chopped dried root, may be blended with other herbs, such as hyssop, peppermint and thyme, for an effective cold remedy tea blend.

Add 1 tsp (5 mL) echinacea tincture to stocks, soups and stews when colds and flu threaten.

Fennel Seeds

Foeniculum vulgare

Fennel grows wild in Mediterranean Europe and Asia and has naturalized in many other parts of the world where the fleshy bulb is harvested and used as a vegetable. Fennel looks like a larger version of the dill plant. Stout, solid stems support bright yellow, large umbel clusters of flowers. Thread-like and feathery green leaves alternately branch out from joints of the stem. Flowers appear in summer, followed by gray-brown seeds.

Parts Used: Seeds. For the fennel bulb, see page 77.

Actions: Soothing diuretic, anti-inflammatory, antispasmodic, soothing digestive, promote milk flow, mild expectorant.

Uses: Indigestion, flatulence, increase milk flow in breastfeeding, relieve colic in babies when taken by the nursing mother and used directly for colic and coughs.

Caution: Avoid high doses in pregnancy, as it is a uterine stimulant.

Availability: Harvest fennel seeds in late summer, early fall. Dried seeds are readily available in whole or natural food stores and supermarkets.

Culinary Use: Fennel seeds are lightly anise-flavored, with astringent citrus tones. They are often combined with cinnamon, cumin, allspice, fenugreek, thyme and cumin for spice blends. The anise flavor complements both sweet and savory dishes, especially custards, rice and egg dishes. Cabbage, lentils, beets and potatoes go well with fennel seeds.

Fenugreek

Trigonella foenum-graecum

Grown as a fodder crop in southern and central Europe, fenugreek is widely naturalized from the Mediterranean to southern Africa and Australia. This annual legume has aromatic trifoliate leaves and solitary or paired yellow-white flowers, followed by beaked pods with yellow-brown seeds shaped like a pyramid.

Parts Used: Aerial parts and seeds.

Actions: Expectorant, soothing digestive, protects intestinal surfaces, reduces blood sugar and increases milk in breastfeeding.

Uses: Bronchitis, coughs, diabetes, diverticular disease, ulcerative colitis, Crohn's disease, menstrual pain, peptic ulcer, stomach upsets.

Availability: Dried seeds are found in whole or natural food stores and some supermarkets. The dried (and rarely fresh) leaves may be found in Indian markets when in season.

Culinary Use: Fresh fenugreek leaves are mildly pungent with a hint of lemon. Dried seeds are pungent, bitter and give the "curry" aroma to spice blends. Toasting the seeds brings out a slightly sweeter, nutty taste with maple overtones. For a nutritious soup stock, simmer 1 to 2 tsp (5 to 10 mL) lightly crushed seeds and 1 cup (250 mL) water for 10 minutes. Let cool. Strain and discard seeds. Add to the liquid in the recipe. Fenugreek seeds are combined with cumin, cinnamon, coriander, allspice, fennel, chiles and garlic in seasonings. Toasted fenugreek works well with other sweet spices (cinnamon and nutmeg) in sweet custards and desserts.

Garlic

Allium sativum

A hardy perennial plant with an edible root bulb made up of four to 15 cloves enclosed in a white, tan or pinkish papery skin. At the tip of the round, hollow and sturdy stem, white flowers appear encased in a teardrop-like membrane that tapers to a sharp, green point. Just before the flowers open, the bud causes the stem to curl and the flower stalk forms a twisted shape. The edible green flower stalks with unopened buds are called "scapes." Flowers form a round ball when in full bloom.

Parts Used: Bulb or head, sometimes called "bud" at the root of the plant. Fresh scapes (the green tops) are eaten as green vegetables.

Actions: Antimicrobial, antibiotic, cardioprotective, hypotensive, anticarcinogen, promotes sweating, reduces blood pressure, anticoagulant, lowers blood sugar levels, expectorant, digestive stimulant, diuretic, antihistaminic, antiparasitic.

Uses: Research has shown that garlic inhibits cancer cell formation and proliferation. It lowers serum total and low-density lipoprotein cholesterol in humans and reduces the tendency of the blood to clot, thereby reducing the risk of blocked arteries and heart disease. Garlic is an antioxidant and helps stimulate the immune system. It has strong antibiotic and anti-inflammatory properties that make it a good wound medicine. Garlic protects organs from damage induced by synthetic drugs, chemical pollutants and the effects of radiation.

One raw garlic clove provides 6 g protein, 29 mg calcium, 202 mg phosphorus, 529 mg potassium and 15 mg vitamin C.

Caution: Dried garlic salt has no medicinal value.

Availability: Fresh whole organic bulbs are found at farmers' markets, food stores and supermarkets. Scapes are found at farmers' markets and Asian markets in mid to late summer.

Culinary Use: Garlic's hot, sharp and strong unique taste is due to the active compound *allicin*. Fresh cloves have the highest medicinal value. It is beneficial to add half to 1 whole fresh raw clove to ingredients in dips and spreads.

To get reliable medicinal benefit from garlic, it is recommended that about two medium-size whole garlic bulbs (about 2 oz/60 g) be taken per week. That requires that almost every main dish you consume contain a minimum of two cloves each. Start to increase your fresh garlic consumption by blending minced fresh garlic into prepared sauces, dips and salad dressings and adding a minimum of one garlic clove to every main dish you make.

The whole head or bulb is often roasted to caramelize the sugars for use in spreads, dips, sauces, vegetable and pasta dishes and spreads. (For Roasted Garlic, see page 258.) Whole, blanched (boiled 30 seconds in water) cloves add subtle flavor to dressings or stir-fries, spiced oils and vinegars. Puréed blanched cloves are used to thicken sauces. Slivered whole garlic works in stir-fries, rice, legume and grain dishes. Chopped, fresh, raw cloves are combined with other herbs and spices for salad dressings, aïoli, pesto, hummus, salsas and seasonings.

Fresh, chopped scapes are mixed into dips, salads, sauces, salad dressing, used as a garnish, stir-fried with butter and lemon or added to grilled or baked vegetable and rice dishes.

Garlic's flower is a beautiful garnish and enlivens vinegars and oils, salads, stir-fries and other main dishes.

German Chamomile

Matricaria recutita

A low-growing hardy annual easily grown in North America. Flowers have daisy-like petals surrounding rounded yellow centers.

Parts Used: Flower heads and petals.

Actions: Gentle sedative, anti-inflammatory, mild antiseptic, prevents vomiting, antispasmodic, carminative, nervine, emmenagogue, mild pain reliever.

Uses: Anxiety, insomnia, indigestion, peptic ulcer, travel sickness and inflammations (such as gastritis) and menstrual cramps are often eased with chamomile. Chamomile also reduces flatulence and pain caused by gas.

Phytonutrients: To date, more than 120 chemical components have been identified from chamomile's clear blue essential oil. Chamazulene, alpha-bisabolol and matricinare have been evaluated individually and found to reduce inflammation. Alpha-bisabolol is also strongly antispasmodic, antimicrobial and mildly sedative.

Availability: Whole dried flower heads and chamomile tincture are available in whole or natural food stores.

Culinary Use: Use fragrant, apple-tasting chamomile to flavor jams, jellies, syrups and sauces. Fresh or dried petals may be used in salads and as an edible garnish, in baked goods and other desserts such as puddings. To relieve an acute upset stomach, take chamomile tea between meals on an empty stomach so the tea will have direct contact with the mucous lining.

Ginger

Zingeber officinalis

The fleshy root we use in cooking is the edible rhizome of a tender perennial plant that is native to Southeast Asia.

Parts Used: Root.

Actions: Antinausea, relieves headaches and arthritis, anti-inflammatory, circulatory stimulant, expectorant, antispasmodic, antiseptic, diaphoretic, guards against blood clots, peripheral vasodilator, prevents vomiting, carminative, antioxidant.

Uses: Ginger root calms nausea and morning sickness and prevents vomiting. Take $\frac{1}{4}$ to $\frac{1}{2}$ tsp (1 to 2 mL) ground ginger in water every 3 to 4 hours to relieve nausea and motion sickness. It is a cleansing herb with warming effects. Ginger is used to stimulate blood flow to the digestive system and to increase absorption of nutrients and increases the action of the gall bladder, while protecting the liver against toxins and preventing the formation of ulcers. Studies show that ginger offers some relief from the pain and swelling of arthritis without side effects. Ginger is also used in flatulence, circulation problems, impotence, and to prevent nausea after chemotherapy.

Caution: Ginger can be irritating to the intestinal mucosa, and should be taken with or after meals. Ginger is contraindicated in kidney disease.

Availability: Fresh gingerroot and dried powdered ginger are widely available in supermarkets, Asian and Indian markets and whole or natural food stores.

Culinary Use: Fresh gingerroot is hot and pungent with a sweet, spicy-citrus bite. The dried powder has a stronger, more bitter taste. Both fresh and dried ginger possess therapeutic properties, so use fresh or dried, ground ginger liberally in cooking, as a general tonic (hormone balancer) and to ward off colds and flu. Cook with fresh and dried ginger daily if you or someone in your family suffers from migraine headaches, influenza threatens, rheumatoid arthritis is diagnosed, joint stiffness is a problem, or embarking on a weight loss program.

Fresh and clean tasting, with a hot bite, fresh ginger blends well with most fruits and many vegetables. Add sliced fresh ginger to vinegars, oils or stocks. Use julienned ginger in stir-fries and vegetable dishes. Chop or grate raw ginger into salad dressings, marinades, Asian sauces and spreads. Ginger enhances all main dishes, stir-fries, cakes, baked goods, preserves and pickles. Use ginger juice to flavor salad dressings, marinades or sauces and candied ginger in fruit salads, desserts, salad dressings and sauces. Peel and chop fresh ginger, dry and blend with other herbs for teas.

To store fresh gingerroot: If left in a cool, dry place, fresh ginger will only keep for several days. Wrap fresh ginger in a paper towel and set in an open plastic bag to keep for several weeks in the refrigerator or seal in a plastic bag, freeze and cut off as needed. Fresh ginger keeps indefinitely when peeled, sliced, placed in a glass jar, covered with vodka, sealed and refrigerated.

Use candied or preserved ginger where fresh ginger is called for, especially in desserts and drinks. Candied ginger keeps for a year or longer, and is easy to use in cooking.

If fresh leaves are available, use them as a decorative plate liner, to wrap fish for the grill, or to serve finger foods and hors d'oeuvres. If fresh flowers are available, use for salads and as an edible garnish.

Dried ground or powdered ginger is used in cooking as you would fresh.

Ginseng

Siberian *Eleutherococcus senticosis,* North American *Panax quinquefolius,* Asian *Panax ginseng*

A hardy perennial, native to cool, wooded areas of Eastern and Central North America.

Parts Used: Root (from plants older than 4 years) and leaves if organic.

Actions: Antioxidant, adaptogen, tonic, stimulant, regulates blood sugar and cholesterol levels, stimulates immune system.

Uses: Ginseng helps the body resist and adapt to stress. It is a mild stimulant and as a tonic, it promotes long-term overall health. Along with increasing the body's resistance to diabetes, cancer, heart disease and various infections, the medical literature claims that ginseng can improve memory, increase fertility, protect the liver against many toxins and protect the body from radiation. It is also used in impotence and depression.

Caution: Avoid ginseng if you have a fever, asthma, bronchitis, emphysema, high blood pressure or cardiac arrhythmia. Avoid in pregnancy and with hyperactivity in children. Do not take with coffee. Do not take continuously for periods of longer than one month.

Availability: Dried root (whole or chopped), tea, powder and tincture are all found in whole or natural food stores and Asian markets. Fresh ginseng is sometimes found in Chinese and Asian markets. While native to North American woodlands, ginseng has been harvested to near extinction. Please do not collect from the wild or purchase wild crafted North American ginseng.

Culinary Use: The flavor of ginseng is pungent, bitter and astringent with notes of lime but when cooked in dishes, ginseng imparts only a slight flavor to the food. Use in the same way as ginger. Dried ginseng root is very hard and brittle. A good grater, such as those used for nutmeg, will shred the root fine. Whole fresh or dried root is excellent in soups, stocks and stews. Dried whole, grated or flaked ginseng is used in long-simmering soups and stews, and strained off.

Chopped fresh or dried ginseng is added to muesli and granola and dessert bars, whole-grain toppings for desserts and mixed with other herbs for tea blends.

Ground dried ginseng is more bitter than the fresh and works best in milkshakes and smoothies, salad dressings, puddings and other cooked desserts, as part of an antibiotic herbal seasoning, chili pastes and roux. The dried organic leaves are brewed into teas, then added to soups, broths, stews and puddings.

Hemp

Cannabis sativa

A tall woody plant that grows on multi-cellular stalks. Leaves consist of five, deeply cut lobes.

Parts Used: Leaves, stalks, seeds, flowering tops and fruit.

Actions: Promotes healthy menstruation, carminative, treats glaucoma, anti-emetic, aids breathing and inhibits lung tumor growth.

Uses: Hemp has been used to treat digestive disorders, neuralgia, insomnia, depression, migraines, asthma and inflammation.

Tetrahydrocannabinol (THC), cannabinol (CBN) and cannabidiol (CBD) are the active compounds in hemp. Hemp seed contains 26 to 31% pure protein with the essential amino acids and fatty acids.

Availability: Seeds low in THC and hemp oil are available in Canada and Europe. Medicinal use of marijuana is still controversial, but available with prescription in some Canadian provinces, and is legislated in 12 states in the United States.

Culinary Use: Hemp oil is thick and green with a rich, pleasant earthy taste. Hemp oil is rich in linoleic and linolenic fatty acids. It is used without heating, in dressings, sauces, dips and spreads. Hemp seeds are used in commercial snacks and a tahini-like paste and may be used in desserts, soups, baked vegetable and grain dishes and stews. In the Middle East a nutritious drink called *Bhang* is made using hemp leaves, black pepper, cloves, nutmeg and mace as the seasoning base. Water, watermelon juice or cucumber juice is added to the spices for a refreshing drink.

Hyssop

Hyssopus officinalis

An evergreen, bushy, woody perennial, hyssop is native to central and southern Europe, western Asia and northern Africa. The square, upright stem bears linear, opposite leaves and purple flowers in whorls from the dense spikes at the top of the stems.

Parts Used: Leaves and flowering tops.

Actions: Antispasmodic, expectorant, promotes sweating, mild painkiller, diuretic, antiviral against herpes simplex, reduces phlegm, soothing digestive.

Uses: Relieves asthma, bronchitis, colds, coughs, influenza, fevers and flatulence. The green tops, boiled in soup, have actually been used in the treatment of asthma. Caffeic acid and unspecified tannins in extracts of hyssop have been shown to have strong anti-HIV activity.

Availability: Hyssop is easy to grow and is harvested from May through fall. Dried leaves are available from whole or natural food stores.

Culinary Use: A fresh, minty, peppery, slightly bitter and pungent taste makes the fresh leaves and flowers excellent additions to salads, fruit cocktails and wraps. The fresh or dried leaves and/or flowers are added to baked goods (especially brownies and date squares), fruit flans and pies, dessert and cough syrups, jams, jellies, sauces, dessert dishes, soups, stews, stocks and stuffing. Hyssop is also dried and mixed with green tea and other herbs for beverages.

Lavender

Lavandula spp

A shrub-like plant with dense, woody stems from which linear, pine-like, gray-green leaves grow. The flowers grow in whorls of tiny flowers on spikes from long stems.

Parts Used: Leaves, stems and flowering tops.

Actions: Relaxant, antispasmodic, antidepressive, nervous system tonic, circulatory stimulant, antibacterial, antiseptic, carminative, promotes bile flow.

Uses: Lavender relieves colic, depression, exhaustion, indigestion, insomnia, and stress and tension headaches.

Laboratory research on the anticancer activity of perillyl alcohol distilled from lavender shows promise in the fight against cancer of the breast, pancreas, colon and prostate.

Caution: Avoid high doses in pregnancy because it is a uterine stimulant.

Availability: Easily grown in temperate climates, harvest lavender from June through fall. Organic, food grade dried flower buds are available in whole or natural food stores.

Culinary Use: Lavender is fragrant and distinctly floral. It can overwhelm the flavors of any dish if over used, so it is best to start with small amounts and increase in very small increments. Dried lavender is three times as potent as the fresh. Fresh or dried flowers are best in baked goods such as cookies, cakes, scones, quick breads, sauces, jellies, sorbets and vinegars. They can also be used as a garnish, to flavor honey and vinegar and in jams, jellies and candies. Dried flowers and leaves are often included in Herbes de Provence spice blend and in sugar substitutes or blended with other herbs

and green tea. Lavender teams nicely with lemon in tarts and other desserts and was used to flavor condiments.

Lemon Balm

Melissa officinalis

Opposite, oval, strongly lemon-scented leaves grow on thin, square stems. Flowers are tubular, white or yellow, growing in clusters, at the base of the leaves.

Parts Used: Leaves and flowering tops.

Actions: Antioxidant, antihistamine, carminative, antispasmodic, antiviral, antibacterial, nerve relaxant, antidepressive, stimulates bile flow, lowers blood pressure.

Uses: Lemon balm eases anxiety, depression, stress, flatulence, indigestion and insomnia.

Availability: An easily grown perennial, harvest leaves and flowers from June through autumn. Organic dried leaves are available in whole or natural food stores.

Culinary Use: Lemon balm is distinctly lemon flavored but it can have a slightly soapy taste. For this reason, it is usually blended with other lemon herbs such as lemon thyme and lemon verbena. Dried lemon balm blends are used in teas or the teas are used in sauces, custards and puddings. The fresh leaves are added to salads and dressings, puddings, egg dishes and rice pilafs. Lemon balm may be added in small amounts to recipes whenever lemon juice is an ingredient but it does not replace the lemon juice.

Lemon Verbena

Aloysia triphylla

A fast-growing, deciduous shrub, and native to South America, lemon verbena grows to over 6 feet (1.8 m) in zones 8 to 10. Long, pointed green leaves grow on erect stems with green to brown bark that turn woody with maturity. Lavender-colored flowers are tiny and grow in spikes.

Parts Used: Leaves.

Actions: Antispasmodic, digestive.

Uses: Indigestion, flatulence.

Availability: Dried leaves may be available in whole or natural food stores.

Culinary Use: Lemon verbena imparts a clear, strong, sweetly lemon taste to foods. Dried lemon verbena leaves are combined with fennel seeds for a refreshing pre- or after dinner tonic beverage that aids digestion and helps to reduce gas. Fresh or dried leaves are blended with thyme, basil, mint and chives for seasoning. Lemon verbena leaves are used with whole grains, baked vegetables and desserts.

Licorice

Glycyrrhiza glabra

A tender perennial, hardy in zones 7 to 9, native to the Mediterranean region and southwest Asia.

Parts Used: Root.

Actions: Gentle laxative, tonic, anti-inflammatory, antibacterial, anti-arthritic, soothes gastric and intestinal mucous membranes, expectorant.

Uses: Licorice root is considered to be one of the best tonic herbs because it provides nutrients to almost all body systems. It detoxifies, regulates blood sugar levels and recharges depleted adrenal glands. It has also been shown to heal peptic ulcers and is used to soothe irritated membranes and loosen and expel phlegm in the upper respiratory tract. It is also used to treat sore throat, urinary tract infections, coughs, bronchitis, gastritis and constipation.

Caution: Large amounts taken over long periods of time may cause fluid retention and a reduction in blood potassium levels. Avoid or use sparingly if you have high blood pressure. Extracts lack the tonic action.

Availability: Whole or powdered dried root available in whole or natural food stores.

Culinary Use: Licorice has a sweet, earthy flavor. Although we think of licorice as a flavor, the taste most people associate with licorice is actually anise. The terms anise and licorice are commonly interchangeable now, however, the medicinal qualities are not. Licorice root is 50 times as sweet as table sugar. Brewers use licorice because it gives port and stout their characteristic black color and thick consistency. It can also be used in cooking for the same purpose in sauces, puddings and gravies.

To use licorice in desserts and sauces, make a tea by simmering 1 tsp (5 mL) of the cut and sifted dried root in a cup of boiling water for 5 minutes. Strain the tea and use for sauces and in baked goods such as cookies and puddings.

Linden Flower

Tilia x *europaea*

Found throughout northern temperate regions, common linden is a deciduous tree with dark green, shiny, heart-shaped leaves and yellow-white flowers that appear in mid-summer. It is often grown as an ornamental in North American cities.

Parts Used: Flowering tops.

Actions: Antispasmodic, promotes sweating when taken as a hot tea, diuretic when taken as a warm tea, lowers blood pressure, relaxant, mild astringent.

Uses: Linden flower tea is a pleasant-tasting, relaxing remedy for stress, anxiety, tension headache and insomnia. It relaxes and nourishes blood vessels, making it useful in high blood pressure and heart disease. In promoting sweating, it is useful in colds, flu and fevers. The tea can be given to children as a calming remedy or to reduce fevers.

Availability: Harvest leaves and flowers in mid-June and leaves from early summer through autumn. Dried aerial parts are available in whole or natural food stores. Linden tea bags are often found in supermarkets.

Culinary Use: The actions in linden is partially due to its essential oils, which are only released with heat. For this reason, dried or fresh linden is not added to raw dishes. The easiest method to incorporate the pleasant and mildly lime taste of linden into recipes is by making a tea with the fresh or dried leaves. Use the strained infusion to replace some or all of the liquid in grains, sauces, puddings and desserts.

Mustard

Brassica spp

A hearty annual indigenous to North America, the mustard plant is tall, with bright green oval leaves. Yellow flowers appear in mid-summer and seedpods develop late summer to early fall.

Parts Used: Seeds (and leaves for cooking) (see Leafy Greens, page 77).

Actions: Blood cholesterol regulator, blood sugar regulator, heartbeat regulator, reduces flatulence.

Uses: Mustard seeds are a good source of magnesium (1 tbsp/15 mL ground mustard seed contains 33 mg magnesium) which helps regulate cholesterol, blood sugar and heartbeat. Native Americans used it to treat asthma, bronchitis, congestion, constipation, dropsy, fever, indigestion, sore muscles and toothache. It has been found to boost energy levels of people with chronic fatigue syndrome.

Availability: Yellow, white, black or brown dried mustard seeds are widely available in food stores. Easily grown from seed.

Culinary Use: Dried mustard seeds are sharp, hot and biting. They are ground into a paste and combined with other spices, vinegar and liquids to make a pungent and hot paste. Mustard seeds or paste may be added to soups, stews, legume and baked vegetable dishes. Use mustard leaves as you would other green leafy vegetables.

Nutmeg

Myristica fragrans

Native to tropical rainforest in the Moluccas and the Banda Islands, the bushy evergreen nutmeg tree is now grown for commercial production in Asia, Australia, Indonesia and Sri Lanka. Pale yellow flowers are followed by fleshy, yellow, round or pear-shaped fruits (generally called seeds).

Parts Used: Dried kernel of the nutmeg fruit.

Actions: Anti-inflammatory, antispasmodic, carminative, digestive stimulant, sedative.

Uses: Nutmeg relieves colic, diarrhea, flatulence, nausea, vomiting and muscle tension.

Caution: Do not use in pregnancy.

Availability: Whole, dried nutmeg seeds are available in whole or natural food stores. Ground nutmeg is widely available.

Culinary Use: Sweetly aromatic with a woodsy clove tone, nutmeg adds depth to savory dishes such as soups, stews, sauces and grain and pasta dishes. It is equally good in desserts and milk puddings. Nutmeg combines well with cinnamon, cloves, allspice, cardamom, coriander, fennel and ginger.

Parsley

Petroselinum crispum

A hardy biennial, native to the Mediterranean and grown as an annual in colder climates.

Parts Used: Leaves, stems and roots.

Actions: Antioxidant, tonic, digestive, diuretic.

Uses: As a diuretic, parsley helps the body expel excess water and flushes the kidneys. Always look for and treat underlying causes of water retention. As a nutrient, it is one of the richest food sources of vitamin C. Parsley's chlorophyll and myristicin may also inhibit the development of some cancers.

Parsley is an excellent source of vitamin A. One hundred grams of fresh parsley contains 3,200 I.U. beta-carotene along with 390 mg calcium, 281 mg vitamin C, 200 mg phosphorus and 17.9 mg iron.

Caution: Parsley should not be used in high doses during pregnancy because it stimulates the womb. Parsley is contraindicated in kidney inflammation.

Availability: Fresh sprigs are found in most supermarkets year-round.

Culinary Use: Parsley's fresh citrus taste has a hint of anise to it. It has the unique ability to enhance the flavors of other ingredients and so it is widely used in vegetarian cooking. One-third to $\frac{1}{2}$ cup (75 to 125 mL) chopped fresh parsley may be added to soups, stews, legume and grain dishes and baked vegetables.

Peppermint

Mentha piperita

An invasive, hardy perennial, native to Europe and Asia but easily grown in North America, peppermint supports bright green, oval aromatic leaves on purple stems. Small pink, white or purple flowers form elongated conical spikes at the tops of the stems.

Parts Used: Leaves and flowers.

Actions: Antispasmodic, digestive tonic, prevents vomiting, carminative, peripheral vasodilator, promotes sweating, promotes bile flow, analgesic.

Uses: Taking peppermint before eating helps stimulate liver and gall bladder function by increasing bile flow to the liver and intestines. Peppermint is well known for its ability to quell nausea and vomiting. Peppermint is used in ulcerative colitis, Crohn's disease, diverticular disease, travel sickness, fevers, colds, flu and to improve the appetite.

Menthol is the constituent that gives peppermint its antiseptic, decongestant, analgestic and mildly anesthetic (the cooling, numbing sensation) properties.

Caution: Do not use during pregnancy or give to children.

Availability: Fresh sprigs in some markets and supermarkets year-round. Dried leaves are found in whole or natural food stores. Peppermint teas in bulk and bags are widely available.

Culinary Use: Whole fresh sprigs are used in sauces, as a garnish and in teas or drinks. Fresh or dried leaves are great in jellies, sauces, teas, beverages, desserts, salads, marinades, and vegetable and fruit dishes. Fresh flowers enhance salads, stir-fries, and vegetable and fruit dishes. Peppermint tea from fresh or dried leaves and flowers is delicious hot or iced. Blend peppermint with other tea herbs to lend its characteristic fresh and minty flavor.

Purslane

Portulaca oleracea

A wild, low-growing and sprawling perennial that grows throughout much of the world. Leaves are oval, thick (almost succulent) and grow opposite along the horizontal stem. Purslane is considered a weed in North America but eaten as an important food in Europe and the Middle East.

Parts Used: Leaves and tender stems.

Actions: Antioxidant, anti-inflammatory, heart protective.

Uses: Medicinal doses are used to treat heart disease, arthritis and other inflammatory diseases.

Low in saturated fat, purslane is a good source of vitamins B_1 (thiamin), B_3 (niacin) and B_6 (pyridoxine), and a very good source of vitamin A, C, B_2 (riboflavin), calcium, iron, magnesium, phosphorus, potassium, copper and manganese. It is also high in pectin and essential fatty acids.

Caution: Purslane contains oxalic acid and if consumed in very large doses, may be toxic.

Availability: The plant often appears unwanted in gardens and cultivated plots. Fresh leaves may be found in some Greek and Turkish markets but otherwise, must be harvested from the wild.

Culinary Use: Purslane is a very good addition to fresh green salads because of its fresh, astringent citrus taste and juicy leaves that add crunch. Fresh leaves complement beets, zucchini, tomato sauces, beans, and spinach and potato dishes.

Red Clover

Trifolium pratense

A perennial with tubular pink to red flowers throughout the summer, red clover grows in fields throughout North America. Its three long oval leaflets distinguish it as a clover.

Parts Used: Flowering tops.

Actions: Antispasmodic, expectorant, hormone balancing, nutrient, blood thinning, lymphatic cleanser.

Uses: Coughs, bronchitis, whooping cough, menstrual problems.

Caution: Because it contributes to blood thinning, avoid red clover in times of heavy menstrual flow.

Availability: The flowering tops can be harvested May through September from the wild or cultivated gardens. Dried flowers are available in whole or natural food stores. Dried clover that has turned brown is of little use; be sure that the flowers are still pink.

Culinary Use: Fresh red clover leaves and buds are pleasantly green and woodsy and are added to summer salads. Remove the bitter green centers from the flowers before using. Blend dried red clover with other herbs for a medicinal tea.

Red Raspberry

Rubus idaeus

A deciduous shrub with prickly stems and pinnately divided leaves, widespread in Europe, Asia and North America. Small white flowers appear in clusters with aromatic, juicy red fruit following in early summer.

Parts Used: Leaves (see Fruits for berry information, page 69).

Actions: Antispasmodic, astringent, promotes milk in breastfeeding.

Uses: Red raspberry leaves have long been used to tone the uterus during pregnancy and labor, resulting in less risk of miscarriage, relief of morning sickness and a safer, easier birth. As an astringent, raspberry leaf is useful in sore throat and diarrhea.

Availability: Harvest leaves from early summer through autumn. Dried leaves are available in whole or natural food stores.

Culinary Use: The leaves have a slight raspberry taste but with astringent and lemon tones. Fresh raspberry leaves may be included in fresh green salads or chopped and added to soups and baked vegetable dishes. Dried leaves are blended with thyme or sage for a soothing tea that eases coughs. Red raspberry tea is easy to make and take during pregnancy.

Rose

Rosa

Cultivation of roses dates back thousands of years with *R. rugosa*, *R. gallica*, *R. rubra* and *R. damascena* being among the oldest varieties. *Rosa rugosa* is a

deciduous shrub with thorny stems and dark green, oval leaves. Dark pink or white flowers appear in summer and are followed by large, globular, bright red hips (fruit). Wild roses (including the dog rose of North America) grow all over northern temperate regions throughout the world.

Parts Used: Petals and rose hips.

Actions: Rose hips from *Rosa canina* contain vitamin C and are diuretic, astringent and a mild laxative. Rose petals from *Rosa gallica, R. damascena, R. centifolia, R. rugosa* are antidepressant, anti-inflammatory, astringent, blood tonic.

Uses: Their nutrient value makes rose hips useful in prevention of the common cold and as a tasty addition to herbal teas used to improve immune functioning. As an astringent, they are used in diarrhea. Rose petals can be added to teas for their relaxing and uplifting fragrance. Used in a bath, they have been known to ease the pains of rheumatoid arthritis.

Availability: Harvest fresh petals from organic bushes from mid-summer through autumn and hips in the fall. Dried edible rose petals and rose water are available in Middle Eastern markets. Do not use petals from roses purchased from florist shops.

Culinary Use: Rose petals are perfumed and pleasantly fragrant. Use fresh or dried rose petals to flavor syrups and sauces. Because hips are an important source of vitamin C, use fresh or dried rosehips in teas, syrups and fruit drinks, steep in water, then add to stocks, soups, sauces and gravy. Rose water can replace some of the liquid in desserts and dessert sauces.

Rosemary

Rosmarinus officinalis

An evergreen shrub that grows to 6 feet (180 cm) in warm climates, rosemary is native to the Mediterranean.

Parts Used: Leaves and flowers.

Actions: Antioxidant, anti-inflammatory,

astringent, nervine, carminative, antiseptic, diuretic, diaphoretic, promotes bile flow, antidepressant, circulatory stimulant, antispasmodic, nervous system and cardiac tonic.

Uses: An effective food preservative. Rosemary may be effective in preventing breast cancer, and it fights against the deterioration of brain functions (improves memory). It is also useful in treating migraine and tension headaches, nervous tension, flatulence, depression, chronic fatigue syndrome and joint pain.

Caution: Avoid large amounts of rosemary during pregnancy.

Availability: Fresh sprigs found in some ethnic markets and supermarkets year-round. Dried whole and powdered leaf found in supermarkets, whole or natural food stores.

Culinary Use: Rosemary is used in smaller amounts than other culinary herbs due to its resinous pine and citrus taste with camphor and spice tones. A combination of rosemary, thyme, garlic and sea salt makes an excellent rub for roasted vegetables and a versatile seasoning for dressings, stuffing and sauces. Rosemary is very good in baked goods such as scones, cookies, focaccia and quick breads. Use a whole sprig the same way you would whole vanilla beans, to impart the spicy essence to egg dishes, syrups and puddings and then remove.

Sage

Salvia officinalis

A hardy, woody perennial evergreen shrub that is native to western United States and Mexico. Tender and hardier varieties of sage grow easily all over Mexico, the United States and southern Canada. Sage has wrinkled, gray-green, oval leaves and purple, pink or white flowers.

Parts Used: Leaves and flowers.

Actions: Antioxidant, antimicrobial, antibiotic, antiseptic, carminative, antispasmodic, anti-inflammatory, circulatory stimulant, estrogenic, peripheral vasodilator, reduces perspiration, uterine stimulant.

Uses: Sage's volatile oil kills bacteria and fungi, even those resistant to penicillin. It is very good as a gargle for sore throat, laryngitis and mouth ulcers. Also used to reduce breast milk production, and to relieve night sweats and hot flashes of menopause.

Caution: Sage can cause convulsions in very high doses. Do not use where high blood pressure or epilepsy is evident, or during pregnancy. Sage should not be consumed during pregnancy. Sage contains steroid-like factors and can encourage miscarriage.

Availability: Fresh sprigs are found at some supermarkets and farmers' markets. Dried, whole, cut, rubbed or ground sage is available at most supermarkets.

Culinary Use: Sage is pungent with balsamic and camphorous notes. Dried sage is often bitter and more potent than the fresh leaves. Small amounts of fresh or dried sage leaves enhance apples, cheese, whole grains, potatoes, tomatoes and legumes. Sage combines well with thyme, garlic, bay, oregano and marjoram, parsley and savory. It is used in stuffing, sauces, and baked vegetable dishes and with legumes and pasta. For a throat-soothing tea, blend sage with thyme, sweet cicely, peppermint and/or licorice. The flower is used chopped fresh in salads, vegetable dishes and as a garnish.

Spearmint

Mentha spicata

Spearmint is a hardy perennial found growing wild in wet soil in most of North America. It is invasive and, like all mints, has a square stem with bright green, lanceolate leaves, lilac, pink, or white flowers borne in a terminal, cylindrical spike.

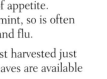

Parts Used: Leaves and flowering tops.

Actions: Antispasmodic, digestive, induces sweating.

Uses: To relieve the common cold, influenza, indigestion, flatulence and lack of appetite. Spearmint is milder than peppermint, so is often used in treating children's colds and flu.

Availability: The leaves are best harvested just before the flowers open. Dried leaves are available in health food stores.

Culinary Use: Spearmint has a milder, sweeter mint flavor than peppermint and for cooking, fresh spearmint sprigs are preferred. Fresh spearmint leaves are used with potatoes, zucchini and peas. While mint jelly and sauce are usually made with peppermint, salsas are made with the sweeter spearmint. Spearmint combines well with cardamom, coriander, cumin, marjoram and thyme. Spearmint is the mint most often used in Mint Juleps. Lentil and whole grain dishes and some stews can benefit from dried spearmint.

Stevia

Stevia rebaudiana

A small, tender shrub, native to northeastern Paraguay and adjacent sections of Brazil.

Parts Used: Leaves.

Actions: Energy booster, natural, low caloric sweetener, tonic, digestive, diuretic.

Uses: Stevia's main benefit is in its use as a safe sweetener and sugar alternative. With its powerful sweet, licorice taste (stevia is 200 to 300 times sweeter than sugar), stevia prevents cavities and does not trigger a rise in blood sugar. It increases energy and improves digestion by stimulating the pancreas without feeding yeast or fungi.

Availability: Dried, cut and powdered leaves and liquid extract available in whole or natural food stores.

Culinary Use: Fresh stevia leaves are sweet with a slight citrus taste. They are best used in cooking if made into an infusion. Make a tea from a handful of fresh stevia sprigs and 2 cups (500 mL) boiling water, let steep overnight. Strain and add the liquid to sauces, syrups, dressings, puddings and other desserts.

Substitute 2 tbsp (25 mL) stevia powder for 1 cup (250 mL) sugar in recipes. Add stevia liquid drops to tea, juices, desserts, syrups and other beverages to sweeten.

Note: Some sugar is required for the success of baked goods, so stevia cannot be substituted for sugar in all recipes.

Stinging Nettle

Urtica dioica

Widespread in temperate regions of Europe, North America and Eurasia, this perennial has bristly, stinging hairs on the stem and ovate, toothed leaves that cause minor skin irritation when touched. Minute green flowers appear in clusters during the summer.

Parts Used: Leaves.

Actions: Leaves and flowers are astringent, blood tonic, circulatory stimulant, diuretic, eliminate uric acid from the body, high in iron, chlorophyll and vitamin C, promote milk in breastfeeding. Fresh stinging nettle root is astringent, diuretic.

Uses: A valuable herb, stinging nettle leaves and flowers are useful as a general, daily nourishing tonic, as well as specifically to treat iron-deficiency anemia, gout, arthritis, kidney stones and as a blood tonic in pregnancy, diabetes, poor circulation and chronic skin disease such as eczema.

The fresh root has a strong action on the urinary system. It is useful in water retention, kidney stones, urinary tract infection, cystitis, prostate inflammation and swelling.

Availability: Gather leaves and flowers while flowering in summer, and harvest the root in autumn. Use gloves to protect bare skin from uric acid. Dried leaves and flowers are available in whole or natural food stores.

Culinary Use: Enjoy the peppery and slightly citrus taste of stinging nettle in soups and salads and add to recipes as you would fresh spinach. Cooking and drying neutralizes the uric acid in the hairs on the leaves and stems that causes the sting.

Tea

Camellia sinensis

Green and black tea comes from the shrub or small tree indigenous to the wet forests of Asia and cultivated commercially in Asia, Africa, South America, and North Carolina.

Green tea is heated and dried after harvesting and undergoes no further processing. Black tea is dried, exposed to air (and fermented) before it is heated, causing the antioxidant catechins to oxidize and form equally potent antioxidants called theaflavins.

Parts Used: Leaves.

Actions: Antioxidant, stimulant, astringent, antibacterial, diuretic, antitumor, anti-obesity, prevents gum disease and cavities, lowers blood pressure and blood sugar levels, lowers cholesterol.

Uses: Green tea is a good tonic beverage and can be mixed with other herbs for teas.

Epidemiological studies of Japanese people, heavy consumers of green tea, show that they have lower death rates from cancer of all types, especially cancer of the stomach. A recent Swedish study revealed that women who drank a minimum of two cups of tea daily developed 46% less ovarian cancer than non-tea drinkers.

Catechins in green tea and theaflavins in black tea are strongly antioxidant, protect against cancer, fight viral infection, streptococcus mutans and lower LDL or low-density lipoprotein. The fluoride content in green tea prevents cavities. Vitamins B and C, proanthocyanidins and phenolic compounds are potent antioxidants in green tea.

Caution: Tea (both green and black) contains caffeine — about 3 to 4%, about one-quarter to one-third the amount in coffee and the stronger the tea, the greater the quantity of caffeine in the drink.

Tea interferes with iron intake from foods of plant origin and vegetarians in particular should take tea between meals and not with them.

Availability: Dried green tea in bulk is found in Oriental markets and whole or natural food stores or individually wrapped in supermarkets.

Culinary Use: Green tea is astringent, some are strong tasting while others are refreshingly sweet and mild. Use green tea for syrups, dressings and puddings. Blend dried green tea with other dried herbs for a beverage.

Thyme

Thymus

A bushy, low-growing shrub easily grown in North America.

Parts Used: Leaves.

Actions: Antioxidant, expectorant, antiseptic, antispasmodic, astringent, tonic, antimicrobial, antibiotic, heals wounds, carminative, calms coughs, nervine.

Uses: Thyme is ideal for deep-seated chest infections such as chronic coughs and bronchitis. It is also used for sinusitis, laryngitis, asthma and irritable bowel syndrome.

Thyme is high in calcium (1,890 mg in 100 mg fresh leaves), phosphorus, potassium and beta-carotene (3,800 I.U.).

Caution: Avoid in pregnancy. Children under 2 years of age and people with thyroid problems should not take thyme.

Availability: Fresh sprigs available in farmers' markets in season and most supermarkets year-round. Dried whole leaves in whole or natural food stores.

Culinary Use: The taste of thyme is peppery, pungent, slightly sweet and clove-like. It is extremely versatile and can be added to most dishes. It stands up to long cooking in soups, stews, tomato sauces, gumbos and chowders. Used daily, thyme's antioxidant effect is beneficial. Use thyme in canning and preserving because of its antibacterial, antifungal activity.

Fresh flowering sprigs are great in fruit and vegetable preserves, to flavor vinegar, oils and wine, in long-simmering dishes. Dried sprigs are used in bouquet garni and to release flavor when burned with coals for grilling foods.

Fresh thyme leaves are added to salads, vegetable dishes, soups, casseroles, stuffing, vegetable pâtés, breads, spreads, dips, vinegars, mustards and herb blends. Use lemon thyme with sea vegetables, lemon-flavored baked goods, syrups, puddings and desserts.

The fresh flowers lend a mild taste and rosy color to vinegar, butter and sauces or can be used as a garnish on soups, pasta, rice and desserts. Dried leaves and flowers are blended with other tea herbs.

Turmeric

Curcuma longa

A deciduous tender perennial belonging to the ginger family, hardy to zone 10 and native to southeast Asia. The long rhizome resembles ginger but is thinner and rounder with brilliant orange flesh.

Parts Used: Fleshy root.

Actions: Antioxidant, anti-inflammatory, antimicrobial, antibacterial, antifungal, antiviral, anticoagulant, analgesic, reduces cholesterol, reduces post-exercise pain, heals wounds, antispasmodic, protects liver cells, increases bile production and flow.

Uses: Turmeric appears to inhibit colon and breast cancer and is used in hepatitis, nausea, digestive disturbances, and where gall bladder has been removed. It boosts insulin activity and reduces the risk of stroke. Turmeric is also used in rheumatoid arthritis, cancer, candida, AIDS, Crohn's disease, eczema and digestive problems.

Availability: Asian stores stock fresh or frozen whole rhizomes at times when it is seasonal in the countries where it grows. Oriental markets or whole or natural food stores offer the dried, whole rhizomes, and supermarkets sell ground turmeric.

Culinary Use: The flavor of turmeric is pungent and charged with a fresh, peppery, camphorous, slightly acrid taste and is at its peak in freshly grated turmeric. Dried, whole rhizomes retain a warm,

sweetish, woody character. Dried, powdered turmeric is weaker and slightly bitter in taste but still gives a yellow color to foods. Turmeric is one of the ingredients in traditional Indian curries. Use the fresh root whenever possible, cutting or grating it as required. Use turmeric to add warmth and a bright yellow hue to rice dishes, cheeses, lentils, pickles, chicken, fish, salsas and liqueurs. The fresh chopped root is also added to stocks, soups, sauces and stews. Fresh sliced root is used to flavor vinegar, oils soups or stocks and the julienne strips are added to stir-fries. Finely chopped or grated, raw fresh turmeric is excellent in salad dressings, marinades, baked vegetable or legume dishes, stir-fries, preserves and pickles. Turmeric juice is used to flavor salad dressings, marinades or sauces. Candied turmeric is used much like candied ginger in fruit salads, salad dressings, syrups and sauces.

Blend fresh or dried turmeric with other spice or herbs such as sweet cinnamon or cloves, hot pepper or mustard, earthy cumin or fenugreek and sharp dill, bay or thyme.

To store fresh root: Wrap the whole fresh root in a dry towel and set in an open plastic bag to keep for several weeks in the refrigerator. To keep longer, seal the fresh root in a plastic bag, freeze and cut off as needed. To keep fresh turmeric indefinitely, peel and slice, place in a glass jar, cover with vodka, seal and refrigerate.

Whole Food Ingredients

Definition: Whole food ingredients are foods used in small amounts to add flavor or to thicken foods. Whole food ingredients are naturally processed. They are products obtained from whole foods without the use of synthetic means. Whole food ingredients retain as many nutrients from their original foods as possible because they have been gently processed, that is, they are not subjected to heat, chemicals or harsh refining methods and do not contain harmful additives or trans fats. Organic whole food ingredients are the very best products we can purchase and use in vegetarian and whole food cooking.

Whole Food Flavorings

Carob

Ceratonia siliqua

Carob beans grow in pods produced by the evergreen carob tree or shrub originating in the Mediterranean region. The beans are ground to a dark powder. Because its taste is similar to cocoa powder or chocolate, carob replaces those ingredients in recipes.

Actions/Uses: Carob does not contain caffeine and is low in saturated fat, cholesterol and sodium. It is a good source of B_2 (riboflavin), calcium, dietary fiber, potassium, copper and manganese.

Forms Available: Powder, flour, chips, chunks, granules.

Culinary Use: Carob is naturally sweeter than cocoa powder and chocolate and may be used in smaller amounts in recipes. Because it does not have the fat, flavor or texture of pure chocolate, carob does not perform the same in baked products. Carob is used in cookies and dessert recipes including puddings, syrups, sauces and fruit bars.

Chocolate

Theobroma cacao

Cocoa and chocolate are derived from the cacao bean, which grows in pods on the tropical cocoa tree. The beans and pulp from the pods are fermented and dried before undergoing a sophisticated process that turns chocolate liquor into the chocolate we eat and use in cooking. For cocoa powder, dried chocolate liquor is ground to a dark powder. Both chocolate and cocoa powders are not naturally sweet, but so bitter, they are inedible.

Actions/Uses: Even though the fats in chocolate are saturated along with the monounsaturated oleic acid, regular consumption of cocoa butter and chocolate has been shown not to raise blood cholesterol levels. This may be due to the relatively high concentrations of stearic acid found in chocolate. Chocolate is rich in magnesium, copper, potassium and manganese. Dark chocolate is rich in flavonoids, which not only act as natural antioxidants (chemicals that combat the damage oxygen does to the body), but that also improve blood vessel flexibility in apparently healthy people. Scientists have found that eating dark chocolate appears to improve the function of important cells lining the wall of blood vessels for at least three hours. Eating dark chocolate seems to make the blood vessels more flexible, which helps prevent the hardening of arteries that leads to heart attacks.

Caution: Chocolate contains caffeine and sugar is usually added in large amounts. Dark, lightly sweetened chocolate is the form to use for health benefits. Check labels and avoid chocolate with wax, vegetable oils or gums as an ingredient or where sugar is listed first.

Forms Available: Unsweetened chocolate with 50 to 58% cocoa butter has no sugar added. To make bittersweet, semisweet and sweet chocolate, cocoa butter, sugar, vanilla and lecithin are added to chocolate liquor in varying degrees. Basically, the sweeter the chocolate, the less cocoa butter and the more sugar it contains. Semisweet chips have a lower cocoa butter content than blocks or squares to keep them from melting when baked in cookies or bars. Milk chocolate is sweetened chocolate with dried milk solids. Milk chocolate is low in cocoa butter (10% minimum by law). White chocolate is made with cocoa butter and not chocolate liquor (so technically it's not a real chocolate) and with milk solids and sugar added. Unsweetened cocoa powder is best for baking. Sweetened cocoa or hot chocolate powders are high in sugar and perhaps milk solids.

Culinary Use: Bittersweet or semisweet dark chocolate (if not too bitter) in block form are the obvious healthy choices for eating chocolate. Generally, expensive dark chocolate has a higher cocoa butter content than the less expensive brands. Unsweetened, bittersweet and semisweet dark chocolate (in squares or blocks) impart a strong chocolate flavor and are all good choices for cooking and baking. However, there must be some sugar in the recipe if these forms of chocolate are used.

Coconut

See Nuts, page 95.

Miso

Miso is a thick, high-protein paste made from soybeans, salt and a fermenting agent. It is similar in taste and color to soy sauce. Sometimes a grain, such as rice and barley, is fermented with the soybeans for additional flavor.

Culinary Use: Small amounts of miso are added to soups, sauces, dressings and stews.

Natto

Natto is made of fermented, cooked whole soybeans, and offers nutritional values similar to those found in miso. It has a sticky, viscous coating and is strong smelling, with a cheese-like texture.

Culinary Use: Natto is used as a spread or in soups.

Sea Salt

Both sea and land salt are the mineral sodium chloride, an essential nutrient that the body requires in small amounts. Sea salt is evaporated from salt water and contains iodine, not naturally found in land-mined salts.

Caution: Excess salt increases the volume of blood in the vessels, causing constriction, which leads to hypertension or high blood pressure.

Culinary Use: Sea salt is added to recipes during the last half hour of cooking or passed at the table for seasoning foods.

Seitan

Made from the gluten in wheat flour, seitan is a high-protein food often used to replace meat in recipes. It has a chewy texture and nutty taste. Purchase seitan in whole or natural food stores.

Caution: The wheat gluten is not appropriate for people with gluten allergies.

Culinary Use: Sold by weight, seitan is broken or crumbled and simmered in liquids.

Tamari Sauce

Similar to soy sauce, tamari is dark brown in color and slightly thicker. Unlike regular soy sauce, which is made by fermenting soybeans with roasted wheat or barley and salt, tamari is fermented naturally. Tamari contains only soybeans, water and sodium and is wheat- and gluten-free.

Actions/Uses: Tamari improve circulation, aid digestion and promote the growth of healthy intestinal bacteria. They are good sources of vitamin B_3 (niacin), manganese and protein.

Culinary Use: Like soy sauce, tamari adds saltiness to foods and should be used in moderation.

Umeboshi

Umeboshi is the name of a Japanese apricot (often called a plum) that is salted or pickled and used as a condiment.

Actions/Uses: Thought to settle an upset and nauseous stomach, umeboshi plums are added to green tea to relieve cold and flu symptoms. Umeboshi is thought to help maintain a low alkaline pH in the blood and this is helpful in neutralizing the acids created by sugars.

Culinary Use: Use umeboshi vinegar as you would rice vinegar. Add small amounts of the salty, pickled umeboshi plums to grains, legumes and baked vegetable dishes. They may be eaten on their own following a meal to improve digestion.

Vanilla

Vanilla planifolia

Vanilla is the edible fruit of a plant that is a member of the orchid family. Bourbon and Tahitian are the two types of vanilla that are used commercially. Pure vanilla extract is an alcohol that has the flavor and fragrance of vanilla. Pure natural vanilla does not contain alcohol; it is made in a glycerin base and contains as much vanilla as the extract.

Actions/Uses: Vanilla has been used medicinally to ease upset stomach and treat asthma, congestion and coughs. A paste made from the vanilla beans is used to treat poisonous bites.

Caution: Beware of inexpensive synthetic vanilla. Pure vanilla extract contains three ingredients — vanilla, alcohol and water.

Forms Available: Liquid extract and whole bean.

Culinary Use: Vanilla may be used to intensify the flavors in both sweet and savory foods. Use vanilla in baked goods, drinks, custards, sauces and syrups. Whole beans are used in sauces to impart flavor, then removed.

Wasabi

Wasabia japonica

Bright green and dangerously hot, wasabi is a Japanese plant that is part of the cabbage family. Known as Japanese horseradish, the green root of the plant is grated and used in ways that are similar to horseradish, that is, in small amounts as a condiment.

Actions: Wasabi's hot taste comes from isothiocyanates that have been known to inhibit microbe growth. The camphor-like vapors burn the nasal passages.

Forms Available: Fresh wasabi is not often seen in North America, but the paste and a powdered wasabi product is found in Japanese food stores, and wasabi-coated peas and peanuts are popular in whole and natural food stores.

Caution: Some products labeled wasabi are actually mixtures of European horseradish, mustard and green food coloring.

Culinary Use: Raw wasabi paste is used in very small amounts and is used most often to accompany sushi or sashimi. It can be used in small amounts in recipes to replace horseradish.

Green Plants

Cereal Grasses

Wheat and barley grass are grown from the seeds or berries of the wheat or barley plant. Harvested when 5 to 6 inches (12.5 to 15 cm) high, the fresh grass is then eaten fresh or juiced. It can also be dried and used in powdered form or pressed into pills.

Actions/Uses: Antioxidant, anti-inflammatory, anticancer, antibiotic, blood cleanser, protective against radiation. High in chlorophyll, which is a powerful healing agent and infection fighter. Also high in beta-carotene and vitamins C and E, these green foods are easily added to juices, blended drinks and uncooked recipes. They have high levels of protein — even higher than soy and legumes — making them the best plant sources of this nutrient.

Culinary Use: Whisk 1 or 2 tsp (5 or 10 mL) powdered wheat or barley grass with 1 or 2 cups (250 to 500 mL) juice, smoothie mixture or other liquids for uncooked spreads, sauces or dips. Chop (or cut with scissors) the fresh green grasses and use as you would parsley in baked vegetable or grain dishes.

Micro-Algae

Chlorella, Spirulina

Rich in carotenoids, protein and chlorophyll, green algae are microscopic single-celled sea vegetables. Ocean or sea algae, including larger sea vegetables (see page 98) are a rich natural source of minerals and trace minerals.

Actions/Uses: Antioxidant, anticancer, immune boosting, reduce heavy-metal toxicity, lower blood pressure. Green algae have been shown to be effective in reducing the effects of radiation and may be helpful in treating HIV infection.

Forms Available: The micro green algae are sold in capsules or bulk loose powder in whole and natural food stores.

Culinary Use: Add up to 1 tbsp (15 mL) to smoothie and other drink recipes. Algae may be added to uncooked foods such as dips, spreads and sauces.

Psyllium Seeds

Plantago ovata

The seed or husk of an annual herb native to Asia and naturalized in the Mediterranean region and North Africa is called psyllium. Psyllium seeds or husks have long been part of traditional and herbal medicine.

Actions/Uses: Psyllium seeds are high in fiber making them an effective natural laxative. By adding bulk to the stool, which causes it to press against the bowel wall, psyllium seeds trigger the contractions leading to a bowel movement. When taking psyllium seeds, you need to drink at least eight glasses of water a day to avoid bowel obstruction. A diet high in whole fresh fruit and vegetables will soon reduce the need for taking psyllium seeds.

Caution: Psyllium can cause an allergic reaction in sensitive individuals, and should be avoided if you have asthma. If you experience an allergic reaction, discontinue immediately. Psyllium must not be taken in cases of bowel obstruction.

Dose: One to 3 tsp (5 to 15 mL) of the seeds mixed in juice or a smoothie, followed by a full glass of water, taken first thing in the morning for 1 week. Another seven glasses of water must be taken during the day.

Plant Thickeners

Agar (or Agar-Agar)

Agar is a substance obtained from some species of red algae (sea vegetable) gathered on the East Indian coast and the Far East. Dissolved in hot water and cooled, agar becomes gelatinous due to its high quantities of mucilage.

Caution: Do not confuse agar with isinglass, which is collagen obtained from the swim or gas bladders of sturgeon and other cold-water ocean fish. Isinglass was extensively used for elaborate molded desserts before gelatin was available. Beer that uses isinglass finings to clarify it is unsuitable for vegetarian diets.

Actions/Uses: Laxative.

Forms Available: Dried granules or flakes are the most common form but whole strips of agar are sometimes available.

Culinary Use: Agar is used as a thickener for sauces, soups, desserts and a clarifying agent in brewing. It is also used to replace gelatin in recipes.

To Use in Recipes: In a saucepan, combine 1 tbsp (15 mL) agar in $2\frac{1}{2}$ cups (625 mL) water, broth or juice. Bring to a boil over medium heat. Reduce heat and simmer for 5 minutes. Let cool and mix with ingredients. Agar sets upon chilling.

Arrowroot

Maranta arundinacea

The root of a tropical rainforest herb that yields a starch that is easily digested, arrowroot is preferred to flour and cornstarch because those ingredients are irritating to people who suffer from food allergies.

Caution: Arrowroot has been known to be adulterated with potato and other vegetable starches.

Culinary Use: Asians use arrowroot in biscuits, puddings, jellies and cakes and in broths and milk puddings. Use arrowroot in place of flour and cornstarch to thicken sauces, custards, puddings and soups. Substitute the same amount of arrowroot as cornstarch in recipes.

Kudzu (or Kuzu)

Pueraria lobata

A cooking starch derived from the roots of a plant belonging to the pea family that is native to Japan. It is used to thicken sauces, custards, puddings and soups. In Japan, along with the roots, which are boiled, the fresh leaves and flowers of the plant are eaten. In southeastern United States, kudzu has taken over large tracts of wasteland along highways and in industrial areas to the point where it is considered a noxious pest.

Actions/Uses: Anti-inflammatory, anticancer, prevents migraines, antimicrobial.

In Japan, kudzu is used to treat cold and flu symptoms, relax muscles and aid digestion. Studies show that it reduces both the ill affects from alcohol consumption and the craving for alcohol itself.

Culinary Use: Kudzu may be used as a substitute for flour or cornstarch to thicken liquids.

Sweeteners

Blackstrap Molasses

Molasses is a thick syrup by-product of the sugar refining process in which the sucrose (sugar) is separated from the liquid and nutrients in the raw cane plant. Several grades of molasses are available, but of the three major types (unsulphured, sulphured and blackstrap), blackstrap contains the least sugar and the most nutrients — iron, six of the B vitamins and calcium, phosphorous and potassium.

In blackstrap molasses, the carbohydrates are quickly assimilated and it is a good source of iron and is totally fat free. Two teaspoons (10 mL) of blackstrap molasses delivers 13.3% of the daily recommended value for iron and 11.8% RDA for calcium. It is also an excellent source of copper and manganese and a very good source of potassium and magnesium.

Sulphured molasses is made by a process that treats green sugarcane with sulphur dioxide fumes during the sugar extraction process.

Culinary Use: Use sparingly in savory dishes or smoothies that require additional sweetening. Molasses adds its own, distinct flavor to baked goods and desserts.

Brown Rice Syrup

When brown rice is cultured with enzymes and the liquid is strained off and cooked, a sweet, dark syrup is the result. Unlike white sugar, brown rice syrup is comprised of about 50% soluble complex carbohydrates that take up to three hours to be digested, providing a steady supply of energy.

Caution: Some rice syrup is produced with the aid of a cereal enzyme that could potentially pose a problem for the gluten intolerant. Look for gluten-free brown rice syrup that uses a fungal enzyme, which produces a superior product safe for people with Celiac disease to consume.

Culinary Use: Brown rice syrup is about half as sweet as table sugar so it cannot be substituted directly. Brown rice syrup and honey may be interchanged in recipes.

Honey

Honey is almost as sweet as granulated white sugar. The difference between the two is that honey has small amounts of B vitamins, calcium, iron, zinc, potassium and phosphorous. And some vitamin A and vitamin C.

Actions/Uses: Antioxidant, antibacterial, antimicrobial, calms nerves, prevents diarrhea. It also acts as a potent killer of bacteria. Generally, honey's antioxidant value is higher in the darker colored types.

Forms Available: Liquid honey is a thick, viscous liquid form of honey that is extracted from the combs by a centrifugal method. It is easy to use in cooking and is the most widely used form of honey.

Granulated or "sugared" honey is partly or wholly solidified honey crystals. This form of honey is solid and melts easily in hot liquids or sauces.

Creamed honey is finely crystallized honey that is mixed with liquid honey to give it a thick, smooth texture.

Comb honey is the only unprocessed honey and is actually a section of the bee comb along with the honey stored by the bees in the sections.

Chunk honey is small pieces of comb honey that is placed into containers and covered with liquid honey.

Caution: The National Honey Board, along with other health organizations, recommends that honey not be fed to infants less than one year of age because most unpasteurized honey contains yeasts from nectar and pollen that may ferment.

Culinary Use: Use honey as a sweetener for both savory and sweet dishes. Honey is added to hot toddies and cold remedies because it soothes sore throats.

Malt Syrup

When barley or other grains are malted, a natural sugar is extracted in the process. The ground, malted grains are heated with water and reduced to syrup. B vitamins and iron are present in malt syrups.

Caution: All malt syrup is produced from grains that could potentially pose a problem for people that are gluten intolerant.

Culinary Use: Barley malt syrup may replace honey or maple syrup in recipes. It sweetens baked products, desserts and drinks.

Maple Syrup

Acer

The clear sap from sugar maples (*Acer saccharum*), red maples (*Acer rubrum*) and silver maples (*Acer saccharinum*) is collected in the spring when it is flowing from the roots into the aerial parts of the tree to provide energy for growth. The sap is 95 to 97% water but when it is boiled down, thick sweet syrup, composed of 65% sucrose, is left behind. The syrup also contains organic acids, minerals (mainly potassium and calcium), and traces of amino compounds and vitamins. One-quarter cup (50 mL) maple syrup provides 6% of the recommended daily intake of calcium and thiamin and 2% of magnesium and riboflavin.

Caution: Avoid maple-flavored syrup because it is primarily corn syrup with artificial flavor.

Culinary Use: Stir 1 to 2 tbsp (15 to 25 mL) pure maple syrup into 1 to 2 cups (250 to 500 mL) of the liquid in sauces, soups, custards or other desserts when a sweetener is required. Fresh maple sap — a thin, watery, clear liquid — may be used as a liquid in soups, stock, syrups, puddings, custards and other desserts, when available in spring.

Organic Cane Syrup Crystals

Cane syrup crystals are produced from the first crystallization of juice pressed from the sugar cane stalk. They are about half as processed as white sugar and contain slightly more molasses and some of the nutrients found in molasses.

Caution: Cane syrup crystals are as high in simple carbohydrates as white or brown sugars.

Culinary Use: Cane syrup crystals lend a mild cane flavor, full sweetness and pale golden color in a fine granulated or powdered form. They may be substituted for white or brown sugar in any recipe.

White Sugar Equivalents

For 1 cup (250 mL) white granulated sugar, substitute any of the following:

- 1⅓ cups (325) unsulphured molasses, minus ⅓ cup (75 mL) liquid specified in recipe, minus baking powder in the recipe, and plus ¾ tsp (4 mL) baking soda
- 1¼ cups (300 mL) honey or rice syrup, minus 2⅔ tbsp (35 mL) liquid in the recipe, plus a pinch of baking soda
- 1¼ cups (300 mL) honey or rice syrup, plus 2⅔ tbsp (35 mL) flour (if no liquid in recipe) plus ½ tsp (2 mL) baking soda

Vinegar

Apple Cider Vinegar

Juice extracted from certified organic apples that is naturally fermented (without heat or the addition of clarifiers, enzymes or preservatives) yields natural vinegar that contains some pectin, trace minerals and beneficial bacteria and enzymes. Organic, natural cider vinegar is usually only available in whole and natural food stores.

Culinary Use: Apple cider vinegar is more robust than the common, non-food distilled white vinegar and should be used in small amounts. It is used in dressings, sauces, soups and other savory or sweet-sour dishes.

Balsamic Vinegar

Called *aceto balsamico* in Italy where it originated in Modena, the production of balsamic vinegar dates back to the Middle Ages. Balsamic vinegar is produced by fermenting and aging white grape juice in wood casks similar to those used in wine making. The longer the grape must ages, the more complex the flavor, texture and sweetness of the resulting vinegar. Balsamic vinegar is priced according to the quality, which is a direct result of the aging process. Labels with the words *tradizionale* and *condimento* indicate vinegars that are made following the ancient methods.

Caution: Some less expensive brands are simply wine vinegar with coloring and sugar added.

Culinary Use: Young balsamic vinegars (3 to 5 years) are used in salad dressing, soups, and sauces and baked dishes. Mid-aged balsamic vinegars (6 to 12 years) enhance sauces, pastas and risottos. Use expensive, long-aged (15 years or older) rich and thick balsamic vinegars in small amounts in simple dishes where the complex aroma, taste and texture will be detected. Good quality, aged balsamic vinegars complement fresh fruit such as strawberries and melon, are brilliant in custards, crème caramel and zabaglione and are sometimes served as a digestive at the end of a meal.

Rice Vinegar

Fermented rice or rice wine is used in China and Japan to produce mild, sweet vinegar that is mellow and light in color. Chinese rice vinegars are slightly darker and stronger than Japanese rice vinegars. Black rice vinegar originated in the eastern Jiangsu province of China and is made with glutinous rice. Black rice vinegar is earthy and smoky in flavor.

Caution: Some inexpensive rice vinegar has salt and sugar added.

Culinary Use: Use rice vinegar in stir-fries, baked vegetable dishes, sweet-and-sour dishes, soups and stews.

Wine Vinegar

Adding some of the vinegar "mother" from organic apple cider vinegar to red or white wine helps the wine to ferment and produce natural wine vinegar. Natural wine vinegars contain a smaller amount of acetic acid than non-food white vinegar, along with smaller amounts of tartaric and citric acids.

Culinary Use: Use wine vinegar in marinades, salad dressings and where a milder taste is preferred for soups, stir-fries, baked vegetable dishes, sweet-and-sour dishes and sauces.

The Vegetarian Diet

The recipes in this book are designed to allow you to follow a sensible, plant-based diet. By using fresh, locally grown, preferably organic fruit, vegetables, legumes, whole grains, nuts, seeds, sea vegetables, soy foods, herbs and whole food ingredients wherever possible, a healthy balance is achieved.

To really take advantage of the benefits of vegetarian practice, knowing when local produce is at its peak and using common sense are essential. Eating produce that is grown outside of our province or state is neither economical, nor is it ecologically sound. Because the seasons each bring a wide range of local plant foods at different times around the globe, individuals must choose those recipes that best reflect what the local market has to offer. For people living in the northern hemisphere, it makes more sense in winter to maximize fresh root vegetables, pairing them occasionally with canned, organic fruits and vegetables packed in their own juices than to reach for genetically modified produce that was picked green, may be subjected to gas for preserving and has been in transit for days.

As we reduce meat and fat and fill up our plates with plant foods, we will come to rely more and more on herbs and whole food condiments. Fat as an ingredient is full of flavor and what food professionals call "mouth feel." Cutting the fat in recipes can result in a bland imitation of the foods most people love. The food industry has met this challenge with a variety of artificial flavors, gums and other non-food additives. Home cooks, on the other hand, have natural, life-supporting ingredients to fill the flavor gap — namely, low-fat yogurt, fresh lemon, miso, tahini, and garlic, ginger and other herbs.

Classic vegetarian dishes have evolved in almost every culture, and those dishes instinctively combine incomplete vegetable proteins. When grains and legumes or dairy products and grains or nuts and legumes are eaten together, the result is complete protein that can be used by the body to build and repair tissue. Many recipes in this book incorporate that basic principle of pairing incomplete plant proteins to satisfy the body's fundamental need for complete protein.

Calcium, vitamin D, iron and vitamin B_{12} are nutrients easily available in animal foods but are not readily available in a strict vegetarian regime and need to be considered. As might be expected, regular, weight-bearing exercise, such as walking, dancing and jogging, keeps bone tissue vibrant, and if calcium-rich foods, such as sea vegetables, quinoa, dark leafy greens, tofu and almonds, are a regular part of the diet, calcium should not be an issue. Eating a wide variety of colorful fresh fruits and vegetables, whole grains, legumes, nuts, seeds and herbs should account for our need for most essential nutrients, but as always, checking with a nutritionist or health care professional is advised when making significant changes to the diet.

One happy result of eating whole foods is that dietary fiber — that delicious snap, crunch and chewy texture that comes only from fresh plant foods — will reappear in our daily meals to help absorb toxins, keep us eliminating regularly and, most importantly, help protect against colon cancer and other diet-related diseases.

There are few frozen (with the exceptions of whole ingredients), bottled, processed, boxed or bagged shortcuts to good health. At the same time, preparing fresh, dynamic, organic food every day can be a challenge. That is why wherever possible, and without sacrificing great taste and appeal, the recipes herein are simple and full of flavor because the extent to which we meet that challenge will determine how vibrant and healthy we are.

Whether you choose to forgo animal food completely or simply begin to reduce them, the best advice for a healthy diet is simple. Eat more fruit. Eat more vegetables. Eat more legumes, whole grains, nuts, seeds, sea vegetables and herbs. Eat less meat, animal fats and dairy products.

Appetizers, Dips and Spreads

Use any large, fleshy mushroom, such as portobello for these tasty bites.

Almond and Herb-Stuffed Mushrooms

- *Preheat oven to 375°F (190°C)*
- *Baking sheet, lightly oiled*

| 16 | large mushrooms | 16 |
| 1 cup | Almond-Herb Filling (see recipe, below) | 250 mL |

1. Remove, trim and finely chop mushroom stems. Set aside. Arrange mushroom caps, hollow side up, on prepared baking sheet.

2. In a small bowl, combine Almond-Herb Filling with reserved mushroom stems. Spoon about 2 tbsp (25 mL) of the filling into mushroom caps. Bake in preheated oven for 12 to 15 minutes or until filling is bubbly.

Variation

- Substitute Almond-Herb Filling with 1 cup (250 mL) of any of the following: Artichokes in Italian Dressing (see recipe, page 141), Olive Tapenade (see recipe, page148), Creamy Red Pepper Spread (see recipe, page 149), Salsa (see recipes, page 303).

Makes 1 cup (250 mL)

This almond and herb filling is one of several that can be used to stuff mushrooms and other vegetables, such as zucchini, bell peppers, tomatoes, potatoes and eggplant.

Vegan Version

- Substitute soy cheese for Parmesan cheese.

Almond-Herb Filling

¾ cup	Basic or Tangy Almond Spread (see recipes, page 151)	175 mL
¼ cup	chopped almonds or Brazil nuts	50 mL
¼ cup	chopped fresh parsley	50 mL
3 tbsp	freshly grated Parmesan cheese	45 mL
2 tbsp	chopped fresh rosemary	25 mL
½ tsp	salt	2 mL

1. In a small bowl, combine Almond Spread, almonds, parsley, cheese, rosemary and salt. Stir well.

Variation

- Omit the Almond Spread. In a blender or food processor, blend1 to 2 tbsp (15 to 25 mL) olive oil with chopped almonds, parsley, Parmesan, rosemary and salt, until well mixed. Continue with Step 2. This variation makes about ¼ cup (50 mL).

Sweet Potato Crisps

Vegan Friendly

Make these when children want french fries or potato chips — they will love the sweet taste and the lower-fat content delivers a healthy alternative.

Tip
- Herbs that work well here are rosemary, oregano, sage, marjoram, savory or thyme

- *Preheat oven to 375°F (190°C)*
- *2 baking sheets, lightly oiled*

2	large sweet potatoes	2
3 tbsp	olive oil	45 mL
2 tbsp	finely chopped garlic or fresh herb (see Tip, left)	25 mL
½ tsp	salt	2 mL
	Freshly ground pepper	
½ cup	Basic or Tangy Almond Spread (see recipes, page 151), optional	125 mL

1. Peel potatoes and slice diagonally into elongated rounds, keeping the slices as thin as possible, about ⅛ inch (0.25 cm).

2. In a large bowl, toss potato slices with oil and garlic. Spread potato slices in a single layer on prepared baking sheets. Bake in preheated oven for 10 to 12 minutes or until light brown on the bottom.

3. Remove baking sheets from oven. Flip slices and return to oven and bake potatoes for another 7 to 12 minutes or until lightly brown and crisp. (Some crisps may cook faster than others. Remove from oven as soon as they are done.)

4. Season with salt and pepper. Let cool on wire racks. Serve slightly warm or at room temperature with Almond Spread, if using.

Baked Vegetable Falafel

Make small falafel "cookies" to use as a canapé base for spreads or salsas. If you make large falafels, they are perfect for filling wraps or pita pockets.

Tip

- In Step 3, drop by the tablespoon (15 mL) for smaller, canapé-size falafel "cookies" and reduce baking time to 12 to 17 minutes.

Serving Suggestion

- Serve large falafels over shredded lettuce with Salsa recipes (page 303) or Harissa (page 145). If using as a base for various toppings (see Spread recipes, page 303), transfer to a serving platter and spoon topping over; garnish with chopped nuts or herbs.

- *Preheat oven to 400°F (200°C)*
- *2 baking sheets, lightly oiled*

1	can (19 oz/540 mL) chickpeas or fava beans, drained and rinsed, or 2 cups (500 mL) cooked chickpeas or fava beans	1
2 tbsp	freshly squeezed lemon juice	25 mL
1 tbsp	Ras el Hanout seasoning (see recipe, page 334)	15 mL
2 tbsp	olive oil	25 mL
1	large egg, beaten	1
2 cups	coarsely grated zucchini or yellow summer squash	500 mL
1/4 cup	finely chopped green onions	50 mL
1/4 to 1/2 cup	toasted chickpea flour or brown rice flour	50 to 125 mL
3/4 tsp	baking powder	4 mL
1 cup	Yogurt Cheese (see recipe, page 145) or store-bought or homemade Tzatziki (see recipe, page 144), optional	250 mL

1. In a food processor, process chickpeas, lemon juice, Ras el Hanout and olive oil for 30 seconds or until smooth. Transfer to a bowl.

2. Stir egg into chickpea purée and mix well. Stir in zucchini and green onions. Sprinkle 1/4 cup (50 mL) of the flour and baking powder over mixture and stir to make a moist, thick batter. If too thin to hold together, add more flour by the tablespoon (15 mL) until the desired consistency is achieved.

3. Using a 1/4 cup (50 mL) measure, drop falafel mixture onto prepared baking sheets, about 1 inch (2.5 cm) apart, and flatten slightly with back of a spoon. Continue to form falafels until pans are full. Stagger pans on oven racks and bake in preheated oven for 15 to 20 minutes or until bottoms are lightly browned. Serve immediately, garnished with a dollop of Yogurt Cheese, if using.

Variations

- Replace Ras el Hanout with 1 tbsp (15 mL) store-bought or homemade Garam Masala Spice Blend (page 333) and 1 tsp (5 mL) salt.

- Substitute grated sweet potato, parsnip or carrot for zucchini.

Roasted Red Peppers

Vegan Friendly

Both sweet and hot red peppers peak around the end of the summer in the northern hemisphere and that's when farmers' markets are afire with the brilliant red tear-shaped fruit. Either may be roasted, but for the roasted pepper recipes in this book, it is the sweet variety that is used. Roasted peppers take time to make in quantity but with many hands the whole process becomes a social event — an autumn tradition.

Tips

- For Step 1, char peppers over barbecue flame instead of in the oven.

- To make large quantities, multiply the recipe ingredients by up to 10. Freeze in 2-cup (500 mL) quantities in freezer bags for up to 3 months.

- Preheat broiler, position oven rack on top rung
- Baking sheet

4	red bell peppers, halved and seeded	4
1/3 cup	olive oil	75 mL
3 tbsp	balsamic vinegar	45 mL
6	large basil leaves, chiffonade (see Tip, page 179)	6
4	cloves garlic, thinly sliced lengthwise	4

1. Place bell pepper halves cut side down on baking sheet. Broil in preheated oven on top rack directly under heat, turning pan often, for 5 to 8 minutes, until skin is evenly charred.

2. Meanwhile, in a bowl, whisk together oil, vinegar, basil and garlic. Set aside.

3. Remove blackened peppers from oven. Set baking sheet on a cooling rack and cover peppers with a clean towel. Let cool. Remove the charred skin from peppers. It should slip off easily when rubbed. Slice pepper halves into $1/2$-inch (1 cm) wide strips and place in bowl with oil mixture. Toss pepper slices to coat evenly. Cover dish tightly with plastic wrap and marinate for at least 2 hours at room temperature or for up to 3 days in the refrigerator.

Variation

- In place of basil leaves, in Step 2, add 3 tbsp (45 mL) store-bought or homemade Basil Pesto (see recipe, page 308).

Serving Suggestions

- As an appetizer, divide roasted peppers into 4 equal portions and spoon into 4 ovenproof dishes. Top each with a $1/2$ oz (15 g) slice of creamy goat's cheese. Bake in a 350°F (180°C) oven for 5 to 10 minutes or until cheese is melted and peppers are bubbly. Serve warm.

- As a pasta sauce, toss 2 cups (500 mL) roasted peppers with $1/2$ cup (125 mL) chopped fresh basil and 4 servings of cooked spaghetti.

Black Bean Quesadillas

These quesadillas are perfect for appetizers when cut into small wedges or use the larger size for a light lunch. Make double batches and freeze these tasty Mexican-inspired sandwiches to use as quick snacks or light main meals.

Vegan Version
- Substitute soy cheese for Swiss cheese.

½ cup	Olive Tapenade (see recipe, page 148) or store-bought	125 mL
1 cup	cooked or canned black beans	250 mL
1 tbsp	chopped fresh oregano leaves	15 mL
½ cup	tomato sauce, divided	125 mL
6	7-inch (18 cm) flour tortillas	6
1 cup	shredded Swiss or mozzarella cheese, divided	250 mL
1½ cups	Yogurt Cheese or Basic Almond Spread (see recipes, pages 145 and 151), optional	375 mL

1. In a food processor or blender, process tapenade, black beans and oregano just until mixed. Set aside.

2. Spread 1 tbsp (15 mL) of the tomato sauce over one half of each tortilla to within ½ inch (1 cm) of the edge. Spoon one-sixth of the bean filling over tomato sauce and sprinkle 2 tbsp (25 mL) of the cheese over the filling. Moisten tortilla edges with water. Fold tortilla in half over filling and press edges lightly to seal.

3. In a lightly oiled large skillet, cook quesadillas over medium heat, 2 or 3 at a time, for 3 to 5 minutes on each side, until lightly browned on each side. Cut each quesadilla into 3 triangles for appetizers, or serve whole for a light lunch. Serve warm, garnished with Yogurt Cheese or Almond Spread, if desired.

Variations
- Use cooked or canned black-eyed peas, fava or kidney beans in place of the black beans.
- Substitute Artichokes in Italian Dressing (see recipe, page 141) or other spreads (see pages 145 to 152) for Olive Tapenade.
- Use tomato salsa for tomato sauce.

Apple-Spinach Pâté

If possible, use a sweet onion variety such as Vidalia, Sweet Imperial, Walla Walla or Maui in this recipe. The sweet onions are milder and have higher water content, which help to keep this pâté rich and moist.

- *9-by 5-inch (2 L) loaf pan, lightly oiled*
- *13-by 9-inch (3 L) baking dish*

2 tbsp	olive oil	25 mL
2	apples, coarsely chopped	2
½ cup	chopped onion	125 mL
1 lb	fresh spinach, trimmed	500 g
1 ¼ cups	chopped walnuts	300 mL
¾ cup	fresh bread crumbs	175 mL
2 tbsp	freshly ground flaxseeds	25 mL
1 tbsp	chopped fresh tarragon or oregano leaves	15 mL
½ tsp	salt	2 mL
	Freshly ground pepper	
2	large eggs, lightly beaten	2

1. In a skillet, heat oil over medium heat. Stir in apples and onion. Sauté for about 10 minutes or until soft. Add spinach to skillet and stir. Cover, reduce heat to medium-low and cook for 2 to 4 minutes or until spinach is wilted. Drain off liquid. Transfer vegetables to a food processor or blender and process for 30 seconds or until smooth.

2. Meanwhile, in a large bowl, combine walnuts, bread crumbs, flaxseeds, tarragon, salt and pepper, to taste. Stir in apple-spinach purée and eggs. Stir well to combine. Spread pâté mixture in prepared loaf pan. Pat the top of the loaf with a spoon to compact it and cover with foil. Refrigerate a minimum of 1 hour or overnight. Bring to room temperature before baking.

3. Preheat oven to 350°F (180°C) and bring a kettle of water to boil. Set loaf pan in center of baking dish. Pour boiling water into the baking dish to within 1 inch (2.5 cm) of the top. Place baking dish with loaf pan in preheated oven and poach for 45 minutes or until pâté is firm.

4. Remove loaf pan from water bath and let cool on a wire rack. Refrigerate for 1 hour or overnight. Slice and serve cold or at room temperature.

Variation

- Use sunflower or pumpkin seeds in place of walnuts.

Serving Suggestion

- Serve this vegetable pâté on shredded greens, such as spinach, lettuce, cabbage, kale or Swiss chard. Drizzle Raspberry Coulis (see recipe, page 357) over top or serve on the side. Stuff slices of the pâté into pita pockets as a light meal.

The traditional way to make this Turkish delicacy is to bread and deep-fry stuffed eggplant "sandwiches" but I prefer to skip the last steps and serve this lighter version warm or at room temperature.

Cheese-Stuffed Eggplant Rolls

- *Preheat oven to 375°F (190°C)*
- *2 baking sheets, lightly oiled*

2	long thin eggplants, ends trimmed	2
3 tbsp	salt	45 mL
3 tbsp	olive oil (approx.)	45 mL
1½ cups	Cheese Filling (see recipe, right)	375 mL

1. Slice eggplants lengthwise ⅛-inch (0.25 cm) thick. Place one layer in a large colander and sprinkle slices with salt. Repeat until all eggplant slices have been salted. Leave to drain for 1 hour. Rinse and pat dry.

2. Place eggplant slices on prepared baking sheets in a single layer, working in batches as necessary. Brush lightly with oil. Bake in preheated oven for 7 to 10 minutes or until lightly browned. Remove from oven, flip slices over and bake for another 3 minutes to brown the other side. Using tongs, lift slices from pan and transfer to drain on paper towels. Repeat with remaining slices.

3. Place 1 tbsp (15 mL) of the Cheese Filling on one end of an eggplant slice and roll eggplant around it. Continue until all slices are rolled. Serve warm or cover and refrigerate overnight and reheat in a 350°F (180°C) oven for 10 minutes or until warmed through.

Variation

- Arrange stuffed eggplant rolls in a lightly greased 11-by 7-inch (2 L) baking dish. Cover with 2 cups (500 mL) tomato sauce. Bake in preheated 350°F (180°C) oven for 20 to 30 minutes or until sauce is bubbly and rolls are heated through. Serve warm with rice or couscous for a light meal.

Cheese Filling

1 cup	Yogurt Cheese (see recipe, page 145)	250 mL
4 oz	lower-fat cream cheese	125 g
2	cloves garlic, minced	2
1 tsp	Garam Masala Spice Blend (see recipe, page 333) or store-bought	5 mL
1	large egg, lightly beaten	1
2 tbsp	chopped fresh cilantro	25 mL

1. In a bowl, combine Yogurt Cheese, cream cheese, garlic, garam masala, egg and cilantro. Stir to mix well.

Teriyaki Tempeh with Peanut Sauce

Makes 30 appetizers

Vegan Friendly

Tempeh is usually sold frozen and there is no need to thaw before making this dish because it must marinate in the refrigerator for several hours or overnight before it is cooked.

- *10-inch (25 cm) pie plate or shallow dish*
- *8 cocktail skewers*

8 oz	frozen tempeh	250 g
¼ cup	tamari or soy sauce	50 mL
2 tbsp	freshly squeezed lemon juice	25 mL
1	clove garlic, minced	1
1 tbsp	grated fresh gingerroot	15 mL
1 tbsp	rice syrup or liquid honey	15 mL
1 tbsp	chopped fresh cilantro or Thai basil	15 mL
2 tsp	peanut oil	10 mL
1 cup	shredded iceberg lettuce, optional	250 mL
¾ cup	Cocktail Peanut Sauce (see recipe, page 326)	175 mL

1. Cut tempeh into ¾-inch (2 cm) cubes. In pie plate, combine tamari, lemon juice, garlic, ginger, rice syrup, cilantro and peanut oil. Stir to mix well. Add tempeh cubes. Cover tightly and marinate for several hours or overnight in the refrigerator. Stir several times while marinating. Bring to room temperature before broiling.

2. Move oven rack to highest position and preheat broiler. Broil tempeh in pie plate with marinade, stirring once, for 6 minutes. Let cool slightly. Using a slotted spoon, transfer tempeh cubes onto serving platter, lined with lettuce, if using. Skewer each cube and serve, passing Cocktail Peanut Sauce separately.

Open-Faced Samosas

Vegan Friendly

This healthy version of
a spicy Indian specialty
uses less pastry, omits
the deep-frying, and is
baked instead. Choose
regular-shaped, long
sweet potatoes.

- *Preheat oven to 375°F (190°C)*
- *2 muffin tins, lightly oiled*

Spicy Sweet Potato Filling

2	medium sweet potatoes (about 1½ lbs/750 g)	2
¼ cup	chopped fresh parsley	50 mL
1	carrot, shredded	1
2	green onions, finely chopped	2
1	clove garlic, finely chopped	1
2 tbsp	freshly squeezed lemon juice	25 mL
1 tbsp	Ras el Hanout seasoning (see recipe, page 334) or store-bought curry powder	15 mL
1 tsp	salt	5 mL
1 tsp	Garam Masala Spice Blend (see recipe, page 333) or store-bought	5 mL
1	dried chile pepper, crumbled, optional	1
1 tbsp	olive oil	15 mL

1. Scrub and cut potatoes into quarters. In a saucepan, cover potatoes with water. Bring to a boil over high heat. Cover and reduce heat and simmer for about 20 minutes or until tender. Drain off liquid in a colander (freeze for another use) and run cold water over potatoes to stop the cooking. Drain and let cool.

2. Meanwhile, in a bowl, combine parsley, carrot, green onions, garlic, lemon juice, Ras el Hanout, salt, garam masala, chile pepper and oil.

3. When potatoes are cool enough to handle, slip off the skins and discard. Cut each chunk into quarters and add to vegetables in the bowl. Mash roughly with a fork and combine all ingredients well. Use right away or make ahead and refrigerate for up to 3 days before using. Bring to room temperature before filling pastry.

Samosas

4	sheets phyllo pastry	4
2 to 3 tbsp	olive oil or melted butter	25 to 45 mL
2½ cups	Spicy Sweet Potato Filling (see recipe, left)	625 mL
¾ cup	Asian Dipping Sauce (see recipe, page 143), optional	175 mL

1. On a clean surface, stack 2 sheets of phyllo pastry, keep remaining sheets in plastic until ready to use. Lightly brush the top sheet with oil. Cut pastry into 12 4-inch (10 cm) squares. Line each cup of prepared muffin tin with a pastry square to form 12 pastry cups.

2. Spoon 2 tbsp (25 mL) of the Spicy Sweet Potato Filling into each pastry cup. Bake in preheated oven for 12 minutes, until pastry is golden. Let cool in pan on a wire rack. Repeat with remaining pastry and filling. Serve warm with Asian Dipping Sauce, if desired.

Variations

• Substitute whole wheat pie pastry or puff pastry for phyllo dough, or use 24 thin slices lightly oiled, whole-grain bread, crusts removed to line muffin wells.

• Add 1 cup (250 mL) cooked peas to the filling in Step 2.

Vegan Friendly

The smoky flavor of the chipotle chiles complements the rather bland artichoke. Use this dish as the filling for the stuffed mushrooms (see recipe, page 132) or Black Bean Quesadillas (see recipe, page 136). As an appetizer, serve over torn fresh spinach, mesclun, watercress or other fresh greens.

Artichokes in Italian Dressing

1	can (14 oz/389 mL) artichoke hearts (8 whole hearts), drained and rinsed	1
2	dried or canned chipotle chiles, thinly sliced	2
½ cup	Italian Dressing (see recipe, page 305)	125 mL
2 cups	torn mixed salad greens	500 mL

1. Cut artichoke hearts into quarters. In a bowl, combine artichokes and chile slices. Add dressing and toss to coat. Cover and refrigerate for 1 to 2 hours or overnight.

2. Bring artichokes to room temperature before serving. Divide greens evenly among 4 small salad plates. Spoon equal portions of artichoke mixture over greens. Serve immediately.

Variation

• Use hearts of palm in place of the artichoke hearts.

Sushi is not hard to prepare but there are several steps, and since the recipe serves 6, consider having all of the ingredients prepared ahead of time for guests to roll their own as part of the fun.

Tips

• Nori is a Japanese seaweed that can be purchased in the specialty section of supermarkets or in Asian food stores. Toast nori by holding over a gas flame or barbecue or electric element for a few seconds each side.

• Keep a bowl of vinegar water for dipping fingers and knife while making sushi rolls. For vinegar water, in a small bowl, combine 1 cup (250 mL) warm water and 1 tsp (5 mL) rice vinegar.

Vegetable Sushi with Wasabi Mayonnaise

2 cups	short-grain brown or white rice	500 mL
3 cups	water	750 mL
1/4 cup	rice vinegar	50 mL
2 tbsp	brown rice syrup	25 mL
2 tbsp	sake	25 mL
1	large zucchini	1
1	large carrot	1
1	large sweet potato	1
1	ripe avocado, cut into 1/4-inch (0.5 cm) sticks	1
	Juice of 1 lemon	
6	nori sheets, toasted (see Tips, left)	6
1 cup	Wasabi Mayonnaise (see recipe, page 306), divided	250 mL
1/4 cup	toasted sesame seeds, divided	50 mL

1. Rinse rice in a colander under cool water. In a saucepan, bring water to a boil over high heat. Stir in rice. Cover, reduce heat and simmer for 20 minutes for brown rice; 15 minutes for white, or until water is absorbed and rice is tender but not mushy. Transfer to a large bowl.

2. Meanwhile, in a small saucepan, heat vinegar and brown rice syrup over medium-high heat, until syrup dissolves. Remove from heat and stir in sake. Set aside to cool.

3. When rice is cooked, pour sweetened vinegar over rice. Gently stir with a fork making sure all grains are coated. Cover and let cool.

4. Bring a large saucepan filled to the halfway point with water to a boil. Meanwhile, cut zucchini, carrot and sweet potato into 1/4-inch (0.5 cm) slices. Drop sweet potato into boiling water and cook for 2 minutes. Add carrot and cook for 1 minute. Add zucchini and cook for 1 minute. Transfer slices from boiling water directly into a sink half-filled with cold water. Let cool completely in the cold water. Pat dry and cut slices into 1/4-inch (0.5 cm) sticks. Cover tightly and set aside in refrigerator, until ready to assemble sushi.

5. In a small bowl, combine avocado with lemon juice. Cover tightly and set aside in the refrigerator, until ready to assemble sushi.

To Assemble Sushi

1. Place a sheet of waxed paper or a sushi rolling mat on a work surface and center one sheet of nori, shiny side down and long side facing you, on top. Spread 1 cup (250 mL) of the rice on nori, leaving a 1-inch (2.5 cm) border along the top edge. Spread 1 tbsp (15 mL) of the Wasabi Mayonnaise over rice. Sprinkle with 2 tsp (10 mL) of the sesame seeds.

2. Lay 2 or 3 sticks of each vegetable in a horizontal line across center of rice, letting them stick out slightly at ends. Top with 2 sticks of avocado.

3. Moisten fingers in vinegar water (see Tips, left) and roll evenly and tightly away from you, using waxed paper to help lift and roll. Rub vinegar water on edge of nori and press seam by rolling back and forth.

4. Dip a sharp knife into the vinegar water and tip to coat the whole blade. Trim ends of the roll. Cut the roll in half and each half into 3 equal pieces. Repeat assembly procedure with remaining sheets of nori and filling. Serve immediately.

Variation

- Sake is a Japanese wine. Substitute a sweet white wine if sake is not available.

Asian Dipping Sauce

½ cup	tamari or soy sauce	125 mL
3 tbsp	freshly squeezed lemon juice	45 mL
1 tbsp	rice vinegar	15 mL
2 tbsp	finely chopped green onions	25 mL
1 tbsp	Asian chili sauce (see Tips, left)	15 mL
2 tsp	liquid honey	10 mL
1 tsp	sesame oil	5 mL

1. In a small bowl, whisk together tamari, lemon juice and vinegar. Stir in green onions, chili sauce, honey and sesame oil.

Variation

- Add 1 tbsp (15 mL) finely chopped fresh or candied ginger.

Use this healthy dip to accompany grilled vegetables, as a salad dressing, in place of mayonnaise in sandwich fillings and as a dip for fresh vegetables.

Tips

- Store tightly covered, in the refrigerator for up to 2 days.

- It is wise to peel non-organic vegetables because the peel is loaded with herbicides and washing will not eliminate them. Cucumbers are waxed in winter and they and other top-growing veggies are exposed to more chemicals than most root vegetables.

Tzatziki

1	English cucumber	1
1⅓ cups	Yogurt Cheese (see recipe, page 145)	325 mL
1	clove garlic, finely chopped	1
2 tbsp	chopped fresh mint (approx.)	25 mL
2 tsp	freshly squeezed lemon juice (approx.)	10 mL
¼ tsp	salt (approx.)	1 mL
	Freshly ground pepper	

1. Scrub cucumber (peel if not organic) and shred into a colander. Let stand in the sink or over a bowl for 30 minutes. Squeeze lightly to expel excess liquid.

2. In a bowl, combine cucumber, Yogurt Cheese, garlic, mint, lemon juice, salt and pepper, to taste. Stir to mix well. Taste and add more mint, lemon juice, salt or pepper as required.

Variation

- Use 1 cup (250 mL) chopped watercress in place of the cucumber.

Use this creamy dip on everything from baked potatoes to bagels and nachos.

Tip

- Store dip, tightly covered, in the refrigerator for up to 2 days.

Herbed Feta Dip

½	English cucumber	½
1⅓ cups	Yogurt Cheese (see recipe, page 145)	325 mL
1 cup	crumbled drained feta cheese	250 mL
2 cups	fresh spinach leaves, chopped	500 mL
¼ cup	chopped fresh chives or green onions	50 mL
2	cloves garlic, minced	2

1. Scrub cucumber (peel if not organic) and shred into a colander. Let stand in the sink or over a bowl for 30 minutes. Squeeze lightly to expel excess liquid.

2. In a bowl, combine cucumber, Yogurt Cheese, feta cheese, spinach, chives and garlic. Stir to mix well.

Variation

- Substitute a mix of other greens such as watercress, bok choy, Swiss chard, mesclun and up to ⅓ cup (75 mL) of green herbs for the spinach.

Sweet Potato Crisps with Basic Almond Spread (pages 133 and 151)

Apricot Granola Biscuits (page 161)

Mâche with Fruit, Nuts and Blue Cheese Dressing (page 182)

Roasted Squash and
Red Pepper Salad (page 193)

Chilled Fruited Gazpacho (page 206)

Sea Gumbo (page 218)

Asparagus Three-Cheese Burritos (page 229)

Stir-Fried Vegetables and Bulgur
with Ginger-Citrus Sauce (page 230)

Yogurt Cheese

2 cups	natural yogurt	500 mL

The longer the yogurt drains, the thicker the resulting "cheese" will be. This is a healthy, low-fat alternative for the mayonnaise and cream cheese in dips and spreads.

1. Spoon yogurt into a sieve lined with cheesecloth, cover with plastic wrap. Set over a bowl to drain. Refrigerate for 2 to 3 hours or until yogurt is thick and reduced to about 1⅓ cups (325 mL).

Tip

• Store cheese, tightly covered, in the refrigerator for up to 2 days.

Harissa

Vegan Friendly

Popular in North Africa, fiery harissa is used almost in the same way that North Americans use ketchup. It is offered as a dip for grilled vegetables and couscous, stirred into soups and stews or used as a hot sauce in other recipes.

12	dried red chile peppers (see Caution, left)	12
¾ cup	boiling water	175 mL
1 tbsp	whole coriander seeds	15 mL
2 tsp	whole cumin seeds	10 mL
1 tsp	whole fennel seeds	5 mL
½ tsp	whole fenugreek seeds, optional	2 mL
2	cloves garlic	2
½ tsp	salt	2 mL
½ cup	olive oil	125 mL

1. Trim stems off chiles and discard along with some of the seeds. Using kitchen scissors, cut chiles into small pieces. Place in a small bowl and pour boiling water over. Soak for about 30 minutes until soft. Drain.

2. Meanwhile, in a small dry heavy skillet, toast coriander, cumin, fennel and fenugreek seeds, if using, over medium heat for about 3 minutes or until fragrant and light brown. Remove from heat and let cool.

3. Using a mortar and pestle or small food processor, pound or process garlic with salt. Add toasted spices and drained chiles and pound or process until smooth. Add olive oil slowly and grind or process until sauce is well mixed. Harissa should be the consistency of mayonnaise.

Tip

• Store harissa in a small clean jar with lid in the refrigerator for up to 3 weeks.

Caution

• Use protective gloves when handling hot chiles. Wash hands and utensils thoroughly afterward.

Hummus

Use this easy yet sophisticated dip with pita wedges or a mix of chopped raw vegetables.

Tips

• Store hummus, tightly covered, in the refrigerator for up to 1 week.

• Keep a tin of chickpeas in the pantry and you have what it takes to boost the protein in salads and wraps.

1	can (19 oz/540 mL) chickpeas, drained and rinsed, or 2 cups (500 mL) cooked chickpeas	1
2	cloves garlic	2
2 tbsp	tahini paste (sesame seed paste)	25 mL
1/3 cup	olive oil	75 mL
1/3 cup	freshly squeezed lemon juice	75 mL
1/2 tsp	salt	2 mL
1/2 tsp	ground cumin	2 mL
1/4 cup	water	50 mL
1 to 2 tbsp	flavored olive oil, optional	15 to 25 mL

1. In a food processor or blender, process chickpeas and garlic for about 30 seconds until finely chopped. Stop and add tahini paste. With motor running, add olive oil and lemon juice through opening in the lid and process for about 15 seconds or until well mixed. Stop and scrape down the sides of the bowl. Add salt and cumin. With motor running, add water through opening in the lid and process for about 15 seconds or until smooth.

2. Scrape purée into a serving dish. Make a few wells in the top with the back of a spoon. Drizzle flavored oil, if using, over the top. Serve at room temperature.

Variations

• Add 1/4 cup (50 mL) chopped fresh parsley to the mixture in Step 1.

• Freshly ground cashews or peanuts without sugar and additives serve as a substitute for the tahini.

• Use cooked or canned cannellini beans in place of the chickpeas.

Black Bean and Roasted Garlic Spread

The roasted garlic lends a sweetly subtle garlic flavor to the robust beans.

Tip

- Store spread, tightly covered, in the refrigerator for up to 3 days.

- *Preheat oven to 375°F (190°C)*
- *8-inch (2 L) baking dish with lid or foil*

4	whole garlic heads	4
3 tbsp	olive oil, divided	45 mL
1	can (19 oz/540 mL) black beans, drained and rinsed, or 2 cups (500 mL) cooked black beans	1
1 tbsp	freshly squeezed lemon juice (approx.)	15 mL
2 tsp	balsamic vinegar (approx.)	10 mL
	Salt and freshly ground pepper	

1. Remove the loose, papery skin from the garlic heads and slice and discard ¼ inch (0.5 cm) off the tips of the cloves in the entire head, leaving the whole head intact. Place garlic heads cut side up in baking dish, drizzle each with 1½ tsp (7 mL) of the olive oil. Cover with a lid or foil and bake in preheated oven for 45 minutes, until garlic is quite soft. Transfer to a cooling rack.

2. When garlic is cool enough to handle, place black beans in bowl of food processor. Squeeze cloves from their skins into the food processor and process for about 30 seconds until smooth. With the motor running, add remaining 1 tbsp (15 mL) of the olive oil, lemon juice and vinegar and process for about 10 seconds or until combined. Taste and add salt and pepper, adjust lemon juice and vinegar as required.

Variation

- Use canned or cooked cannellini beans or black-eyed peas in place of the chickpeas.

Serving Suggestion

- Use this easy-to-prepare spread on crackers or crudités for canapés. Stuff into wraps or pita pockets or spread on toasted whole wheat bread slices and combine with a salad for a light meal.

Olive Tapenade

I	large clove garlic	I
2 tbsp	pine nuts or sunflower seeds	25 mL
2 cups	pitted black or green olives	500 mL
	(about 65 medium or I 14 oz/398 mL can)	
I tbsp	fresh thyme leaves	15 mL
I tbsp	chopped fresh oregano or parsley	15 mL
I tsp	capers	5 mL
¼ cup	olive oil	50 mL

1. In a food processor or blender, process garlic and nuts for about 30 seconds or until finely chopped. Add olives, thyme, oregano and capers. Pulse 2 to 3 times to chop. With motor running, add olive oil through opening in lid. Process just until oil is mixed in well. Spoon mixture into a small serving dish.

Guacamole

I	large ripe avocado	I
I tbsp	freshly squeezed lemon juice (approx.)	15 mL
3 tbsp	drained natural yogurt or Yogurt Cheese	45 mL
	(see recipe, page 145)	
I	clove garlic, minced	I
2	green onions, finely chopped	2
	Salt and freshly ground pepper	
	Tortilla chips, optional	

1. Slit avocado lengthwise from stem end around base and back to stem. Twist the two halves apart. Remove pit from one half and skin from both halves. Coarsely chop flesh into a bowl. Using a fork, mash lemon juice into avocado.

2. Stir in yogurt, garlic and green onions. Taste and add more lemon, and salt and pepper as required. Spoon into a small bowl and serve with tortilla chips, if using.

Variation

• Add a tomato, skinned, seeded and chopped, in Step 2.

Vegan Friendly

I love the striking color
of this spread. It is very
dramatic when used in
appetizers.

Tip

- Store spread, tightly
  covered, in the
  refrigerator for up
  to 3 days.

Creamy Red Pepper Spread

2	red bell peppers, seeded and thinly sliced	2
1	clove garlic, minced	1
1 tbsp	olive oil	15 mL
11 oz	firm tofu, drained	350 g
1 tbsp	tahini paste	15 mL
2 tbsp	freshly squeezed lemon juice	25 mL
2 tbsp	Basic Almond Spread (see recipe, page 151)	25 mL
1 tbsp	maple syrup or liquid honey	15 mL

1. In a large skillet, combine bell peppers, garlic and oil. Sauté over medium heat for 7 minutes or until tender. Transfer to a bowl and let cool.

2. In a food processor or blender, combine pepper mixture, tofu, tahini, lemon juice, Almond Spread and maple syrup. Process for about 30 seconds or until smooth. Transfer to a bowl or serving dish.

Two ounces (60 g)
taken daily provides a
therapeutic dose of the
amino acids alanine,
glycine and glutamic
acid (thought to reduce
the symptoms of
prostate enlargement).

Tips

- Store spread, covered
  tightly, in the
  refrigerator for up
  to 5 days.

- Use organic
  ingredients to reduce
  strain on the body
  while it uses the
  active components
  to repair itself.

Pumpkin Seed Spread

1 cup	hulled pumpkin seeds (see Tips, left)	250 mL
1/2 cup	sesame seeds	125 mL
1/4 cup	organic almonds	50 mL
3 tbsp	liquid honey	45 mL
2 tbsp	flaxseeds	25 mL
3 tbsp	cold-pressed hemp oil or walnut oil (approx.)	45 mL

1. In a blender, combine pumpkin seeds, sesame seeds, almonds, honey and flaxseeds. Process for 30 seconds or until blended. With motor running, add oil through the opening in the lid using just enough oil to achieve a smooth consistency.

Serving Suggestion

- Spread on whole-grain toast or serve as a dip with fruit or vegetables.

Herbed Vegetable Spread

- *Ramekins or custard cups*

Vegetable or fruit spreads offer a lower-fat alternative to butter or mayonnaise. Fresh herbs are the key to the great flavor.

Vegan Version
- Use 1 tbsp (15 mL) olive oil in place of the butter.

Tips
- Use chives, thyme, oregano, basil, sage or savory in this spread.
- Store spread, tightly covered, in the refrigerator for up to 2 weeks.

1 lb	parsnips or carrots, cut into chunks	500 g
1	can (19 oz/540 mL) chickpeas, drained and rinsed, or 2 cups (500 mL) cooked chickpeas	1
2 tbsp	butter	25 mL
1 tbsp	chopped fresh herb (see Tips, left)	15 mL
1 tbsp	liquid honey	15 mL

1. In a pot, cover parsnips with water. Bring to a boil over high heat. Cover, reduce heat and simmer for 10 minutes or until soft. Drain and let cool.

2. In a food processor or blender, process parsnips, chickpeas, butter, herb and honey for about 30 seconds or until smooth. Pack into custard cups or ramekins and cover with plastic wrap.

Variation
- Use cooked or canned cannellini beans in place of the chickpeas.

Fruit Spread

- *Ramekins or custard cups*

Use this sweeter spread on toast or with hot cereals in place of jam.

Vegan Version
- See above.

Tip
- Store spread, tightly covered, in the refrigerator for up to 2 weeks.

Variation
- In place of the apples, use peaches, nectarines or plums or 1 cup (250 mL) berries.

4	large apples, peeled and quartered	4
1/2 cup	dried apricots, coarsely chopped	125 mL
1	can (19 oz/540 mL) chickpeas, drained and rinsed, or 2 cups (500 mL) cooked chickpeas	1
2 tbsp	butter	25 mL
1/4 tsp	ground cinnamon	1 mL
1 tbsp	liquid honey	15 mL

1. In a pot, cover apples and apricots with water. Bring to a boil over high heat. Cover, reduce heat and simmer for 10 minutes or until fruit is soft. Drain and let cool.

2. In a food processor or blender, process apples, apricots, chickpeas, butter, cinnamon and honey for about 30 seconds or until smooth. Pack into custard cups or ramekins and cover with plastic wrap.

Basic Almond Spread

This recipe is so
versatile and healthy.
When savory herbs and
garlic are used it
replaces commercial
spreads and dips and
sauces and yet if berries
and soft fruits are
added, it becomes a
sweet topping or light
pudding with all sorts of
applications for healthy
desserts. My refrigerator
is never without this
mixture and I have
come to rely on it for
wraps, as an emulsifier
of ingredients in
sandwich fillings, salads
and sauces, to finish
canapés and as a
substitute for
mayonnaise.

1 cup	whole almonds (unblanched)	250 mL
2 cups	water, divided	500 mL
2 tbsp	olive oil	25 mL
2 tbsp	freshly squeezed lemon juice (approx.)	25 mL
2	cloves garlic	2
½ tsp	salt, optional	2 mL

1. In a small bowl, mix almonds with 1 cup (250 mL) of the
water. Cover and let stand in the refrigerator for at least
6 hours or overnight.

2. Drain and rinse almonds well. Place remaining 1 cup
(250 mL) of the water in a blender. Add almonds, olive
oil, lemon juice, garlic and salt, if using, and process for
30 seconds or until mixture is smooth and creamy. Taste
and add more salt or lemon juice, if required. Use right
away or store, tightly covered in the refrigerator for up
to 5 days.

Variation

• In Step 2 after processing, fold in ¼ cup (50 mL) chopped
toasted almonds.

Tangy Almond Spread

Vegan Friendly

Tip

• Store spread, tightly
covered, in the
refrigerator for up
to 5 days.

1 cup	whole almonds (unblanched)	250 mL
2 cups	water, divided	500 mL
2 tbsp	olive oil	25 mL
1 tbsp	apple cider vinegar (approx.)	15 mL
2	cloves garlic	2
2 tsp	Dijon mustard	10 mL
¼ tsp	salt, optional	1 mL

1. In a small bowl, mix almonds with 1 cup (250 mL) of the
water. Cover and let stand in the refrigerator for at least
6 hours or overnight.

2. Drain and rinse almonds well. Place remaining 1 cup
(250 mL) of the water in a blender. Add almonds, olive oil,
vinegar, garlic, mustard and salt, if using, and process for
30 seconds or until mixture is smooth and creamy. Taste
and add more salt or vinegar.

Spicy Almond Spread

1 cup	whole almonds (unblanched)	250 mL
2 cups	water, divided	500 mL
2 tbsp	olive oil	25 mL
1 tbsp	white wine vinegar	15 mL
1 tbsp	freshly squeezed lemon juice (approx.)	15 mL
1 tbsp	Ras el Hanout seasoning or Garam Masala Spice Blend (see recipes pages 334 and 333) or store-bought	15 mL
1	dried chile pepper, crushed	1

1. In a small bowl, mix almonds with 1 cup (250 mL) of the water. Cover and let stand in the refrigerator for at least 6 hours or overnight.

2. Drain and rinse almonds well. Place remaining 1 cup (250 mL) of the water in a blender. Add almonds, olive oil, vinegar, lemon juice, Ras el Hanout and chile pepper and process for 30 seconds or until mixture is smooth and creamy. Taste and add more lemon juice, if required.

Sweet Almond Spread

1 cup	whole almonds (unblanched)	250 mL
1 1/3 cups	water, divided	325 mL
1/2 cup	fresh berries or soft fruit (see Tips, left)	125 mL
2 tbsp	freshly squeezed lemon juice (approx.)	25 mL
2 tbsp	liquid honey (approx.)	25 mL
1 tbsp	olive oil	15 mL

1. In a small bowl, mix almonds with 1 cup (250 mL) of the water. Cover and let stand in the refrigerator for at least 6 hours or overnight.

2. Drain and rinse almonds well. Place remaining 1/3 cup (75 mL) of the water in a blender. Add almonds, fruit, lemon juice, honey and oil and process for 30 seconds or until mixture is smooth and creamy. Taste and add more lemon juice or honey, if required.

Breakfast and Brunch Dishes

Potato and Leek Tart

Vegan Friendly

This tart is a versatile and all-season dish for breakfast, lunch or dinner.

- *Preheat oven to 375°F (190°C)*
- *10-inch (3 L) springform pan or round tart pan, lightly oiled*

Potato Base

3 cups	thinly sliced potatoes	750 mL
1 cup	thinly sliced peeled sweet potato	250 mL
3 tbsp	honey mustard	45 mL
2 tbsp	olive oil	25 mL
½ tsp	salt	2 mL
	Freshly ground pepper	

Topping

¼ cup	sliced leek, white and light green parts	50 mL
4	cloves garlic, slivered	4
3 cups	thinly sliced onions (about 3 onions)	750 mL
2 tbsp	olive oil	25 mL
3 tbsp	chopped fresh basil	45 mL
¼ cup	freshly grated Parmesan cheese	50 mL

1. Potato Base: In a large bowl, toss potatoes with mustard and oil. Spread in bottom of prepared pan. Press potatoes with the back of a spoon to compress. Sprinkle salt and pepper, to taste, over top.

2. Topping: Distribute leek and garlic evenly over potato base. Scatter onions over top. Drizzle with oil. Bake in preheated oven for 40 minutes or until potatoes are tender and onions are golden. Sprinkle basil and Parmesan over top and bake for another 3 minutes or until cheese is lightly browned. Transfer to a wire cooling rack and let stand for 10 minutes before serving.

Serving Suggestion
- Serve it with grilled or sliced fresh tomatoes in summer and Warm Root Vegetable Salad (see recipe, page 198) in the winter.

Vegetable Frittata

This makes a great company brunch dish because it can be made the night before and refrigerated.

- *Preheat oven to 375°F (190°C)*
- *9-inch (2.5 L) square baking dish, lightly oiled*

2 cups	trimmed fresh spinach	500 mL
2 tbsp	olive oil	25 mL
1/2 cup	chopped onion	125 mL
2/3 cup	sliced leek, white and tender green parts	150 mL
1/2 cup	chopped red bell pepper	125 mL
1/2 cup	shredded carrot	125 mL
6	large eggs	6
1/3 cup	rice or soy milk	75 mL
1/4 cup	shredded Swiss cheese	50 mL
1/4 cup	shredded Cheddar cheese	50 mL
1 tbsp	chopped fresh basil	15 mL
2 tsp	chopped fresh sage	10 mL
2 tsp	fresh thyme leaves	10 mL
1/2 tsp	salt	2 mL
	Freshly ground pepper	

1. Wash spinach, drain and transfer wet leaves to a saucepan. Cover and cook on medium-high heat for about 2 minutes or until spinach is wilted. Remove from heat, drain and cool. Squeeze out excess moisture and coarsely chop.

2. Meanwhile, in a large skillet, heat oil over medium heat. Add onion, leek, bell pepper and carrot. Cook, stirring, for 7 minutes or until soft. Stir in spinach and distribute it evenly. Set aside and let cool.

3. In a large bowl, beat together eggs and milk. Add Swiss cheese, Cheddar cheese, vegetable mixture, basil, sage, thyme, salt and pepper. Pour into prepared baking dish. Mixture may be prepared to this point and refrigerated several hours or overnight. Return to room temperature before baking.

4. Bake in preheated oven for 25 to 30 minutes or until lightly browned and set. Let cool for 10 minutes before cutting. Serve warm or at room temperature.

Variation

- Reduce eggs to 4, increase milk to 1/2 cup (125 mL) and add 1 cup (250 mL) stale bread cubes in Step 3.

Use any cooked vegetable in this recipe — chopped cauliflower, carrots, squash, onions or peas in any combination will work.

Tip

• Crêpes may be made up to 2 days in advance. For storage, stack with a square of waxed paper between each crêpe. Place in a large freezer bag and refrigerate for up to 3 days or freeze for up to 3 months. Return to room temperature before using in recipes.

Cheesy Broccoli Crêpes

• *Preheat oven to 350°F (180°C)*
• *7-inch (18 cm) crêpe pan or heavy skillet*
• *11-by 7-inch (2 L) baking dish, lightly oiled*

Crêpes

¾ cup	unbleached all-purpose flour	175 mL
1 tbsp	organic cane sugar	15 mL
1½ cups	rice or soy milk	375 mL
2	large eggs, lightly beaten	2
2 tbsp	olive oil (approx.), divided	25 mL

Broccoli Filling

2 tbsp	butter	25 mL
2	green onions, finely chopped	2
3 tbsp	whole wheat flour	45 mL
1½ cups	rice or soy milk	375 mL
⅓ cup	shredded Cheddar cheese	75 mL
¼ tsp	ground nutmeg	1 mL
3 cups	cooked broccoli florets	750 mL
	Salt and freshly ground pepper	
¼ cup	freshly grated Parmesan cheese	50 mL

1. Crêpes: In a large bowl, combine flour and sugar. In a small bowl or 2-cup (500 mL) measuring cup, combine milk, eggs and 1 tbsp (15 mL) of the olive oil and beat with a fork. Make a well in the center of the flour mixture and gradually whisk in the milk-egg mixture (batter will be thin). Cover with plastic wrap and let stand for 30 minutes.

2. Lightly oil crêpe pan. Place crêpe pan over medium-high heat. Pour 2 to 3 tbsp (25 to 45 mL) of the batter into hot pan and tip pan to coat the surface evenly. Cook crêpe for about 1 minute or until brown underneath. Turn crêpe and cook for about 45 seconds or until lightly browned on the other side. Repeat with remaining batter to make 7 more crêpes, adding more oil as needed. Layer crêpes between waxed paper. Set aside.

3. Broccoli Filling: In a saucepan, melt butter over medium-low heat. Add green onions and cook, stirring, for 1 minute. Stir in flour until a smooth paste is achieved. Using a wire whisk, gradually whisk in milk. Reduce heat and gently simmer sauce, stirring constantly, for 2 minutes or until thick. Stir in Cheddar cheese, nutmeg and broccoli. Cook for 2 minutes or until cheese is melted into the sauce. Add salt and pepper, to taste.

4. To assemble crêpes: Spoon $\frac{1}{4}$ cup (50 mL) of the filling on a crêpe. Fold crêpe in half over filling and in half again to form a triangle. Place in prepared dish. Repeat with remaining filling and crêpes, overlapping as necessary. Sprinkle with Parmesan. Bake in preheated oven for 10 minutes or until heated through. Serve immediately.

Variation
- Replace Broccoli Filling with Spinach-Ricotta Filling (see recipe, below).

Makes 3 cups (750 mL)

Tip
- Store filling, tightly covered, in the refrigerator for up to 3 days.

Spinach-Ricotta Filling

3	cloves garlic	3
$\frac{1}{4}$ cup	toasted sunflower seeds	50 mL
$1\frac{1}{2}$ cups	ricotta cheese	375 mL
$1\frac{1}{2}$ cups	packed fresh basil leaves	375 mL
$\frac{1}{2}$ cup	fresh parsley, stems trimmed	125 mL
2 cups	packed and trimmed spinach leaves	500 mL
$\frac{1}{4}$ cup	freshly grated Parmesan cheese	50 mL

1. In a food processor or blender, combine garlic and sunflower seeds. Process for 30 seconds or until finely chopped. Add ricotta, basil and parsley. Process for 30 seconds or until greens are incorporated. Add spinach and Parmesan. Process for about 1 minute or until well blended.

Make these soufflés just before serving because they will not stay puffed for long.

Greek Soufflés

- *Preheat oven to 350°F (180°C)*
- *4 1-cup (250 mL) ramekins, lightly oiled*
- *Baking sheet*

1½ cups	grated zucchini	375 mL
3 tbsp	butter	45 mL
¼ cup	unbleached all-purpose flour	50 mL
1 cup	rice or soy milk	250 mL
4	large eggs, separated, yolks beaten	4
1	can (14 oz/398 mL) artichoke hearts, drained and chopped	1
4 oz	feta cheese, drained and crumbled	125 g
½ cup	Olive Tapenade (see recipe, page 148) or store-bought, optional	125 mL

1. In a colander, set zucchini aside to drain in the sink or over a bowl until ready to use.

2. In a saucepan, melt butter over medium heat. Stir in flour. Cook, stirring, for 3 minutes or until a smooth paste is achieved. Using a wire whisk, gradually whisk in milk. Reduce heat and gently simmer sauce, stirring constantly, for 2 minutes or until thick. Pour sauce into a large bowl and let cool slightly.

3. Meanwhile, in a bowl, beat egg whites until soft peaks form.

4. Stir zucchini, artichokes and feta cheese into white sauce. Gradually stir in egg yolks. Fold egg whites into zucchini mixture in 2 batches.

5. Gently spoon mixture into prepared ramekins. Place ramekins on baking sheet. Bake in preheated oven for about 25 minutes or until puffed and golden brown. Serve immediately with Olive Tapenade, if using.

Vegan Friendly

Serve this pâté on whole-grain toast with a salad as a light lunch or on seasonal greens as an appetizer.

Tips

- Dulse is a sea vegetable that is harvested off the east coast of Canada. It is widely available in health/alternative stores and some supermarkets.

- Store pâté, tightly covered, in the refrigerator for up to 3 days.

Non-Vegan Version

- Beat an egg into the pâté in Step 3. Pack into a lightly oiled 9-by 5-inch (2 L) loaf pan and bake in a 350°F (180°C) oven for 40 minutes. Let cool and serve at room temperature or chill before serving.

Country Vegetable Pâté

- *Preheat oven to 400°F (200°C)*
- *Baking sheet, lightly oiled*

15	small shiitake mushrooms	15
6	cloves garlic	6
1	onion, quartered	1
1	leek, white and light green parts, cut into large chunks	1
1	zucchini, cut into large chunks	1
1	eggplant, cut into large chunks	1
2 tbsp	olive oil	25 mL
1 tsp	salt	5 mL
½ cup	dulse (see Tips, left)	125 mL
½ cup	hot water	125 mL
½ cup	chopped toasted pecans	125 mL
½ cup	cooked brown rice	125 mL
½ cup	whole wheat bread crumbs	125 mL
2 tbsp	fresh thyme leaves	25 mL

1. Remove and discard mushroom stems. In a large bowl, toss together mushrooms, garlic, onion, leek, zucchini, eggplant and oil. Spread onto prepared baking sheet and sprinkle with salt. Roast in preheated oven for 40 minutes, stirring once or twice, or until tender and browned, removing vegetables as they are done. (The smaller vegetables will cook faster than the larger ones.)

2. Meanwhile, in a small bowl, cover dulse with hot water. Let stand for 5 minutes. Drain, pressing lightly and reserving soaking liquid.

3. In a food processor or blender, combine roasted vegetables, dulse, pecans, rice, bread crumbs and thyme. Pulse on and off until well mixed and chunky. If too dry to hold together, add a little reserved dulse soaking liquid until the consistency is right for spreading. Pack into a serving dish, cover tightly and chill for at least 1 hour before serving.

Variations

- Substitute almonds, Brazil nuts, chestnuts or walnuts for pecans.

- Use any cooked whole grain in place of the brown rice.

Whole-Grain Granola

Vegan Friendly

The amounts may be cut in half but the mixture is so versatile, you will want to keep a good quantity in the refrigerator to use when rolled oats are called for in recipes. As well as a healthy cereal, this granola mix is great in pie crusts and as a topping (see Serving Suggestion, right).

Tips

- Don't confuse quick-cooking or instant rolled oats with rolled oats, which are oat groats (kernels) that are steamed, rolled and flaked. Rolled oats are more nutritious than either of the fast-cooking types because the whole oat kernel (minus the hull) is still intact.

- Store granola in an airtight container in the refrigerator for up to 2 months.

- *Preheat oven to 375°F (190°C)*
- *2 rimmed baking sheets, lightly oiled*

2 cups	spelt flakes	500 mL
1 cup	rolled oats (see Tips, left)	250 mL
1/2 cup	natural bran or bran flakes cereal	125 mL
2/3 cup	chopped almonds (unblanched)	150 mL
1/2 cup	sunflower seeds	125 mL
1/3 cup	sesame seeds	75 mL
1/4 cup	chopped walnuts	50 mL
1/2 cup	honey	125 mL
2 tsp	ground cinnamon	10 mL
1 tsp	ground ginger	5 mL
1/2 cup	chopped dried apricots	125 mL
1/2 cup	raisins	125 mL
1/2 cup	dried cranberries	125 mL

1. On one prepared baking pan, spread spelt, oats and bran. On the other pan, spread almonds, sunflower seeds, sesame seeds and walnuts. Stagger the sheets in preheated oven and toast for 8 minutes. Remove nuts and seeds from oven and let cool. Stir grains and continue toasting for another 6 to 8 minutes or until lightly browned.

2. Meanwhile, in a small saucepan, heat honey, cinnamon and ginger over medium heat until just simmering. Turn off heat and keep pan on the element to keep the mixture warm.

3. Transfer toasted grains to a large bowl. Stir in toasted seeds and nuts. Drizzle with warm honey mixture. Add apricots, raisins and cranberries and stir lightly to mix. Let cool.

Variation

- Use chestnuts or pecans in place of the walnuts.

Serving Suggestions
- Use this healthy cereal mix as a crumb crust in pies (Cheese Tart with Blueberry Sauce, see recipe, page 362), in quick breads (Apple-Carrot Popovers, see recipe, page 162), in bars (Date and Nut Bars, see recipe, page 364) or as a topping for both savory and sweet dishes.

Apricot Granola Biscuits

Great to have on hand for breakfast on the run or snacks at any time of the day, the whole grains, nuts and fruit are high-energy and nutritious.

Tip

• Store biscuits in an airtight container for up to 5 days or in the freezer for up to 2 months.

• *Preheat oven to 350°F (180°C)*
• *2 baking sheets, lightly oiled*

½ cup	rice or soy milk	125 mL
1	large egg	1
2 tbsp	olive oil	25 mL
2 cups	Whole-Grain Granola (see recipe, page 160) or store-bought	500 mL
½ cup	whole wheat flour	125 mL
¼ cup	chopped apricots	50 mL
3 tbsp	organic cane sugar	45 mL
¼ cup	unsweetened shredded coconut, optional	50 mL

1. In a large bowl, beat milk and egg together until frothy. Beat in oil. Stir in granola, flour, apricots, sugar and coconut, if using. Drop by the tablespoon (15 mL) about 1 inch (2.5 cm) apart onto prepared baking sheets. Flatten slightly with a fork.

2. Bake in preheated oven for 10 minutes or until golden brown. Transfer to a cooling rack and let cool.

Although made like a muffin, the texture of these lower-fat snacks is not cake-like, but very moist, almost custardy. One of these popovers with a chunk of Cheddar cheese makes a very good start to the day.

Tips

- Use large-flake rolled oats (sometimes called "old fashioned"), not the instant or quick-cooking varieties.

- Store popovers in a resealable plastic bag for up to 3 days or in the freezer for up to 2 months.

Apple-Carrot Popovers

- *Preheat oven to 375°F (190°C)*
- *2 muffin tins, lightly oiled*

I cup	unbleached all-purpose flour	250 mL
½ cup	whole wheat flour	125 mL
½ cup	spelt flour	125 mL
¼ cup	Whole-Grain Granola (see recipe, page 160) or rolled oats (see Tips, left)	50 mL
I tbsp	baking powder	15 mL
½ tsp	salt	2 mL
2	apples, peeled and chopped	2
I cup	grated carrot	250 mL
I	large egg	I
I cup	natural yogurt	250 mL
¾ cup	unsweetened applesauce	175 mL
¼ cup	liquid honey or brown rice syrup	50 mL
2 tbsp	olive oil	25 mL

1. In a large bowl, combine all-purpose flour, whole wheat flour, spelt flour, granola, baking powder and salt. Using a whisk, stir in apples and carrot. Make a well in the center.

2. In a bowl, whisk egg. Stir in yogurt, applesauce, honey and oil and mix well. Pour liquid ingredients into dry ingredients and stir just until blended.

3. Spoon about ⅓ cup (75 mL) of the batter into 16 muffin cups, filling wells almost to the top. Bake in preheated oven for 20 minutes or until cake tester comes out clean and tops are golden brown. Serve warm.

Variation

- To add some protein, reduce grated carrot to ½ cup (125 mL) and add ½ cup (125 mL) shredded Cheddar cheese.

Scottish Oatcakes

Make these oatcakes ahead and freeze or bake fresh on a weekend. Either way, these portable breakfast cakes will be much enjoyed.

Tips

• Use large-flake rolled oats (sometimes called "old fashioned"), not the instant or quick-cooking varieties.

• Store oatcakes in a resealable plastic bag for up to 3 days or in the freezer for up to 2 months.

• *Preheat oven to 375°F (190°C)*
• *Baking sheet, lightly oiled*

1 1/2 cup	rolled oats (see Tips, left) or spelt flakes	375 mL
1/2 cup	Whole-Grain Granola (see recipe, page 160) or store bought	125 mL
2 tbsp	whole wheat flour	25 mL
1 tsp	baking powder	5 mL
Pinch	salt	Pinch
2 tbsp	butter, softened	25 mL
1/3 cup	liquid honey	75 mL
3 tbsp	boiling water	45 mL
1	large egg, beaten	1

1. In a large mixing bowl, combine oats, granola, flour, baking powder and salt. Using a fork, stir butter and honey into the dry ingredients. Add boiling water, stir well and let cool. Beat egg into the mixture.

2. Turn dough out onto prepared baking sheet. Using a fork, pat into a 10-by 1/2-inch (25 x 1 cm) compact round.

3. Bake in preheated oven for 5 to 7 minutes or until lightly browned. Transfer pan to a cooling rack. Let cool for 10 minutes before cutting into wedges.

Toothsome and heavy with fruit and nuts, these pancakes are quite a change from the lighter variety made with refined white flour.

Tip

• Use large-flake rolled oats (sometimes called "old fashioned"), not the instant or quick-cooking varieties.

Buckwheat Apple Pancakes

1/2 cup	rolled oats (see Tip, left) or Whole-Grain Granola (see recipe, page 160)	125 mL
1/2 cup	spelt flakes	125 mL
1 cup	boiling water	250 mL
1/4 cup	unbleached all-purpose flour	50 mL
1/4 cup	buckwheat flour	50 mL
2 tbsp	organic cane sugar	25 mL
1 tbsp	baking powder	15 mL
1/4 tsp	ground cinnamon	1 mL
Pinch	salt	Pinch
1	apple, shredded	1
1/4 cup	finely chopped walnuts or pecans	50 mL
1 cup	rice or soy milk	250 mL
1	large egg, lightly beaten	1
3 tbsp	olive oil, divided (approx.)	45 mL
	Pure maple syrup, optional	

1. In a bowl, combine oats and spelt. Stir in boiling water and let stand for 5 minutes.

2. Meanwhile, in a large bowl, combine all-purpose and buckwheat flours, sugar, baking powder, cinnamon and salt and stir with a whisk. Add apple and nuts. Make a well in the center.

3. Stir in milk, egg and 2 tbsp (25 mL) of the oil into soaked grains. Pour into dry ingredients and stir just enough to mix.

4. In a large skillet or griddle, heat 1 tbsp (15 mL) of the oil over medium heat. Spoon 1/4 cup (50 mL) of the pancake batter onto hot skillet, cook for 2 to 3 minutes or until lightly browned on underside and bubbles have formed throughout the batter. Flip and cook for 1 minute more or until lightly browned on other side. Repeat with remaining batter, re-oiling the pan when necessary. Serve immediately with maple syrup, if desired.

Variations

• Use 1/2 cup (125 mL) fresh or drained frozen blackberries, black currants, blueberries or elderberries in place of the apple.

• Use cashews or chestnuts in place of the walnuts.

The nut butter provides some protein in this tasty bread.

Tips

- Store bread, tightly covered, in the refrigerator for up to 1 week.

- Two bananas will provide enough for this moist and nutritious breakfast or snacking bread. The sugar is adjusted for natural nut butter. If using a commercial peanut butter, reduce the amount of sugar to 2 tbsp (25 mL).

Peanut Butter and Banana Bread

- *Preheat oven to 375°F (190°C)*
- *9-by 5-inch (2 L) loaf pan, lightly oiled*

1 cup	whole wheat flour	250 mL
1 cup	Whole-Grain Granola (see recipe, page 160) or store-bought	250 mL
3 tbsp	organic cane sugar	45 mL
1 tbsp	baking powder	15 mL
½ tsp	salt	2 mL
¾ cup	mashed ripe banana	175 mL
¼ cup	natural peanut or cashew butter	50 mL
2	large eggs, lightly beaten	2
2 tbsp	soy or rice milk	25 mL
2 tbsp	olive oil	25 mL

1. In a large bowl, combine flour, granola, sugar, baking powder and salt and stir to mix well. Make a well in the center.

2. In a bowl, using a fork, beat banana with peanut butter. Beat in eggs, milk and oil. Pour liquid ingredients into dry ingredients and stir just until mixed. Scrape into prepared loaf pan. Bake in center of preheated oven for 35 to 45 minutes or until cake tester comes out clean. Transfer to a wire rack and let cool.

This bread has grit! The variety of flours lends a dense, nutty taste to this breakfast classic.

Tip

- Store gingerbread, tightly covered, in the refrigerator for up to 1 week.

Gingerbread with Hot Spiced Applesauce

- *Preheat oven to 375°F (190°C)*
- *8-inch (20 cm) square cake pan, lightly greased*

1 ½ cups	whole wheat pastry flour	375 mL
½ cup	teff flour	125 mL
½ cup	rye flour	125 mL
1 tbsp	ground flaxseeds	15 mL
1 tsp	baking powder	5 mL
⅓ cup	organic cane sugar	75 mL
1 tsp	salt	5 mL
1 tsp	ground cinnamon	5 mL
½ tsp	ground ginger	2 mL
¼ tsp	ground nutmeg	1 mL
¼ tsp	ground allspice	1 mL
Pinch	ground cloves	Pinch
1	large egg	1
1 cup	rice or soy milk	250 mL
¼ cup	organic canola oil	50 mL
¼ cup	blackstrap molasses	50 mL
1 cup	Hot Spiced Applesauce (see recipe, page 317), optional	250 mL

1. In a large bowl, combine whole wheat flour, teff flour, rye flour, flaxseeds and baking powder. Using a whisk, stir in sugar, salt, cinnamon, ginger, nutmeg, allspice and cloves. Make a well in the center.

2. In a small bowl, whisk egg. Whisk in milk, oil and molasses. Pour liquid ingredients into dry ingredients and stir with a wooden spoon just until combined.

3. Pour batter into the prepared pan. Bake in preheated oven for 30 minutes or until cake pulls away from the sides of the pan and a toothpick inserted in the center comes out clean.

4. Transfer to a wire rack and let cool slightly. Cut into squares and serve warm with Hot Spiced Applesauce, if desired.

Variations

- Omit teff and rye flours and use 2½ cups (625 mL) whole wheat pastry flour or any combination of whole-grain flours.
- Serve gingerbread with Sweet Almond Spread (see recipe, page 152) instead of Hot Spiced Applesauce.

Kasha Pudding with Apple and Raisins

This is a great breakfast or family dessert dish. It can be made and baked the day before, refrigerated overnight and reheated in a 350°F (180°C) oven for 15 to 20 minutes.

Vegan Version

- Omit the eggs and do not bake. Substitute soy cheese for cottage cheese and use $\frac{1}{2}$ cup (125 mL) Sweet Almond Spread (see recipe, page 152) in place of the yogurt. Cook kasha following Step 1. Add soy cheese, Fruit Almond Spread, apple, raisins, vanilla and cinnamon, mix well and serve hot.

- *Preheat oven to 375°F (190°C)*
- *8-inch (20 cm) baking dish with lid or foil, lightly oiled*

I cup	rice or soy milk	250 mL
$\frac{1}{2}$ cup	kasha	125 mL
2	large eggs	2
I cup	lower-fat cottage cheese	250 mL
$\frac{1}{2}$ cup	natural lower-fat yogurt	125 mL
I	small apple, finely chopped	I
$\frac{1}{4}$ cup	raisins	50 mL
I tsp	vanilla	5 mL
I tsp	ground cinnamon	5 mL

1. In a small saucepan, bring milk to a boil over medium-high heat. Stir in kasha. Reduce heat and simmer, stirring occasionally, for 10 to 12 minutes or until all liquid has been absorbed. Transfer to a wire rack and let cool.

2. Meanwhile, in a large bowl, beat eggs. Stir in cheese and yogurt, mashing cheese with a fork to break up the curds.

3. Stir apple and raisins into kasha. Add vanilla and cinnamon. Using a spatula, scrape kasha mixture into cheese mixture and mix well. Spread into prepared baking dish. Bake in preheated oven for 30 to 40 minutes or until lightly browned. Serve warm or at room temperature.

Variation

- For a sweeter pudding, substitute $\frac{1}{4}$ cup (50 mL) chopped dates for the raisins.

Serving Suggestions

- For breakfast, serve with fresh fruit (bananas, blueberries, peaches) and milk. As a satisfying afternoon snack or dessert, garnish with 1 cup (250 mL) drained natural yogurt or Sweet Almond Spread (see recipe, page 152).

Baked Apple Polenta Custard

Whole cornmeal or corn grits work equally well in this recipe. Make on the weekend, keep tightly covered in the refrigerator and heat individual servings every morning for a fast, delicious breakfast through the week — if it lasts that long.

Vegan Version

- Increase cornmeal to 1 cup (250 mL). Follow directions in Step 1. Omit egg and all of Step 2. In Step 3, stir dates, pecans, apples and remaining $\frac{1}{3}$ cup (75 mL) milk into cornmeal, serve immediately as a hot breakfast cereal.

- *Preheat oven to 350°F (180°C)*
- *8-inch (20 cm) baking dish, lightly oiled*

2$\frac{1}{3}$ cups	rice or soy milk, divided	575 mL
2 tbsp	organic cane sugar	25 mL
1 tbsp	butter	15 mL
1 tbsp	grated lemon zest	15 mL
$\frac{3}{4}$ cup	cornmeal or grits	175 mL
1	large egg	1
$\frac{1}{2}$ cup	chopped dates	125 mL
$\frac{1}{2}$ cup	chopped pecans	125 mL
1	large apple, finely chopped	1
$\frac{1}{3}$ cup	Whole-Grain Granola (see recipe, page 160), optional	75 mL

1. In a saucepan, combine 2 cups (500 mL) of the milk, sugar, butter and zest. Slowly bring to a boil over medium heat. Gradually whisk in cornmeal. Reduce heat to medium-low. Cook, whisking for about 5 minutes until polenta is smooth and thick. Remove from heat and let cool.

2. In a small bowl, whisk egg. Whisk in remaining $\frac{1}{3}$ cup (75 mL) of the milk and set aside.

3. Stir dates, pecans and apple into cornmeal. Slowly add egg mixture, stirring well. Pour into prepared pan. Sprinkle granola over top, if desired. Bake in preheated oven for 30 minutes or until browned and coming away slightly from the sides of the pan. Serve warm.

Variation

- Use pistachio nuts or pumpkin or sunflower seeds in place of the pecans.

Serving Suggestions

- Serve with fresh fruit and milk or yogurt as a hot breakfast cereal or hearty snack. This dish also makes a comforting dessert.

Use fresh fruits when in season for this great breakfast dish.

Tips

- Fresh fruits, such as peaches, nectarines, apricots or pitted cherries or berries (fresh or drained frozen blackberries, black currants, blueberries or elderberries) are all suitable here.

- Two cans (each 14 oz/ 398 mL) low-sugar fruit, drained, works when fresh local fruit is not available.

Roasted Fruit with Custard

- *Preheat oven to 350°F (180°C)*
- *10-inch (25 cm) pie plate, lightly oiled*

| 4 cups | pitted, peeled and sliced soft fruit or berries (see Tips, left) | 1 L |
| 2 tbsp | organic cane sugar | 25 mL |

Custard

½ cup	unbleached all-purpose flour	125 mL
¼ cup	organic cane sugar	50 mL
Pinch	salt	Pinch
2	large eggs, lightly beaten	2
1 cup	rice or soy milk	250 mL
1 tsp	vanilla	5 mL
¼ tsp	ground nutmeg	1 mL
1 cup	natural yogurt, drained, optional	250 mL

1. Spread fruit evenly over bottom of prepared pie plate. Sprinkle with 2 tbsp (25 mL) sugar.

2. Custard: In a blender or large bowl, combine flour, sugar, salt, eggs, milk, vanilla and nutmeg. Process for 15 seconds or whisk until batter is smooth. Pour over fruit. Bake in preheated oven for 45 minutes or until puffy and golden brown. Serve warm with a dollop of yogurt, if desired.

Breakfast Cocktail

This smoothie is a vitamin A dynamo.

½ cup	carrot juice	125 mL
1	mango, sliced	1
1	papaya, sliced	1
1	ripe banana, cut into pieces	1
1	piece (½ inch/1 cm) fresh gingerroot, peeled and sliced, optional	1
¼ cup	natural yogurt	50 mL
	Honey to taste, optional	

1. In a blender, combine carrot juice, mango, papaya, banana, ginger, if using, and yogurt. Cover with lid and blend on low for 30 seconds. Gradually increase speed to high and blend for 30 seconds or until smooth. Taste and add honey, if desired, and blend for 10 seconds to mix in honey.

B-Vitamin Smoothie

Adding whole wheat germ and flaxseeds is an easy way to boost the vitamin B content of any smoothie recipe.

½ cup	orange juice	125 mL
1 cup	chopped pineapple (see Variation, below)	250 mL
¼ cup	rice or soy milk	50 mL
¼ cup	chopped, pitted apricots, peaches or nectarines	50 mL
1	ripe banana, cut into pieces	1
1 tbsp	wheat germ	15 mL
2 tsp	whole or ground flaxseeds	10 mL
1 tsp	cod liver or hemp oil	5 mL

1. In a blender, combine orange juice, pineapple, milk, apricots, banana, wheat germ, flaxseeds and oil. Cover with lid and blend on low for 30 seconds. Gradually increase speed to high and blend for 30 seconds or until smooth.

Variation
• Substitute 1 can (14 oz/398 mL) pineapple chunks and their juice for the orange juice and fresh pineapple.

Citrus Cocktail

Serves 2

Teenagers are especially fond of frozen yogurt in smoothies.

½ cup	orange juice	125 mL
¼ cup	grapefruit juice	50 mL
12	strawberries, hulled and halved	12
1	piece (½ inch/1 cm) fresh gingerroot, peeled and sliced, optional	1
¼ cup	natural or frozen yogurt	50 mL

1. In a blender, combine orange juice, grapefruit juice, strawberries, ginger, if using, and yogurt. Cover with lid and blend on low for 30 seconds. Gradually increase speed to high and blend for 30 seconds or until smooth.

Fruit Explosion

Serves 2

Vegan Friendly

The beautiful sunrise color and rich fruity taste of this smoothie will start your day off beautifully.

½ cup	grapefruit juice	125 mL
¼ cup	apple juice	50 mL
¼	cantaloupe, cut into pieces	¼
6	fresh or frozen strawberries	6
¼ cup	fresh or frozen raspberries	50 mL

1. In a blender, combine grapefruit juice, apple juice, cantaloupe, strawberries and raspberries. Cover with lid and blend on low for 30 seconds. Gradually increase speed to high and blend for 30 seconds or until smooth.

Orange Aid

Serves 4

Vegan Friendly

Not your ordinary glass of orange juice, this smoothie is a morning glory.

¾ cup	orange juice	175 mL
1 tbsp	freshly squeezed lemon juice	15 mL
2	nectarines, sliced	2
1	orange, segments separated	1
¼	cantaloupe, cut into pieces	¼
3	fresh or frozen strawberries	3

1. In a blender, combine orange juice, lemon juice, nectarines, orange, cantaloupe and strawberries. Cover with lid and blend on low for 30 seconds. Gradually increase speed to high and blend for 30 seconds or until smooth.

Prune Smoothie

I cup	rice or soy milk	250 mL
¼ cup	pitted prunes	50 mL
I	ripe banana, cut into pieces	I

I. In a blender, combine milk, prunes and banana. Cover with lid and blend on low for 30 seconds. Gradually increase speed to high and blend for 30 seconds or until smooth.

Sunrise Supreme

Vegan Friendly

With their cancer-fighting phytonutrients, adding grapes to smoothies makes good health sense.

½ cup	white grape juice	125 mL
I cup	seedless red grapes, halved	250 mL
12	fresh or frozen strawberries	12
½ cup	fresh or frozen raspberries	125 mL
I	orange, segments separated	I

I. In a blender, combine grape juice, grapes, strawberries, raspberries and orange. Cover with lid and blend on low for 30 seconds. Gradually increase speed to high and blend for 30 seconds or until smooth.

Watermelon-Strawberry Splash

Vegan Friendly

Here's a great summer thirst quencher with lots of vitamin C.

½ cup	raspberry or cranberry juice	125 mL
2 tbsp	freshly squeezed lemon juice	25 mL
I cup	chopped, seeded watermelon	250 mL
6	frozen strawberries	6

I. In a blender, combine raspberry juice, lemon juice, watermelon and strawberries. Cover with lid and blend on low for 30 seconds. Gradually increase speed to high and blend for 30 seconds or until smooth.

Salads

Moroccan Orange and Onion Salad

6	blood oranges, peeled, seeded and thinly sliced	6
1 tbsp	Moroccan Seasoning (see recipe, below)	15 mL
1	small red onion, thinly sliced	1
1/4 cup	fresh pomegranate seeds	50 mL
3 tbsp	coarsely chopped black olives	45 mL
2 tbsp	chopped fresh mint	25 mL
1/4 cup	Lemon-Ginger Dressing (see recipe, page 175)	50 mL
1/4 cup	Dukkah (see recipe, page 336) or chopped pistachio nuts, optional	50 mL

1. Line the bottom of a shallow serving dish with orange slices, overlapping if necessary. Sprinkle Moroccan Seasoning over top. Separate onion slices into rings and arrange over orange slices. Distribute pomegranate seeds, olives and mint over orange and onion slices.

2. Drizzle Lemon Ginger Dressing over salad. Cover and let stand at room temperature for 1 to 2 hours. Just before serving, taste and adjust Moroccan Seasoning and garnish with Dukkah, if using.

Moroccan Seasoning

2 tsp	cumin seeds	10 mL
1 tsp	coriander seeds	5 mL
1 tsp	allspice berries	5 mL
1 tsp	black peppercorns	5 mL
1/2 tsp	fenugreek seeds	2 mL

1. In a small heavy skillet, combine cumin, coriander, allspice, peppercorns and fenugreek seeds. Toast over medium heat for about 2 minutes or until fragrant. Seeds will start to pop just before toasted. Remove before or immediately if seeds start to smoke. Let cool. Grind in a mortar or small electric grinder.

In addition to the
nutritional boost, sea
herbs add tang and
natural saltiness to
salads, soups, chowders
and other dishes.

Vegan Version

- Substitute soy cheese
  for feta or omit
  cheese altogether.

Variation

- Use arame or dulse in
  place of the wakame
  in this recipe.

Wakame Cabbage Salad

½ oz	wakame	15 g
2 cups	shredded green cabbage	500 mL
2	green onions, chopped	2
2	carrots, shredded	2
I	apple, shredded	I
¼ cup	chopped walnuts	50 mL
¼ cup	chopped dried apricots	50 mL
¼ cup	raisins	50 mL
½ cup	Lemon Ginger Dressing (see recipe, below)	125 mL
¼ cup	cubed, drained feta cheese	50 mL
3 tbsp	sunflower seeds	45 mL

1. In a bowl, cover wakame with warm water. Let stand for 10 minutes. Drain and pat dry.

2. Meanwhile, in a large salad bowl, toss cabbage, green onions, carrots, apple, walnuts, apricots and raisins. Stir in wakame.

3. Drizzle Lemon-Ginger Dressing over salad and toss to combine. Sprinkle feta cheese and sunflower seeds over salad and serve immediately.

Vegan Friendly

Lemon and ginger
make a refreshing
combination in this
dressing. Use it with
grilled vegetables and
even fruit.

Lemon-Ginger Dressing

¼ cup	olive oil	50 mL
3 tbsp	tamari or soy sauce	45 mL
2 tbsp	freshly squeezed lemon juice	25 mL
I to 2	cloves garlic, minced	I to 2
I tbsp	chopped candied ginger	15 mL

1. In a jar with lid or small bowl, combine oil, tamari, lemon juice, garlic and ginger. Shake or whisk to mix well.

Vegan Friendly

Every household and every café in North Africa has a personalized version of this salad (called *fattoush*), and each season brings different ingredients to be included so there is never one way of making it. Some Variations are listed at the top of page 177, but use your own favorites to make this salad your own.

Vegan Version

• Omit feta cheese or use soy cheese in its place.

Serving Suggestion

• On a large round or oval platter, spread greens or cucumber. Arrange salad in a ring on the greens. Mound Bread Dressing in the center of the ring. Sprinkle cheese over salad. Serve immediately.

Mediterranean Red Pepper and Tomato Salad

Bread Dressing

3 tbsp	freshly squeezed lemon juice, divided	45 mL
2 tbsp	water	25 mL
2	slices dry brown bread, cubed	2
3 tbsp	olive oil	45 mL
1	clove garlic, minced	1
1 tsp	crushed coriander seeds	5 mL
1/2 tsp	crushed caraway seeds	2 mL
1/4 tsp	salt or to taste	1 mL
1/8 tsp	Harissa (see recipe, page 145), optional	0.5 mL

Salad

2 cups	Roasted Red Pepper slices (see recipe, page 135) or chopped red bell pepper	500 mL
2	tomatoes, coarsely chopped	2
2	green onions, thinly sliced on the diagonal	2
1/4 cup	coarsely chopped pitted black olives	50 mL
2 tbsp	capers, rinsed, optional	25 mL
2 tsp	grated lemon zest	10 mL
2 cups	mixed greens or thinly sliced cucumber	500 mL
1/2 cup	crumbled, drained feta cheese	125 mL

1. Bread Dressing: In a bowl, mix 1 tbsp (15 mL) of the lemon juice with water. Stir in bread cubes. Cover and set aside to soften while making salad (see Step 3).

2. When bread is soft, using a fork, whisk remaining 2 tbsp (25 mL) of the lemon juice, oil, garlic, coriander, caraway, salt and Harissa, if using, into softened bread cubes. Taste and adjust seasonings, if required. Cover and set aside until ready to use.

3. Salad: In a salad bowl, toss red pepper slices, tomatoes, green onions, olives, capers, if using, and lemon zest together to mix well.

4. Add dressing and toss to combine with salad ingredients or see Serving Suggestion, left. Sprinkle feta cheese over salad. Serve immediately.

Serves 4

Vegan Friendly

If you grow herbs, use both the leaves and the flowers in this simple but dramatic salad.

Tip

• Edible Flowers: Use flowers and herbs that are pesticide-free and not harvested from the wild. Good choices include bergamot, borage, calendula, chicory, chives, clove pinks, dandelion, day lilies, hollyhock, hyssop, lavender, nasturtium, pansy, rose, rosemary, sage, thyme, white or red clover.

Summer Flower Salad

3 cups	mesclun or tender greens, such as watercress	750 mL
1/2 cup	bean sprouts	125 mL
2 tbsp	raisins, chopped	25 mL
2 tbsp	chopped apricots	25 mL
2 tbsp	chopped almonds	25 mL
1/3 cup	Raspberry Dressing (see recipe, below)	75 mL
2 cups	edible flowers (see Tip, left)	500 mL

1. In a large bowl, combine greens, sprouts, raisins, apricots and almonds. Toss with Raspberry Dressing. Garnish top of salad with flowers and serve immediately.

Variation
• When available, use broccoli or sunflower sprouts in place of bean sprouts.

Makes 1/3 cup (75 mL)

Vegan Friendly

Raspberry is such a summer flavor. It is the perfect foil for the summer greens and flowers in above salad.

Raspberry Dressing

1/4 cup	olive oil	50 mL
3 tbsp	raspberry vinegar	45 mL

1. In a jar with lid or small bowl, combine oil and vinegar. Shake or whisk to mix well.

Variation
• Use 2 tbsp (25 mL) each raspberry purée and freshly squeezed lemon juice in place of raspberry vinegar.

Vegan Friendly

Bitter tastes have a tonic effect on the body and should not be sweetened with fruit if their digestive tonic action is to be fully enjoyed.

Dandelion Salad with Citrus Dressing

2 cups	fresh dandelion leaves or other greens (see Variations, below)	500 mL
2 cups	fresh spinach, trimmed and patted dry	500 mL
1/2 cup	bean sprouts	125 mL
1/4 cup	sliced green onions	50 mL
1/4 cup	chopped fresh parsley	50 mL
1/4 cup	fresh dandelion petals, optional	50 mL
1/4 cup	Citrus Dressing (see recipe, below)	50 mL

1. In a large salad bowl, combine dandelion leaves, spinach, sprouts, green onions, parsley and dandelion petals, if using. Drizzle Citrus Dressing over top and toss well. Serve immediately.

Variations

• Adding any or all of the following will soften the bitterness of the salad, but will also lessen the positive effects the bitter quality holds for the body: 1 cup (250 mL) cooked lentils, lima beans, flageolets or chickpeas; 1/2 cup (125 mL) chopped apricots; 1/2 cup (125 mL) bean sprouts; 1/2 cup (125 mL) raisins; 1/2 cup (125 mL) chopped mango, papaya or melon; 1/4 cup (50 mL) almond slivers.

• Use radicchio, endive, chicory, watercress or sorrel for greens with the same bitter qualities as dandelion.

Makes 1/2 cup (125 mL)

Vegan Friendly

The light citrus dressing allows the tangy, bitter taste of the dandelion leaves to have their effect on the body.

Citrus Dressing

1/3 cup	olive oil	75 mL
1/4 cup	freshly squeezed orange juice	50 mL
1 tsp	grated lemon zest	5 mL
1 tbsp	freshly squeezed lemon juice	15 mL
1 tbsp	fresh lemon thyme leaves	15 mL
1 tbsp	chopped fresh lemon balm	15 mL
	Salt	

1. In a jar with lid or small bowl, combine oil, orange juice, lemon zest and juice, thyme and lemon balm. Shake or whisk to mix well. Taste and add salt or extra lemon juice, if required.

Autumn Harvest Salad

Shaving or shredding the root vegetables makes them easy to combine and digest. For a different looking salad, cut the vegetables into thin strips.

1 cup	shredded carrot	250 mL
½ cup	shredded turnip	125 mL
½ cup	shredded beet	125 mL
1	apple, diced	1
2	green onions, thinly sliced on the diagonal	2
2 tbsp	fresh thyme leaves	25 mL
1 tbsp	chopped fresh sage	15 mL
⅓ cup	Harvest Dressing (see recipe, below)	75 mL
¼ cup	coarsely chopped cashew nuts	50 mL
3 tbsp	sesame seeds	45 mL

1. In a large salad bowl, combine carrot, turnip, beet, apple, green onions, thyme and sage. Toss well to combine. Drizzle Harvest Dressing over top and toss well. Scatter cashew nuts and sesame seeds over top and serve immediately.

Harvest Dressing

This light and complementary dressing allows the bounty of harvest vegetables to shine through.

Tip

• Chiffonade: Any finely shredded herb or leaf vegetable is termed "chiffonade." Use a large-leaf basil, such as "Genoa" or "Mammouth" for chiffonade. Stack 3 to 5 leaves and roll up tightly. Using a sharp knife, cut the roll of leaves into very fine slices. This yields about 2 tbsp (25 mL) shredded basil.

1	whole head garlic, roasted (see page 258) or 1 clove garlic, finely chopped	1
3 tbsp	olive oil	45 mL
1 tbsp	tamari or soy sauce	15 mL
1 tbsp	freshly squeezed lemon juice	15 mL
2 tbsp	chiffonade basil (see Tip, left)	25 mL
	Salt, optional	

1. In a jar with lid or small bowl, combine garlic, oil, tamari, lemon juice and basil. If using roasted garlic, squeeze soft cloves into the container and mash with a fork. Shake or whisk ingredients to mix well. Taste and adjust seasonings, adding salt, if needed.

Watercress (*Nasturtium officinale*) grows in and around shallow water and is often gathered from the wild. The only caution if wild crafting is that the water should not be standing and should be clear of any field run-off.

Watercress, Raspberry and Avocado Salad

2	firm ripe avocados	2
2 tbsp	freshly squeezed lemon juice	25 mL
4 cups	tender watercress sprigs, torn	I L
I cup	fresh raspberries	250 mL
¼ cup	Raspberry Dressing #2 (see recipe, below)	50 mL

1. Slit avocados lengthwise from stem end around base and back to stem. Twist the two halves apart. Remove pit from one half and skin from both halves. Slice flesh into a small bowl. Sprinkle lemon juice over top.

2. Line a serving platter with watercress. Arrange avocado slices and raspberries over watercress. Drizzle Raspberry Dressing #2 over top and serve immediately.

Variations

• Use 2 kiwifruits or 1 cup (250 mL) sliced mango or melon or papaya in place of the avocados.

• Tender young spinach leaves may be used to replace the watercress.

Makes ¼ cup (50 mL)

Vegan Friendly

Use fresh pressed raspberry purée when raspberries are in season.

Raspberry Dressing #2

3 tbsp	organic canola oil	45 mL
I tbsp	raspberry vinegar or purée	15 mL
I tbsp	liquid honey, optional	15 mL
I tbsp	chopped fresh chervil or parsley	15 mL
	Salt and freshly ground pepper	

1. In a jar with lid or small bowl, combine oil, vinegar, honey, if using, and chervil. Shake or whisk to mix well. Add salt and pepper, to taste, and extra raspberry vinegar, if required.

Fresh dates and figs are available only at certain times of the year. Look for them and use them in this recipe when they are soft, plump and full of flavor.

Tips

- Before cooking beets with the skin, be sure to scrub under cool running water to remove any grit.

- Feta cheese is available dried and crumbled. It's much easier to work with than feta packed in liquid.

Grated Beet and Apple Salad

3	small beets (see Tips, left)	3
3	apples	3
	Juice of 1 lemon	
1/4 cup	crumbled feta cheese (see Tips, left)	50 mL
1/4 cup	chopped dates	50 mL
1/4 cup	sliced figs	50 mL
1/4 cup	slivered toasted almonds or pine nuts	50 mL
1/3 cup	natural yogurt	75 mL
2 tbsp	rose water or orange flower water	25 mL
1 tbsp	chopped fresh mint	15 mL
1/4 tsp	crushed fennel seeds	1 mL

1. In a saucepan, cover beets with water. Bring to a boil over high heat. Reduce heat and simmer for 5 minutes. Drain, cool and slip peels off. Slice beets thinly. Cut into fine matchsticks and place in a serving bowl.

2. Meanwhile, core apples. Slice thinly and cut into fine matchsticks. Sprinkle lemon juice over top and toss with beets. Add feta cheese, dates, figs and almonds. Toss to combine with apples and beets.

3. In a small bowl, whisk yogurt with rose water. Drizzle over salad. Sprinkle mint and fennel seeds over salad. Serve immediately.

Variations

- Use cooled mint or herb tea in place of the rose water.
- Use dried figs and dates when fresh are not available.

Serving Suggestions
- Add 1/2 cup (125 mL) cooked peas, beans or lentils and use as a filling with lettuce and/or tomatoes for wraps or pita halves.
- Serve over cooked whole grains for a light meal.

Mâche (*Valerianella locusta*), also known as lamb's lettuce, is often one of the leaves in a mesclun blend. The small, dark green leaves have a fine, silky texture and a slightly sharp, nutty taste.

Mâche with Fruit, Nuts and Blue Cheese Dressing

2	soft ripe pears	2
2 tbsp	freshly squeezed lemon juice	25 mL
4 cups	mâche greens (see Introduction, left)	1 L
¼ cup	Blue Cheese Dressing (see recipe, below)	50 mL
4	soft ripe figs, halved lengthwise	4
2 tbsp	coarsely chopped hazelnuts	25 mL

1. Halve and core pears. Slice lengthwise and place in a small bowl. Sprinkle lemon juice over top. Set aside.

2. In a large bowl, toss mâche with Blue Cheese Dressing.

3. Divide greens evenly among 4 salad plates. Place 2 fig halves and 1 pear half on each salad. Garnish each with hazelnuts.

Variations

• Use spinach, watercress or mesclun greens in place of the mâche greens.

• Use ¼ cup (50 mL) chopped dried figs or dates when fresh figs are not available.

Any blue-veined cheese, such as Danish Stilton or gorgonzola, will work in this recipe.

Tip

• Store dressing, tightly covered, in the refrigerator for up to 3 days.

Blue Cheese Dressing

3 tbsp	hazelnut oil	45 mL
1 tbsp	balsamic vinegar	15 mL
3 oz	blue cheese, crumbled	90 g
	Salt and freshly ground pepper	

1. In a small bowl, combine oil, vinegar and cheese. Whisk to mix well. Taste and add salt and pepper, if required.

Vegan Friendly

Cucumbers are cooling, so this salad goes well with hot and spicy foods.

Cucumber in Sake and Rice Vinegar Dressing

| 2 | English cucumbers | 2 |
| 1 cup | Sake and Rice Vinegar Dressing (see recipe, below) | 250 mL |

1. Trim the ends of the cucumbers and slice each in half lengthwise. Cut the halves into 2-inch (5 cm) pieces. Place cut side of each piece down on a cutting surface and slice each piece lengthwise as thin as possible, place ribbons in a bowl.

2. Toss Sake and Rice Vinegar Dressing with cucumber slices. Cover and refrigerate for up to 1 hour. Serve cold.

Vegan Friendly

The taste of this dressing is sharp and sweet. As well as with cucumbers, use it with other grated vegetables such as daikon radish or horseradish to make a fresh condiment for fish and roasted vegetables, but eat in small quantities.

Sake and Rice Vinegar Dressing

¾ cup	rice vinegar	175 mL
3 tbsp	sake or sweet white wine	45 mL
3 tbsp	granulated sugar	45 mL
1 tbsp	grated fresh gingerroot	15 mL
⅛ to ¼ tsp	salt	0.5 to 1 mL

1. In a small bowl, combine rice vinegar, sake, sugar and ginger. Whisk to mix well. Taste and add salt, in small amounts, as required.

A simple, raw and nutritious salad, this dish can become a staple in the winter when fresh carrots are still plentiful.

Grated Carrots with Dates and Walnuts

4	carrots, grated	4
2	green onions, thinly sliced diagonally	2
1/3 cup	chopped dates	75 mL
1/4 cup	coarsely chopped walnuts	50 mL
1/3 cup	Citrus Dressing (see recipe, page 178) or Raspberry Dressing (see recipe, page 177)	75 mL

1. In a large bowl, combine carrots, green onions, dates and walnuts. Toss with Citrus-Dressing to coat. Serve immediately.

Variations

• Add shredded apple or turnip.

• Use raisins or dried cranberries in place of the dates.

• Substitute other favorite nuts and seeds for the walnuts.

The slightly anise flavor of the fennel and the tart-sweet fruit combine to make this a light and tangy starter. Use with pasta or other robust dishes.

Fennel, Celery and Apple Salad

2 cups	finely sliced fennel bulb	500 mL
2	apples, coarsely chopped	2
1 cup	finely sliced celery	250 mL
1/4 cup	slivered dried apricots	50 mL
3 tbsp	chopped nuts or seeds	45 mL
1/3 cup	Citrus Dressing (see recipe, page 178) or Blue Cheese Dressing (see recipe, page 182)	75 mL

1. In a large bowl, combine fennel, apples, celery, apricots and nuts. Toss with Citrus Dressing to coat. Serve immediately.

Variations

• Add 1/2 cup (125 mL) shredded turnip or bean sprouts.

• Use raisins in place of the apricots.

Basil and tomatoes are perfect together and they are both available around the same time at farmers' markets in late summer.

Tomatoes and Goat Cheese with Pesto and Balsamic Vinegar

2	large ripe tomatoes, thinly sliced	2
$\frac{1}{3}$ cup	Basil Pesto (see recipe, page 308) or store-bought	75 mL
$\frac{1}{2}$	red onion, thinly sliced	$\frac{1}{2}$
3 tbsp	balsamic vinegar	45 mL
3 oz	soft goat cheese, crumbled	90 g

1. Spread tomato slices in one layer on a serving platter. Spread a small amount of pesto on each slice. Scatter onion slices over top. Drizzle balsamic vinegar over top and top with goat cheese. Cover and let stand at room temperature for 30 minutes or in refrigerator for 1 hour. Serve at room temperature.

Variation
• Add $\frac{1}{2}$ cup (125 mL) Roasted Red Pepper slices (see recipe, page 135) before adding cheese.

Pink and perfectly seasoned, this salad is pretty served over fresh, tender spring greens.

Beet and Feta Cheese Salad

4	beets, cooked and sliced	4
$\frac{1}{4}$ cup	chopped red onion	50 mL
$\frac{1}{4}$ cup	chopped fresh parsley	50 mL
3 tbsp	olive oil	45 mL
1 tbsp	rice vinegar	15 mL
1 tsp	fresh thyme leaves	5 mL
1 tsp	chopped fresh rosemary	5 mL
$\frac{1}{4}$ cup	crumbled feta cheese	50 mL

1. In a salad bowl, toss together beets, onion and parsley.

2. In a small jar with a lid or small bowl, combine oil, vinegar, thyme and rosemary. Shake or whisk to mix well.

3. Pour dressing over salad ingredients. Toss gently to mix. Sprinkle with feta cheese and serve immediately.

Mediterranean Bean Salad

Make this salad your own by adding your favorite vegetables. In the winter, 1 cup (250 mL) shredded cabbage or root vegetables add texture and vitamins. Summer squash or peas or beans, steamed just until they crunch, make great warm weather ingredients.

1	can (19 oz/540 mL) cannellini beans, rinsed and drained, or 2 cups (500 mL) cooked navy beans or Great Northern beans	1
½ cup	cooked red lentils	125 mL
½ cup	coarsely chopped drained canned artichoke halves or hearts of palm	125 mL
½ cup	diced red onion	125 mL
¼ cup	chopped fresh parsley	50 mL
¼ cup	coarsely chopped black or green olives	50 mL
¼ cup	Mediterranean Dressing (see recipe, below)	50 mL

1. In a large bowl, combine beans, lentils, artichokes, onion, parsley and olives. Toss with Mediterranean Dressing. Cover and let stand for at least 30 minutes or refrigerate overnight. Serve at room temperature.

Variations

- Use chopped nuts for the lentils but add just before serving.
- Chopped red or green bell pepper may replace the olives.
- Add any of the following: 1 cup (250 mL) cooked green beans; 2 chopped hard-boiled eggs; 3 oz (90 g) drained, crumbled feta cheese; or ½ cup (125 mL) cherry tomato halves.

Mediterranean Dressing

Olive oil, lemons and garlic are classic Mediterranean ingredients. The light and zippy dressing complements other ingredients of the area such as olives, artichokes, legumes and red pepper.

2 tbsp	olive oil	25 mL
2 tbsp	apple cider vinegar	25 mL
1 tbsp	freshly squeezed lemon juice	15 mL
1	clove garlic, minced	1
2 tsp	miso	10 mL
	Freshly ground pepper	

1. In a jar with lid or small bowl, combine oil, vinegar, lemon juice, garlic, miso and pepper. Shake or whisk to mix well. Taste and add more lemon juice, if required.

Serves 6

Vegan Friendly

This refreshing salad also works well as a summer fruit salad (see Variations, below).

Summer Vegetable and Millet Salad

1 cup	cooked millet or couscous	250 mL
8 oz	snow peas, trimmed and sliced	250 g
2	carrots, cut into medium dice	2
1	small zucchini or summer squash, cut into medium dice	1
½ cup	diced red onion	125 mL
½ cup	chopped fresh parsley	125 mL
1	red or green bell pepper, seeded and chopped	1
⅓ cup	Summer Vegetable Dressing (see recipe, below)	75 mL

1. In a bowl, combine millet, snow peas, carrots, zucchini, onion, parsley and bell pepper. Toss with Summer Vegetable Dressing. Serve immediately.

Variations

• Make this a summer fruit salad by replacing the peas, carrots, zucchini and onion with 4 cups (1 L) mixed fresh chopped or sliced peaches, berries, nectarines, plums and cherries.

• Use 1 cup (250 mL) cooked fresh peas in place of snow peas.

Makes ⅓ cup (75 mL)

Vegan Friendly

The lemon and the milder wine vinegar in the dressing are perfect for bringing out the delicate taste of summer vegetables and fruit.

Summer Vegetable Dressing

3 tbsp	olive oil	45 mL
2 tbsp	freshly squeezed lime juice	25 mL
1 tbsp	white wine vinegar	15 mL
1 tbsp	grated fresh gingerroot	15 mL
2 tsp	organic cane sugar, optional	10 mL

1. In a jar with lid or small bowl, combine oil, lime juice, vinegar, ginger and sugar, if using. Shake or whisk to mix well.

When yet another green salad seems a bit mundane, try this salad for a nutritious and enjoyable change. It makes a light meal.

Vegan Version

- Substitute ¼ cup (50 mL) chopped nuts in place of Parmesan cheese.

Tip

- If you don't have time to roast a red pepper, use one red bell pepper, seeded and sliced, and make twice the amount of dressing.

Cannellini with Roasted Peppers and Shaved Parmesan

1	can (19 oz/540 mL) cannellini beans, rinsed and drained, or 2 cups (500 mL) cooked navy beans or Great Northern beans	1
2 cups	arugula leaves, torn	500 mL
1 cup	Roasted Red Pepper slices (see recipe, page 135) (see Tip, left)	250 mL
¼ cup	Lemon Dressing #2 (see recipe, below)	50 mL
3 oz	Parmesan cheese, thinly shaved	90 g

I. In a large bowl, combine beans, arugula and red peppers. Toss with Lemon Dressing #2. Sprinkle Parmesan over salad. Serve at room temperature.

Makes ¼ cup (50 mL)

Use this as a "standard" dressing. It goes with most salad ingredients.

Lemon Dressing #2

2 tbsp	olive oil	25 mL
2 tbsp	freshly squeezed lemon juice	25 mL
1	clove garlic, minced	1
2 tbsp	chopped fresh parsley	25 mL
1 tbsp	fresh thyme leaves	15 mL
½ tsp	salt	2 mL

I. In a jar with lid or small bowl, combine oil, lemon juice, garlic, parsley, thyme and salt. Shake or whisk to mix well. Taste and add more salt and lemon juice, if required.

A dramatic start for any meal, the flavors in the dressing combine to make the taste buds dance.

Tip

• Use portobello, shiitake, oyster, chanterelle or porcini mushrooms or a mixture.

Warm Mushrooms with Goat Cheese

• *Preheat oven to 375°F (190°C)*
• *Baking sheet, lightly oiled*

8 oz	mixed mushrooms (see Tip, left)	250 g
¼ cup	olive oil, divided	50 mL
¼ cup	finely chopped onion	50 mL
I	clove garlic, finely chopped	I
	Salt and freshly ground pepper	
4 oz	goat cheese, divided into 4 rounds	125 g
4 cups	mesclun or French sorrel	I L
2 tbsp	chopped fresh chives	25 mL
2 tbsp	chopped fresh tarragon	25 mL
2 tbsp	Balsamic vinegar	25 mL

1. Wash and trim mushrooms, pat dry. Slice and set aside.

2. In a large skillet, heat 2 tbsp (25 mL) of the oil over medium heat. Add onion and cook, stirring, for 4 minutes. Add garlic and cook for 2 minutes. Stir in mushrooms and cook for 2 minutes or until barely tender. Remove from heat. Add salt and pepper, to taste.

3. Using a slotted spoon, lift mushrooms out of skillet onto prepared baking sheet. Set skillet aside for Step 5. Divide mushroom mixture into 4 equal portions. Place one round of goat cheese in center of each. Bake in preheated oven for about 4 minutes or until cheese begins to soften. Immediately remove from oven.

4. Meanwhile, in a bowl, toss mesclun with chives and tarragon. Distribute equal portions on 4 salad plates.

5. Add remaining 2 tbsp (25 mL) of the oil to the skillet and heat over medium heat. Add vinegar and stir to collect pan juices and bits. Bring to a boil. Reduce heat and simmer for about 5 minutes or until slightly reduced.

6. Lift hot mushrooms and cheese portions off baking sheet and slide on top of greens. Drizzle each plate with vinegar reduction. Serve immediately.

Swiss Chard with Almond Butter Sauce

Vegan Friendly

The nut sauce here is thinned with water so as not to overpower the greens. Make the sauce first so that it is ready to drizzle over the greens as soon as they are wilted. Use less water in the sauce if using with tempeh or cooked vegetables. Swiss chard is not as delicate as many other greens but when braised, it is tender and lighter in taste.

Tip

• Be sure to use a high quality, freshly made nut butter that contains no hydrogenated oils, sugar and preservatives.

• *Warmed serving bowl or platter*

Almond Butter Sauce

½ cup	freshly ground almond butter (see Tip, left)	125 mL
¼ cup	freshly squeezed lemon juice	50 mL
2 tbsp	tamari or soy sauce	25 mL
2 tsp	freshly grated gingerroot	10 mL
⅓ cup	warm water	75 mL

1. In a small bowl, combine almond butter, lemon juice, tamari and ginger. Gradually stir in warm water until sauce reaches a creamy consistency.

Braised Swiss Chard

1	bunch Swiss chard or kale leaves	1
2 tbsp	olive oil	25 mL
1	onion, coarsely chopped	1
2	cloves garlic, finely chopped	2
1 cup	Almond Butter Sauce (see recipe, above)	250 mL
¼ cup	raisins	50 mL
¼ cup	coarsely chopped natural almonds	50 mL

1. Remove tough center stem from Swiss chard leaves and coarsely chop stems (to make about 6 cups/1.5 L). In a large saucepan, bring 2 quarts (2 L) water to boil over high heat. Drop leaves and chopped stems into water. Reduce heat and simmer for 1 to 2 minutes or just until tender. Drain and rinse with cold water.

2. In a large skillet, heat oil over medium heat. Add onion and cook, stirring, for 5 minutes. Stir in garlic and cook for another 2 minutes. Add blanched Swiss chard to skillet and toss to mix with onion and garlic. Transfer to warmed serving bowl or platter and drizzle with Almond Butter Sauce. Sprinkle raisins and nuts over top. Serve immediately.

Variations

• Use freshly ground peanut butter or cashew butter for almond butter.

• Mix mustard, beet or turnip greens, or spinach for the Swiss chard and adjust cooking time to suit the greens, 1 to 1½ minutes or until tender.

Broccoli Pesto Salad

Vegan Friendly

A popular summer salad to make as a "potluck" dish because it can be made in advance and doesn't need refrigerating right up to serving time.

Tip

• Store salad, tightly covered, in the refrigerator for up to 1 day.

2	bunches broccoli	2
⅔ cup	Basil Pesto (see recipe, page 308) or store-bought	150 mL
2 tbsp	Balsamic vinegar	25 mL
1 tbsp	tamari or soy sauce	15 mL
½	red onion, chopped	½
½ cup	raisins or chopped dried apricots	125 mL

1. Trim broccoli and cut into florets, reserving stalks for another use. You should have about 6 cups (1.5 L) florets. In a large saucepan of boiling water, cook broccoli for 3 to 4 minutes or just until tender. Drain and rinse with cold water. Let cool.

2. Meanwhile, in a large bowl, whisk together pesto, vinegar and tamari. Add broccoli, onion and raisins and toss. Cover tightly and chill until serving time.

Variation

• Add 1 cup (250 mL) cooked macaroni in Step 2.

Vegan Friendly

Indian food stores often
have many different
varieties of lentils and
beans. Mung beans,
also known as moong
beans, are delicate and
small — perfect for this
unusual potato salad.

Tip

• If using store-bought
Cajun spice, start
with 1½ tsp (7 mL)
because it may be
stronger than the
homemade version.
Taste and add more
as required.

Cajun Blackened Potato and Mung Bean Salad

½ cup	yellow mung beans, rinsed	125 mL
1½ cups	water	375 mL
6	medium potatoes, scrubbed	6
3 tbsp	olive oil	45 mL
1 tbsp	freshly squeezed lemon juice	15 mL
1 to 2 tbsp	Cajun Black Spice or store-bought (see recipe, page 330) (see Tip, left)	15 to 25 mL
1 tsp	salt	5 mL
1 cup	fresh or frozen corn kernels, cooked	250 mL

1. In a saucepan, combine beans and water. Bring to a boil over medium-high heat. Reduce heat and simmer gently for 20 minutes or until tender. Drain and rinse in a colander. Let cool slightly.

2. Meanwhile, in a saucepan, cover potatoes with water. Bring to a boil over high heat. Cover, reduce heat and simmer for about 20 minutes or until tender. Drain and rinse with cold water. Let cool and slip off skins.

3. In a large bowl, whisk together olive oil, lemon juice, 1 tbsp (15 mL) of the Cajun spice and salt. Slice potatoes directly into the oil mixture. Stir in lentils and corn. Taste and add more Cajun Seasoning or salt, if required.

Variation

• Substitute any lentil for the mung beans or use 1 cup (250 mL) cooked fava beans or flageolets in place of the beans and add in Step 3.

Serves 4

Easy to make, this simple salad or side dish can be made in advance and brought to room temperature before serving.

Vegan Version

- Replace Parmesan cheese with Whole-Grain Granola (see recipe, page 160) or Dukkah (see recipe, page 336).

Roasted Squash and Red Pepper Salad

- *Preheat oven to 400°F (200°C)*
- *9-inch (2.5 L) baking dish*

1	small butternut or acorn squash	1
4	thin whole slices red onion	4
2 cups	Roasted Red Pepper slices (see recipe, page 135)	500 mL
4 tbsp	shredded Parmesan cheese, divided	60 mL

1. Prick squash in several places with a knife and place in baking dish. Bake in preheated oven for 45 minutes or until tender when pierced with a sharp knife. Remove from oven and let cool enough to handle.

2. Trim ends and cut squash in half lengthwise. Scoop out and discard seeds. Scrape peel away from flesh. Cut each half crosswise into 6 slices. Cut onion slices in half.

3. Arrange 3 slices of squash on each of 4 individual salad plates. Between squash slices, place a half slice of onion. Spoon about ¼ cup (50 mL) of the red pepper over top of squash slices. Sprinkle 1 tbsp (15 mL) of the Parmesan over each. Serve warm or at room temperature.

Warm Beet Salad

Vegan Friendly

Slightly sweet, this salad is often enjoyed by ardent beet haters.

4	medium beets	4
2 tbsp	olive oil	25 mL
½ cup	chopped onion	125 mL
½ cup	sliced fennel bulb or celery	125 mL
½ cup	vegetable stock	125 mL
⅓ cup	apple juice	75 mL
2	apples, quartered	2
¼ cup	quartered dried apricots	50 mL
2 tbsp	rice vinegar	25 mL
1 to 2 tbsp	honey	15 to 25 mL
	Salt and freshly ground pepper	

1. Trim and scrub beets. Cut into wedges.

2. In a large saucepan with a lid, heat oil over medium heat. Add onion and cook, stirring, for 5 minutes or until soft. Add beets, fennel, stock and apple juice. Bring to a boil over high heat. Cover, reduce heat and simmer for about 20 minutes or until beets are tender.

3. Stir in apples, apricots, vinegar and honey. Simmer for about 7 minutes or until apples are soft and sauce is reduced slightly. Add salt and pepper, to taste. Serve warm.

Fast, simple, yet a very dramatic start to a meal or main course accompaniment.

Vegan Version
- Replace goat cheese with ¼ cup (50 mL) chopped pecans or walnuts.

Maple Pear and Portobello Mushroom Salad

- *Preheat broiler or barbecue*
- *Baking sheet*

2	pears	2
4	portobello mushroom caps	4
2 tbsp	olive oil	25 mL
2 tbsp	freshly squeezed orange juice	25 mL
2 tbsp	pure maple syrup	25 mL
3 oz	soft goat cheese, crumbled	90 g

1. Cut pears in half, core and place cut side up on baking sheet. Place mushroom caps, hollow side up, on the same baking sheet.

2. In a small saucepan, combine oil, orange juice and maple syrup. Whisk to mix well. Brush some of orange mixture over pears and mushroom caps. Reserve remaining sauce. Broil or grill pears and mushroom caps for 3 to 5 minutes or until soft. Let cool slightly.

3. Meanwhile, bring orange sauce to a boil over medium-high heat. Reduce heat and simmer, stirring occasionally for about 7 minutes or until sauce thickens slightly.

4. Slice pears and mushrooms. Arrange on a platter or 4 individual salad plates. Drizzle orange sauce over top and sprinkle with cheese. Serve warm.

Hot Sweet Potato Salad

4	medium sweet potatoes, scrubbed and quartered	4
3 tbsp	olive oil	45 mL
I	leek, white and light green parts sliced	I
I	onion, chopped	I
½ cup	vegetable stock	125 mL
I tbsp	blackstrap molasses or liquid honey	15 mL
2 tsp	Ras el Hanout seasoning (see recipe, page 334) or store-bought curry powder	10 mL
½ tsp	ground nutmeg	2 mL
½ tsp	salt	2 mL

1. In a large saucepan, cover sweet potatoes with water. Bring to a boil over high heat. Reduce heat and simmer for 20 minutes or until tender. Drain, let cool and remove skins. Cut into large dice and transfer to a large serving bowl. Cover tightly.

2. Meanwhile, in a large skillet, heat oil over medium heat. Add leek and onion. Sauté for 7 minutes or until soft. Stir in stock and molasses. Increase heat and bring to a boil. Reduce heat and simmer, stirring occasionally, for 10 to 12 minutes or until liquid is slightly reduced.

3. Toss leek mixture with sweet potatoes. Add Ras el Hanout, nutmeg and salt. Taste and add more seasonings, if required. Serve warm or at room temperature.

Variation
• Add ¼ cup (50 mL) any of the following: nuts or seeds, long flake coconut or raisins.

Vegan Friendly

Make this salad when the tomatoes are at their peak. Heritage varieties are perfect in this salad because the lemon in the dressing and the subtle eggplant allow the rich tomato essence to come through.

Grilled Eggplant and Tomato Salad

- *Preheat broiler*
- *Baking sheet, lightly oiled*

1	eggplant, peeled and sliced 1/4-inch (0.5 cm) thick	1
1 tbsp	salt	15 mL
1/2 cup	Lemon Dressing (see recipe, below), divided	125 mL
4	tomatoes, sliced and cut into strips	4
	Salt and freshly ground pepper	

1. In a large colander in the sink or over a bowl, layer eggplant slices and sprinkle each layer with 1 tsp (5 mL) of the salt. Set aside for 15 to 20 minutes.

2. Rinse and pat eggplant dry. Arrange in one layer on prepared baking sheet. Brush 3 tbsp (45 mL) of the Lemon Dressing over top. Broil in preheated oven for 2 minutes or until browned. Turn slices over and broil for 1 to 2 minutes on other side. Remove and let cool enough to handle.

3. Cut eggplant into strips and place in a large bowl with tomato strips. Toss with remaining dressing. Taste and add salt and pepper. Serve warm.

Makes 1/2 cup (125 mL)

Fresh lemon herbs are versatile and easy to grow. Try lemon varieties of sage, thyme and basil.

Lemon Dressing

1/3 cup	olive oil	75 mL
1 tsp	grated lemon zest	5 mL
2 tbsp	freshly squeezed lemon juice	25 mL
1 tbsp	organic cane sugar	15 mL
1 tbsp	fresh lemon thyme leaves	15 mL
1 tbsp	chopped fresh lemon balm	15 mL
1/2 tsp	salt, or to taste	2 mL

1. In a jar with lid or small bowl, combine oil, lemon zest and juice, sugar, thyme, lemon balm and salt. Shake or whisk to mix well. Taste and adjust seasonings, if required.

Variation

- When fresh lemon herbs are not available, use 1 tbsp (15 mL) each fresh chopped parsley and an additional 1 tbsp (15 mL) grated lemon rind.

Vegan Friendly

This easy winter salad lends itself to using leftovers.

Variations

- When fresh turnips are not in season, use 1 cup (250 mL) diced rutabaga in their place.
- Use 1 cup (250 mL) blanched cabbage, broccoli or green beans in place of the beets.

Warm Root Vegetable Salad

2	beets, trimmed and quartered	2
2	small turnips, trimmed and quartered	2
2	carrots, cut into large chunks	2
1	parsnip, cut into large chunks	1
1/2	onion, chopped	1/2
1	can (10 oz/300 g) water chestnuts, drained and chopped	1
1/3 cup	Winter Vegetable Dressing (see recipe, below)	75 mL

1. In a small saucepan, cover beets with water. Cover and bring to a boil over medium heat. Reduce heat and simmer for 30 minutes or until tender. Drain and let cool slightly. Slip skins off.

2. Meanwhile, in a saucepan, cover turnips, carrots and parsnip with water. Cover and bring to a boil over medium heat. Reduce heat and simmer for 20 minutes or until tender. Drain and let cool slightly.

3. In a large bowl, toss beets, turnips, carrots and parsnip with onion, water chestnuts and Winter Vegetable Dressing. Serve warm or at room temperature.

Makes 1/3 cup (75 mL)

Use this tangy dressing with greens as well as warm vegetables.

Winter Vegetable Dressing

3 tbsp	olive oil	45 mL
2 tbsp	freshly squeezed orange juice	25 mL
1 tbsp	white wine vinegar	15 mL
1 tbsp	Ras el Hanout seasoning (see recipe, page 334) or store-bought curry powder	15 mL
2 tsp	organic cane sugar	10 mL

1. In a jar with lid or small bowl, combine oil, orange juice, vinegar, Ras el Hanout and sugar. Shake or whisk to mix well.

Soups, Stews and Chowders

Vegetable Stock

Makes 8 cups (2 L)

Vegan Friendly

The backbone of whole, fresh cooking is often a good vegetable stock. One way to ensure a supply of vegetables for the stockpot is to freeze clean organic trimmings — the tougher asparagus or broccoli stalks, peelings and leafy tops of celery — and drop them directly into the simmering stock. Similarly, freezing homemade stock makes it easy to thaw and use in recipes.

The ingredients in the stock recipe (right) are only suggestions. Use vegetables, herbs and spices you have on hand and omit those you don't have. Cooking with this broth boosts the nutrients in recipes. Use it in every recipe (even baked goods) that calls for water.

- *Preheat oven to 400°F (200°C)*
- *Baking sheet*
- *Large stockpot*

1	onion, peeled and quartered	1
4	cloves garlic, peeled, left whole	4
1	leek, trimmed and cut into large chunks	1
2 tbsp	olive oil	25 mL
8 cups	water	2 L
½	green cabbage, quartered	½
1 cup	coarsely chopped broccoli or asparagus stems, optional	250 mL
1	stalk celery, cut into chunks	1
1	carrot, cut into chunks	1
1	apple, cut into chunks	1
1	whole dried cayenne pepper	1
6	fresh parsley sprigs	6
5	allspice berries	5
5	whole cloves	5
5	black peppercorns	5
1	bay leaf	1
Few	sprigs thyme	Few
Few	sprigs sage	Few
3	dried astragalus root wafers	3
1	piece (1 inch/2.5 cm) fresh gingerroot	1
1	piece (1 inch/2.5 cm) burdock root	1
1	piece (1 inch/2.5 cm) dandelion root	1

1. On baking sheet, toss onion, garlic and leek with olive oil. Roast in preheated oven, stirring once, for 30 to 40 minutes or until vegetables are soft and brown (some edges may be charred) (see Tips, right).

2. In a large stockpot, bring water to a boil over high heat. Add cabbage, broccoli, celery, carrot, apple, cayenne, parsley, allspice, cloves, peppercorns, bay leaf, thyme, sage, astragalus, ginger, burdock, dandelion root and roasted vegetables. Cover, reduce heat and simmer for 1 hour. Remove from heat and let cool slightly. Strain off and discard solids. Let stock cool completely and store.

Tips

- Roasting onion, garlic and leek lends a more complex taste and rich color to the stock. If time does not permit roasting, simply sauté onion, garlic and leek with oil in the stockpot first, then add all other items. Or, for an extremely easy and fat-free stock, omit the oil and toss all ingredients into the pot, simmer for 1 hour and strain.

- Omit any ingredient, except onion, garlic and cabbage.

- Potatoes and beets are not suitable for this broth.

- Other vegetables to use: parsnips, mushrooms, rutabaga, fennel bulb, zucchini, tomatoes, kale, bok choy and Swiss chard.

- To boost the potassium level of this stock, add sea vegetables (such as dulse, kelp or nori), alfalfa, chamomile, stinging nettles or plantain leaves.

- To boost the calcium level of this stock, add sea vegetables (see list above), dandelion greens, kale, Swiss chard or spinach.

- Store stock in clean jars with lids in the refrigerator for up to 2 days or freeze in 2- or 4-cup (500 mL or 1 L) portions in freezer containers for up to 2 months.

When Homemade Isn't Handy

When healing herbs and fresh vegetables are combined and simmered to release their essential qualities, the result has no commercial equivalent. However, to enjoy the goodness of soups when homemade vegetable stock is not on hand, the following may be used in its place:

- Dried organic vegetable bouillon and water — see package directions for mixing with water.

- Organic brown rice milk — generally, the original or plain variety is best for savory soups, however, the vanilla-flavored version has been used with success in the mushroom soups in this book, but it does lend a distinctly different flavor.

- Coconut milk — 1 can (14 oz/398 mL) coconut milk plus water can be used especially in chowders and creamy soups.

- Mushroom stock — simmer 8 oz (250 g) mushroom pieces or stems, chopped with 4 cups (1 L) water for 30 minutes. Strain and discard solids.

- Mushroom liquor — when dried mushrooms are reconstituted, strain, save and freeze soaking water to use as a stock or as an ingredient in the Vegetable Stock recipe, left.

- Vegetable cooking water — when vegetables are cooked in water, save and freeze the cooking water to use as a stock or as an ingredient in the Vegetable Stock recipe left.

Spring Tonic Broth

Vegan Friendly

Spring herbs are valued for their role as natural digestion and liver stimulants. They gently nourish the liver and gall bladder, allowing the body to balance and renew itself. Take this broth if following a spring cleanse routine.

Tip

• Store broth, tightly covered, in the refrigerator for up to 2 days or freeze for up to 3 months in 2-cup (500 mL) portions in freezer containers.

1	fresh burdock root or parsnip	1
2	fresh dandelion roots or carrots	2
¼	green cabbage, cut into 4 pieces	¼
1	onion, quartered	1
2	apples, quartered	2
2	whole cloves	2
2	peppercorns	2
2	allspice berries	2
2	dried astragalus root wafers	2
6 cups	water or vegetable stock	1.5 L

1. Scrub burdock and dandelion roots. Cut into large chunks.

2. In a large stockpot, combine burdock, dandelion, cabbage, onion, apples, cloves, peppercorns, allspice and astragalus. Cover with water and bring to a boil over medium-high heat. Skim off foam that rises to the surface. Reduce heat. Cover and gently simmer for 2 hours.

3. Remove from heat and let cool slightly. Strain off and discard solids. Serve broth in small cups, once or twice per day if cleansing.

Serving Suggestion

• Use this broth to cook breakfast grains or as the cooking liquid for soups, stews, risotto and other pasta dishes.

Mushroom Broth

This mushroom soup is nothing like the canned version. It is brown and brothy, full of the earthy mushroom essence.

8 oz	shiitake mushrooms	250 g
I	leek, white and light green parts, sliced	I
I cup	chopped onion	250 mL
I	clove garlic, finely chopped	I
2 tbsp	olive oil	25 mL
3 cups	vegetable stock, divided	750 mL
I tbsp	pure maple syrup	15 mL
I tsp	salt	5 mL
I cup	coconut, rice or soy milk, optional	250 mL

1. Trim and discard mushroom stems. Slice caps and set aside.

2. In a large saucepan, combine leek, onion, garlic and oil. Sauté over medium heat for about 10 minutes or until very soft. Add mushrooms and $\frac{1}{2}$ cup (125 mL) of the stock. Bring to a gentle boil. Cover, reduce heat and simmer for 15 minutes.

3. Add remaining $2\frac{1}{2}$ cups (625 mL) of the stock, maple syrup and salt. Bring to a boil. Cover, reduce heat and simmer for 45 minutes.

4. Using a slotted spoon, lift out half the vegetables and transfer to a food processor or blender. Process for 30 seconds or until smooth. Pour into a bowl. Repeat with remaining vegetables. Keep remaining cooking liquids hot in the saucepan over low heat.

5. Return purée to the saucepan and stir well. Taste and add more salt, if required. Add milk, if using. Heat through and serve immediately.

Vegan Friendly

A thick purée is the perfect foil for the slightly crisp, nutty-tasting strands of wakame in this soup. Serve with a salad and bread for a hearty lunch.

Spinach and Sea Vegetable Soup

1 cup	chopped onion	250 mL
2 tbsp	olive oil	25 mL
2	cloves garlic, finely chopped	2
1	carrot, chopped	1
1	leek, white and light green parts, chopped	1
1	turnip, chopped	1
6 cups	vegetable stock (approx.), divided	1.5 L
8 oz	spinach, trimmed	250 g
$\frac{1}{2}$ cup	wakame or arame	125 mL
2 tbsp	fresh thyme leaves	25 mL

1. In a large saucepan, sauté onion in oil over medium heat for 7 minutes or until soft. Stir in garlic, carrot, leek, turnip and $\frac{1}{2}$ cup (125 mL) of the stock. Bring to a boil. Cover, reduce heat and simmer, stirring occasionally, for 10 minutes.

2. Stir in 4 cups (1 L) of the stock. Bring to a boil. Cover, reduce heat and simmer for 10 minutes or until vegetables are tender. Stir in spinach. Cook for 2 minutes or until wilted. Let cool slightly.

3. Using a slotted spoon, lift out half the vegetables and transfer to a food processor or blender. Process for 30 seconds or until smooth. Pour into a bowl. Repeat with remaining vegetables. Keep remaining cooking liquids hot in the saucepan over low heat.

4. Return purée to the saucepan. Add wakame and thyme. Stir in remaining $1\frac{1}{2}$ cups (375 mL) of the stock, a small amount at a time, until desired consistency is achieved. Cover and simmer over medium heat for 10 minutes or until wakame is tender. Serve immediately.

Hot and Sour Summer Soup

If you have the time, simmer the soup on low heat for 2 or 3 hours the way Asian cooks do. Keep the lid on to trap water-soluble nutrients that would otherwise escape in the steam.

I cup	finely chopped onion	250 mL
2 tbsp	olive oil	25 mL
2 cups	finely diced turnip or rutabaga	500 mL
2	cloves garlic, finely chopped	2
I cup	thinly sliced shiitake mushrooms	250 mL
5 cups	vegetable stock	1.25 L
3 tbsp	rice vinegar	45 mL
2 tbsp	tamari or soy sauce	25 mL
2 tbsp	blackstrap molasses	25 mL
¼ to ½ tsp	Harissa (see recipe, page 145) or hot pepper sauce	I to 2 mL
	Summer Soup Garnish (see recipe, below)	
	Salt	

Summer Soup Garnish

8 oz	firm tofu, cut into ½-inch (I cm) cubes	250 g
2	green onions, thinly sliced on the diagonal	2
I	carrot, cut into matchsticks	I
¼ cup	chopped fresh cilantro or parsley	50 mL

1. In a large saucepan, sauté onion in oil over medium heat for 7 minutes or until soft. Stir in turnip and garlic. Cook, stirring often, for 5 minutes. Stir in mushrooms, stock, vinegar, tamari and molasses. Cover, reduce heat and simmer for about 25 minutes or until vegetables are tender.

2. Meanwhile, make garnish: In a small bowl, combine tofu, green onions, carrot and cilantro. Cover and set aside or refrigerate until serving time.

3. Remove soup from heat. Stir in Harissa ¼ tsp (1 mL) at a time, tasting after each addition, until hot enough. Add salt, to taste. Divide garnish among 4 bowls. Ladle hot soup over top. Serve immediately.

A refreshing change from the savory chilled summer classic gazpacho, this soup is welcome during the hottest days of summer.

Chilled Fruited Gazpacho

4 cups	sliced fresh strawberries	1 L
2 cups	chopped, seeded, peeled tomatoes	500 mL
¾ cup	seeded, diced, peeled cucumber	175 mL
3 tbsp	chopped fresh chives	45 mL
1 cup	apple juice	250 mL
3 tbsp	freshly squeezed lemon juice	45 mL
2 tbsp	raspberry vinegar (see Tip, page 271)	25 mL
2 tbsp	Basil Pesto (see recipe, page 308) or store-bought	25 mL
½ tsp	salt	2 mL
½ to 1 cup	vegetable stock	125 to 250 mL
4 to 6	whole strawberries, optional	4 to 6

1. In a large bowl, combine strawberries, tomatoes, cucumber, chives, apple juice, lemon juice, vinegar, pesto and salt, stirring to mix well. Using a slotted spoon, lift out about 3 cups (750 mL) solids and transfer to a food processor or blender. Process for 30 seconds or until smooth. Return to remaining mixture in bowl. Mix well. Stir stock into soup in ¼-cup (50 mL) portions until desired consistency is achieved.

2. Cover and refrigerate for a minimum of 2 hours or for up to 24 hours. Taste and add more salt, lemon juice or vinegar, if required. Serve well chilled and garnish with a whole strawberry, if using.

Curried Sweet Potato Soup

The taste combination of the curry and the sweet potatoes along with the coconut milk makes this complex and mildly flavorful soup a great starter for a lunch meal or for a soup-salad combo.

1 cup	chopped onion	250 mL
1 tbsp	Yellow or Red Curry Spice (see recipes, page 331) or store-bought	15 mL
2 tbsp	olive oil	25 mL
2	sweet potatoes, peeled and cut into large dice	2
1 cup	chopped carrot	250 mL
3 cups	vegetable stock	750 mL
1/4 cup	chopped raisins	50 mL
1 tsp	salt	5 mL
1	can (14 oz/398 mL) coconut milk	1
1/3 cup	chopped red bell pepper	75 mL

1. In a large saucepan, sauté onion and curry spice in oil over medium-low heat, stirring occasionally, for 6 minutes. Stir in sweet potatoes and carrot. Cook, stirring constantly, for 3 minutes.

2. Stir in stock. Increase heat and bring to a boil. Reduce heat and simmer for 15 minutes. Add raisins and salt. Cook for 5 minutes or until all vegetables are soft. Remove from the heat.

3. Using a potato masher, roughly mash sweet potato mixture. Stir in coconut milk and return to medium-high heat and heat through. Ladle soup into 4 bowls. Float 1 tbsp (15 mL) chopped bell pepper on top of each bowl. Serve immediately.

This soup can simmer for as long as several hours (before the cheese and milk are added) or it can be ready in less than an hour. If you wish to have it simmer for a while, keep an eye on the liquid and add more when required.

Vegan Version

• Substitute soy cheese for Cheddar.

Cheddar Cheese and Root Vegetable Soup

I	leek, white and light green parts, chopped	I
I cup	chopped onion	250 mL
2	cloves garlic, minced	2
I	parsnip, chopped	I
I	carrot, chopped	I
I cup	chopped potato	250 mL
I cup	chopped rutabaga	250 mL
I tbsp	fresh thyme leaves	15 mL
I tbsp	chopped fresh sage	15 mL
3 tbsp	olive oil	45 mL
2 cups	vegetable stock, divided	500 mL
I tsp	salt	5 mL
2 cups	rice or soy milk	500 mL
I $\frac{1}{2}$ cups	shredded Cheddar cheese	375 mL

1. In a large saucepan, combine leek, onion, garlic, parsnip, carrot, potato, rutabaga, thyme, sage, oil and $\frac{1}{2}$ cup (125 mL) of the stock. Gently simmer over medium heat, stirring occasionally, for 10 minutes.

2. Add remaining $1\frac{1}{2}$ cups (375 mL) of the stock and salt. Return soup to a light simmer. Cover and simmer for 15 to 20 minutes or until vegetables are tender. Remove from the heat.

3. Using a slotted spoon, lift out about 1 cup (250 mL) of the vegetables to a bowl. Using a potato masher, roughly mash and return to the pot. Stir in milk and cheese. Heat, stirring often, for 2 to 3 minutes or until cheese is melted (do not allow soup to boil at this point). Serve immediately.

Tomato-Thyme Soup

This is a winter soup —
its comforting tomato
taste is welcome on
those days when dinner
comes from a can and
whatever the pantry
holds.

1 tbsp	olive oil	15 mL
1 cup	finely chopped onion	250 mL
1	clove garlic, finely chopped	1
1 cup	shredded carrot or rutabaga	250 mL
1/2 cup	finely chopped kohlrabi or celery	125 mL
1	can (28 oz/796 mL) tomatoes, including juice	1
1 cup	vegetable stock	250 mL
2 tbsp	blackstrap molasses	25 mL
1 tbsp	apple cider vinegar	15 mL
1 tbsp	dried thyme leaves	15 mL
1/2 tsp	salt	2 mL
1/2 tsp	ground nutmeg	2 mL

1. In a large saucepan, heat oil over medium heat. Add onion and cook, stirring, for 7 minutes or until soft. Stir in garlic, carrot and kohlrabi. Cook, stirring occasionally, for 5 minutes.

2. Add tomatoes with juice, stock, molasses, vinegar, thyme, salt and nutmeg. Bring to a gentle boil. Cover, reduce heat and simmer for 35 minutes.

3. Using a slotted spoon, lift out half the vegetables and transfer to a food processor or blender. Process for 30 seconds or until smooth. Pour into a bowl. Repeat with remaining vegetables. Keep remaining cooking liquids hot in the saucepan over low heat. Return tomato purée to the pan.

4. Taste and add more vinegar, thyme, salt or nutmeg, if required. Heat through and serve immediately.

Variation
• Omit Step 3 for a more chunky soup.

Vegan Friendly

My personal favorite, this recipe makes a large amount of soup so that individual portions can be frozen.

Roasted Squash, Caramelized Onion and Garlic Soup

- *Preheat oven to 400°F (200°C), adjust racks to allow squash to sit on the lower rack and onions on the top rack*
- *Shallow baking dish*
- *Baking sheet, lightly oiled*

1	large butternut squash	1
3	large red onions, peeled and cut into eighths	3
3 tbsp	olive oil	45 mL
1 tsp	salt	5 mL
1/2 tsp	freshly ground pepper	2 mL
12	cloves garlic, peeled and left whole	12
2 tbsp	chopped fresh rosemary, divided	25 mL
2 tbsp	fresh thyme leaves, divided	25 mL
4 1/2 to 6 cups	vegetable stock, divided	1.125 to 1.5 L
2 tbsp	balsamic vinegar	25 mL
1 tbsp	blackstrap molasses	15 mL
1/2 to 1 cup	natural yogurt, drained, or Basic or Tangy Almond Spread (see recipes, page 151), optional	125 to 250 mL

1. Prick squash and place in baking dish. Bake on lower oven rack in preheated oven for 1 hour, turning once, until soft (test by inserting a sharp knife into the flesh). Let cool.

2. Meanwhile, in a large bowl, toss onions with oil, salt and pepper. Spread on prepared baking sheet and bake on top rack in preheated oven for 20 minutes. Remove sheet from oven and stir onions. Add garlic and sprinkle 1 tbsp (15 mL) each rosemary and thyme over top. Return to oven and roast for another 20 minutes or until vegetables are very soft and golden brown (some edges may be charred). Let cool.

3. When squash is cool enough to handle, cut in half lengthwise. Remove and discard seeds and scoop out flesh. In a food processor or blender, blend roughly 1 cup (250 mL) of the squash, 1 cup (250 mL) of the onion mixture, 1/2 cup (125 mL) of the stock, vinegar, molasses and remaining rosemary and thyme.

4. Transfer mixture to a large saucepan or bowl. Repeat with remaining 2 batches of 1 cup (250 mL) of the squash, 1 cup (250 mL) of the onion mixture and $\frac{1}{2}$ cup (125 mL) of the stock. Stir purée to blend well. The purée may be frozen at this point in 2-cup (500 mL) portions or refrigerated until ready to serve for up to 2 days.

5. When ready to serve, in a large saucepan, bring purée to a gentle simmer over medium heat. Stir in 3 to $4\frac{1}{2}$ cups (750 to 1.125 L) remaining stock, 1 cup (250 mL) at a time, until desired consistency is achieved. Blend well and heat through. Serve hot. Garnish the soup with a dollop of yogurt, if desired.

Borscht

This soup has a dual personality. If made following the method below, it is thick and chunky, very much a peasant-style soup. Yet, if the cooked vegetables are strained and blended in a food processor and returned to the pot with the cooking liquid, a smooth and creamy sophisticated texture is achieved.

Vegan Version
• Omit butter and use 2 tbsp (25 mL) olive oil in total instead.

1 lb	beets, peeled and finely chopped	500 g
1	onion, finely chopped	1
1	stalk celery, finely chopped	1
1	apple, finely chopped	1
1	carrot, shredded	1
1	parsnip, shredded	1
5 cups	vegetable stock, divided	1.25 L
1 tbsp	olive oil	15 mL
1 tbsp	butter	15 mL
2 tbsp	freshly squeezed lemon juice	25 mL
1 tbsp	fresh thyme leaves	15 mL
1 tsp	salt	5 mL
$\frac{1}{2}$ cup	Basic Almond Spread (see recipe, page 151), optional	125 mL

1. In a large saucepan, combine beets, onion, celery, apple, carrot, parsnip, $\frac{1}{2}$ cup (125 mL) of the stock, oil and butter. Bring to a gentle boil over medium-high heat. Cover, reduce heat to medium and gently simmer for 15 minutes.

2. Stir in remaining $4\frac{1}{2}$ cups (1.125 L) of the stock, lemon juice, thyme and salt. Bring to a boil. Cover, reduce heat and gently simmer for 30 minutes or until the vegetables are soft. Garnish with a dollop of Almond Spread, if using. Serve immediately.

Minestrone Soup

To make this classic soup seasonal, use new potatoes, peas and asparagus in the spring; green beans, snap peas and spinach when summer vegetables are at their peak; and winter roots, such as turnips, carrots, parsnips or cabbage.

Tip

• Flageolets are a pale haricot bean available dried or canned in specialty food stores. Soak and cook in the same manner as any dried bean.

2 tbsp	olive oil	25 mL
1	large onion, coarsely chopped	1
3	cloves garlic, minced	3
1	medium zucchini, coarsely chopped	1
1	stalk celery, coarsely chopped	1
½	red bell pepper, coarsely chopped	½
3 cups	vegetable stock, divided	750 mL
1 cup	green beans, trimmed and cut into 1-inch (2.5 cm) pieces	250 mL
1	can (19 oz/540 mL) tomatoes, including juice	1
1 tbsp	chopped fresh oregano leaves	15 mL
1	can (19 oz/540 mL) flageolets or white kidney beans, drained and rinsed (see Tip, left), or 2 cups (500 mL) cooked flageolets or white kidney beans	1
3 tbsp	chopped fresh parsley	45 mL
1 tbsp	fresh thyme leaves	15 mL
1 tsp	salt, or to taste	5 mL
	Freshly ground pepper	
¼ cup	Basil Pesto (see recipe, page 308) or store-bought, optional	50 mL

1. In a large stockpot or Dutch oven, heat oil over medium heat. Stir in onion and cook, stirring frequently, for 7 minutes or until soft. Stir in garlic. Reduce heat to low and cook, stirring frequently, for 1 minute or until fragrant.

2. Stir in zucchini, celery, bell pepper and 1 cup (250 mL) of the stock. Increase heat to medium-low and simmer, stirring frequently, for 5 minutes or until vegetables are soft.

3. Stir in remaining 2 cups (500 mL) of the stock, green beans, tomatoes with juice and oregano. Increase heat and bring to a boil. Skim off foam and adjust heat so that the liquid gently simmers. Simmer soup until green beans are tender, about 7 minutes.

4. Stir in flageolets, parsley and thyme. Cook for another 2 to 3 minutes, until heated through. Taste and add salt and pepper, if required. Ladle into soup bowls and garnish each with pesto, if using.

Variation

• Substitute any cooked or canned bean for the flageolets in this recipe including kidney, navy or chickpea.

Mushroom and Barley Soup

Dried mushrooms are widely available and because they take up little room and store easily, they make a good pantry staple. Reconstituted dried mushrooms or a mixture of fresh mushrooms can be used in this recipe. Try portobello, shiitake, oyster, chanterelles or porcini.

1 lb	fresh mixed mushrooms	500 g
1 cup	chopped onion	250 mL
1	leek, white and light green parts, thinly sliced	1
2	cloves garlic, finely chopped	2
4⅓ cups	vegetable stock, divided	1.075 L
3 tbsp	sherry or 2 tbsp (25 mL) red wine vinegar	45 mL
1 tbsp	olive oil	15 mL
½ cup	steel-cut barley	125 mL
2 tbsp	tamari or soy sauce	25 mL
1 tbsp	grated semisweet or bittersweet dark chocolate	15 mL
	Salt and freshly ground pepper	
6 tbsp	freshly grated Parmesan cheese, optional	90 mL

1. Slice mushroom caps and chop tender stems. Discard any tough stems. Set aside.

2. In a large saucepan, combine onion, leek, garlic, ⅓ cup (75 mL) of the vegetable stock, sherry and oil. Bring to a gentle boil over medium-low heat. Reduce heat to medium and simmer for 8 to 10 minutes or until onions are soft.

3. Stir in mushrooms and 1 cup (250 mL) of the stock. Bring to a boil. Cover, reduce heat and gently simmer for 15 minutes.

4. Add remaining 3 cups (750 mL) of the stock, barley and tamari and stir well. Simmer, uncovered, for 45 minutes. Skim off any foam that rises to the surface.

5. Add chocolate and stir until melted. Add salt and pepper, to taste. Ladle into soup bowls. Top each with 1 tbsp (15 mL) of the Parmesan, if using. Serve immediately.

Variation

- In place of the barley, use ½ cup (125 mL) farro, an heirloom grain from the Tuscany region of Italy. Available in specialty food markets.

Kale and Lentil Soup with Mango Chutney

Vegan Friendly

Kale is available late into the autumn. Try it in this exotic tasting soup.

6	kale leaves	6
I tbsp	olive oil	15 mL
I	onion, finely chopped	I
I	clove garlic, minced	I
½ cup	finely chopped mushrooms	125 mL
¼ tsp	ground nutmeg	I mL
I cup	dried red lentils, rinsed and drained	250 mL
I	apple, finely chopped	I
6 cups	vegetable stock, divided	1.5 L
I tbsp	tamari or soy sauce	15 mL
I	bay leaf	I
I tbsp	fresh thyme leaves	15 mL
	Salt	
6 to 8 tbsp	Mango Chutney (see recipe, page 314), or store-bought, optional	90 to 120mL

1. Wash kale and cut each leaf in half along one side of the center rib. Cut off rib from other side of the leaf. Finely chop rib and set aside. Stack the two leaf halves, roll tightly and cut crosswise into ¼-inch (0.5 cm) shreds. Set aside separate from ribs. Repeat with remaining leaves.

2. In a large saucepan, heat oil over medium heat. Add kale ribs, onion, garlic, mushrooms and nutmeg. Sauté for 5 to 7 minutes or until onions are soft. Stir in lentils, apple and 1½ cups (375 mL) of the stock. Bring to a boil. Cover, reduce heat and simmer gently for 15 minutes or until lentils are tender and most of the stock has been absorbed.

3. Stir in the remaining 4½ cups (1.125 L) of the stock, shredded kale, tamari, bay leaf and thyme. Slowly bring to a boil. Cover, reduce heat to low and gently simmer for 20 minutes.

4. Remove bay leaf. Add salt, to taste. Ladle into bowls and float 1 tbsp (15 mL) of the Mango Chutney, if using, on top. Serve immediately.

Variations
• Use 1 bunch bok choy or Swiss chard in place of kale and proceed as instructed.

• Use 2 cups (500 mL) spinach leaves in place of kale and add to the soup in Step 4, heating just until wilted.

Ginger warms this healing and delicious soup.

Udon Noodle Soup with Shiitakes and Bok Choy

8 oz	fresh udon noodles	250 g
6 oz	shiitake mushrooms	175 g
4	green onions, sliced on the diagonal	4
3 tbsp	freshly squeezed lemon juice	45 mL
3 tbsp	tamari or soy sauce	45 mL
2 tsp	toasted sesame oil	10 mL
4 cups	vegetable stock, divided	1 L
1 tbsp	grated fresh gingerroot	15 mL
1	bunch bok choy, greens only, shredded	1

1. Rinse noodles in a large colander. In a medium or large saucepan, bring 8 cups (2 L) water to a boil over high heat. Add noodles and cook for about 3 minutes or until soft. Drain and rinse in cold water. Set aside.

2. Remove and discard stems of mushrooms. Slice caps thinly. Transfer to a saucepan. Add green onions, lemon juice, tamari, oil and $\frac{1}{4}$ cup (50 mL) of the stock. Bring to a gentle boil over medium heat. Reduce heat and simmer gently for 10 minutes or until mushrooms are tender.

3. Add the remaining $3\frac{3}{4}$ cups (925 mL) of the stock, ginger, bok choy and noodles. Simmer for 1 minute or until the bok choy is wilted and noodles are heated through. Ladle into soup bowls. Serve immediately.

Variations

- Use soba noodles in place of udon noodles.
- Finely chopped candied ginger may replace the fresh ginger.
- Two cups (500 mL) trimmed spinach leaves or shredded cabbage may replace the bok choy.
- In Step 3, add 1 cup (250 mL) fried tofu squares, cubed cooked sweet potato.

Easy to make, this soup
is enough for a light
winter lunch.

Curried Vegetable and Lentil Soup

2 tbsp	Yellow or Red Curry Spice (see recipes, page 331) or store-bought	25 mL
1 tbsp	olive oil	15 mL
1 tsp	toasted sesame oil	5 mL
1 cup	chopped onion	250 mL
5 cups	vegetable stock	1.25 L
1 cup	dried red or green lentils, rinsed and drained	250 mL
1 cup	chopped green cabbage	250 mL
1	zucchini, finely chopped	1
1	carrot, finely chopped	1
1	parsnip, finely chopped	1
1	stalk celery, finely chopped	1
	Salt and freshly ground pepper	
¼ cup	chopped fresh parsley, optional	50 mL

1. In a large saucepan, stir curry spice with olive oil and sesame oil to make a paste. Heat gently over medium-low heat. Cook, stirring constantly, for 1 minute. Add onion and cook, stirring constantly, for 3 minutes.

2. Add stock. Bring to a boil over high heat. Reduce heat and add lentils. Cover and simmer for 45 minutes or until the lentils are tender.

3. Add cabbage, zucchini, carrot, parsnip and celery. Cover and simmer, stirring occasionally, for 25 minutes. Add salt and pepper, to taste. Ladle into soup bowls and garnish with parsley, if using.

Roasted Vegetable and Tomato Ratatouille

Full of sweet roasted flavor and chunky in texture, this is a hearty dish. Serve with rice or a whole grain, or simply dish up and pass homemade bread.

- *Preheat oven to 400°F (200°C)*
- *Baking sheet, lightly oiled*

1	large onion, peeled and cut into eighths	1
6	cloves garlic, peeled and left whole	6
3	carrots, cut into 1-inch (2.5 cm) chunks	3
2	parsnips, cut into 1-inch (2.5 cm) chunks	2
1	red bell pepper, seeded and cut into 1-inch (2.5 cm) pieces	1
1	zucchini, cut into 1-inch (2.5 cm) pieces	1
2 tbsp	olive oil	25 mL
8	large tomatoes, peeled and cut into wedges	8
1 tbsp	chopped fresh basil or rosemary	15 mL
1 tsp	salt	5 mL
1/3 cup	Basil Pesto (see recipe, page 308) or store-bought	75 mL
1/2 cup	vegetable stock	125 mL
2 tbsp	balsamic vinegar	25 mL
2 tbsp	blackstrap molasses, optional	25 mL
1/4 cup	chopped fresh parsley, optional	50 mL

1. On prepared baking sheet, toss onion, garlic, carrots, parsnips, pepper, zucchini and oil. Roast in preheated oven, stirring once or twice, for 40 minutes. Remove from oven. Stir in tomatoes, basil and salt. Return to oven and roast for 20 minutes longer.

2. Transfer roasted vegetables to a large saucepan. Add pesto, stock, vinegar and molasses, if using. Bring to a boil over high heat. Reduce heat and simmer, uncovered, for 20 minutes Serve immediately. Garnish each serving with parsley, if desired.

Variation

- When fresh local tomatoes are not available, use 1 can (28 oz/796 mL) tomatoes, including juice, and add in Step 2.

Sea Gumbo

Vegan Friendly

Arame, a sea vegetable commonly used in Japanese cooking, can be added directly to the pot, no need to presoak. The okra thickens the gumbo and adds an authentic flavor to the dish, but if not available, can be replaced with chopped green pepper with a thinner result.

Tip

• Arame is black, shredded sea vegetable available dehydrated, in packets, in Asian grocery stores. It usually requires a few minutes of soaking to reconstitute, but isn't necessary for this recipe.

1 cup	chopped onion	250 mL
1	leek, white and light green parts, sliced	1
3	cloves garlic, finely chopped	3
1	red bell pepper, chopped	1
1	celery stalk, chopped	1
2 tbsp	olive oil	25 mL
1 cup	vegetable stock, divided	250 mL
1	can (28 oz/796 mL) tomatoes, including juice	1
1 cup	chopped okra or green bell pepper	250 mL
1	bay leaf	1
3 tbsp	fresh thyme leaves	45 mL
1 cup	arame	250 mL
1/2 to 2 tsp	ground cayenne pepper	2 to 10 mL

1. In a large saucepan, combine onion, leek, garlic, bell pepper, celery, oil and 1/4 cup (50 mL) of the stock. Bring to a gentle boil over medium heat. Reduce heat and simmer gently for 10 to 12 minutes or until vegetables are soft.

2. Stir in the remaining 3/4 cup (175 mL) of the stock, tomatoes with juice, okra, bay leaf, thyme and arame. Cover and simmer, stirring occasionally, for 35 minutes or until arame is tender. Taste and add cayenne pepper, a little at a time, until desired taste is achieved. Ladle into soup bowls and serve.

Jambalaya

Vegan Friendly

This version of jambalaya, that southern United States Bayou country classic dish that usually contains mussels or shrimp, has all the spicy punch of a traditional jambalaya, without the seafood.

Tip

• If using store-bought Cajun spice, start with $1\frac{1}{2}$ tsp (7 mL) because it may be stronger than the homemade version. Taste and add more as required.

1 to 2 tbsp	Cajun Black Spice (see recipe, page 330) or store-bought, divided (see Tip, left)	15 to 25 mL
3 tbsp	olive oil	45 mL
2 cups	chopped onion	500 mL
$\frac{1}{2}$ cup	chopped celery	125 mL
$\frac{1}{2}$ cup	chopped red bell pepper	125 mL
$\frac{1}{2}$ cup	chopped mushrooms	125 mL
4	cloves garlic, finely chopped	4
1 cup	tomato sauce	250 mL
1 tbsp	grated lemon zest	15 mL
3 tbsp	freshly squeezed lemon juice	45 mL
4 cups	vegetable stock, divided	1 L
$\frac{1}{2}$ cup	brown rice	125 mL
$\frac{1}{2}$ cup	wild rice	125 mL
2	green onions, sliced on the diagonal	2
$\frac{1}{4}$ cup	chopped fresh parsley	50 mL
1	bay leaf	1
1 tbsp	fresh thyme leaves	15 mL
1 tbsp	chopped fresh basil	15 mL
$\frac{1}{2}$ tsp	salt	2 mL
$\frac{1}{2}$ cup	wakame or arame	125 mL

1. In a large saucepan, combine 1 tbsp (15 mL) of the Cajun spice and oil to make a paste. Heat gently over medium heat. Stir in onion and cook, stirring, for 5 minutes. Stir in celery, bell pepper, mushrooms, garlic, tomato sauce, lemon zest and juice and $\frac{1}{4}$ cup (50 mL) of the stock. Reduce heat and simmer gently for 10 minutes.

2. Stir in the remaining $3\frac{3}{4}$ cups (925 mL) of the stock. Increase heat and bring to a boil. Stir in brown rice, wild rice, green onions, parsley, bay leaf, thyme, basil, salt and wakame. Cover, reduce heat to low and simmer for 40 minutes. Do not lift the lid or stir the jambalaya, but be sure that heat is turned low.

3. Taste and add remaining 1 tbsp (15 mL) of the Cajun spice or more salt, if required. Remove bay leaf and serve immediately.

Barley and Vegetable Ragout

For years, pot barley was the only type of barley widely available to North Americans. Milled six times to remove all traces of the grain's outer husk and bran layer, pot barley is white and cooks fast (in half the time as its more natural counterparts) — but is bereft of nutrients. Now, hulled barley, the form with the bran layer intact and Scotch barley (milled three times) are finding their way into supermarkets as consumers ask for healthier forms of grains.

Tip

• If using prepared vegetable stock that is salted, do not add salt in Step 3. Add to taste in Step 4.

I cup	chopped celery	250 mL
I cup	chopped carrots	250 mL
I cup	chopped parsnips	250 mL
2	cloves garlic, finely chopped	2
I	onion, chopped	I
I	leek, white and light green parts, chopped	I
3 tbsp	Basil Pesto (see recipe, page 308) or store-bought	45 mL
¼ cup	apple cider or apple juice	50 mL
5 cups	vegetable stock	1.25 L
I cup	steel-cut, Scotch or pot barley	250 mL
I cup	tomato sauce	250 mL
I cup	broccoli florets	250 mL
I cup	cauliflower florets	250 mL
3 tbsp	chopped fresh parsley	45 mL
2 tbsp	chopped fresh basil	25 mL
2 tsp	fresh thyme leaves	10 mL
I tsp	salt, or to taste (see Tip, left)	5 mL
	Freshly ground pepper	

1. In a large bowl, combine celery, carrots, parsnips, garlic, onion and leek. Toss with pesto.

2. In a large saucepan, bring cider to a boil over high heat. Stir in pesto-coated vegetables. Reduce heat and simmer gently, stirring occasionally, for 7 minutes or until cider is almost gone.

3. Stir in stock and bring to a boil over high heat. Add barley. Cover, reduce heat to medium-low and simmer for 40 minutes. Stir in tomato sauce, broccoli, cauliflower, parsley, basil, thyme, salt and pepper. Simmer gently, covered, for 12 minutes or until broccoli and cauliflower florets are just tender.

4. Taste and add more salt and pepper, if required. Serve hot.

Variations

• Replace Basil Pesto with 2 tbsp 25 mL) olive oil and 2 tbsp (25 mL) chopped fresh parsley or oregano leaves.

• Use turnip, zucchini or mushrooms in place of celery, carrots or parsnips.

Winter Cassoulet

This is one of those weekend dishes that can simmer on the stove most of the day — just keep adding stock to the mixture as the cooking thickens and concentrates the flavors.

Tip

• Add ½ tsp (2 mL) salt if olives are omitted.

¼ cup	whole wheat flour	50 mL
I tbsp	dry mustard powder	15 mL
I	small eggplant, cut into 1-inch (2.5 cm) pieces	I
2 to 6 tbsp	olive oil (approx.)	25 to 90 mL
I cup	chopped onion	250 mL
I cup	chopped celery	250 mL
I	can (28 oz/796 mL) tomatoes, including juice	I
I cup	vegetable stock	250 mL
I	can (5 oz/156 mL) tomato paste	I
I	bay leaf	I
3	carrots, sliced	3
8 oz	mushrooms, sliced	250 g
¼ cup	water	50 mL
½ cup	black olives, pitted and sliced, optional	125 mL
I tbsp	chopped fresh savory	15 mL
	Freshly ground pepper	
	Salt, optional	

1. In a bowl, combine flour and mustard powder. Add eggplant and toss to coat.

2. In a large saucepan, heat 2 tbsp (25 mL) oil over medium heat. Using tongs, lift enough eggplant into saucepan to cover bottom in one layer. Brown lightly on all sides. Transfer to a plate. Add more oil if required and continue browning eggplant in batches, until all are done. Set eggplant and any remaining flour mixture aside.

3. Drizzle more oil in the pan if required, heat and add onion and celery. Sauté for 5 minutes. Stir in tomatoes with juice, stock, tomato paste, bay leaf and eggplant (with any juices that have accumulated in the bowl). Bring to a boil, reduce heat and simmer for 45 minutes.

4. Stir in carrots and mushrooms. Simmer for 15 minutes or until vegetables are tender. Slowly stir water into the reserved flour mixture to make a smooth paste. Stir into the vegetable cassoulet. Add olives, if using, savory and pepper. Simmer for another 15 minutes. Remove bay leaf. Taste and add salt, if desired. Serve immediately.

Vegetable Red Curry

Flavorful and nutritious, this is both a family and a casual company entrée.

4 oz	green beans, trimmed and cut into 1-inch (2.5 cm) pieces	125 g
1 tbsp	Red Curry Spice (see recipe page 331) or store-bought	15 mL
2 tbsp	olive oil	25 mL
1 cup	chopped onion	250 mL
1 lb	potatoes, peeled and cut into 1-inch (2.5 cm) cubes	500 g
1	carrot, sliced on the diagonal	1
1	stalk lemongrass, tops and outer leaves removed	1
1	clove garlic, finely chopped	1
1 tsp	salt	5 mL
1/2 cup	vegetable stock or water	125 mL
2 1/2 cups	Makrut Lime Leaf Sauce (see recipe, page 316)	625 mL
2	zucchini, cut into 1-inch (2.5 cm) pieces	2
1	red bell pepper, coarsely chopped	1
1	can (14 oz/398 mL) hearts of palm, drained and coarsely chopped	1

1. In a small saucepan, cover beans with water and bring to a gentle boil over medium heat. Cover, reduce heat and simmer for 7 minutes or just until tender. Drain and set aside.

2. Meanwhile, in a large saucepan, combine curry spice and oil to make a paste. Gently heat over medium heat. Add onion and sauté for 5 minutes or until soft. Stir in potatoes, carrot, lemongrass, garlic, salt and stock. Cover, reduce heat to low and simmer gently for 7 minutes or until stock is almost gone.

3. Stir in Makrut Lime Leaf Sauce, zucchini, bell pepper and hearts of palm. Cover and simmer gently for 15 minutes. Add cooked green beans and heat through. Remove lemongrass stalk. Serve immediately.

Variations

• Use 1 cup (250 mL) sliced green cabbage in place of the green beans. In Step 1, blanch for 3 to 4 minutes until soft, drain and set aside. Add to the curry with the potatoes in Step 2.

• Substitute Mango Chutney (see recipe, page 314) or store-bought for Makrut Lime Leaf Sauce.

Here we have the perfect balance of incomplete proteins together in one dish — corn, rice and beans.

Tip
• Use fresh corn kernels sliced off the cob when available; at all other times frozen corn is best.

Corn and Rice Chowder with Parsley Persillade

3 cups	rice or soy milk	750 mL
I cup	chopped onion	250 mL
I	leek, white and light green parts, chopped	I
I ⅓ cups	sweet corn kernels (see Tip, left)	325 mL
I	can (14 oz/398 mL) lima beans, drained and rinsed, or I ⅔ cups (400 mL) cooked lima beans	I
I cup	cooked wild rice	250 mL
½ tsp	salt	2 mL
¼ cup	Parsley Persillade (see recipe, below)	50 mL

1. In a large saucepan, heat milk to just under a boil over medium heat. Add onion and leek. Cover, reduce heat to low and simmer gently for 10 minutes. Add corn. Cover and simmer for 5 minutes.

2. Stir in lima beans, wild rice and salt and heat through. Taste and add more salt, if required. Ladle into soup bowls. Garnish with about 1 tbsp (15 mL) Parsley Persillade.

Persillade is the term given to a fine mince of garlic and parsley that is usually added at the end to sautéed dishes, vegetables, stews and soups. Use it as a substitute for salt or butter on vegetables.

Tip
• Store persillade, tightly covered, in the refrigerator up to 4 days.

Parsley Persillade

¼ cup	finely chopped fresh parsley	50 mL
I	clove garlic, finely chopped	I
2 tbsp	finely ground almonds	25 mL

1. In a small bowl, combine parsley, garlic and almonds.

Rainbow Chowder

Bursting with the color
and flavor of summer,
this soup can be
doubled easily.

Tip

- To freeze this
chowder, cool
and ladle 2 cups
(500 mL) into a
freezer container.
Seal, label and store
in the freezer for up
to 3 months.

Variations

- Acorn squash or
sweet potatoes may
be used in place of
butternut squash.
- Replace Red Pepper
Sauce with a mild to
medium-hot tomato
salsa.

1 cup	chopped onion	250 mL
1/2 cup	chopped celery	125 mL
2 tbsp	olive oil	25 mL
2 cups	vegetable stock	500 mL
2 cups	coarsely chopped peeled butternut squash	500 mL
1/2 tsp	salt	2 mL
2 cups	corn kernels	500 mL
1 cup	spinach leaves, trimmed	250 mL
3 1/4 cups	Red Pepper Sauce (see recipe, below)	800 mL
1 tbsp	fresh thyme leaves	15 mL

1. In a large saucepan, combine onion, celery and oil. Heat
gently over medium heat and sauté for 5 minutes or until
onions are soft. Add stock. Increase heat and bring to a boil.
Stir in squash and salt. Cover, reduce heat and simmer
gently for 20 minutes or until squash is soft.

2. Add corn, spinach, Red Pepper Sauce and thyme. Simmer
gently, uncovered, for 5 minutes. Taste and add more salt
or thyme, if required. Ladle into soup bowls and serve
immediately.

**Makes 3 1/4 cups
(800 mL)**

Red Pepper Sauce

Tip

- To replace Roasted
Red Pepper slices: In a
small saucepan, bring
3 cups (750 mL) water
to a boil over high
heat. Add 1 cup (250
mL) sliced red bell
pepper. Reduce heat
and simmer for 2 to 3
minutes or until
pepper is soft. Drain
peppers and toss with
2 tsp (10 mL) olive oil
and use where Roasted
Red Pepper slices are
called for.

1 cup	Roasted Red Pepper slices (see recipe, page 135 or Tip, left)	250 mL
1/4 cup	coarsely chopped dried or canned chipotle chiles	50 mL
2 tsp	Red Curry Spice (see recipe, page 331) or store-bought	10 mL
2 cups	coconut milk or soy milk	500 mL

1. In a blender or food processor, combine Roasted Red
Pepper slices, chiles and curry spice. Process for
15 seconds. With the motor running, slowly add milk
through the opening in the lid and process for about
5 seconds or until smooth.

Mushroom-Almond Bisque

20	shiitake mushrooms	20
I	leek, white and light green parts, sliced	I
2 tbsp	olive oil	25 mL
2 cups	vegetable stock, divided	500 mL
I	medium potato, peeled and cut into large chunks	I
2 tbsp	tahini paste	25 mL
2 tbsp	miso	25 mL
2 cups	rice or soy milk, divided	500 mL
¼ cup	Basic Almond Spread (see recipe, page 151) or ground almonds	50 mL
2	green onions, thinly sliced on the diagonal, optional	2

1. Remove and discard stems from mushrooms. Slice caps thinly and set aside.

2. In a large saucepan, combine leek and oil. Sauté over medium heat for 5 minutes or until soft. Add mushrooms and ¼ cup (50 mL) of the stock. Simmer for 5 minutes.

3. Stir in the remaining 1¾ cups (425 mL) of the stock. Increase heat to high and bring to a boil. Add potato. Cover, reduce heat to low and simmer gently for 15 minutes or until tender. Let cool.

4. Using a slotted spoon, transfer solids to a food processor or blender. Add tahini, miso and 1 cup (250 mL) of the milk. Process for 1 minute or until smooth.

5. In a large bowl, combine purée, soup liquids from the saucepan, the remaining 1 cup (250 mL) of the milk and Almond Spread. Stir to blend. Let cool and refrigerate until chilled for at least 2 hours or for up to 24 hours.

6. Ladle chilled soup into bowls. Garnish each with about 1 tbsp (15 mL) green onions, if desired.

Sea Vegetable Chowder

This recipe includes instructions for both a slow cooker, if you have one, and a stove top method. Using a slow cooker makes sense for busy households.

3	garlic cloves, minced	3
3	carrots, chopped	3
1	onion, chopped	1
1	stalk celery, chopped	1
1	medium potato, chopped	1
1	leek, white and light green parts, chopped	1
2 cups	vegetable stock	500 mL
1	can (14 oz/398 mL) coconut milk	1
1 cup	arame	250 mL
½ cup	dried red lentils, rinsed and drained	125 mL
½ cup	freshly ground almond or cashew butter	125 mL
1 tbsp	chopped candied ginger	15 mL
	Salt and freshly ground pepper	

Slow Cooker Method

1. In slow cooker stoneware, combine garlic, carrots, onion, celery, potato, leek, stock, milk, arame, lentils, almond butter and ginger. Stir well and cook on Low for 4 to 6 hours, until vegetables and lentils are tender. Taste and add salt and pepper, if required. Serve hot.

Stove Top Method

1. In a large saucepan, combine garlic, carrots, onion, celery, potato, leek and stock. Bring to a boil over high heat. Cover, reduce heat and simmer for 10 minutes.

2. Add milk, arame and lentils. Bring to just under a boil. Cover, reduce heat and simmer for 15 minutes or until lentils are tender.

3. Remove from heat. Stir in almond butter and ginger. Taste and add salt and pepper, if required. Serve hot.

Main Dishes

Nut and Lentil Wraps

Nuts and legumes are
an excellent protein
source. Serve these
bite-size rolls as hot
appetizers or the whole
wrap for lunch or
snacks to go.

Tip
• Recipe can easily be
doubled or tripled.

- *Preheat oven to 375°F (190°C), optional*
- *Baking sheet*

½ cup	Basil Pesto (see recipe, page 308) or store-bought	125 mL
4	7-inch (17.5 cm) whole wheat tortillas	4
1 cup	Nut-Lentil Filling (see recipe, below)	250 mL
6 tbsp	shredded mozzarella cheese	90 mL

1. Spoon 2 tbsp (25 mL) of the pesto into center of a tortilla. Spread to within ½ inch (1 cm) of the edges. Spread 2 tbsp (25 mL) of the Nut-Lentil Filling over pesto. Sprinkle with 1½ tbsp (22 mL) of the cheese. Repeat with remaining tortillas and filling.

2. Roll each tortilla into a compact cylinder. Serve immediately as a sandwich wrap or cut each wrap into five ½-inch (1 cm) slices. Place seam side down on baking sheet. Bake in preheated oven for 12 to15 minutes or until cheese is bubbly. Transfer to a serving platter and serve immediately.

Nut-Lentil Filling

Vegan Version
• Substitute soy cheese
for mozzarella cheese.

½ cup	Basic Almond Spread (see recipe, page 151) or Hummus (see recipe, page 146) or store-bought	125 mL
¼ cup	cooked red lentils or split peas	50 mL
¼ cup	finely chopped pecans	50 mL
2 tbsp	finely chopped green onions	25 mL

1. In a bowl, combine Savory Almond Spread, lentils, pecans and green onions.

Variations
- Any cooked, chopped legumes (such as black-eyed peas or beans, chickpeas or black beans) may be used in this recipe.
- Substitute chopped walnuts, peanuts or almonds for the pecans.

These burritos are a great way to enjoy fresh asparagus in season, but steamed or blanched broccoli and other vegetables step in as a replacement at other times of the year.

Asparagus Three-Cheese Burritos

- *Preheat oven to 375°F (190°C)*
- *Baking sheet, lightly oiled*

1 lb	asparagus	500 g
1 cup	ricotta cheese	250 mL
1/3 cup	shredded mozzarella cheese	75 mL
1/4 cup	freshly grated Parmesan cheese	50 mL
3 tbsp	fresh thyme leaves	45 mL
1 tsp	sesame oil	5 mL
	Salt and freshly ground pepper	
4	large, soft flour tortillas	4
2 cups	tomato sauce	500 mL
8	fresh thyme sprigs, optional	8

1. Trim tough ends from asparagus and discard (or freeze for vegetable stock). In a large saucepan, bring 6 cups (1.5 L) water to a boil over high heat. Drop asparagus into the water. Reduce heat and simmer for 3 to 5 minutes or just until tender. Drain and let cool.

2. Meanwhile, in a bowl, combine ricotta, mozzarella and Parmesan cheeses, thyme and oil. Add salt and pepper, to taste.

3. Spoon about one-quarter of the cheese mixture into center of a tortilla. Spread to within 1/2 inch (1 cm) of the edges. Divide asparagus into 4 portions. Lay one portion in the center of tortilla. Fold in bottom and one side and roll the tortilla around the asparagus allowing the tips to extend out the top of burrito. Repeat with remaining tortillas and filling.

4. Place burritos seam side down on prepared baking sheet. Bake in preheated oven for 12 to 15 minutes, until heated through.

5. Meanwhile, in a small saucepan, heat tomato sauce over medium heat. Transfer burritos to serving plates and spoon about 1/2 cup (125 mL) of the sauce over top each. Garnish with thyme springs, if using, and serve immediately.

This is a spectacular weekday dinner. Complete in itself, it is ready in less than 30 minutes.

Stir-Fried Vegetables and Bulgur with Ginger-Citrus Sauce

• *Heated serving platter*

1 ½ cups	boiling water	375 mL
¾ cup	bulgur	175 mL
2 tbsp	olive oil	25 mL
½ cup	chopped onion	125 mL
½ cup	chopped red bell pepper	125 mL
2	cloves garlic, minced	2
2 cups	sliced shiitake mushroom caps	500 mL
8 oz	green beans, cut into 1-inch (2.5 cm) pieces	250 g
8 oz	asparagus, trimmed and cut into 1-inch (2.5 cm) pieces	250 g
1 cup	fresh peas	250 mL
¾ cup	Ginger Citrus Sauce (see recipe, right)	175 mL

1. In a small bowl, pour boiling water over bulgur. Cover and set aside until ready to serve. Fluff with a fork just before serving.

2. Meanwhile, in a wok or large skillet, heat oil over medium-high heat. Add onion and bell pepper and cook, stirring constantly, for 3 minutes. Add garlic, mushrooms, green beans and asparagus. Cook, stirring often, for 3 to 5 minutes or until green beans are tender-crisp.

3. Stir in peas and Ginger Citrus Sauce. Reduce heat and simmer for 3 minutes or until sauce is slightly thickened. Transfer bulgur to serving platter. Spoon vegetables and sauce over top and serve immediately.

Variations

• When local fresh green beans and asparagus are out of season, use broccoli and carrots in their place.

• Use couscous instead of bulgur.

• Use cooked millet or amaranth in place of bulgur and omit Step 1.

Ginger-Citrus Sauce

Easy to make, this sauce enlivens stir-fried vegetables, as in the recipe left, but also makes a flavorful dipping sauce and sauce for steamed vegetables and greens.

1	piece (1 inch/2.5 cm) fresh gingerroot, peeled	1
1	small jalapeño pepper, seeded and quartered	1
1	stalk lemongrass, tops and outer leaves removed, coarsely chopped	1
⅓ cup	freshly squeezed orange juice	75 mL
3 tbsp	freshly squeezed lemon juice	45 mL
1 tbsp	rice vinegar	15 mL
1 tbsp	tamari or soy sauce	15 mL
2 tbsp	peanut butter	25 mL
2 tbsp	finely chopped fresh basil	25 mL
	Salt and freshly ground pepper	

1. In a small food processor or blender, chop ginger, jalapeño pepper and lemongrass. With motor running, add orange juice, lemon juice, vinegar and tamari through opening in lid. Process for 10 seconds. Stop and add peanut butter. Process for 10 seconds or until sauce is smooth.

2. Scrape mixture into a small bowl. Stir in basil. Add salt and pepper, to taste. Taste and adjust other seasonings, if required. Sauce may be used right away or made ahead and refrigerated, tightly covered, for up to 3 days. Bring to room temperature before using in recipes.

To enjoy a taste of the summer during the winter months, make extra casseroles at harvest time and freeze.

Tip

• To freeze: In Step 3, spoon vegetables into prepared ramekins, cover tightly with plastic wrap and place in resealable freezer bags and freeze. Mixture keeps in the freezer for up to 2 months. Thaw overnight in refrigerator before baking.

Summer Vegetable Casseroles

• *Preheat oven to 375°F (190°C)*
• *Six 2-inch (5 cm) ramekins, lightly oiled*

3	cobs fresh corn	3
2 tbsp	olive oil	25 mL
1½ cups	chopped zucchini	375 mL
½ cup	chopped red onion	125 mL
3 cups	shredded beets	750 mL
1 cup	cooked spelt kernels	250 mL
⅔ cup	shredded Swiss cheese	150 mL
3 tbsp	fresh thyme leaves	45 mL

1. Slice kernels from cobs over a bowl and set kernels aside. Run the blunt end of a knife down each cut cob over a small bowl, allowing remaining solids and corn "milk" or liquor to collect in bowl. Reserve liquor and discard cobs.

2. In a large skillet, heat oil over medium heat. Add corn kernels, zucchini and onion. Sauté for 5 minutes or until onions are soft. Stir in beets, spelt, cheese, thyme and corn liquor and stir to combine.

3. Spoon vegetable mixture equally into prepared ramekins. Bake in preheated oven for 15 to 20 minutes or until cheese is melted and mixture is bubbly. Serve immediately.

Here is the Summer
Vegetable Casseroles
recipe using winter
vegetables.

Tip

• To freeze: In Step 3,
  spoon vegetables into
  prepared ramekins,
  cover tightly with
  plastic wrap and
  place in resealable
  freezer bags and
  freeze. Mixture keeps
  in the freezer for up
  to 2 months. Thaw
  overnight in
  refrigerator before
  baking.

Winter Vegetable Casseroles

- *Preheat oven to 375°F (190°C)*
- *Six 2-inch (5 cm) ramekins, lightly oiled*

2 cups	frozen corn kernels or 1 can (14 oz/540 mL) corn kernels and liquid	500 mL
2 tbsp	olive oil	25 mL
1 cup	chopped carrot	250 mL
1 cup	chopped parsnip or rutabaga	250 mL
½ cup	chopped red onion	125 mL
1	can (14 oz/540 mL) diced beets, drained	1
1 cup	cooked spelt kernels	250 mL
⅔ cup	shredded Swiss cheese	150 mL
3 tbsp	fresh thyme leaves	45 mL

1. In a saucepan, cover corn kernels with water. Bring to a boil over high heat. Reduce heat and simmer for 2 minutes. Drain and reserve kernels and ¼ cup (50 mL) of the cooking liquid. If using canned corn, drain and reserve kernels and ¼ cup (50 mL) of the liquid.

2. In a large skillet, heat oil over medium heat. Add corn kernels, carrot, parsnip and onion. Sauté for 5 minutes or until onions are soft. Stir in beets, spelt, cheese, thyme and reserved corn liquid and stir to combine.

3. Spoon vegetable mixture equally into prepared ramekins. Bake in preheated oven for 15 to 20 minutes or until cheese is melted and mixture is bubbly. Serve immediately.

Herbed Nut and Bean Patties

While the patties hold together quite nicely for baking, they are still soft and fragile, definitely not suited to grilling on a barbecue.

Tip

- If using store-bought Cajun spice, start with 1½ tsp (7 mL) because it may be stronger than the homemade version. Taste and add more as required.

Serving Suggestions

- Lightly toast hamburger buns and serve patties in buns with assorted condiments.

- For a light lunch, toss 3 cups (750 mL) mixed greens with a light salad dressing and divide among 6 plates. Slide a patty on top and spoon Barbecue Sauce over top, if using.

- *Preheat oven to 375°F (190°C)*
- *Baking sheet, lightly oiled*

1	can (19 oz/540 mL) chickpeas, drained and rinsed, or 2 cups (500 mL) cooked chickpeas	1
1	small onion, cut into quarters	1
2	cloves garlic	2
1	carrot, cut into chunks	1
1	small apple, quartered	1
1	slice candied ginger or piece (½-inch/1 cm) fresh gingerroot	1
½ cup	spelt flakes	125 mL
¼ cup	natural almonds	50 mL
¼ cup	sunflower seeds	50 mL
2 tbsp	ground flaxseeds	25 mL
4	parsley sprigs, stems trimmed	4
1 tbsp	Cajun Black Spice (see recipe, page 330), or store-bought (see Tip, left)	15 mL
1 tbsp	fresh thyme leaves	15 mL
1 tsp	salt	5 mL
2 tbsp	olive oil	25 mL
1	egg	1
½ cup	Barbecue Sauce (see recipe, page 320) or store-bought, optional	125 mL
6	hamburger buns, optional	6

1. In a food processor, combine chickpeas, onion, garlic, carrot, apple and ginger. Pulse until chopped. Add spelt, almonds, sunflower seeds, flaxseeds, parsley, Cajun spice, thyme and salt. Process until finely chopped. With motor running, add oil and egg through opening in the lid. Process until well mixed and holding together.

2. Spoon about one-sixth of the mixture directly onto prepared baking sheet, and pat into a compact patty, about 4 inches (10 cm) in diameter. Repeat until 6 patties are formed. Bake in preheated oven for 15 minutes. Top each patty with Barbecue Sauce, if using, and place in hamburger buns, if using (see Serving Suggestion, left).

Variation

- For a meatless main course loaf, pack the mixture into a lightly oiled 9-by 5-inch (2 L) loaf pan and bake in a 375°F (190°C) oven for 20 minutes or until mixture is set and begins to come away from sides of the pan. Let stand for 10 minutes before serving. Slice and top with Barbecue Sauce. Serve hot or cold.

Serves 4

Vegan Friendly

The tangy barbecue sauce and heat from the ginger combine to add an East-meets-southwestern flavor to the grilled tempeh.

Tip

- Although nothing beats the homemade version, a store-bought organic barbecue sauce, available at alternative or fine food stores, is a good substitution in this recipe.

Gingered Tempeh in Barbecue Sauce

- *13-by 9-inch (3 L) baking pan, lightly oiled*
- *4 wooden skewers, lightly oiled*

8 oz	tempeh, thawed	250 g
1 cup	Barbecue Sauce (see recipe, page 320)	250 mL
2 tbsp	chopped candied ginger	25 mL
8	cherry tomatoes	8
1	onion, cut into 8 wedges	1

1. Cut tempeh into nine 1-inch (2.5 cm) squares. In prepared pan, combine Barbecue Sauce with ginger. Toss tempeh squares in sauce. Cover and marinate for a minimum of 2 hours or overnight in the refrigerator.

2. About 30 minutes before serving, bring tempeh to room temperature and preheat barbecue to high or oven to broil. Slide 2 tomatoes, 2 onion wedges and 2 tempeh squares on each skewer, alternating vegetables with tempeh, reserving Barbecue Sauce marinade. Grill, basting with reserved Barbecue Sauce occasionally, for 3 minutes per side. Serve hot and pass remaining Barbecue Sauce separately.

Eggplant strips replace pasta in this flavorful dish. Make ahead and serve for an elegant dinner dish.

Eggplant Manicotti with Spinach Pesto

- *Preheat oven to broil*
- *Baking sheet(s), lightly oiled*
- *8-inch (2 L) square baking dish, lightly oiled*

2	small eggplants, cut lengthwise into $\frac{1}{4}$-inch (0.5 cm) strips	2
1 cup	tomato sauce, divided	250 mL
2 cups	Spinach Pesto Filling (see recipe, right)	500 mL
$\frac{1}{2}$ cup	shredded mozzarella cheese	125 mL

1. Arrange eggplant strips in a single layer on prepared baking sheet. (If necessary, use 2 baking sheets, broiling separately.) Broil for 3 minutes. Flip eggplant strips using tongs and broil other side for 2 minutes or until eggplant is softened and lightly browned. Let cool.

2. Spread $\frac{1}{2}$ cup (125 mL) of the tomato sauce in the bottom of prepared baking dish.

3. Place 2 tbsp (25 mL) of the Spinach Pesto Filling on the short end of an eggplant strip. Roll up jelly-roll style into a ball around the filling. Place seam side down in baking dish. Repeat with remaining eggplant strips and filling. Pour remaining $\frac{1}{2}$ cup (125 mL) of tomato sauce over top and sprinkle with mozzarella cheese.

4. Bake in preheated oven for 25 to 30 minutes or until cheese is melted and sauce is bubbly. Let stand for 5 minutes before serving.

Spinach Pesto Filling

This is a creamy, low-fat version of the classic Basil Pesto (see recipe, page 308). As well as in this eggplant manicotti, use it in wraps and sandwiches or in appetizers and crêpes.

Tips

* Store pesto, tightly covered, in the refrigerator for up to 3 days.

* This recipe is doubled or halved with ease.

2	cloves garlic	2
3 tbsp	toasted sunflower seeds	45 mL
2 cups	packed spinach leaves	500 mL
1 cup	packed fresh basil leaves	250 mL
1 cup	lower-fat ricotta cheese	250 mL
1/2 cup	fresh parsley, stems trimmed	125 mL
2 tbsp	freshly grated Parmesan cheese	25 mL
	Salt and freshly ground pepper	

1. In a food processor or blender, combine garlic and sunflower seeds. Process for 20 seconds or until chopped. Add spinach, basil, ricotta, parsley and Parmesan. Process for 1 minute or until well blended. Add salt and pepper, to taste.

Variations

* Chopped walnuts or almonds may be used to replace sunflower seeds.

* Cottage cheese can take the place of ricotta cheese.

Fall Vegetable Paella

This dish is a colorful celebration of fall flavors. It's a one-dish meal that can be served for both family or as a potluck contribution.

3 tbsp	olive oil	45 mL
I cup	chopped onion	250 mL
2	cloves garlic, finely chopped	2
I cup	brown rice, rinsed	250 mL
2 tbsp	Turmeric Spice Paste (see recipe, page 335) or store-bought curry powder	25 mL
3 cups	vegetable stock, divided	750 mL
I cup	chopped zucchini	250 mL
½ cup	chopped green bell pepper	125 mL
½ cup	chopped red bell pepper	125 mL
½ cup	chopped mushrooms	125 mL
½ cup	cauliflower florets	125 mL
½ cup	broccoli florets	125 mL
½ cup	chopped carrot	125 mL
I tsp	salt	5 mL
	Freshly ground pepper	

1. In a large wok or saucepan, heat oil over medium-high heat. Add onion and garlic. Sauté for 5 minutes or until onions are soft. Stir in rice and Turmeric Spice Paste. Reduce heat and cook, stirring often, for 2 minutes.

2. Stir in 2 cups (500 mL) of the stock and bring to a boil over high heat. Cover, reduce heat and simmer for 25 minutes.

3. Stir in the remaining 1 cup (250 mL) of the stock, zucchini, green and red bell peppers, mushrooms, cauliflower, broccoli, carrot, salt and pepper, to taste. Cover and simmer gently for 10 minutes or until rice is soft and vegetables are tender-crisp without lifting the lid. Serve hot.

Variation

• Add 1 cup (250 mL) drained canned artichoke hearts in the last minute of cooking in Step 3.

Three-Bean Enchiladas with Green Tomato and Apple Salsa

The three beans in the filling make this a nutrient- and protein-rich main dish. A salad or vegetable dish balances out the meal.

Vegan Version

- Omit Asiago cheese or substitute soy cheese.

Tips

- Refried beans (*frijoles refritos*) are traditionally prepared by mashing red or pinto beans, adding seasonings and frying them in lard. Only packages labeled "vegetarian" will be sure to contain no lard.

- Enchiladas can be prepared to the end of Step 3 and refrigerated for 1 day or frozen for up to 3 months. Bring to room temperature before baking.

- *Preheat oven to 375°F (190°C)*
- *13-by 9-inch (3 L) baking dish, lightly oiled*

1	can (19 oz/540 mL) cannellini beans, drained and rinsed, or 2 cups (500 mL) cooked Great Northern White beans	1
1	can (19 oz/540 mL) chickpeas, drained and rinsed, or 2 cups (500 mL) cooked chickpeas	1
1/3 cup	chopped red bell pepper	75 mL
1	clove garlic, minced	1
1/2 cup	grated Asiago cheese	125 mL
1	can (14 oz/398 mL) refried beans (see Tips, left)	1
6	large, soft flour tortillas	6
1 cup	Green Tomato and Apple Salsa (see recipe, page 312) or regular tomato salsa	250 mL

1. Coarsely chop beans and chickpeas and transfer to a bowl. Stir in bell pepper, garlic and cheese.

2. Spread one-sixth of the refried beans evenly over each tortilla to within 1 inch (2.5 cm) of the edges.

3. Mound one-sixth of the bean-cheese filling down the center of each tortilla. Fold bottom and top in and fold sides in. Place seam side down in prepared baking dish. Cover with a lid or foil.

4. Bake in preheated oven for 15 to 20 minutes or until heated through. Serve with salsa.

Variations

- Substitute Swiss cheese for Asiago.
- In place of the refried beans, use 1 1/2 cups (375 mL) of any one of the following: Basic Almond Spread (page 151), Tzatziki (page 144), Hummus (page 146), Olive Tapenade (page 148) or Guacamole (page 148).

Black Bean Chili

Vegan Friendly

Serve this robust chili over baked potatoes for a main dish or with whole-grain nachos for an appetizer or party dish. Because many of the water-soluble nutrients are in the canned liquid, try to use both the beans and the liquid from the tin (if using home-cooked dried beans, do not use cooking liquid).

Tips

• Freezing tofu overnight or for a few hours and then thawing gives it a meaty texture. It crumbles nicely and seems to absorb more of the cooking liquid. Omit this step if time does not permit.

• If using store-bought Cajun spice, start with 2 tsp (10 mL) because it may be stronger than the homemade version. Taste and add more as required.

1 cup	chopped onion	250 mL
1 1/2 cups	chopped red bell pepper	375 mL
2 tbsp	olive oil	25 mL
1/2 cup	chopped celery	125 mL
3	cloves garlic, finely chopped	3
2	dried chiles, crushed	2
1 1/2 tbsp	Cajun Black Spice (see recipe, page 330) or store-bought (see Tips, left)	22 mL
1 lb	firm tofu, frozen, thawed and crumbled (see Tip, left)	500 g
1	can (28 oz/796 mL) tomatoes, including juice	1
1	can (19 oz/540 mL) black beans with liquid	1
1	can (19 oz/540 mL) dark red kidney beans with liquid	1
1/4 cup	chopped fresh parsley	50 mL
1 tbsp	chopped fresh savory	15 mL
1 tbsp	blackstrap molasses, optional	15 mL
	Salt and freshly ground pepper	

1. In a large saucepan, combine onion, bell pepper and oil. Sauté over medium heat for 7 minutes. Add celery, garlic, chiles, Cajun spice and tofu. Reduce heat and gently simmer, stirring occasionally, for 5 minutes.

2. Add tomatoes with juice. Increase heat and bring to a boil, stirring up browned bits in bottom of pan. Reduce heat and simmer for 10 minutes. Add black and red beans with liquid, parsley and savory. Simmer for 5 to 10 minutes or until heated through. Add molasses, if using. Add salt and pepper, to taste.

Variation

• Use chickpeas or black-eyed peas in place of either the black or kidney beans.

Fall Vegetable Paella (page 238)

Vegetable Pie with Sweet Potato Topping (page 244)

Golden Cauliflower with Split Peas (page 264)

Tomatoes Stuffed with Basil and Shiitake Mushrooms (page 265)

Kamut with Sautéed Summer Vegetables (page 288)

Fettuccine and Fiddleheads in Thyme Vinaigrette (page 298)

Peach Cobbler Cocktail (page 343)

Apple and Cheddar Cheese Flan (page 353)

Vegetable Cakes

Kids love these cakes and are oblivious to the vegetables that make them so nutritious.

- *Preheat oven to 400°F (200°C)*
- *Baking sheet, lightly oiled*

½	rutabaga, cut into 1-inch (2.5 cm) cubes	½
2	carrots, cut into 1-inch (2.5 cm) pieces	2
½ cup	shredded Cheddar cheese	125 mL
3 cups	fresh whole wheat bread crumbs, divided	750 mL
2	cloves garlic, minced	2
1 cup	chopped onion	250 mL
1	piece (1 inch/2.5 cm) fresh gingerroot	1
1 tbsp	chopped fresh parsley	15 mL
1 tsp	salt	5 mL
1	large egg, beaten	1
1 tbsp	ground flaxseeds	15 mL

1. In a steamer or colander over boiling water, steam rutabaga and carrots for 15 minutes or until tender. Drain and let cool. Transfer to a bowl and mash using a potato masher.

2. Meanwhile, in a large bowl, combine cheese, 2 cups (500 mL) of the bread crumbs, garlic, onion, ginger, parsley and salt. Stir in egg and rutabaga-carrot mixture.

3. Sprinkle the remaining 1 cup (250 mL) bread crumbs and flaxseeds over a sheet of waxed paper. Divide vegetable mixture into 8 balls. Place one at a time on bread crumbs. Flatten to a 4-inch (10 cm) diameter cake. Flip to coat other side with crumbs. Transfer to prepared baking sheet. Repeat with remaining vegetable balls.

4. Bake in preheated oven for 12 minutes. Flip cakes and bake for another 10 to 12 minutes or until lightly browned. Serve immediately.

Serving Suggestion
- Serve these vegetable cakes as a main course with rice or whole grain and a sauce, such as Salsa Verde (see recipe, page 315) or Miso Gravy (see recipe, page 322).

Potato and Adzuki Latkes

A fast and nutritious meal that is both satisfying and great tasting, this dish can be adapted to almost any vegetable that is in your refrigerator. The egg holds the ingredients together and the flour absorbs the liquid from the freshly grated vegetables to keep the pancakes from falling apart.

- *Preheat oven to 325°F (160°C)*
- *Baking sheet, lined with paper towel*

2	medium potatoes, shredded and drained	2
1 cup	cooked adzuki beans	250 mL
1	carrot, shredded	1
½	onion, chopped or shredded	½
½ cup	shredded Swiss or Cheddar cheese	125 mL
1	clove garlic, minced	1
1 tbsp	chopped fresh savory	15 mL
1 tbsp	chopped fresh oregano	15 mL
½ tsp	salt	2 mL
1	large egg, beaten	1
¼ cup	unbleached all-purpose or whole wheat flour (approx.)	50 mL
2 to 4 tbsp	olive oil	25 to 60 mL
1 cup	drained yogurt or Yogurt Cheese (see recipe, page 145), optional	250 mL

1. In a large bowl, combine potatoes, beans, carrot, onion, cheese, garlic, savory, oregano and salt, mixing well. Stir in egg. Sprinkle in flour, 1 tbsp (15 mL) at a time, stirring until the mixture holds together well.

2. In a large skillet, heat 1 tbsp (15 mL) of the oil over medium heat. Drop ¼ cup (50 mL) of the potato mixture into the skillet and flatten lightly with a fork (keep latke compact and at least ½-inch/1 cm thick). Repeat to make 1 or 2 more latkes. Cook for 4 minutes on one side. Flip and cook for 3 to 4 minutes on the other side or until browned. Using a slotted lifter, transfer to prepared baking sheet and keep warm in preheated oven. Repeat with remaining vegetable mixture, adding more oil as necessary. Serve hot with a dollop of yogurt, if using.

Variation
- Use any cooked legume (lima, red kidney or pinto beans) or lentils (red or green) in place of the adzuki beans.

Vegetables and Tempeh au Gratin

- *Preheat oven to 350°F (180°C)*
- *9-inch (2.5 L) square baking dish, lightly oiled*

1 cup	broccoli florets	250 mL
1 cup	sliced carrots	250 mL
1 cup	coarsely chopped leeks, white and light green parts	250 mL
2 cups	cubed tempeh (12 oz/340 g)	500 mL
3 tbsp	tamari or soy sauce	45 mL
2 cups	cooked brown rice	500 mL
1 ½ cups	Cheese Sauce (see recipe, page 324)	375 mL
¼ cup	shredded Swiss cheese	50 mL
¼ cup	whole wheat bread crumbs	50 mL

1. In a steamer or colander over a pot of boiling water, steam broccoli, carrots and leeks for 10 to 15 minutes or until tender-crisp.

2. Meanwhile, in a bowl, combine tempeh with tamari. Set aside.

3. Spread rice in bottom of prepared baking dish. Lift tempeh out of tamari and distribute over rice. Spread broccoli, carrots and leeks evenly over rice. Pour Cheese Sauce over top and sprinkle with Swiss cheese and bread crumbs. Bake in preheated oven for 20 minutes or until mixture is well heated and sauce is bubbly and golden brown.

Variations

- Use Whole-Grain Granola (see recipe, page 160) in place of bread crumbs.
- Replace Swiss cheese and bread crumbs with ½ cup (125 mL) Savory Oatmeal Topping (see recipe, page 253).

The roasted vegetables are naturally sweet and when combined with the sweet potato topping, it makes a memorable buffet or company dinner entrée.

Vegetable Pie with Sweet Potato Topping

- *Preheat oven to 400°F (200°C)*
- *13-by 9-inch (3 L) baking dish*

1 cup	boiling water	250 mL
4	large dried black mushrooms	4
3 cups	1-inch (2.5 cm) cubes rutabaga	750 mL
2	carrots, cut into 1-inch (2.5 cm) pieces	2
2	parsnips, cut into 1-inch (2.5 cm) pieces	2
3 tbsp	olive oil, divided	45 mL
2	potatoes, cut into eighths	2
2	onions, cut into eighths	2
6	cloves garlic, peeled and left whole	6
1	leek, white and light green parts, cut into 1-inch (2.5 cm) pieces	1
2 tbsp	chopped fresh sage	25 mL
2 tbsp	fresh thyme leaves	25 mL
1 cup	broccoli florets	250 mL
1 cup	frozen peas	250 mL
2 tbsp	cornstarch	25 mL
1 cup	tomato juice, divided	250 mL
1/2 cup	dry red wine	125 mL

Topping

3	large sweet potatoes, each cut into 4 chunks	3
2 tbsp	butter	25 mL
1/4 cup	natural yogurt	50 mL
1/2 tsp	salt	2 mL
1/2 tsp	ground nutmeg	2 mL

1. In a bowl, pour water over mushrooms and set aside to soak for 20 minutes. Drain, reserving 1/2 cup (125 mL) of the soaking liquid, and squeeze mushrooms dry. Set aside.

2. Meanwhile, in baking dish, combine rutabaga, carrots, parsnips and 1 1/2 tbsp (22 mL) of the oil. Toss to coat well.

- Recipe may be prepared to the end of Step 6. Cover tightly and refrigerate over night or freeze for up to 3 months. Return to room temperature before baking.

Roast in preheated oven for 30 minutes. Add potatoes, onions, garlic, leek, sage, thyme and remaining 1½ tbsp (22 mL) of the oil. Toss to combine. Roast for 40 to 50 minutes or until vegetables are browned and tender (onions may be slightly charred). Remove dish from oven. Reduce oven temperature to 375°F (190°C).

3. Meanwhile, make Topping: Fill a large saucepan to the halfway point with cold water and add sweet potatoes. Bring to a boil over high heat. Cover, reduce heat and simmer for 20 minutes or until soft. Drain and rinse with cold water. Remove and discard skins. Return sweet potatoes to the pan. Using a potato masher, mash sweet potatoes. Beat in butter, yogurt, salt and nutmeg. Set aside.

4. Add reserved mushrooms, broccoli and peas to roasted vegetables in baking dish and stir to mix well.

5. In a small saucepan, mix cornstarch with ¼ cup (50 mL) of the tomato juice to make a smooth paste. Whisk in the remaining ¾ cup (175 mL) of tomato juice, red wine and reserved mushroom soaking liquid. Bring to a boil over medium heat. Reduce heat and simmer, stirring often, for 4 minutes or until sauce is thickened.

6. Pour sauce over roasted vegetables in baking dish. Stir to mix well. Spoon sweet potato topping over vegetables and smooth with a spatula.

7. Bake in preheated oven for 20 minutes or until topping is browned and vegetable mixture is bubbly around the edges. Let stand for 5 minutes before serving.

Variations

- Omit cornstarch and replace tomato juice with 1 cup (250 mL) of tomato sauce and follow directions for sauce in Step 5.

- For protein, add ⅔ cup (150 mL) shredded Swiss or Cheddar cheese or 1 cup (250 mL) cooked legumes or chopped nuts in Step 4.

A new take on a classic, this vegetarian lasagna uses a Mushroom Sauce that makes for a complex and smoky flavor.

Artichoke and Mushroom Lasagna

- *Preheat oven to 375°F (190°C)*
- *13-by 9-inch (3 L) baking pan, lightly oiled*

1½ lbs	lower-fat cottage or ricotta cheese	750 g
1	egg, beaten	1
¼ cup	freshly grated Parmesan cheese	50 mL
2 tbsp	fresh chopped oregano	25 mL
2 tbsp	fresh thyme leaves	25 mL
1 tsp	salt	5 mL
6 to 8 oz	lasagna noodles (9 or 10 whole)	175 to 250 g
1 cup	finely chopped onion	250 mL
2 lbs	mushrooms, sliced	1 kg
½ cup	dry white wine	125 mL
1	can (14 oz/398 mL) artichoke hearts, drained and coarsely chopped	1
4 cups	Mushroom Sauce (see recipe, page 321)	1 L

1. In blender or food processor, combine cottage cheese, egg, Parmesan, oregano and thyme. Process for 1 minute or until puréed. Transfer to a small bowl. Cover and set aside.

2. Fill a large saucepan to the halfway point with water and bring to a boil over high heat. Add salt and noodles. Reduce heat and keep water gently boiling. Cook noodles for about 10 minutes or until tender (al dente). Using tongs, transfer noodles to a bowl filled with cold water. When cool, drain and lay flat on clean kitchen towels (not paper).

3. Meanwhile, in a saucepan, simmer onion, mushrooms and wine over medium heat for 7 minutes or until onions are soft and mushrooms are half their original volume. Stir in artichokes and remove from heat.

4. To assemble lasagna: Spread one-half of the Mushroom Sauce in bottom of prepared baking pan. Lay 3 or 4 lasagna noodles over sauce. Spread one-half of the cheese mixture over noodles and one-half of the mushroom mixture over cheese. Repeat another layer of noodles, cheese and mushrooms. Lay remaining 3 or 4 noodles on top and pour remaining Mushroom Sauce over top.

5. Cover with lid or foil and bake in preheated oven for 30 minutes. Let stand for 10 minutes before serving.

Variation

- Spread $3/4$ cup (175 mL) shredded mozzarella cheese over top of lasagna after baking in Step 5. Return to oven and bake for 5 to 10 minutes more or until cheese is melted and sauce is bubbly. Let stand for 10 minutes before serving.

Imam is the Persian word for "holy man." The Middle Eastern name of this dish - *imam bayildi* — literally means "the holy man fainted," implying that he was so enraptured he collapsed after taking a whiff of the fragrant spices in the baked dish.

Turkish-Stuffed Baked Eggplant

- *Preheat oven to 375°F (190°C)*
- *Baking sheet, lightly oiled*

2	medium eggplants	2
3 tbsp	olive oil	45 mL
1	onion, coarsely chopped	1
1 cup	thinly sliced fennel bulb or celery	250 mL
3	cloves garlic, minced	3
2	large tomatoes, seeded and diced	2
1 tsp	ground coriander seeds	5 mL
1/2 tsp	ground cinnamon	2 mL
1/2 tsp	ground cumin	2 mL
1/2 tsp	ground turmeric	2 mL
1/2 tsp	salt	2 mL

1. Trim ends from eggplants and discard. Fill a large saucepan to the halfway point with water and bring to a boil over high heat. Add eggplants and cook for 7 minutes. Remove and rinse under cold water to stop the cooking. When cool, cut each in half lengthwise. Scoop out the flesh leaving a 1/4-inch (0.5 cm) thick shell. Place shells cut side up on prepared baking sheet. Coarsely chop and reserve flesh.

2. Meanwhile, in a large skillet, heat oil over medium heat. Add onion and sauté for 10 minutes or until soft. Stir in fennel and garlic and sauté for 5 minutes. Stir in tomatoes, coriander, cinnamon, cumin, turmeric, salt and reserved eggplant. Cook, stirring, for 3 minutes or until vegetables are tender.

3. Spoon stuffing equally into each eggplant shell. Cover with foil and bake in preheated oven 30 minutes. Serve immediately or let cool and serve at room temperature.

Squash Tagine

Tagine is the name for North African stew — unique and luscious because of its combinations of delicately spiced vegetables and fruit that are slow-cooked for long periods of time until the components are transformed into rich, velvet-smooth sauces. The traditional clay utensil, also called tagine, has a conical lid, which allows moisture and steam to circulate up and around the food so that it poaches as it cooks and becomes very tender.

Tips

- Any local autumn squashes, such as turban, acorn, patty pan or butternut, are suitable for this recipe.

- If you have a tagine, but it isn't flameproof (a flameproof base will be clearly marked on the bottom), use a large skillet in Steps 2 and 3 and transfer to tagine for Step 4.

- If using store-bought Cajun spice, start with $1\frac{1}{2}$ tsp (7 mL) because it may be stronger than the homemade version. Taste and add more as required.

- *Preheat oven to 350°F (180°C)*
- *Flameproof tagine or Dutch oven*

2 lbs	squash (see Tips, left)	1 kg
1	large onion, chopped	1
4	cloves garlic, finely chopped	4
3 tbsp	olive oil	45 mL
1 tbsp	Cajun Black Spice (see recipe, page 330) or Ras el Hanout seasoning (see recipe, page 334) or store-bought (see Tips, left)	15 mL
1 tsp	Yellow or Red Curry Spice (see recipes, page 331) or store-bought	5 mL
1 tsp	Garam Masala Spice Blend (see recipe, page 333) or store-bought	5 mL
$1\frac{1}{4}$ cup	vegetable stock	300 mL
6	dried apricots, chopped, or $\frac{1}{4}$ cup (50 mL) dried cranberries	6
1	apple, chopped	1
$\frac{1}{2}$ cup	chopped raisins	125 mL
	Salt	
	Cooked couscous or bulgur	

1. Peel and seed squash and cut into 1-inch (2.5 cm) cubes. You will have about 5 to 6 cups (1.25 to 1.5 L). Set aside.

2. In bottom of tagine or Dutch oven, combine onion, garlic and oil. Cook over medium heat for 7 minutes or until onions are soft. Add Cajun spice, curry spice and garam masala. Cook, stirring continuously, for 1 minute.

3. Stir in vegetable stock. Increase heat and bring to a boil. Stir in squash, apricots, apple, raisins and salt to taste and stir well to coat squash cubes.

4. Cover and bake in preheated oven for 45 minutes to 1 hour or until squash is tender and sauce has thickened. Serve over cooked couscous or bulgur.

Variations

- Add $\frac{1}{2}$ cup (125 mL) pitted, quartered prunes to the mixture in Step 3.
- Garnish with $\frac{1}{2}$ cup (125 mL) toasted pistachio nuts or almonds.

Cantonese Noodles

Tofu is now available in tetra-packs so can be kept in a cupboard to have readily on hand. All the other ingredients are easily available for this fast and easy dinner dish.

Tip

- If using store-bought Cajun spice, start with 1½ tsp (7 mL) because it may be stronger than the homemade version. Taste and add more as required.

1 tbsp	Cajun Black Spice (see recipe, page 330) or store-bought (see Tip, left)	15 mL
1 tbsp	Chinese black bean sauce	15 mL
½ cup	chopped onion	125 mL
4 cups	vegetable stock, divided	1 L
1 tbsp	tamari or soy sauce	15 mL
6 oz	dried somen (buckwheat) noodles	175 g
4	oyster mushrooms, sliced	4
4 oz	firm tofu, cut into small dice	125 g
2 cups	spinach, shredded	500 mL
1	sheet nori, shredded	1
	Salt and freshly ground pepper	
2	green onions, thinly sliced, optional	2

1. In a wok or large saucepan, combine Cajun spice and black bean sauce. Heat gently over medium-low heat for 1 minute. Stir in onion and 2 tbsp (25 mL) of the stock. Increase heat to medium and cook for 5 minutes or until onions are soft.

2. Stir in remaining stock and tamari. Increase heat to high and bring to a boil. Add noodles and mushrooms. Reduce heat and simmer for 8 minutes or until noodles are tender.

3. Add tofu, spinach and nori and simmer for 2 minutes. Taste and add more black bean sauce, tamari or salt, if required. Add salt and pepper, to taste. Ladle into soup bowls and garnish with green onions, if using.

Variations

- Soy or rice milk can replace the vegetable stock.
- Use frozen spinach or canned lima or green beans in place of the spinach.

Make this bread pudding the night before and refrigerate so that all you have to do is pop it in the oven when you come home. It makes great leftovers for breakfast or snacks.

Tips

- Lower-fat milk also works well in this recipe.

- Pudding can be prepared through Step 3 and refrigerated overnight. Bring to room temperature before baking.

Mediterranean Savory Bread Pudding

- *Preheat oven to 375°F (190°C)*
- *11-by 7-inch (2 L) baking dish, lightly oiled*

2	red bell peppers, cut into large dice	2
I	onion, chopped	I
I tbsp	fresh chopped basil	15 mL
I tbsp	fresh thyme leaves	15 mL
1/3 cup	white wine	75 mL
4 oz	feta cheese, drained and crumbled	125 g
3 tbsp	freshly grated Parmesan cheese	45 mL
6 to 8	black olives, pitted and chopped	6 to 8
3	large eggs	3
2 cups	milk (see Tips, left)	500 mL
8	slices whole wheat bread	8

1. In saucepan, combine bell peppers, onion, basil, thyme and wine. Simmer gently over medium heat for 10 minutes or until vegetables are soft.

2. Meanwhile, in a bowl, combine feta cheese, Parmesan and olives and set aside. In a another bowl, beat eggs with milk and set aside.

3. Line bottom of prepared dish with one layer of bread slices, cutting to make fit, as necessary. Spread vegetable mixture over bread slices. Spread cheese mixture over vegetables. Top with remaining bread slices. Pour eggs and milk over top. Cover with foil. Refrigerate for 1 hour or overnight. Return to room temperature before baking.

4. Bake in preheated oven for 30 minutes. Remove foil and bake for another 5 to 10 minutes or until puffed up and golden. Let stand for 3 minutes and serve hot.

Variations

- Sprinkle 1/3 cup (75 mL) grated mozzarella cheese over top of pudding after baking for 30 minutes in Step 4. Bake another 5 to 10 minutes or until mozzarella cheese is melted and pudding is puffed up and golden.

Black-Eyed Pea Casserole

Here is another easy, after-work dinner dish and the bonus is that the casserole ingredients are mixed and served in the baking dish.

- *Preheat oven to 375°F (190°C)*
- *8 cups (2 L) casserole dish, lightly oiled*

Casserole

I	can (19 oz/540 mL) black-eyed peas, drained and rinsed, or 2 cups (500 mL) cooked black-eyed peas	I
I	can (28 oz/796 mL) tomatoes, including juice	I
2 tbsp	tomato paste	25 mL
I cup	chopped onion	250 mL
I cup	chopped green or red bell pepper	250 mL
I cup	chopped zucchini	250 mL
2	cloves garlic, finely chopped	2
2 tbsp	chopped fresh parsley	25 mL
2 tbsp	chopped fresh savory	25 mL
I cup	fresh, frozen or canned corn kernels, drained, if canned	250 mL

Biscuit Topping

I cup	whole wheat flour	250 mL
I½ tsp	baking powder	7 mL
I tbsp	chopped fresh parsley	15 mL
I tbsp	chopped fresh savory	15 mL
½ tsp	salt	2 mL
3 tbsp	butter	45 mL
⅓ cup	drained natural yogurt (see Tip, right)	75 mL
2 to 3 tbsp	rice or soy milk	25 to 45 mL

I. Casserole: In prepared casserole dish, combine peas, tomatoes with juice and tomato paste. Stir to mix well. Add onion, bell pepper, zucchini, garlic, parsley, savory and corn. Cover and bake in preheated oven for 25 minutes.

- Some brands of natural yogurt are slightly more watery than others. This is because there are no gum or thickeners added and the liquid collects on the top. Before using in recipes, drain some of this watery liquid (use it in soup or add to the casserole) by positioning the lid over the container and easing out some of the excess liquid.

Makes 1½ cups (375 mL)

Tip

- Any nut or combination of nuts and seeds will work in this recipe.

2. Meanwhile, make Biscuit Topping or Savory Oatmeal Topping (see recipe, below): In a bowl, whisk together flour, baking powder, parsley, savory and salt. Using a pastry cutter or 2 knives, cut in butter until it is the size of peas. Stir in yogurt. Add milk, 1 tbsp (15 mL) at a time, until dough holds together. On a lightly floured surface, knead dough lightly once or twice and roll out to ½-inch (1 cm) thick. Using a round cookie cutter, cut out 2-inch (5 cm) rounds, rerolling scraps once.

3. Remove dish from oven and arrange biscuit rounds on top of hot casserole. Bake for another 25 minutes or until topping is browned and a cake tester or toothpick comes out clean. Serve immediately.

Savory Oatmeal Topping

½ cup	large flake rolled oats or spelt	125 mL
½ cup	chopped nuts (see Tip, left)	125 mL
⅓ cup	shredded mozzarella	75 mL
¼ cup	chopped fresh parsley	50 mL
1 to 2 tbsp	olive oil	15 to 25 mL

1. In a small bowl, combine oats, nuts, cheese and parsley. Stir in oil, a small amount at a time, mixing until it resembles a coarse crumb.

Variations

- Use soy cheese, or Cheddar or Parmesan cheese in place of the mozzarella cheese.

A tasty and complete meal, this casserole travels well and makes a great potluck dish. As an added bonus it can be made ahead up to two days before baking.

Tip

- Casserole can be prepared through Step 4, covered and refrigerated for up to 2 days. Bring to room temperature before baking.

Vegetable Oatmeal Crumble

- *8-inch (2 L) baking dish, lightly oiled*

I cup	vegetable stock	250 mL
½ cup	brown rice, rinsed	125 mL
I cup	chopped onion	250 mL
I cup	chopped red bell pepper	250 mL
½ cup	white wine	125 mL
I	can (28 oz/796 mL) tomatoes, drained, reserving juice	I
I ½ cups	cauliflower florets	375 mL
I ½ cups	broccoli florets	375 mL
I cup	Spinach-Ricotta Filling (½ recipe, see page 157), divided	250 mL
I ½ cups	Savory Oatmeal Topping (see recipe, page 253)	375 mL

1. In a saucepan, bring stock to a boil over high heat. Stir in rice. Cover, reduce heat and simmer gently for 35 minutes or until rice is tender. Drain if any liquid remains.

2. Meanwhile, in another saucepan, combine onion, bell pepper and wine. Simmer over medium-high heat for 7 minutes or until vegetables are soft. Add tomatoes, cauliflower and broccoli. Increase heat to high and bring to a boil. Reduce heat and simmer gently for 7 minutes or until florets are tender-crisp, adding some of the reserved tomato juice if mixture gets too dry.

3. Preheat oven to 350°F (180°C).

4. In bottom of prepared baking dish, combine rice and ½ cup (125 mL) of the Spinach-Ricotta Filling. Spread evenly over bottom of dish. Spoon vegetables over rice. Spread remaining filling over vegetables. Scatter Savory Oatmeal Topping evenly over top.

5. Bake in preheated oven for 20 minutes or until vegetables are bubbly and topping is browned.

Vegan Stroganoff

The Mushroom Sauce may be made up to two days in advance, making this elegant dish very quick and easy to prepare for company.

1 tsp	salt	5 mL
6 to 8 oz	linguine noodles	175 to 250 g
3 tbsp	olive oil, divided	45 mL
3 cups	seitan, cut into thin pieces	750 mL
2	cloves garlic, finely sliced	2
1 cup	chopped onion	250 mL
1 lb	mushrooms, sliced	500 g
1/3 cup	white wine	75 mL
2 cups	Mushroom Sauce (see recipe, page 321)	500 mL
1/3 cup	chopped fresh parsley, optional	75 mL

1. Fill a large saucepan to the halfway point with water and bring to a boil over high heat. Add salt and noodles. Reduce heat to keep water gently boiling. Cook noodles for 8 to 10 minutes or until tender (al dente). Drain and rinse under cool water. Transfer to a large bowl. Toss with 2 tbsp (25 mL) of the oil and set aside.

2. In a large saucepan, heat remaining 1 tbsp (15 mL) of oil over medium heat. Add seitan and garlic. Sauté for 3 minutes or just until lightly brown. Using a slotted spoon, transfer to a bowl and set aside.

3. In the same saucepan, simmer onion, mushrooms and wine over medium heat for 7 minutes or until onions are soft and mushrooms are half their original volume. Stir in Mushroom Sauce and seitan-garlic mixture. Cook for 2 to 3 minutes or until heated through.

4. Divide noodles among 4 plates. Spoon stroganoff over top. Garnish with parsley, if using, and serve immediately.

Traditional moussaka is baked with ground lamb, thick cream sauce, piles of cheese, and sometimes even topped with mashed potatoes. Try this lighter, vegetarian version.

Baked Eggplant with Tomatoes and Mozzarella

• *13-by 9-inch (3 L) baking pan, lightly oiled*

1	medium eggplant, trimmed and cut into $1/4$-inch (0.5 cm) slices	1
1 tbsp	salt (approx.)	15 mL
2 tbsp	olive oil	25 mL
$1/2$ cup	finely chopped fresh parsley	125 mL
2 tbsp	Chinese black bean sauce	25 mL
2	cloves garlic, minced	2
1	onion, thinly sliced	1
2	large tomatoes, peeled and cut in $1/4$-inch (0.5 cm) slices	2
1 cup	shredded mozzarella cheese	250 mL

1. In a large colander, spread eggplant slices in one layer. Sprinkle with 1 tsp (5 mL) of the salt. Keep layering eggplant and salt until all slices are salted. Drain for 30 minutes. Rinse and pat dry. Meanwhile, preheat oven to 350°F (180°C).

2. In prepared baking pan, overlap eggplant slices to form one layer. Drizzle olive oil over top. Bake in preheated oven for 20 minutes.

3. In a small bowl, combine parsley, black bean sauce and garlic. Spread onion slices evenly over eggplant and sprinkle with parsley mixture. Spread tomato slices over vegetables and top with cheese. Cover with foil.

4. Bake in preheated oven for 30 minutes. Remove foil and continue to bake for another 10 to 15 minutes or until cheese is melted and golden brown. Serve hot or at room temperature.

Vegetables and Legumes

Roasted Vegetables

Vegan Friendly

Roasted fruit and
vegetables blacken
slightly around the
edges and are shriveled
in appearance. For this
reason, they are often
used in soups and
puréed dishes.

Tip

• Use rosemary, sage,
thyme, chives,
parsley, basil or savory
in any combination.

• *Preheat oven to 400°F (200°C)*
• *Baking sheet, lightly oiled*

3 cups	quartered scrubbed vegetables	750 mL
2 tbsp	olive oil	25 mL
¼ cup	chopped fresh herbs (see Tip, left)	50 mL

1. Toss vegetables with oil and herbs on prepared baking
sheet. Roast in the lower half of the preheated oven for
25 to 45 minutes or until browned and tender.

Roasted Garlic

Vegan Friendly

When roasted, garlic is
mellow and sweet and
usually the whole head
is used in a recipe.

Tip

• Bake several heads
at a time and store
in the refrigerator
for up to 5 days. Or
squeeze the cloves
out of skin and place
in resealable freezer
bags and freeze for
up to 3 months.

• *Preheat oven to 400°F (200°C)*
• *Small heatproof baking dish with lid or foil*

1	whole head garlic	1
1 tsp	olive oil	5 mL

1. Remove the loose, papery skin from the garlic head and
slice and discard ¼ inch (0.5 cm) off the tips of the
cloves in the entire head. Place the garlic head cut side up
in baking dish and drizzle with oil. Cover with a lid or foil.
Bake in preheated oven for about 40 minutes or until garlic
is quite soft. Transfer to a cooling rack. If using a clay
garlic roaster with a lid, roast at 375°F (190°C) for 35 to
40 minutes.

2. When garlic is cool enough to handle, squeeze cloves from
their skins. It is now ready to use in any recipe that calls
for roasted garlic.

Vegan Friendly

The creamy center of roasted eggplant is contrasted in this dish by the crispy browned texture of the outside as a result of roasting. One of the keys to roasting eggplant is to slice it at a thickness of $^3/_8$ inches (0.9 cm) because if thinner, the slices will dry out and if thicker, they will not cook on the inside. This recipe is easily doubled.

Roasted Eggplant with Walnut Sauce

- *Preheat oven to 400°F (200°C)*
- *Baking sheet, lightly oiled*
- *Warmed serving platter or individual plates*

I	medium eggplant, trimmed	I
I tbsp	salt	15 mL
	organic canola or olive oil	
$^1/_2$ cup	Walnut Sauce ($^1/_4$ recipe, see page 325)	125 mL

1. Slice eggplant crosswise in $^3/_8$-inch (0.9 cm) thick rounds. In a large colander, arrange one layer of rounds and sprinkle 1 tsp (5 mL) of the salt over top. Repeat layering and salting. Let stand for 30 minutes. Rinse and pat dry. Arrange in one layer on prepared baking sheet. Brush the tops lightly with oil.

2. Bake in preheated oven for 8 to 10 minutes, in batches if necessary. Turn and bake another 8 to 10 minutes or until both sides are golden brown. Transfer to a warmed platter. Spoon Walnut Sauce over top and serve immediately.

Roasting and Caramelizing Vegetables

Roasting vegetables or fruit is a technique that requires a higher heat than baking. This fast-cooking method caramelizes the natural sugars on the outside, concentrating and deepening the flavors. Thick, firm and juicy-fleshed fruit such as plums, apricots and cherries, and all manner of vegetables such as beets, onions, squash, turnip, carrots, parsnips, eggplant, sweet potatoes, corn on the cob and asparagus benefit from roasting.

Vegan Friendly

Many other sauces complement the vegetables and greens in this dish. Instead of the Citrus Dressing, try Cocktail Peanut Sauce or Red Pepper Sauce (see recipes, page 326 and 224) next time you make it.

Braised Greens with Citrus Dressing

• *Heated serving platter*

4 cups	vegetable stock or water	I L
8	small new potatoes	8
I	onion, quartered	I
8 oz	Swiss chard or kale	250 g
I lb	asparagus, trimmed and cut into 2-inch (5 cm) pieces	500 g
I cup	snow peas, trimmed	250 mL
½ cup	Citrus Dressing (see recipe, page 178)	125 mL

1. In a large skillet with lid, bring stock to a boil over high heat. Add potatoes. Cover, reduce heat and simmer for 5 minutes. Add onion and simmer for 3 minutes. Add Swiss chard and asparagus and simmer for 2 minutes. Add snow peas and simmer for 2 minutes or until vegetables are tender-crisp.

2. Drain vegetables (reserve cooking liquid for stock). Transfer to serving platter. Drizzle Citrus Dressing over top and serve immediately.

Scalloped Turnips with Potatoes and Onion

Small, tender and sweet, locally grown turnips appear in the spring and early summer. They are not here for long so as well as in this recipe, use turnips in soups, stews and chowders. Stuff them with sautéed mushrooms and onions and bake them, or simply steam them and serve with herbed butter for a light spring meal.

Tip

- If vegetables, such as potatoes, sweet potatoes and turnips, are organic then there is no need to peel them.

- *Preheat oven to 350°F (180°C)*
- *9-inch (2.5 L) casserole dish, lightly oiled*

3 cups	thinly sliced potatoes (see Tip, left)	750 mL
1⅓ cups	thinly sliced sweet potatoes	325 mL
¼ cup	Basil Pesto (see recipe, page 308) or store-bought	50 mL
½ tsp	salt	2 mL
	Freshly ground pepper	
3 cups	thinly sliced turnips, divided	750 mL
1 cup	thinly sliced onion, divided	250 mL
¼ cup	whole wheat flour, divided	50 mL
1 cup	soy or rice milk, divided	250 mL
½ cup	mozzarella cheese	125 mL

1. In a large bowl, toss potatoes and sweet potatoes with pesto, salt and pepper, to taste, coating well. Spread one-third of potato mixture in bottom of prepared dish. Cover with one-half each of the turnips and onion. Sprinkle with 2 tbsp (25 mL) of the flour. Pour ½ cup (125 mL) of the milk over top.

2. Repeat layers of potato mixture, turnips, onion, flour and milk, ending with a layer of potatoes. Distribute cheese evenly over top. Cover with a lid or foil and bake in preheated oven for 30 minutes or until vegetables are tender. Uncover and bake for another 15 to 20 minutes or until top is brown and cheese is bubbly. Let stand for 3 minutes before serving.

Variation

- Substitute rutabaga for turnips.

Crispy and charred on the outside and sweetly soft on the inside, roasted asparagus is delicious. Whether simply dressed with a dash of fresh lemon juice, or served with warm Spring Green Sauce, this is a superb way to cook the season's crop of fresh asparagus.

Asparagus with Spring Green Sauce

- *Preheat oven to 400°F (200°C)*
- *13-by 9-inch (3 L) baking dish*

2 lbs	fresh asparagus, trimmed	1 kg
2 tbsp	olive oil	25 mL
1 tbsp	fresh thyme leaves	15 mL
1 tsp	salt	5 mL
	Freshly ground pepper	
2 cups	Spring Green Sauce (see recipe, page 328), optional	500 mL

1. In baking dish, toss asparagus with oil, thyme, salt and pepper, to taste. Roast in preheated oven for 30 minutes. Turn and roast for another 15 to 20 minutes or until asparagus is tender-crisp. Drizzle Spring Green Sauce over top, if using.

Full of vitamins, use this stuffing as a filling for peppers, zucchini, tomatoes, squash flowers, phyllo pastry, lettuce, radicchio cups or cabbage leaves.

Tips

- For vegetables, use a combination of chopped leeks, cauliflower, broccoli, legumes, celery, parsnips and rutabaga.

- Use chopped fresh herbs (sage, thyme, savory, chives, oregano or marjoram) or any of the spice blends (see Seasonings, page 329).

- For the cheese, use Gouda, Swiss Cheddar or another favorite cheese.

- Store stuffing, tightly covered, in the refrigerator for up to 2 days or in the freezer for up to 2 months.

Vegan Version

- Omit the cheese.

Whole-Grain and Vegetable Stuffing

3 cups	chopped vegetables (see Tips, left)	750 mL
¼ cup	white wine	50 mL
1 tbsp	chopped fresh herbs or spice blend (see Tips, left)	15 mL
1 cup	brown or wild rice	250 mL
2 cups	vegetable stock	500 mL
½ cup	grated cheese (see Tips, left)	125 mL

1. In a large skillet, combine vegetables and wine. Bring to a gentle simmer over medium heat and cook for 7 minutes or until tender.

2. Stir in herbs and cook for 1 minute. Stir in rice and cook, stirring, for 1 minute. Add stock. Increase heat to high and bring to a boil. Cover, reduce heat and simmer for 40 minutes or until rice is tender and most of the liquid has been absorbed. Drain if necessary. Stir in cheese.

Variation

- Instead of brown or wild rice, use whole soaked spelt, wheat berries or kamut and increase the cooking time to 1 hour or until tender.

Vegan Friendly

Any fresh summer vegetable will work well in this lower-fat recipe.

Golden Cauliflower with Split Peas

¾ cup	dried split green peas	175 mL
2 cups	water	500 mL
2 tbsp	olive oil	25 mL
1	piece (1 inch/2.5 cm) cinnamon, crushed	1
2 tsp	whole cumin seeds	10 mL
2 tsp	whole fennel seeds	10 mL
2 tsp	ground turmeric	10 mL
1 tbsp	minced fresh gingerroot	15 mL
1	small cauliflower, cut into small florets	1
½ cup	vegetable stock	125 mL
1 cup	chopped green onions	250 mL

1. In a saucepan, cover split peas with water. Bring to a boil over medium-high heat. Cover, reduce heat and simmer for 15 to 20 minutes or until peas are tender. Drain and set aside.

2. Meanwhile, in a large skillet or wok, heat oil over medium heat. Add cinnamon, cumin and fennel seeds. Toast, stirring, for 1 minute or until seeds turn brown. Add turmeric, ginger, cauliflower and stock. Bring to a boil over high heat. Reduce heat and cook, stirring occasionally, for 10 minutes. Stir in peas and heat through. Sprinkle green onions over top. Serve immediately.

Variation

• Use mung beans in place of the dried split green peas.

Arriving at harvest time simultaneously, tomatoes and basil are naturals together in cooked dishes. Serve this dish with Swiss Chard with Almond Butter Sauce (see recipe, page 190) or other greens.

Tomatoes Stuffed with Basil and Shiitake Mushrooms

- *Preheat oven to 350°F (180°C)*
- *8-inch (20 cm) pie plate, lightly oiled or shallow baking dish*

4	large tomatoes	4
2 tbsp	olive oil	25 mL
3	cloves garlic, minced	3
I cup	chopped onion	250 mL
½ cup	thinly sliced shiitake mushroom caps	125 mL
I cup	cooked rice	250 mL
½ cup	chopped fresh basil	125 mL
I tbsp	chopped fresh oregano	15 mL
I tbsp	fresh thyme leaves	15 mL
	Salt and freshly ground pepper	
4 tbsp	freshly grated Parmesan cheese, divided	60 mL

1. Core tomatoes and slice ¼ inch (0.5 cm) off top. Scoop out seeds and juice to form a cavity. Chop tops and inside flesh. Set aside. Arrange tomatoes in prepared dish. Set aside.

2. In a saucepan, heat oil over medium heat. Add garlic, onion and mushrooms. Sauté for 5 minutes or until soft. Add reserved chopped tomato, rice, basil, oregano and thyme. Cook, stirring, for 1 minute. Add salt and pepper, to taste.

3. Spoon stuffing equally into tomato cavities. Sprinkle each with 1 tbsp (15 mL) of the Parmesan. Bake in preheated oven for 10 to 15 minutes or until cheese melts and tomatoes begin to soften. Serve immediately.

Roasted Peppers with Wild Rice and Walnuts

Something magic happens when red bell peppers are roasted. In addition to the soft sweetness, there is an earthy quality that is imparted and it seems to engage our sense of the sublime.

- *Preheat oven to 400°F (200°C)*
- *Baking sheet, lightly oiled*

4	red bell peppers, cored and cut in half	4
2 tbsp	olive oil	25 mL
2	cloves garlic, minced	2
2 cups	chopped shiitake mushroom caps	500 mL
1 cup	chopped seeded tomatoes	250 mL
⅓ cup	Basil Pesto (see recipe, page 308) or store-bought	75 mL
1 cup	cooked wild rice	250 mL
¼ cup	chopped walnuts or pecans	50 mL
2 tbsp	freshly grated Parmesan cheese	25 mL
	Salt and freshly ground pepper	

1. Arrange bell peppers cut side down on prepared baking sheet. Roast on top rack of preheated oven for 10 minutes or until slightly softened. Remove from oven (do not turn oven off) and flip peppers over so cut sides are up. Set aside.

2. Meanwhile, in a skillet, heat oil over medium heat. Add garlic and mushrooms. Sauté for 7 minutes or until soft. Stir in tomatoes, pesto and rice. Cook, stirring occasionally, for 3 minutes. Remove from heat, stir in walnuts and Parmesan. Add salt and pepper, to taste.

3. Spoon rice stuffing evenly into pepper halves. Bake for 5 to 10 minutes or until peppers are soft and filling is bubbly. Let stand for 5 to 10 minutes before serving.

Variation

- Use 4 small zucchini or tomatoes in place of the peppers.

We often pair leeks with potatoes, especially in the spring when the new potatoes are abundant, but adding fennel gives an entirely new twist to this team of favorites.

Fennel and Potatoes au Gratin

- *Preheat oven to 350°F (180°C)*
- *8 cups (2 L) baking dish, lightly oiled*

5	small potatoes, quartered	5
1	fennel bulb, cut into ½-inch (1 cm) cubes	1
3 tbsp	olive oil	45 mL
1½ cups	sliced leeks, white and light green parts	375 mL
1 cup	chopped onion	250 mL
¼ cup	whole wheat flour	50 mL
½ tsp	ground cayenne pepper	2 mL
½ tsp	dry mustard	2 mL
½ cup	shredded Swiss cheese	125 mL
	Salt and freshly ground pepper	
1½ cups	Savory Oatmeal Topping (see recipe, page 253)	375 mL

1. In a large saucepan, cover potatoes and fennel with water. Bring to a boil over high heat. Cover, reduce heat and simmer for 10 to 15 minutes or just until tender. Drain, reserving 2 cups (500 mL) of the cooking liquid. Let cool. Slip skins off potatoes and cut in half. Set potatoes and fennel aside.

2. In a large saucepan, heat oil over medium heat. Add leeks and onion. Sauté for 10 minutes or until soft. Stir in flour, cayenne pepper and mustard. Cook, stirring, for 2 minutes. Whisk in reserved cooking liquid and simmer gently for 2 to 3 minutes or until sauce is thickened.

3. Remove sauce from heat, stir in cheese, potatoes and fennel. Add salt and pepper, to taste. Transfer to prepared baking dish and sprinkle with Savory Oatmeal Topping. Bake in preheated oven for 20 minutes or until bubbly.

Variations

- Omit topping. In Step 3, instead of transferring to a baking dish, transfer to a serving dish and serve immediately.

- For a celery taste without the anise from fennel, celery root (also known as celeriac) can be used instead of the fennel flavor.

This is a healthy alternative to the sweet yam and marshmallow side dish traditionally served at Thanksgiving.

Golden Baked Pumpkin with Cranberry

- *9-inch (2.5 L) baking dish, lightly oiled*
- *Preheat oven to 375°F (190°C)*

2 cups	cubed peeled pumpkin	500 mL
2 tbsp	butter	25 mL
½ tsp	salt	2 mL
	Freshly ground pepper	
½	onion, finely chopped	½
1 to 2 tbsp	brown rice syrup	15 to 25 mL
¼ cup	dried cranberries	50 mL
⅛ tsp	ground nutmeg	0.5 mL

1. Bring a large pot of salted water to a boil over medium heat. Add pumpkin and cook for 10 minutes or until easily pierced with a fork. Drain and return to the pot.

2. Using a potato masher, mash pumpkin. Beat in butter, salt and pepper. Stir in onion, rice syrup and cranberries. Spoon into prepared baking dish and bake in preheated oven for 45 minutes. Garnish with nutmeg. Serve immediately.

Yukon Gold or Russet
potatoes work well in
this recipe or use a
combination of sweet
potatoes, turnip and
regular potatoes.

Baked Potatoes with Caramelized Onions and Leeks

- *Preheat oven to 400°F (200°C)*
- *Baking sheet, lightly oiled*

2	large Vidalia or Spanish onions, cut into eighths	2
1	large leek, white and light green parts, cut into 2-inch (5 cm) pieces	1
8	cloves garlic, peeled and left whole	8
3 tbsp	olive oil	45 mL
1 tbsp	fresh thyme leaves	15 mL
1 tsp	salt	5 mL
4	medium potatoes, scrubbed and pricked	4
2 tbsp	balsamic vinegar	25 mL
¼ cup	freshly grated Parmesan cheese	50 mL
¼ cup	chopped fresh parsley	50 mL

1. Combine onions, leek, garlic, oil, thyme and salt on prepared baking sheet. Toss to mix well. Add whole potatoes to the sheet. Roast in preheated oven for 20 minutes.

2. Remove from oven. Stir vegetables and remove garlic and leeks, if soft and browned. Reduce heat to 375°F (190°C). Roast for another 25 to 35 minutes or until onions are golden and potatoes are tender when tested with a knife. Split potatoes in half and transfer to a serving platter or individual plates.

3. In a bowl, toss onion mixture with vinegar. Spoon mixture equally over potato halves. In a small bowl, toss together Parmesan and parsley and sprinkle over potatoes. Serve immediately.

Serve this warming vegetable dish with cooked legumes and whole grains for a high-protein complete meal.

Tip

- If using store-bought Cajun spice, start with 1½ tsp (7 mL) because it may be stronger than the homemade version. Taste and add more as required.

Braised Winter Vegetables

1 tbsp	Cajun Black Spice (see recipe, page 330) or store-bought (see Tip, left)	15 mL
1	onion, chopped	1
2 tbsp	olive oil	25 mL
1	can (28 oz/796 mL) tomatoes, including juice	1
1 cup	vegetable stock	250 mL
1	medium sweet potato, peeled and cut into ½-inch (1 cm) cubes	1
1	large carrot, coarsely chopped	1
1	large parsnip, coarsely chopped	1
½	rutabaga, peeled and cut into ½-inch (1 cm) cubes	½
1 cup	Brussels sprouts, trimmed and cut in half if large	250 mL
	Salt and freshly ground pepper	

1. In a large saucepan, combine Cajun spice with onion and oil. Sauté over medium-low heat for 7 minutes or until onions are soft. Add tomatoes with juice. Increase heat to high. Stir in stock and bring to a boil.

2. Add sweet potato, carrot, parsnip, rutabaga and Brussels sprouts. Cover, reduce heat and simmer gently for 25 to 35 minutes or until vegetables are tender-crisp. Add salt and pepper, to taste. Serve immediately.

Vegan Friendly

Flavored oil lends extra depth, so use one with garlic, herbs or cayenne peppers, if available.

Tip
- If raspberry vinegar is not available combine 1 tbsp (15 mL) each wine vinegar and raspberry jam.

Roasted Eggplant with Plums and Apricots

- *Preheat oven to 350°F (180°C)*
- *10-inch (3 L) casserole with lid, lightly oiled*

2	small eggplants	2
4 tbsp	freshly squeezed lemon juice	60 mL
I cup	coarsely chopped onion	250 mL
I cup	coarsely chopped apple	250 mL
½ cup	coarsely chopped pitted plums or prunes	125 mL
½ cup	coarsely chopped fresh or dried apricots	125 mL
½ cup	applesauce	125 mL
2 tbsp	raspberry vinegar (see Tip, left)	25 mL
½ tsp	salt	2 mL
3 tbsp	olive oil	45 mL

1. Cut eggplants in half lengthwise and scoop out and discard seeds. Brush each half with 1 tbsp (15 mL) of the lemon juice. Arrange eggplant halves cut side up in prepared casserole dish. Set aside.

2. In a bowl, combine onion, apple, plums, apricots, applesauce, vinegar and salt. Spoon fruit mixture equally into eggplant halves. Drizzle oil over top. Cover and bake in preheated oven for 50 to 60 minutes or until tender. Serve immediately.

Serving Suggestions
- Serve with Red Beans and Rice (see recipe, page 274).
- Serve with cooked brown rice or another whole grain.

Steaming the parsnips first means that they are actually tender before they hit the pan to be caramelized and glazed. This method turns an ordinary root vegetable into a sweet treat.

Vegan Version
• Use olive oil in place of the butter.

Herbed-Glazed Parsnips

1 lb	parsnips, cut into matchsticks	500 g
2 tbsp	butter	25 mL
3 tbsp	honey	45 mL
2 tbsp	chopped fresh chives or green onions	25 mL
2 tbsp	rice vinegar	25 mL
	Salt and freshly ground pepper	

1. In a large colander or steamer over a pot of boiling water, steam parsnips for about 6 minutes or until tender-crisp. Drain.

2. In a large skillet, heat butter over medium heat. Add parsnips. Sauté for 3 minutes or until lightly browned. Stir in honey, chives and vinegar. Cook for another 1 to 2 minutes or until glaze is thick and parsnips are well coated. Add salt and pepper, to taste as required. Serve immediately.

Variation
• Turnips and carrots can be substituted for the parsnips or mixed with them for a colorful dish.

Spiced Root Vegetables

Some dishes just simmer away without attention and this is one. Once the ingredients are in the pot, it can be left virtually on its own to gently bubble and that makes it a great recipe for company dinners — a half hour more will not harm either the taste or the presentation.

Vegan Version
• Use 2 tbsp (25 mL) olive oil in place of the butter.

• *Flameproof tagine or Dutch oven*

2	cloves garlic, chopped	2
1 tsp	whole cumin seeds, crushed	5 mL
1 tsp	whole coriander seeds, crushed	5 mL
3 tbsp	butter	45 mL
1 1/2 cups	orange juice	375 mL
2 tbsp	freshly squeezed lemon juice	25 mL
1/4 cup	chopped dates	50 mL
1/2 tsp	salt	2 mL
3	carrots, cut into thick matchsticks	3
3	parsnips, cut into thick matchsticks	3
3	slices (1/4 inch/0.5 cm) rutabaga, trimmed and cut into thick matchsticks	3

1. In bottom of tagine, combine garlic, cumin, coriander and butter. Cook gently over medium heat for 3 minutes. Stir in orange juice, lemon juice, dates and salt. Bring to a gentle simmer. Cover and cook for 10 minutes.

2. Stir in carrots, parsnips and rutabaga. Cover, reduce heat to low and cook for about 30 minutes or until vegetables are tender and sauce is thick. Add more orange juice if cooking time is extended or if vegetables get too dry. Serve immediately.

Red Beans and Rice

A classic dish all over America's south, red beans and rice are traditionally flavored with sausage or ham. This lower-fat vegan version relies on Cajun Black Spice and miso for flavor.

Tip

- If using store-bought Cajun spice, start with $1\frac{1}{2}$ tsp (7 mL) because it may be stronger than the homemade version. Taste and add more as required.

1 cup	chopped onion	250 mL
2	cloves garlic, finely chopped	2
1 cup	coarsely chopped green bell pepper	250 mL
¼ cup	vegetable stock or wine	50 mL
2 tbsp	miso	25 mL
1 tbsp	Cajun Black Spice (see recipe, page 330) or store-bought (see Tip, left)	15 mL
1	can (28 oz/796 mL) tomatoes, drained	1
2	strips (6-inch/15 cm) kombu	2
1	can (19 oz/540 mL) red kidney beans, drained and rinsed, or 2 cups (500 mL) cooked red kidney beans	1
¼ cup	chopped fresh parsley	50 mL
1 tbsp	fresh thyme leaves	15 mL
3 cups	cooked brown rice	750 mL

1. In a large saucepan, combine onion, garlic, bell pepper, stock, miso and Cajun spice. Simmer over medium heat for 7 minutes or until vegetables are tender.

2. Add tomatoes and kombu. Simmer for another 10 minutes. Stir in beans, parsley, thyme and rice. Simmer for 5 minutes or until heated through. Serve immediately.

Variation

- Use black beans in place of the red beans.

Serving Suggestion
- Serve with Roasted Vegetables (see recipe, page 258).

This polished dish is sophisticated enough to serve for company, yet fast and delicious for family meals.

Brussels Sprouts with Walnuts and Blue Cheese

2 cups	Brussels sprouts, trimmed and cut in half if large	500 mL
$1\frac{1}{2}$ cups	halved walnuts	375 mL
1 tbsp	olive oil	15 mL
1 tbsp	honey	15 mL
2 tbsp	freshly squeezed lemon juice	25 mL
$\frac{1}{4}$ cup	crumbled blue cheese	50 mL

1. In a colander or steamer over a pot of boiling water, steam Brussels sprouts for 6 to 10 minutes or until tender-crisp. Drain and set aside.

2. Meanwhile, in a large skillet, combine walnuts and oil. Sauté over medium-high heat for 4 minutes or until walnuts are lightly toasted. Stir in honey, lemon juice and Brussels sprouts. Cook, stirring, for 2 minutes. Remove from heat and stir in cheese. Serve immediately.

Variation

• Use crumbled, drained feta or shredded sharp Cheddar cheese in place of the blue cheese.

Sesame Broccoli

1	bunch broccoli, trimmed	1
1 cup	coarsely chopped red or green bell pepper	250 mL
2	cloves garlic, finely chopped	2
1	dried cayenne pepper, crushed	1
1 tbsp	grated fresh gingerroot	15 mL
2 tbsp	olive oil	25 mL
½ cup	slivered drained canned water chestnuts	125 mL
3 tbsp	rice vinegar	45 mL
3 tbsp	tamari or soy sauce	45 mL
1 tbsp	blackstrap molasses or organic cane sugar	15 mL
1 tsp	toasted sesame oil	5 mL
3 tbsp	sesame seeds	45 mL

1. In a saucepan, bring 4 cups (1 L) water to a boil over high heat. Cut broccoli heads into florets and coarsely chop tender parts of stalks. Drop into boiling water and blanch for 2 to 3 minutes. Using a slotted spoon, transfer broccoli to a colander and rinse under cold water. Drain and set aside.

2. In a wok or large skillet, combine bell pepper, garlic, cayenne, ginger and olive oil. Heat gently over medium-low heat. Sauté for 3 minutes. Add broccoli and water chestnuts. Sauté for 2 minutes.

3. In a small bowl, combine vinegar, tamari, molasses and sesame oil. Add to wok and cook, stirring, for 1 or 2 minutes or until vegetables are coated and sauce is hot. Transfer to serving bowl or individual plates. Sprinkle with sesame seeds and serve immediately.

Roasted Onion and Parsnip Gratin with Greens

Serves 4

Amazingly sweet due to the Vidalia onions and parsnips, this dish offers an unusual twist to the classic French gratin.

Tip

- You can use tender fresh greens, such as collard, kale, Swiss chard, beet tops, bok choy or spinach in this recipe.

- *Preheat oven to 400°F (200°C)*
- *10-cup (2.5 L) casserole dish*

2	Vidalia onions, quartered	2
4	parsnips, quartered lengthwise and cut into 2-inch (5 cm) pieces	4
4	cloves garlic, peeled and left whole	4
3 tbsp	olive oil	45 mL
1 cup	dry whole wheat bread crumbs	250 mL
4 cups	greens, torn (see Tip, left)	1 L
2 cups	Cheese Sauce (see recipe, page 324)	500 mL

1. In casserole dish, toss onions, parsnips and garlic with oil. Roast in preheated oven for 40 minutes. Add bread crumbs and toss to combine. Reduce oven temperature to 350°F (180°C) and bake vegetables for another 20 minutes or until tender.

2. Remove casserole from oven. Stir in greens, pour Cheese Sauce over top and return to oven. Bake for 15 minutes or until sauce is bubbly. Serve immediately.

Serving Suggestion
- Serve over cooked whole grains for a complete meal.

This recipe is a tasty way to enjoy the heart-protective benefits of onions, leeks and cabbage.

Tip

- Using a Dutch oven saves washing an extra pan but if not available, use a large skillet to cook vegetables, then transfer to a lightly oiled 10-cup (2.5 L) casserole dish to bake in the oven.

Baked Onion, Leek and Cabbage Casserole

- *Preheat oven to 400°F (200°C)*
- *Dutch oven or 10-cup (2.5 L) casserole dish (see Tip, left)*

I	small head green cabbage	I
¼ cup	butter or olive oil	50 mL
I	onion, thinly sliced	I
I	leek, white and light green parts, thinly sliced	I
I	clove garlic, finely chopped	I
I tbsp	whole wheat flour	15 mL
I tsp	salt	5 mL
	Freshly ground pepper	
I cup	rice or soy milk	250 mL
3 tbsp	shredded Swiss cheese	45 mL
3 tbsp	freshly grated Parmesan cheese	45 mL
3 tbsp	dry bread crumbs	45 mL

1. In a large saucepan, bring 6 cups (1.5 L) water to a boil over high heat. Cut cabbage into quarters. Cut out and discard core from each quarter. Cut the quarters lengthwise into very thin slices. Drop cabbage into boiling water and blanch for 2 to 3 minutes (in batches if necessary). Using a slotted spoon, transfer cabbage to a colander and rinse under cold water. Drain and set aside.

2. In a Dutch oven, heat butter over medium heat. Just as butter foams, add onion, leek and garlic. Cover, reduce heat to low and cook for 15 to 20 minutes or until very soft. Add cabbage. Cover and cook for 10 to 15 minutes or until cabbage is tender.

3. Stir in flour and salt and pepper, to taste. Increase heat to medium-high and whisk in milk, a little at a time. Cook, stirring, for about 5 minutes or until sauce is thickened. Remove from heat and sprinkle Swiss and Parmesan cheeses and bread crumbs over top. Bake in preheated oven for 20 minutes or until top is browned and edges are bubbly. Serve immediately.

Gado gado, an
Indonesian platter of
vegetables, is served
with a spicy peanut
sauce.

**Serving
Suggestion**
- In summer, serve
  the cooked beans
  over torn lettuce
  and in winter, use
  as a vegetable
  accompaniment
  to legumes and
  whole-grain
  dishes.

Green Beans Gado Gado

- *Heated serving platter*

1 lb	green beans, trimmed and cut in half	500 g
1	small onion, sliced and separated into rings	1
1 tbsp	olive oil	15 mL
⅓ cup	Gado Gado Sauce (see recipe, below)	75 mL
1	can (14 oz/398 mL) lima beans, drained and rinsed, or 2 cups (500 mL) cooked lima beans	1
4 oz	bean sprouts	125 g
3 tbsp	chopped peanuts	45 mL

1. In a saucepan, bring 4 cups (1 L) water to a boil over high heat. Drop green beans into boiling water and blanch for 2 to 3 minutes. Using a slotted spoon, transfer green beans to a colander and rinse under cold water. Drain and set aside.

2. In a wok or large saucepan, combine onion rings and oil. Cook gently over medium heat for 7 minutes or until onion is soft. Add Gado Gado Sauce. Reduce heat and simmer for 2 minutes. Stir in green beans, lima beans and bean sprouts. Cook for 1 or 2 minutes or until heated through. Transfer to serving platter or individual plates. Garnish with peanuts and serve immediately.

Variation
- Any nuts may be used in place of the peanuts.

Variation
- Use soy or rice milk if coconut milk is not available.

Gado Gado Sauce

¼ cup	coconut milk	50 mL
2 tbsp	peanut or cashew butter	25 mL
1 tbsp	freshly squeezed lemon juice	15 mL
2 tsp	tamari or soy sauce	10 mL
2 tsp	grated fresh gingerroot	10 mL
½	dried cayenne pepper, crushed	½

1. In a small bowl, combine milk, peanut butter, lemon juice, tamari, ginger and cayenne. Stir to mix well.

Pumpkin and Black Beans

I	onion, chopped	I
2 tbsp	olive oil	25 mL
2	cloves garlic, minced	2
I	red bell pepper, chopped	I
I cup	vegetable stock	250 mL
2 cups	cubed peeled pumpkin	500 mL
I ½ cups	cooked or canned black beans, rinsed and drained	375 mL
2 tbsp	chopped fresh savory or oregano	25 mL
I tbsp	minced fresh gingerroot	15 mL
I tbsp	freshly squeezed lemon juice	15 mL
I tbsp	tamari or soy sauce	15 mL

1. In a large skillet, combine onion and oil. Sauté over medium heat for 5 minutes. Add garlic and bell pepper and sauté for another 3 minutes.

2. Stir in stock. Increase heat to high and bring to a boil. Stir in pumpkin, black beans, savory, ginger, lemon juice and tamari. Cover, reduce heat to medium-low and cook gently for 8 to 10 minutes or until pumpkin is tender-crisp. Serve immediately.

Variations

• Substitute sweet potatoes or squash for the pumpkin, if desired.

• Use any cooked legume, such as chickpeas, soybeans, lentils or black-eyed peas, in place of the black beans.

Grains and Pasta

Cracked Wheat and Lima Bean Wrap

This recipe makes enough filling for 10 large wraps, but half of the filling may be frozen for use in crêpes or in stir-fried vegetable dishes.

I cup	chopped onion	250 mL
I cup	chopped celery	250 mL
2	cloves garlic, finely chopped	2
2 tbsp	olive oil	25 mL
I tbsp	rice vinegar	15 mL
2 tbsp	finely chopped candied ginger	25 mL
I tsp	ground cumin	5 mL
I cup	cracked wheat	250 mL
3 tbsp	freshly squeezed lemon juice	45 mL
I	can (28 oz/796 mL) tomatoes, including juice	I
I	can (19 oz/540 mL) lima beans, drained, or 2 cups (500 mL) cooked lima beans, coarsely chopped	I
	Salt and freshly ground pepper	
I⅓ cups	Basic or Tangy Almond Spread (see recipes, page 151) or Hummus (see recipe, page 146)	325 mL
10	large soft flour tortillas	10
2½ cups	shredded lettuce	625 mL
I cup	sliced pitted black olives, optional	250 mL

I. In a large skillet, combine onion, celery, garlic and oil. Gently sauté over medium-low heat for 7 minutes. Add vinegar, ginger and cumin. Cook for another 3 minutes.

2. Stir in cracked wheat, lemon juice and tomatoes with juice, breaking up tomatoes with back of a spoon. Cover, reduce heat to low and simmer for 20 minutes or until liquid is absorbed and wheat is tender.

3. Remove from heat and stir in lima beans. Add salt and pepper, to taste. Let cool. Filling can be used immediately in wraps or stored, covered tightly, in the refrigerator for up to 3 days.

4. To assemble wraps: Spread 2 tbsp (25 mL) Almond Spread over a tortilla. Spoon about ½ cup (125 mL) of the filling down center. Top with ¼ cup (50 mL) of the lettuce and 1 rounded tbsp (15 mL) of the olives, if using. Fold the bottom up and both sides in, leaving the top open. Fold the tortilla in half lengthwise. Repeat with remaining wraps. Serve at room temperature or warmed slightly in a 350°F (180°C) oven.

Any spring green —
dandelion, spinach or
spinach — will work
well in this recipe.

Baked Wild Rice with Sorrel and Mustard Greens

- *Preheat oven to 350°F (180°C)*
- *6-cup (1.5 L) casserole dish, lightly oiled*

1 ½ cups	vegetable stock	375 mL
½ cup	wild rice	125 mL
½ cup	brown rice, rinsed	125 mL
1	large egg	1
1 cup	natural yogurt, drained	250 mL
¼ cup	Basil Pesto (see recipe, page 308) or store-bought	50 mL
1 cup	sorrel leaves, torn	250 mL
1 cup	mustard greens, torn	250 mL
½ cup	sunflower seeds	125 mL
	Salt and freshly ground pepper	

1. In a saucepan, bring stock to a boil over medium-high heat. Add wild rice and brown rice. Cover, reduce heat and simmer for 40 minutes. Let rice cool slightly.

2. In a large bowl, beat egg. Whisk in yogurt and pesto. Add sorrel, mustard greens and sunflower seeds and mix well. Stir in cooled rice. Add salt and pepper, to taste.

3. Transfer to prepared dish. Bake in preheated oven for 20 to 30 minutes or until bubbly. Serve immediately.

Variation

- An optional ½ cup (125 mL) topping of whole wheat bread crumbs or Savory Oatmeal Topping (see recipe, page 253) or Whole-Grain Granola (see recipe, page 160), spread over the top in the last 10 minutes of baking gives a crisp finish to the dish.

Spinach Pie

This dish is very easy to make and absolutely delicious, just a little unusual because the raw spinach is piled into the dish, covered and baked. Don't be discouraged — you can't ruin this dish. It takes 15 minutes to assemble, cooks in less than half an hour and is great cold or heated for lunch or as a snack.

Tips

- Use Chinese sticky rice, if available, or Basmati rice.
  Be sure to mix barley with the rice because it thickens and adds a chewy texture to the base. Shorten up the cooking time slightly so that the grain mixture is a little wet. This makes it easier to mash into the baking dish with the back of a spoon.

- If frozen for up to 1 hour, creamy goat cheese will be easier to slice.

- *Preheat oven to 350°F (180°C)*
- *10-inch (25 cm) deep-dish pie plate, lightly oiled*

½ cup	sticky white rice (see Tips, left)	125 mL
½ cup	pot barley	125 mL
¼ tsp	salt	1 mL
2 tbsp	olive oil	25 mL
1	Vidalia onion, coarsely chopped	1
½ cup	finely chopped mushrooms	125 mL
1 tbsp	butter	15 mL
2	cloves garlic, finely chopped	2
1 tbsp	Garam Masala Spice Blend (see recipe, page 333) or store-bought, or Ras el Hanout seasoning (see recipe, page 334)	15 mL
3 cups	spinach, divided	750 mL
3 oz	creamy goat cheese (see Tips, left)	90 g
½ cup	whole-grain bread crumbs	125 mL
¼ cup	finely chopped almonds	50 mL
¼ cup	freshly grated Parmesan cheese	50 mL

1. In a colander, rinse rice and barley. In a saucepan, bring 2 cups (500 mL) water to a boil over high heat. Stir in rice, barley and salt. Cover, reduce heat and simmer for 15 to 20 minutes or until rice and barley are soft and have absorbed most of the water (do not cook until dry). Remove from heat. Stir, cover and set aside.

2. Meanwhile, in a large skillet, heat oil over medium heat. Stir in onion and cook, stirring frequently, for 5 minutes. Stir in mushrooms and butter. Cook, stirring, for 4 minutes or until onions are soft and mushrooms are about half their original size. Stir in garlic and garam masala. Cook for 1 minute and leave skillet on the stove but turn heat off.

3. Transfer about ¾ of the rice mixture from the saucepan into the onion mixture in the skillet. Stir until well mixed. Turn out into prepared pie plate. Using the back of a spoon, mash over the base and up the sides of the pie plate.

4. Wash the spinach well, tear into pieces and drain but keep some of the water on the leaves so that they steam in the pie. Pile half of the spinach over the base. (When you add the spinach to the dish, it may seem that it will not fit, just gently push it down so that it mounds over the base.)

5. Cut goat cheese into pieces and distribute over spinach. Pile remaining spinach over top.

6. Stir bread crumbs, almonds and Parmesan into remaining rice in the pot. Spoon mixture over spinach. (The rice might be a little hard to spread over the spinach but use your hands to smooth and even it over the top. Try to form a sealed "lid" to steam the spinach.) Bake in preheated for 20 to 30 minutes or until crust is bubbly. Let stand for 3 minutes before serving.

Variation
• Use pine nuts or sunflower seeds instead of almonds.

Serves 6

Short-grain Italian Arborio rice works best for this recipe. Brown rice does not take up the stock in the same way. The goodness in the mushrooms and broth are enough to make up for the polished grain.

Vegan Version
• Omit Parmesan cheese.

Leek and Mushroom Pilaf

• *Heated serving bowl*

I	leek, white and light green parts, sliced	I
2 cups	coarsely chopped shiitake mushroom caps	500 mL
3 tbsp	white or red wine	45 mL
I tbsp	olive oil	15 mL
2 tbsp	fresh thyme leaves	25 mL
I cup	Arborio rice	250 mL
2 cups	Mushroom Broth (see recipe, page 203) or vegetable stock, divided	500 mL
I	head roasted garlic (see page, 258)	I
1/2 cup	freshly grated Parmesan Cheese	125 mL

1. In a large skillet, combine leek, mushrooms, wine and oil. Gently simmer over medium heat for 5 minutes. Stir in thyme and rice. Cook, stirring constantly, for another 3 minutes.

2. Stir in $\frac{1}{2}$ cup (125 mL) of the Mushroom Broth and squeeze roasted garlic cloves into the rice mixture. Increase heat to high. Bring to a boil and stir up any browned bits in the skillet. Add remaining $1\frac{1}{2}$ cups (375 mL) of stock. Cover and bring to a boil. Reduce heat and simmer for 20 minutes or until rice is tender and mixture is creamy. Transfer to heated serving bowl. Sprinkle Parmesan over top and serve immediately.

Serve for a colorful and light lunch or dinner meal. The wine eliminates the need for oil but keep the temperature slightly lower than usual to avoid having vegetables stick to the pan.

Whole-Grain Broccoli Stir-Fry

2	carrots, chopped	2
2	stalks celery, chopped	2
I	onion, chopped	I
1/2	red or green bell pepper, chopped	1/2
1/4 cup	white wine	50 mL
I cup	broccoli spears	250 mL
I cup	thinly sliced mushrooms	250 mL
2	cloves garlic, slivered	2
1 1/2 cups	cooked whole spelt or kamut	375 mL
1/3 cup	Ginger Sauce (see recipe, below)	75 mL
1/2 cup	sliced almonds, optional	125 mL

1. In a wok or large skillet, combine carrots, celery, onion, bell pepper and wine. Bring to a gentle simmer over medium-high heat. Reduce heat and simmer, stirring often, for 3 minutes. Stir in broccoli, mushrooms and garlic. Simmer, stirring often, for 3 to 4 minutes or until vegetables are tender-crisp.

2. Stir in spelt. Pour Ginger Sauce over top. Increase heat and bring to a boil. Stir-fry for 1 minute or until grains are heated through. Sprinkle with almonds, if using. Serve immediately.

This sauce can be used with any stir-fry.

Ginger Sauce

2 tbsp	tamari or soy sauce	25 mL
I tbsp	rice vinegar or white wine	15 mL
I tbsp	liquid honey	15 mL
2 tsp	grated fresh gingerroot	10 mL
I tsp	toasted sesame oil	5 mL

1. In a small bowl, whisk together tamari, vinegar, honey, ginger and sesame oil.

The method is a
remnant from the
wood-stove era. The
bread has an unusual
texture, but is great
with soups and stews.

Cheesy Apple Whole Wheat Skillet Bread

- **8-inch (20 cm) cast iron or heavy skillet, lightly oiled**

1 cup	whole wheat flour	250 mL
1 cup	unbleached all-purpose flour	250 mL
2 tbsp	chopped fresh sage	25 mL
2 tbsp	chopped fresh chives	25 mL
1 1/2 tsp	baking powder	7 mL
1/2 tsp	salt	2 mL
1/2 cup	butter	125 mL
1/2 cup	grated apple	125 mL
1/4 cup	shredded sharp Cheddar cheese	50 mL
3/4 cup	rice or soy milk	175 mL
+ 1 tbsp		+ 15 mL
1/4 cup	water, divided	50 mL
2 tbsp	freshly grated Parmesan cheese	25 mL

1. In a large bowl, combine whole wheat and all-purpose flours, sage, chives, baking powder and salt. Using a pastry blender or 2 knives, cut butter into dry ingredients until it resembles coarse crumbs. Stir in apple and cheese.

2. Stir 3/4 cup (175 mL) of the milk and 2 tbsp (25 mL) of the water into dry ingredients and mix well. Add remaining water if necessary to make dough hold together (dough will be sticky). Turn out onto a lightly floured surface. Knead until smooth. Form into a ball.

3. Transfer to prepared skillet and flatten to fill the skillet. Brush with the remaining 1 tbsp (15 mL) of milk and sprinkle with Parmesan. Cover with foil. Heat skillet over medium heat for 3 minutes. Reduce heat to medium-low and cook for 20 minutes. Turn and cook for another 15 minutes or until lightly browned. Cut into wedges and serve hot.

Kamut with Sautéed Summer Vegetables

The large kamut kernels are great in vegetable dishes and salads, adding a chewy texture.

Tip

• Soaking the kamut for a minimum of 4 hours or overnight reduces the cooking time.

1¼ cups	kamut kernels	300 mL
1½ cups	vegetable stock or water	375 mL
2 tbsp	olive oil	25 mL
1 cup	chopped red bell pepper	250 mL
1 cup	chopped zucchini	250 mL
1 cup	fresh or frozen peas	250 mL
1 cup	fresh or frozen corn kernels	250 mL
¼ cup	chopped fresh parsley	50 mL
1 tbsp	tamari or soy sauce	15 mL

1. In a saucepan, combine kamut and stock. Cover and refrigerate for at least 4 hours or overnight (see Tip, left).

2. Bring stock and kamut to room temperature. Bring to a boil over high heat. Cover, reduce heat and simmer for 45 to 60 minutes or until kamut is tender and most of the liquid is absorbed. Drain, rinse and let cool.

3. In a skillet, heat oil over medium-high heat. Add bell pepper, zucchini, peas and corn. Sauté for 4 minutes or until vegetables are tender-crisp.

4. Stir in kamut, parsley and tamari and heat through. Serve immediately or chill before serving.

Variations

• Add a chopped fresh garlic clove in Step 3.

• For protein, add 1 or 2 cups (250 or 500 mL) cooked chickpeas or lentils in Step 4.

• Garnish with ½ cup (125 mL) chopped nuts.

The nutty flavor of the whole grain combined with the earthy mushrooms makes this pilaf remarkable.

Vegan Version
- Omit the Parmesan cheese or substitute soy cheese.

Spelt and Vegetable Pilaf

1 cup	spelt or kamut kernels	250 mL
4 cups	vegetable stock, divided	1 L
2 tbsp	olive oil	25 mL
1 cup	chopped Portobello mushroom caps	250 mL
1 cup	chopped onion	250 mL
1 cup	chopped sweet potato	250 mL
1/4 cup	white wine	50 mL
1	clove garlic, finely chopped	1
2 tsp	chopped fresh sage	10 mL
2 tsp	fresh thyme leaves	10 mL
1/3 cup	freshly grated Parmesan cheese	75 mL

1. In a large bowl, combine spelt with 4 cups (1 L) water. Cover and refrigerate for 4 hours or overnight (see Tip, page 288).

2. Rinse spelt in warm water and drain. In a large saucepan, combine soaked spelt with 3 cups (750 mL) of the stock. Bring to a boil over medium heat. Cover, reduce heat and simmer for 45 minutes or until kernels are tender.

3. Meanwhile, in a large skillet, heat oil over medium heat. Add mushrooms, onion and sweet potato. Sauté for 5 minutes. Add wine, garlic and remaining 1 cup (250 mL) of stock. Cover, reduce heat and simmer for 15 minutes or until vegetables are tender.

4. Stir spelt and any liquid in the pan into vegetables. Add sage, thyme and Parmesan and stir to mix well. Serve immediately.

Serving Suggestion
- Serve as a side dish for Braised Greens with Citrus Dressing, Asparagus with Spring Sauce or Golden Cauliflower with Split Peas (see recipes, pages 260, 262 and 264).

Lemon Risotto

Arborio rice is the best variety to use for risotto because it takes up the stock and goes creamy without breaking down. Butter is used here, as a flavor and texture enhancer.

Vegan Version

• Omit the butter rather than replacing it with oil in this recipe.

2 cups	Mushroom Broth (see recipe, page 203)	500 mL
2 cups	vegetable stock	500 mL
3 tbsp	olive oil	45 mL
2 tbsp	butter, divided	25 mL
1/4 cup	minced onion	50 mL
1 cup	Arborio rice	250 mL
1 tbsp	grated lemon zest	15 mL
	Juice of 1 lemon	
2 cups	chopped fresh spinach	500 mL
1/4 cup	freshly grated Parmesan cheese	50 mL
2 tbsp	chopped fresh basil	25 mL

1. In a saucepan, combine Mushroom Broth and stock. Bring to a gentle simmer over medium heat. Cover, reduce heat to low and keep simmering.

2. In a large saucepan, heat oil and 1 tbsp (15 mL) of the butter over medium heat. Stir in onion. Reduce heat and gently cook for 4 minutes or until transparent. Add rice and sauté, for 3 minutes or until rice looks, sounds and feels like glass.

3. Ladle about 1/2 cup (125 mL) of the hot stock into the rice mixture. Increase heat to maintain a gentle simmer. Stir and cook rice until the stock is almost all gone. Keep adding hot stock, 1/2 cup (125 mL) at a time and stirring until almost all of the stock is absorbed and rice is nearly tender and there is only about 1 cup (250 mL) of stock left. This will take about 15 to 20 minutes.

4. Stir lemon juice into remaining simmering stock. Stir spinach and lemon zest into rice. Add 1/2 cup (125 mL) of stock to rice. Stir until almost all of the liquid has been absorbed. Add the last 1/2 cup (125 mL) of the stock, 1 tbsp (15 mL) at a time. Stir until rice is tender and will not absorb any more liquid. Remove from heat and stir in Parmesan, remaining 1 tbsp (15 mL) of butter and basil. Serve immediately.

Sesame seeds are high in calcium and are a good source of incomplete protein that combines well with legumes or whole grains.

Cauliflower and Wheat Berries with Sesame Dressing

I	head cauliflower, separated into florets	I
I 1/2 cups	wheat berries	375 mL
1/2 cup	Sesame Dressing (see recipe, below)	125 mL
I cup	sliced green onions	250 mL
3 tbsp	sesame seeds	45 mL

I. In a large saucepan, cover cauliflower with 4 to 6 cups (1 to 1.5 L) water. Bring to a boil over high heat. Cover, reduce heat and cook cauliflower for 5 to 7 minutes or until just tender-crisp. Using tongs, transfer cauliflower to a colander and rinse with cold water. Drain and set aside and let cool.

2. Drain off all but 3 cups (750 mL) of cauliflower cooking water. Bring back to a boil over high heat. Add wheat berries. Reduce heat and gently boil, uncovered, for 1 hour or until tender. Drain, rinse and let cool.

3. In a large bowl, toss together Sesame Sauce, cauliflower, wheat berries and green onions. Chill before serving. Transfer to a serving dish and sprinkle sesame seeds over top.

Tip
• Sauce can be made up to 2 days in advance and refrigerated until ready to use. Bring to room temperature before adding to Cauliflower and Wheat Berries.

Sesame Dressing

3 tbsp	olive oil	45 mL
3 tbsp	rice vinegar	45 mL
I tbsp	tamari or soy sauce	15 mL
I tbsp	tahini sauce	15 mL
2 tsp	sesame oil	10 mL
2	cloves garlic, finely chopped	2

I. In a large bowl, whisk together olive oil, vinegar, tamari, tahini, sesame oil and garlic. Cover and refrigerate until ready to use or for up to 3 days.

Serves 6

Vegan Friendly

Couscous is teamed
here with quinoa for
extra nutrients.

Creamy Couscous with Quinoa and Cranberries

I cup	whole wheat couscous, divided	250 mL
¼ cup	natural almonds or Brazil nuts	50 mL
½ cup	quinoa, thoroughly rinsed	125 mL
I	can (14 oz/398 mL) coconut milk	I
½ cup	dried cranberries	125 mL
½ tsp	ground cinnamon	2 mL
I tsp	ground licorice, optional	5 mL

1. In a food processor or blender, grind ½ cup (125 mL) of the couscous and almonds to a fine powder. Place in a small bowl and set aside.

2. In a saucepan, combine quinoa and 2½ cups (625 mL) water. Bring to a boil over high heat. Cover, reduce heat to medium-low and simmer gently for 10 minutes. Stir in remaining couscous. Replace cover and cook for about 5 minutes or until liquid is absorbed and quinoa looks transparent.

3. Stir in ground couscous mixture, coconut milk, cranberries, cinnamon and licorice, if using. Bring to a gentle boil. Reduce heat and simmer, uncovered, stirring once, for 2 minutes or until mixture thickens.

4. Remove from heat. Cover pan and set aside for 5 minutes. Fluff with a fork. Serve warm.

Variation

• Any nut such as walnuts, pecans, cashews or pine nuts, or seeds such as pumpkin or sunflower will work in place of almonds.

Serving Suggestions
• Serve this dish as a warm breakfast cereal, a sweet-tart accompaniment to steamed vegetables or as a satisfying dessert.

Basil and Roasted Pepper Quinoa

Chipotle is the name given to jalapeño peppers that have been smoked and dried. The thick flesh is free of peel and lends a distinctly smoky flavor to dishes. They are most commonly available canned in adobo sauce.

1 cup	chopped red onion	250 mL
2	cloves garlic, finely chopped	2
2 tbsp	olive oil	25 mL
2 cups	Roasted Red Pepper slices (see recipe, page 135), coarsely chopped	500 mL
¼ cup	chopped drained canned chipotle peppers	50 mL
2 cups	cooked quinoa	500 mL
1 tbsp	shredded fresh basil or Basil Pesto (see recipe, page 308) or store-bought pesto	15 mL
1 tbsp	rice vinegar	15 mL
½ tsp	salt	2 mL

1. In a skillet, combine onion, garlic and oil. Gently simmer over medium heat for 7 minutes or until soft. Add roasted peppers, chipotle peppers, quinoa, basil, vinegar and salt. Heat through and serve hot.

Variations

• Use a whole roasted garlic head in place of the raw garlic.

• Substitute 1 cup (250 mL) chopped fresh red bell peppers for the roasted red pepper slices.

Tabbouleh

Vegan Friendly

Fresh tasting and nutty, this fast and delicious grain dish may be served as an appetizer or as a main dish accompaniment. Omit the tomatoes and use it as a stuffing for vegetables and fish. Garnish it with any of the following to create a light lunch: olives, sliced avocado, artichoke hearts, cooked lentils, hard-boiled eggs or grated cheese.

1 cup	bulgur	250 mL
2½ cups	vegetable or mushroom stock	625 mL
1 cup	chopped fresh parsley	250 mL
½ cup	finely chopped onion	125 mL
¼ cup	finely chopped green onions	50 mL
¼ cup	chopped fresh mint	50 mL
2	tomatoes, seeded and coarsely chopped	2
¼ cup	olive oil	50 mL
3 tbsp	freshly squeezed lemon juice	45 mL
2 tsp	Garam Masala Spice Blend (see recipe, page 333) or store-bought	10 mL
½ tsp	salt	2 mL
	Freshly ground pepper	

1. In a saucepan, combine bulgur and stock. Cover and bring to a light simmer over medium heat. Reduce heat to low and cook for 20 to 25 minutes, until grain is soft but still chewy and liquid is absorbed. Remove from heat and let stand, covered, for 10 minutes.

2. Fluff with a fork and transfer to a large bowl. Stir in parsley, onion, green onions, mint and tomatoes. Toss to combine.

3. In a small bowl, whisk oil, lemon juice, garam masala and salt. Toss with bulgur. Add pepper, to taste. Add more seasoning, lemon juice or salt, if required. Serve at room temperature.

Variation

• Instant couscous is widely available and only requires a few minutes of soaking. It may be used in place of bulgur in this recipe. Follow package directions for soaking 1 cup (250 mL) couscous, substituting vegetable or mushroom stock for the water called for. Follow Steps 2 and 3 above.

Amaranth Chili

¼ cup	amaranth grains, thoroughly rinsed	50 mL
4	tomatoes, peeled and coarsely chopped	4
½ cup	chopped onion	125 mL
½ cup	chopped green bell pepper	125 mL
2	cloves garlic, minced	2
2 cups	vegetable stock	500 mL
1 cup	dried green or red lentils	250 mL
1	potato, peeled and coarsely chopped	1
1 cup	chopped carrot	250 mL
2 cups	cooked chickpeas or 1 can (19 oz/540 mL) chickpeas, drained and rinsed	500 mL
2 tbsp	chili powder	25 mL
2 tsp	ground cumin	10 mL
1 tsp	salt	5 mL

1. In a skillet, toast amaranth over medium-high heat, stirring constantly for about 10 or 15 seconds until the seeds pop. Transfer to a small bowl and set aside.

2. In a large saucepan, combine tomatoes, onion, bell pepper and garlic. Simmer over medium heat for 5 minutes. Add stock. Increase heat to high and bring to a boil. Add lentils. Cover, reduce heat to low and simmer gently for 15 minutes until lentils are tender.

3. Add amaranth, potato and carrot. Reduce heat and simmer for 15 minutes or until tender. Stir in chickpeas, chili powder, cumin and salt. Cook for 1 minute or until chickpeas are heated through. Serve immediately.

Variation

• Use ¼ cup (50 mL) couscous instead of amaranth grains.

Vegan Friendly

The *Allium* family is well represented in this dish. Serve it at the first hint of cold or flu and it may be enough to retire the bug.

Tip

• If you don't happen to have stock on hand, use 1 cup (250 mL) of the pasta cooking water in its place.

Soba with Caramelized Onions, Leeks and Chives

• *Heated serving bowl or platter*

4	large red or yellow onions, coarsely chopped	4
1	large leek, white and light green parts, sliced	1
3 tbsp	olive oil	45 mL
1	bay leaf, crushed	1
1 tbsp	chopped fresh rosemary	15 mL
12 oz	soba noodles	375 g
2	cloves garlic, finely chopped	2
3 tbsp	white wine	45 mL
1 cup	vegetable stock (see Tip, left)	250 mL
¼ cup	chopped fresh chives	50 mL

1. In a large skillet, combine onions, leek and oil. Sauté over medium heat for 3 minutes. Stir in bay leaf and rosemary. Reduce heat and gently simmer for 8 to 12 minutes or until onions are golden brown and soft.

2. Meanwhile, in a large saucepan of boiling water, cook noodles for 6 to 8 minutes or until tender but firm. Drain.

3. Add garlic and wine to onion mixture. Cook over medium heat for 5 minutes or until wine is reduced by half. Add stock and simmer for 15 to 20 minutes or until liquid is reduced by about one-third. Remove from heat and transfer to heated bowl. Stir in chives and toss with cooked soba noodles. Serve immediately.

Fruited Pesto Pasta

Serves 4

Vegan Friendly

Any summer fruit works well in this refreshing starter or side dish.

Variation

- Use fresh kiwifruits, blueberries or blackberries in place of any of the fruit listed.

8 oz	whole wheat pasta bows or shells	250 g
2 tbsp	olive oil	25 mL
2 tbsp	raspberry vinegar (see Tip, page 271)	25 mL
¼ cup	Lemon Pesto (see recipe, page 310)	50 mL
½ cup	sliced strawberries	125 mL
½ cup	sliced peaches	125 mL
½ cup	sliced cherries	125 mL
½ cup	diced pears	125 mL

1. In a large saucepan of boiling salted water, cook pasta for about 10 minutes or until tender but firm. Drain and rinse under cold water until cool. Drain and transfer to a large bowl.

2. Meanwhile, in a jar with a tight-fitting lid, combine oil, vinegar and Lemon Pesto. Shake well. Pour over pasta and toss to mix well.

3. Toss strawberries, peaches, cherries and pears with pasta. Serve at room temperature.

Tomato Pesto Udon

Serves 4

If you keep the noodles and sun-dried tomatoes in the pantry, it is likely that you can make this dish without a special trip to the supermarket.

Vegan Version

- Omit the butter and double the olive oil to 2 tbsp (25 mL).

12 oz	whole wheat udon noodles	375 g
1 tbsp	butter	15 mL
1 tbsp	olive oil	15 mL
3 cups	sliced red or Spanish onions	750 mL
¼ cup	white wine	50 mL
2 tbsp	chopped candied gingerroot	25 mL
¼ cup	Sun-Dried Tomato Pesto (see recipe, page 309) or tomato sauce	50 mL
	Salt and freshly ground pepper	

1. In a large saucepan of boiling water, cook noodles for 5 to 7 minutes or until tender but firm. Drain.

2. In a large saucepan, heat butter and oil over medium heat. Add onions and cook, stirring, for 7 minutes or until soft and translucent. Add wine and ginger. Reduce heat to medium-low and cook onions, stirring occasionally, for 10 to 15 minutes or until caramelized. Remove from heat and stir in Sun-Dried Tomato Pesto. Add salt and pepper, to taste. Toss noodles with sauce and serve immediately.

Fettuccine and Fiddleheads in Thyme Vinaigrette

In early spring when the ostrich fern pushes its tightly wound, rounded shoots through the mulch along streams and riverbanks, this is the recipe that highlights that unique-tasting, wild delicacy.

Tip

• Frozen fiddleheads are often available all year.

2 cups	fresh fiddleheads, trimmed	500 mL
12 oz	fettuccine	375 g
2 tbsp	olive oil	25 mL
½ cup	chopped red onion	125 mL
½ cup	chopped rhubarb or dried cranberries	125 mL
2 tbsp	tamari or soy sauce	25 mL
1 tbsp	sesame oil	15 mL
1 tbsp	pure maple syrup	15 mL
2 tbsp	fresh thyme leaves	25 mL

1. In a large saucepan, bring 4 cups (1 L) water to a boil over medium-high heat. Add fiddleheads. Bring back to a boil and cook for 2 minutes or until tender-crisp. Using a slotted spoon, remove to a colander to drain. Discard water.

2. In a large pot of fresh boiling water, cook fettuccine for 6 to 10 minutes or just until tender. Drain.

3. Meanwhile, in a large wok or skillet, heat olive oil over medium heat. Add onion and sauté for 5 minutes or until soft. Stir in rhubarb. Cook, stirring, for another 5 minutes. Drizzle tamari, sesame oil and maple syrup over onion mixture. Stir in fiddleheads and thyme. Cook, stirring, for 1 minute. Toss with cooked noodles and serve immediately.

Variation

• Use 8 oz (250 g) each green and yellow beans, trimmed, instead of the fiddleheads and increase the water to 6 cups (1.5 L).

Vegan Friendly

The "sauce" here isn't a noodle sauce in the traditional sense. It is meant to spice up the noodles but not make them the main course. Served at room temperature or chilled, this dish is still warming due to the ginger, chili pepper and Cajun Black Spice. Frozen green soybeans (edamame) are widely available in whole food stores but green peas or cooked lentils may be substituted.

Tips

• If using store-bought Cajun Spice, start with $1\frac{1}{2}$ tsp (7 mL) because it may be stronger than the homemade version. Taste and add more as required.

• Store, covered tightly, in the refrigerator for up to 3 days.

Spicy Soba Noodles

8 oz	soba noodles	250 g
1 cup	green soybeans	250 mL
$\frac{1}{3}$ cup	cashew butter	75 mL
$\frac{1}{4}$ cup	tamari or soy sauce	50 mL
2 tbsp	rice vinegar	25 mL
2 tbsp	freshly squeezed lemon juice	25 mL
1 to 2 tbsp	Cajun Black Spice (see recipe, page 330) or store-bought, divided (see Tips, left)	15 to 25 mL
2 tbsp	chopped candied ginger	25 mL
2 tsp	toasted sesame oil	10 mL
1	clove garlic, minced	1
1	dried chili pepper, crushed, optional	1
3 tbsp	toasted sesame seeds	45 mL

1. In a large saucepan of boiling water, cook noodles and soybeans for 5 to 7 minutes or until both are tender but firm. Drain and rinse well. Drain again.

2. Meanwhile, in a saucepan over medium heat, combine cashew butter, tamari, vinegar, lemon juice, 1 tbsp (15 mL) of the Cajun spice, ginger, sesame oil, garlic and chili pepper, if using. Whisk until nut butter is blended with other ingredients. Taste and add remaining 1 tbsp (15 mL) Cajun spice, if required. Transfer sauce to a large bowl and toss with noodles and sesame seeds. Serve at room temperature or chilled.

Eight-Treasure Noodle Pot

Traditionally, fish, shrimp and scallops are the three treasures in this dish.

Tip

• Chinese black mushrooms are available in Chinese food stores.

2	dried black Chinese mushrooms (see Tip, left)	2
2 cups	boiling water	500 mL
1 oz	cellophane noodles (bean threads)	30 g
2 tbsp	olive oil	25 mL
2	cloves garlic, minced	2
1 tbsp	chopped fresh gingerroot	15 mL
2 cups	thinly sliced cored Chinese cabbage	500 mL
2 cups	broccoli florets	500 mL
4 cups	vegetable stock	1 L

1. In a bowl, cover mushrooms with boiling water. Set aside. In a large bowl, cover noodles with hot tap water. Set aside to soften.

2. Meanwhile, in a large saucepan or Dutch oven, heat oil over medium heat. Stir in garlic, ginger, cabbage and broccoli. Sauté for 2 to 3 minutes. Do not brown.

3. Stir in stock and bring to a boil. Cover, reduce heat and simmer for 15 to 20 minutes or until vegetables are tender-crisp.

4. Drain mushrooms, pat dry and slice. Drain noodles. Add mushrooms and noodles to the vegetable mixture and simmer for 2 to 3 minutes to heat through. Serve immediately.

Variation

• Substitute 2 fresh portobello mushrooms for the black Chinese mushrooms and slice but do not soak before adding in Step 4.

Using pantry ingredients and a very short time to prepare, this tasty, all-in-one dish makes weekday dinners easy.

Cajun Dirty Rice and Tempeh

- *Preheat oven to 350°F (180°C)*
- *Ovenproof skillet or saucepan*

2 cups	chopped onion	500 mL
2	cloves garlic, finely chopped	2
I	piece candied ginger, chopped (about I tbsp/I5 mL)	I
2 tbsp	olive oil	25 mL
I tbsp	Garam Masala Spice Blend (see recipe, page 333) or store-bought	I5 mL
I tbsp	Ras el Hanout seasoning (see recipe, page 334) or store-bought curry powder	I5 mL
I cup	brown rice, rinsed	250 mL
8 oz	frozen tempeh, cut into cubes	250 g
2 cups	vegetable or mushroom stock	500 mL
2 tsp	brown rice syrup	I0 mL
½ cup	sliced mushrooms	I25 mL
½ tsp	salt	2 mL

1. In a baking pan, combine onion, garlic, ginger and oil. Heat gently over medium-low heat and sauté for 5 minutes. Stir in garam masala and Ras el Hanout. Cook, stirring for 3 minutes.

2. Stir in brown rice and cook, stirring, for 3 minutes. Add tempeh. Stir and cook for 2 minutes. Stir in stock and syrup. Increase heat and bring to a boil. Remove from heat and stir in mushrooms and salt.

3. Cover tightly and bake in preheated oven for 30 minutes or until rice is swollen and tender. Serve hot.

Easy to fix, this dish may be enlivened with greens or roasted red peppers for color.

Spiced Cauliflower with Pasta

I	cauliflower, cut into florets	I
½ tsp	salt	2 mL
I cup	whole wheat macaroni	250 mL
I cup	chopped green beans (1-inch/2.5 cm pieces)	250 mL
3 tbsp	olive oil	45 mL
I	small onion, chopped	I
I	leek, white and light green parts, sliced	I
I cup	grated zucchini or summer squash	250 mL
2	cloves garlic, finely chopped	2
I tbsp	Ras el Hanout (see recipe, page 334) or store-bought curry powder	15 mL
½ cup	shredded mozzarella cheese	125 mL
2 tbsp	freshly grated Parmesan cheese	25 mL

1. Bring a large saucepan of water to a boil over high heat. Add cauliflower and salt. Cover, reduce heat and simmer for 6 to 8 minutes or until cauliflower is tender-crisp. Using a slotted spoon, lift out and set aside in a colander to drain and let cool.

2. Bring the water back to a boil and stir in macaroni. Cover and reduce heat and lightly boil for 5 minutes. Add green beans to the saucepan. Cover and lightly boil for another 5 minutes or until macaroni and green beans are both tender but firm.

3. Meanwhile, in a large skillet, heat olive oil over medium-low heat. Stir in onion and leek. Cook, stirring frequently, for 5 minutes. Stir in zucchini, garlic and Ras el Hanout. Cook, stirring, for 5 minutes. Spoon 2 tbsp (25 mL) or enough of the macaroni cooking water into the onion mixture to keep it moist.

4. Drain macaroni and green beans and immediately return to the pot. Add onion mixture, cauliflower, mozzarella and Parmesan cheeses. Toss well to combine and serve immediately.

Variation
• Use fresh or frozen peas in place of the green beans.

Dressings, Pesto, Salsa and Sauces

Citrus Dressing #2

I tbsp	olive oil	15 mL
2	cloves garlic, finely chopped	2
2 tbsp	fresh lemon thyme leaves	25 mL
I	stalk lemongrass, lightly pounded and cut in half	I
I cup	vegetable stock	250 mL
I tbsp	pure maple syrup	15 mL
I tbsp	grated lemon zest	15 mL
2 tbsp	freshly squeezed lemon juice	25 mL
	Salt and freshly ground pepper	

1. In a small saucepan, heat oil over medium-low heat. Add garlic and cook for 2 minutes or until soft. Stir in thyme, lemongrass and stock. Increase heat to high and bring to a boil. Reduce heat and keep gently boiling for 7 minutes or until liquid is reduced by half. Stir in maple syrup, lemon zest and lemon juice. Simmer for another 2 minutes. Add salt and pepper, to taste. Remove lemongrass before serving.

Roasted Garlic Dressing

¹⁄₄ cup	buttermilk	50 mL
I	head roasted garlic (see recipe, page 258)	I
I tbsp	rice vinegar	15 mL
¹⁄₄ tsp	salt	I mL
¹⁄₄ to ¹⁄₂ tsp	ground cayenne powder	I to 2 mL

1. In a small bowl, combine buttermilk, garlic, vinegar and salt. Using a fork, whisk and add cayenne powder, ¹⁄₄ tsp (1 mL) at a time, tasting after each addition.

Fruit Dressing

½ cup	Yogurt Cheese (see recipe, page 145) or drained natural yogurt	125 mL
3 tbsp	pure maple syrup or liquid honey	45 mL
½ tsp	vanilla	2 mL

1. In a small bowl, combine Yogurt Cheese, maple syrup and vanilla. Using a fork, whisk to mix.

Sweet-and-Sour Oriental Dressing

2 tbsp	tamari or soy sauce	25 mL
2 tbsp	rice vinegar	25 mL
2 tbsp	olive oil	25 mL
2 tbsp	brown rice syrup	25 mL
1 tbsp	freshly squeezed lemon juice	15 mL
1 tsp	sesame oil	5 mL
1	clove garlic, minced	1

1. In a small bowl, combine tamari, vinegar, olive oil, syrup, lemon juice, sesame oil and garlic. Using a fork whisk to mix.

Italian Dressing

¼ cup	olive oil	50 mL
1 tbsp	rice vinegar	15 mL
1 tbsp	freshly squeezed lemon juice	15 mL
1	clove garlic, minced	1
2 tbsp	chopped fresh oregano leaves	25 mL
¼ tsp	salt	1 mL
	Freshly ground pepper	

1. In a jar with a tight-fitting lid, combine olive oil, vinegar, lemon juice, garlic, oregano, salt and pepper to taste and shake well.

Sesame Mayonnaise

I	large egg, at room temperature (see Tips, page 307)	I
I tbsp	rice vinegar	15 mL
I tbsp	Dijon mustard	15 mL
I tbsp	tamari or soy sauce	15 mL
2 tbsp	toasted sesame oil	25 mL
¾ cup	olive oil	175 mL

1. In a food processor or blender, combine egg, vinegar, mustard and tamari. Process about 10 seconds or until combined.

2. Stir sesame oil into olive oil. With the motor running, slowly add oils through the opening in the lid in a thin steady stream until blended and thick. Scrape into a small bowl. Serve immediately or refrigerate until ready to serve.

Tofu Mayonnaise

I	clove garlic	I
8 oz	soft tofu, drained	250 g
2 tbsp	freshly squeezed lemon juice	25 mL
I tsp	Dijon mustard	5 mL
	Salt and freshly ground pepper	

1. In a blender or food processor, chop garlic. Add tofu, lemon juice and mustard and process for 20 seconds or until smooth. Add salt and pepper, to taste. Process for 5 seconds to blend.

Wasabi Mayonnaise

I cup	mayonnaise	250 mL
2 tbsp	wasabi from tube or powder (see Tip, left)	25 mL

1. In a small bowl, whisk together mayonnaise and wasabi.

Aïoli

1 cup	olive oil	250 mL
6	cloves garlic, crushed	6
3	large eggs, at room temperature (see Tips, left)	3
1 tbsp	freshly squeezed lemon juice	15 mL
¼ tsp	salt	1 mL

Aïoli is a traditional Mediterranean egg mayonnaise made to be served with vegetables. The garlic is very subtle in this version.

Tips

• Store, tightly covered, in the refrigerator for up to 2 days.

• In some areas you can purchase a pasteurized liquid egg product, not to be confused with liquid egg substitutes. This is a great product for making recipes with raw eggs when you may have safety concerns. Please consult your medical professional prior to making or serving dishes with raw eggs if this is a concern for you.

1. In a small saucepan, gently heat oil with garlic over low heat for about 15 minutes. Do not let oil smoke. Let cool to room temperature.

2. In a sieve over a small bowl, strain oil, pressing with the back of a spoon to extract soft solids from the garlic. Discard remaining garlic. Let oil cool to room temperature.

3. In a food processor or blender, combine eggs, lemon juice and salt. Process for about 10 seconds or until blended. With the motor running, add oil a few drops at a time through opening in the lid, then in a thin steady stream until all oil is absorbed and mixture has thickened. Scrape into a small bowl. Serve immediately or refrigerate until ready to serve.

Ginger Mayonnaise

½ cup	Aïoli (see recipe, above) or Sesame Mayonnaise (see recipe, page 306)	125 mL
½ cup	Yogurt Cheese (see recipe, page 145) or drained natural yogurt	125 mL
1 tbsp	white wine or rice vinegar	15 mL
3 tbsp	minced candied ginger	45 mL

A much lighter mayonnaise, this version uses only half the amount of oil of traditional recipes.

Tip

• Store, tightly covered, in the refrigerator for up to 2 days.

1. In a small bowl, whisk together Aïoli, Yogurt Cheese and wine. Stir in ginger.

Basil Pesto

2	large cloves garlic	2
½ cup	pine nuts or toasted sunflower seeds	125 mL
3 cups	fresh basil leaves	750 mL
¾ cup	freshly grated Parmesan cheese	175 mL
¾ cup	olive oil (approx.)	175 mL
	Salt	

Often in North America, pesto is thought of as only made with basil. Pesto may be made using different aromatic herbs, such as cilantro, rosemary, mint, oregano, tarragon, thyme and savory, are often mixed together along with or in place of basil.

Tip

• Store, tightly covered, in the refrigerator for up to 1 week or in the freezer for up to 3 months.

1. In a food processor, combine garlic and pine nuts. Process for 10 seconds or until chopped. Add basil and Parmesan to the bowl and pulse 3 to 5 times. With the motor running, slowly add oil through opening in the lid in a thin steady stream. Keep adding oil and blending until pesto has reached the desired consistency. Add salt, to taste. Process for 3 seconds to blend.

Coriander Pesto

2	large cloves garlic	2
¼ cup	pine nuts or toasted sunflower seeds	50 mL
1 tbsp	crushed coriander seeds	15 mL
1	fresh green chile pepper, quartered	1
2 cups	fresh cilantro leaves	500 mL
¼ cup	freshly grated Parmesan cheese	50 mL
½ cup	olive oil (approx.)	125 mL
	Salt	

Both cilantro (the green leaves) and coriander seeds are parts of the same plant, *Coriandrum sativum*.

Tip

• Store, tightly covered, in the refrigerator for up to 1 week or in the freezer for up to 3 months.

1. In a food processor or blender, combine garlic, pine nuts and coriander seeds. Process for 15 seconds or until chopped. Add chile pepper, cilantro and Parmesan. Process for 30 to 40 seconds or until chopped. With motor running, add oil through opening in the lid in a steady stream. Keep adding oil and blending until pesto has reached the desired consistency. Add salt, to taste. Process for 3 seconds to blend.

Roasted Garlic and Red Pepper Pesto

Makes 2 cups (500 mL)

This pesto is bright red. Use it as a colorful garnish or as a sauce for pasta.

Tip

• Store, tightly covered, in the refrigerator for up to 1 week or in the freezer for up to 2 months.

4	heads roasted garlic (see recipe, page 258)	4
2 cups	Roasted Red Peppers (see recipe, page 135), divided	500 mL
1 cup	fresh basil leaves	250 mL
1/4 cup	pine nuts or toasted sunflower seeds	50 mL
1/3 cup	freshly grated Parmesan cheese	75 mL
1/2 tsp	salt	2 mL

1. Squeeze the soft flesh of each garlic clove into the bowl of a food processor or blender. Add 1 cup (250 mL) of the Roasted Red Peppers, basil, pine nuts and Parmesan. Process for 30 seconds or until well blended. Add remaining Roasted Red Peppers and salt and pulse 2 or 3 times to chop peppers (being careful not to purée them).

Sun-Dried Tomato Pesto

Makes 1 cup (250 mL)

Sun-dried tomatoes packed in oil tend to be softer and easier to work with than dry-packed, in this pesto.

Tip

• Store, tightly covered, in the refrigerator for up to 1 week or in the freezer for up to 3 months.

2	large cloves garlic	2
1/4 cup	pine nuts or toasted sunflower seeds	50 mL
2 cups	sun-dried tomatoes, packed in olive oil, drained	500 mL
1/4 cup	fresh basil or oregano leaves	50 mL
1/4 cup	freshly grated Parmesan cheese	50 mL
2 tbsp	balsamic vinegar	25 mL
1/4 to 1/2 cup	olive oil	50 to 125 mL
1/4 tsp	salt	1 mL

1. In a food processor or blender, combine garlic and pine nuts. Process for 10 seconds or until chopped. Add sun-dried tomatoes, basil and Parmesan. Process for 1 minute or until tomatoes are coarsely chopped. With motor running, add vinegar and then oil through opening in the lid in a steady stream. Keep adding oil and blending until pesto has reached the desired consistency. Add salt, to taste. Process for 30 seconds to blend. The pesto should be finely chopped and easy to spread but not excessively oily.

Mediterranean Pesto

With all the flavors of the Mediterranean, this pesto is a natural when teamed with roasted red peppers or other dishes from the Mediterranean region.

Tip

• Store, tightly covered, in the refrigerator for up to 1 week or in the freezer for up to 2 months.

2	large cloves garlic	2
2	slices candied ginger	2
½ cup	natural almonds	125 mL
1 cup	fresh basil leaves	250 mL
½ cup	fresh thyme leaves	125 mL
½ cup	fresh savory or oregano leaves	125 mL
2 tbsp	fresh rosemary leaves, optional	25 mL
¼ cup	freshly grated Parmesan cheese	50 mL
½ cup	olive oil (approx.)	125 mL
	Salt	

1. In a food processor or blender, combine garlic and ginger. Process for 20 seconds or until minced. Add almonds, basil, thyme, savory, rosemary, if using, and Parmesan. Process for 30 to 40 seconds or until chopped. With motor running, add oil through opening in the lid in a steady stream until well blended. Keep adding oil and blending until pesto has reached the desired consistency. Add salt, to taste. Process for 3 seconds to blend.

Lemon Pesto

Lemon is not a usual ingredient in pesto, but if used in small amounts with vegetables, it adds a fresh dimension.

Tips

• Use lemon-flavored herbs, such as lemon balm, lemon verbena or lemongrass (tender parts only), or the lemon varieties of basil, mint, sage or thyme.

• Store, tightly covered, in the refrigerator for up to 1 week or in the freezer for up to 3 months.

2	cloves garlic	2
¼ cup	natural almonds, pine nuts or pistachios	50 mL
2 cups	fresh basil leaves	500 mL
¼ cup	fresh lemon-flavored herb leaves (see Tips, left)	50 mL
¼ cup	freshly grated Parmesan cheese	50 mL
1 tsp	grated lemon zest	5 mL
2 tbsp	freshly squeezed lemon juice	25 mL
¼ to ½ cup	olive oil	50 to 125 mL
	Salt	

1. In a food processor or blender, combine garlic and almonds. Process for 20 seconds or until chopped. Add basil, lemon herbs, Parmesan and lemon zest. Process for 30 to 40 seconds or until chopped. With motor running, add lemon juice and then oil in a steady stream through opening in the lid. Keep adding oil and blending until pesto has reached the desired consistency. Add salt, to taste. Process for 3 seconds to blend.

Vegan Friendly

This makes a party-size amount of dip for nachos, crudités or toasted pita triangles. Use it as a substitute for guacamole, or roast only one eggplant and add a whole avocado for a creamier spread. Either way, roasting the garlic mellows its flavors and brings out the complex and sweeter tastes.

Tip

• Store, tightly covered, in the refrigerator for up to 3 days or in the freezer for up to 2 months.

Eggplant Salsa

• *Preheat oven to 400°F (200°C)*
• *Baking sheet, lightly oiled*

2	medium eggplants	2
3 tbsp	olive oil, divided	45 mL
I	whole head garlic	I
2	tomatoes	2
I tbsp	freshly squeezed lemon juice	15 mL
¼ cup	chopped fresh parsley	50 mL
2	green onions, finely chopped	2
	Salt and freshly ground pepper	
	Raw vegetables or pita triangles, optional	

1. Pierce eggplants in a few places with a skewer. Place on prepared baking sheet and drizzle with ½ tbsp (7 mL) of the olive oil.

2. Rub the loose outer skin off the head of garlic. Cut ⅛ to ¼ inch (0.25 to 0.5 cm) off the tops of the cloves keeping the head intact. Place on a square of foil, drizzle ½ tbsp (7 mL) of the oil over the tops of the cloves and seal foil to form a pouch around the head. Place wrapped garlic on baking sheet with eggplant.

3. Roast eggplant and garlic in preheated oven for 1 hour. Open pouch and test garlic after 45 minutes. If cloves are soft, transfer to a bowl. If not, reseal and continue to roast for remaining 15 minutes, until eggplant is soft when pierced with a sharp knife. Transfer eggplant and garlic to a bowl and let cool.

4. Meanwhile, core and chop tomatoes. Place in a colander and set aside over a bowl or in the sink to drain.

5. When eggplant is cool enough to handle, trim ends and remove blackened outer skin. Coarsely chop flesh and place along with juices into a food processor or blender. Squeeze garlic cloves into eggplant. Add remaining 2 tbsp (25 mL) of olive oil and lemon juice. Process for 30 seconds or until blended and smooth.

6. Pour eggplant purée into a bowl. Stir in tomatoes, parsley and green onions. Add salt and pepper, to taste. Serve immediately with raw vegetables or pita triangles, if using.

Vegan Friendly

A great harvest salsa, especially in those years when the tomatoes don't ripen, as they should. Make double the recipe and freeze (see Tip, below).

Tip

• Store, tightly covered, in the refrigerator for up to 1 week or in the freezer for up to 3 months.

Green Tomato and Apple Salsa

4	green tomatoes, diced and drained	4
4	apples, diced	4
1	onion, chopped	1
¼ cup	apple juice	50 mL
1 tbsp	apple cider vinegar	15 mL
1 tbsp	brown rice syrup or molasses	15 mL
2 tbsp	Yellow Curry Spice (see recipe, page 331) or store-bought	25 mL
	Salt and freshly ground pepper	

1. In a large saucepan, combine tomatoes, apples, onion and apple juice. Bring to a boil over high heat. Reduce heat and simmer for 25 minutes or until mixture is soft, thickened and reduced to about 6 cups (1.5 L).

2. Stir in vinegar, syrup and curry spice. Simmer for another 5 minutes. Add salt and pepper, to taste.

This salsa can be used to accompany savory dishes and a cheese course or as a dessert topping.

Vegan Version

• Replace butter with olive oil.

Tip

• Store, tightly covered, in the refrigerator for up to 1 week or in the freezer for up to 3 months.

Spiced Pear Salsa

3 tbsp	butter	45 mL
1 cup	chopped onion	250 mL
6	pears, peeled, cored and diced	6
¾ cup	pear nectar or apple juice	175 mL
1 tbsp	apple cider vinegar	15 mL
1 tbsp	ground turmeric	15 mL
1 tsp	Garam Masala Spice Blend (see recipe, page 333) or store-bought	5 mL
1 tsp	ground cardamom	5 mL
¼ cup	raisins	50 mL
1 tbsp	honey	15 mL

1. In a large saucepan, melt butter over low heat. Stir in onion and cook, stirring occasionally, for 15 minutes or until soft.

2. Stir in pears, nectar, vinegar, turmeric, garam masala, cardamom, raisins and honey. Increase heat to medium and simmer gently for 20 to 30 minutes or until mixture is thick and pears are tender.

Harvest Salsa

**Makes 2 cups
(500 mL)**

Some of the ingredients in this salsa reflect the classic vegetables used in *Pisto Manchego* — the vegetable "stew" from La Mancha, land of Don Quixote in the central plains of Spain.

Tip

• Store, tightly covered, in the refrigerator for up to 1 week or in the freezer for up to 3 months.

I	fresh jalapeño pepper, chopped	I
I	red or green bell pepper, chopped	I
I	onion, chopped	I
I	medium zucchini, cubed	I
3	cloves garlic, minced	3
3 tbsp	olive oil	45 mL
4	tomatoes, peeled, seeded and diced	4
2	ripe peaches, peeled and chopped	2
2	apples, peeled and chopped	2
2 tbsp	apple cider vinegar	25 mL
I tbsp	freshly squeezed lemon juice	15 mL
I tbsp	blackstrap molasses	15 mL
I tbsp	tamari or soy sauce	15 mL
	Salt and freshly ground pepper	
I tbsp	fresh thyme leaves	15 mL
I tbsp	chopped fresh basil	15 mL

1. In a large nonreactive saucepan or stockpot, combine jalapeño pepper, bell pepper, onion, zucchini, garlic and oil. Bring to a simmer over medium heat. Reduce heat and gently cook, stirring often, for 10 minutes.

2. Add tomatoes, peaches, apples, vinegar, lemon juice, molasses and tamari. Bring to just under a boil. Reduce heat and gently simmer, uncovered, stirring occasionally, for 30 minutes or until vegetables are tender. Increase heat to high and boil for 6 to 12 minutes or until excess liquid is reduced and a thick consistency is achieved. Add salt and pepper, to taste. Add thyme and basil and cook for another 5 minutes.

Mango Chutney

Choose firm, ripe, unblemished fruit for this versatile condiment. Use it with vegetable curry dishes, stirred into yogurt as a dip, to accompany cheeses after dinner or with breakfast egg dishes.

Tip

- Store cooled and labeled jars in a cold place for up to 3 months. Freeze for up to 3 months. Chutney will keep, tightly covered, in the refrigerator for up to 5 days.

- *Freezer bags or six 2-cup (500 mL) preserving jars and lids, sterilized*

I lb	mangoes	500 g
I lb	fresh apricots	500 g
I lb	nectarines	500 g
I cup	raisins	250 mL
1/2 cup	freshly squeezed lime juice	125 mL
2 tbsp	olive oil	25 mL
2 cups	thinly sliced onions	500 mL
1 1/4 cups	white wine vinegar	300 mL
1/4 cup	Tamarind Water (see recipe, right)	50 mL
3/4 cup	organic cane sugar	175 mL
1/2 cup	chopped preserved stem ginger	125 mL
1 tbsp	Ras el Hanout seasoning (see recipe, page 334)	15 mL
1 tbsp	Garam Masala Spice Blend (see recipe, page 333) or store-bought	15 mL
1 tbsp	ground turmeric	15 mL
2 tsp	sea salt	10 mL

1. Peel mangoes, apricots and nectarines. Remove stones and cut flesh into 1/2-inch (1 cm) pieces. Transfer to a large bowl and combine with raisins and lime juice. Set aside.

2. In a large nonreactive saucepan, heat oil over medium-low heat. Add onions and cook, stirring often, for 10 minutes. Stir in fruit and their juices, vinegar and Tamarind Water. Increase heat to medium-high and bring to a gentle boil. Boil, stirring often, for 3 minutes.

3. Stir in sugar, ginger, Ras el Hanout, garam masala, turmeric and sea salt. Reduce heat and simmer gently, stirring occasionally, for 15 minutes or until fruit is soft but not puréed.

4. If freezing, cover and let cool. Spoon into 2-cup (500 mL) freezer bags and label. Spoon hot fruit into sterilized jars, removing air bubbles and leaving 1/2-inch (1 cm) headspace. Seal with two-piece lids and process in a boiling water bath for 15 minutes. Refrigerate any with lids that do not seal.

Variations

- Substitute peaches and plums for any of the fruit.
- Use vegetable stock or apple juice in place of the tamarind water.

Tamarind Water

¹⁄₂ cup	boiling water	125 mL
1	walnut-size piece tamarind pulp, about 1-inch (2.5 cm) square	1

Often used in Middle Eastern recipes, tamarind water is easy to prepare and may be made in larger quantities (see Tip, below).

1. In a small bowl, pour boiling water over tamarind. Let stand for 20 minutes. Strain through a fine mesh sieve over a bowl or measuring cup, pressing pulp and squeezing solids dry. Discard solids.

Tip
- Store, tightly covered, in the refrigerator for up to 2 days or freeze in 1 tbsp (15 mL) portions in ice cube trays.

Salsa Verde

2	slices day-old whole-grain bread	2
2 tbsp	white wine	25 mL
1 tbsp	apple cider vinegar	15 mL
3	cloves garlic	3
3 tbsp	fresh rosemary leaves	45 mL
3 cups	packed fresh parsley leaves	750 mL
¹⁄₂ cup	fresh basil leaves	125 mL
³⁄₄ to 1 cup	olive oil	175 to 250 mL
	Salt and freshly ground pepper	

The flat-leaf Italian parsley is best for this sauce, although the curly leaf variety can be used. This bread pesto adds a fresh taste to raw or cooked fresh vegetables as a dip or as a sauce.

1. Cut bread into ¹⁄₂-inch (1 cm) cubes. In a small bowl, toss bread with wine and vinegar. Let stand for 3 to 5 minutes to soften the bread.

2. In a food processor or blender, combine garlic and rosemary. Process for 10 seconds or until chopped. Add parsley and basil. Pulse 5 or 6 times or until coarsely chopped. Add bread mixture and pulse 5 or 6 times to blend into herbs.

3. With motor running, add oil in a steady stream through opening in the lid. Keep adding oil and blending until pesto has reached the desired consistency. Use less oil to make it thick for spreads, slightly thinner for dips and pouring consistency for sauces. Add salt and pepper, to taste.

Tip
- Store, tightly covered, in the refrigerator for up to 1 day. This sauce does not freeze well.

Makrut Lime Leaf Sauce

This sauce is similar in flavor to the fresh-tasting Malaysian *Laksa* dishes that combine noodles in a creamy, lime-coconut sauce seasoned with a light curry.

Tips

• Wild limes are pear-shaped, bumpy and wrinkled. The leaves and rind of the fruit are used most often in cooking because the juice is bitter and so sour that it is not pleasant. Look for the limes or leaves in specialty food stores.

• Store sauce, tightly covered, in the refrigerator for up to 2 days. This sauce does not freeze well.

1 cup	vegetable stock	250 mL
	Juice of 1 lime	
1 tbsp	Red Curry Spice (see recipe, page 331) or store-bought	15 mL
1 cup	chopped onion	250 mL
1 cup	chopped red bell pepper	250 mL
1	clove garlic, minced	1
½ tsp	salt	2 mL
2	makrut lime leaves	2
1 tbsp	grated fresh gingerroot	15 mL
1 tbsp	minced galangal, optional	15 mL
1	can (14 oz/398 mL) coconut milk	1

1. In a saucepan, combine stock, lime juice and curry spice. Bring to a gentle boil over medium-high heat. Add onion, bell pepper, garlic, salt, lime leaves, ginger and galangal, if using. Cover, reduce heat to low and simmer for 5 minutes. Let cool slightly.

2. Remove lime leaves and set aside. Transfer sauce to a blender or food processor. Process sauce for about 1 minute or until blended and smooth. With motor running, add coconut milk through opening in the lid and process for 30 minutes or until well blended.

3. Pour sauce back into saucepan and add reserved lime leaves. Cover and set aside until needed. Remove lime leaves before serving. Serve at room temperature or heat gently before tossing with noodles or vegetables.

Variation

• Replace makrut lime leaves with 1 tbsp (15 mL) grated lime zest.

With the warming qualities of both ginger and cayenne pepper, this is a good dish to serve to an individual that is recovering from the flu, but also delicious and healthy for anyone. The recipe may easily be doubled.

Tip

• Store, tightly covered, in the refrigerator for up to 1 week or in the freezer for up to 2 months.

Vegan Version

• Replace butter with olive oil.

Hot Spiced Applesauce

5	apples (about 1½ lbs/750 g)	5
½ cup	apple cider or apple juice	125 mL
1 tbsp	butter	15 mL
1 tbsp	brown rice syrup	15 mL
1 tbsp	finely chopped fresh gingerroot	15 mL
2 tsp	apple cider vinegar	10 mL
2	whole cloves, crushed	2
1	whole dried cayenne pepper, crushed, divided	1

1. In a saucepan, combine apples, cider, butter, syrup, ginger, vinegar, cloves and half the cayenne pepper. Bring to a boil over medium heat. Cover, reduce heat and simmer for 15 minutes. Uncover and cook, stirring, for 5 minutes longer if a chunky applesauce is preferred, or for 15 minutes to obtain a smoother sauce.

2. Taste and add remaining cayenne pepper, if desired.

Variations

• Use ¼ tsp (1 mL) ground cloves in place of the whole cloves.

• Substitute ½ to 1 tsp (2 to 5 mL) ground cayenne pepper for the whole pepper.

Vegan Friendly

Use this colorful sauce for breakfast dishes and desserts.

Tip

• Store, tightly covered, in the refrigerator for up to 5 days.

Blueberry Sauce

2 cups	fresh or frozen blueberries, divided	500 mL
⅓ cup	apple juice or water	75 mL
2 tbsp	freshly squeezed lemon juice	25 mL
3 tbsp	organic cane sugar	45 mL

1. In a blender, purée ⅓ cup (75 mL) of the blueberries and apple juice. In a saucepan, combine puréed blueberries, remaining 1⅔ cups (425 mL) whole blueberries, lemon juice and sugar. Bring to a gentle boil over medium heat. Reduce heat and simmer, stirring occasionally, for 10 minutes or until thickened. Serve warm.

Peach-Rose Sauce

3	peaches, peeled and coarsely chopped	3
1 cup	pitted fresh apricots, quartered	250 mL
3 tbsp	rose water	45 mL
2 tbsp	brown rice syrup	25 mL
¼ cup	fresh rose petals, optional (see Tip, left)	50 mL

Vegan Friendly

Serve this pretty sauce chilled and use as you would a jam, with fruit or cheese. Alternately, heat and drizzle it over pancakes or gingerbread.

Tip

• Use organic rose petals, not from florist shops.

1. In a large saucepan, combine peaches, apricots, rose water and syrup. Cover and bring to a gentle boil over medium heat. Reduce heat and gently simmer for 15 minutes or until apricots are soft. Stir in rose petals, if using. Serve warm or refrigerate until chilled.

Variation

• Use orange water or apple juice in place of the rose water.

Green Tea Sauce

2	bags green tea leaves	2
2	bags raspberry herbal tea	2
¼ cup	dried cherries	50 mL
2 cups	boiling water	500 mL
¼ cup	chopped dried apricots	50 mL
½ cup	apple juice	125 mL
1 tbsp	freshly grated gingerroot	15 mL

The cherries make this a tart sauce that complements fruit and egg dishes, but it may be sweetened with honey or brown rice syrup for desserts.

Tips

• Store, tightly covered, in the refrigerator for up to 3 days.

• In place of tea bags, use 2 tsp (10 mL) each loose green and herbal raspberry teas in a tea ball infuser or tied in cheesecloth.

1. In a nonreactive saucepan, combine green tea, raspberry tea and cherries. Pour boiling water over top. Cover and steep for 15 minutes. Remove tea bags, pressing lightly to extract all liquid.

2. Stir apricots, apple juice and ginger into tea liquid and cherries in saucepan. Cover and bring to a boil over medium-high heat. Reduce heat and keep at a gentle boil for 15 minutes or until reduced to about 1½ cups (375 mL).

3. Using a slotted spoon, transfer solids to a food processor or blender. Process for 30 seconds or until puréed. Return to saucepan and stir well to combine purée with liquids. Serve warm or chilled.

Tomato Sauce

Vegan Friendly

Oregano is sometimes called the "pizza herb" because it goes so well with tomatoes. Fresh oregano — *O. x majoricum* — is the best variety for tomato sauce. It and fresh basil are the keys to this great-tasting tomato sauce.

2 lbs	ripe tomatoes	1 kg
2 tbsp	olive oil	25 mL
1	red onion, finely chopped	1
4	large cloves garlic, minced	4
2 tbsp	chopped fresh oregano	25 mL
1 tbsp	chopped fresh parsley	15 mL
½ tsp	sea salt	2 mL
	Freshly ground pepper	
3 tbsp	chopped fresh basil	45 mL

1. In a large saucepan of boiling water, blanch tomatoes for 30 seconds. Plunge into cold water and slip skins off. Cut in half, gently squeeze and discard seeds. Coarsely chop flesh and set aside.

2. In a large skillet or saucepan, heat oil over medium heat. Stir in onion and gently sauté for about 7 minutes or until soft. Do not brown. Add garlic and sauté for 2 to 3 minutes or until fragrant.

3. Add tomatoes and oregano and simmer, stirring occasionally, for 10 minutes or until the sauce has thickened slightly. Stir in parsley, salt and pepper, to taste, and simmer, stirring occasionally, for another 10 minutes or until sauce has reached the desired thickness. Stir in basil and serve immediately.

Barbecue Sauce

- *Preheat oven to 400°F (200°C)*
- *13-by 9-inch (3 L) baking pan, lightly oiled*

Vegan Friendly

Commercial barbecue
sauces are high in
sugar, salt and
preservatives. The
sauce in this recipe
offers the medicinal
qualities of fresh
wholesome ingredients.
Make double batches
when tomatoes are at
their peak and freeze
in 1-cup (250 mL)
amounts (see Tip,
below).

6	large ripe tomatoes (about 4 lbs/2 kg)	6
I	onion, quartered	I
I	whole head garlic	I
3 tbsp	olive oil, divided	45 mL
I	can (5½ oz/156 mL) tomato paste	I
⅓ cup	blackstrap molasses	75 mL
I tbsp	apple cider vinegar	15 mL
2 tbsp	freshly squeezed lemon juice	25 mL
I tbsp	tamari or soy sauce	15 mL
I tsp	mustard powder	5 mL
2 tbsp	fresh thyme leaves	25 mL
	Salt and freshly ground pepper	

Tip

- Store sauce in clean
  quart (1 L) or pint
  (500 mL) jars with
  lids in the refrigerator
  for up to 1 week or
  in freezer bags in
  the freezer for up
  to 2 months.

1. Core tomatoes, cut in half, gently squeeze out and discard seeds and liquid. Arrange tomatoes, cut side down, in prepared baking dish. Add onion wedges to the pan.

2. Remove the loose, papery skin from the garlic head and slice and discard ¼ inch (0.5 cm) off the tips of the cloves in the entire head, leaving the whole head intact. Place the garlic head, cut side up in the baking pan with tomatoes and onion. Drizzle about 1 tbsp (15 mL) of the oil over garlic head and remaining 2 tablespoons (25 mL) oil over tomatoes and onion. Roast in preheated oven for 1 hour. Let cool slightly.

3. Slip skins off tomatoes and using a slotted spoon, transfer to a blender or food processor. Add onion to blender. Reserve pan juices for another use or freeze for vegetable stock. Squeeze roasted garlic cloves into the blender. Process for 30 seconds or until smooth.

4. Pour tomato purée into a saucepan. Add tomato paste, molasses, vinegar, lemon juice, tamari, mustard and thyme. Bring to a boil over high heat. Reduce heat and simmer, stirring occasionally, for 45 minutes. Let cool. Add salt and pepper, to taste.

Mushroom Sauce

Vegan Friendly

Make this sauce for any dish that requires a white or Béchamel Sauce. It contains no fat and does not use flour or eggs to thicken it.

Tip

• For a smooth sauce, purée in a blender or food processor.

1 cup	boiling water	250 mL
1 oz	dried mushrooms, whole or sliced	30 g
1 cup	chopped onion	250 mL
3	cloves garlic, finely chopped	3
1	stalk celery, chopped	1
1/4 cup	ground almonds	50 mL
1/4 cup	white wine	50 mL
1 1/2 cups	rice or soy milk, divided	375 mL
1 tbsp	chopped fresh parsley	15 mL
1 tbsp	chopped fresh oregano	15 mL
1/2 tsp	salt	2 mL

1. In a small bowl, pour hot water over mushrooms. Set aside and let stand for 15 minutes. Strain mushrooms and reserve 1/2 cup (125 mL) of the soaking liquid. Set aside. Chop mushrooms and set aside.

2. In a saucepan, combine onion, garlic, celery, almonds and wine. Sauté gently over medium-low heat for 10 minutes. If mixture gets too dry, add a little of the rice milk.

3. Stir in the remaining milk, parsley, oregano, salt, reserved mushrooms and mushroom liquid. Increase heat to high and bring to a boil. Reduce heat and simmer for 30 to 45 minutes or until sauce is thick. Let cool. Cover tightly and refrigerate until needed (up to 24 hours). Bring to room temperature before using in recipes.

Variation

• Use a whole head of roasted garlic in place of the raw garlic cloves.

Miso Gravy

Vegan Friendly

Miso is a thick, salty
paste made from
cooked and aged
soybeans and grains.
Used as a flavoring for
sauces, soups, stews
and other vegetable
dishes, it is available in
darker or lighter
varieties.

1 tsp	whole cumin seeds	5 mL
1 tsp	whole coriander seeds	5 mL
1 tbsp	olive oil	15 mL
½ cup	finely chopped onion	125 mL
2	cloves garlic, minced	2
½ cup	finely chopped mushrooms	125 mL
¼ cup	red or white wine	50 mL
2 tbsp	cornstarch	25 mL
2 tsp	organic cane sugar	10 mL
1½ cups	vegetable stock, divided	375 mL
1 tbsp	fresh thyme leaves	15 mL
1 tbsp	chopped fresh parsley	15 mL
3 tbsp	red or brown miso	45 mL

1. In a dry saucepan, combine cumin and coriander seeds. Toast over medium heat for 2 minutes or until they begin to pop. Stir in oil and onion and cook, stirring occasionally, for about 6 minutes or until soft.

2. Add garlic and mushrooms and cook, stirring, for 1 or 2 minutes to brown. Stir in wine. Reduce heat and simmer for 5 minutes.

3. Meanwhile, in a small bowl, combine cornstarch and sugar. Stir in ½ cup (125 mL) of the stock to make a smooth paste.

4. Stir remaining 1 cup (250 mL) of stock into mushrooms. Increase heat to high and bring to a boil. Reduce heat and stir in cornstarch paste. Simmer gravy, stirring constantly, for 5 minutes or until thickened. Add thyme, parsley and miso and simmer for 3 minutes. Serve hot.

Medieval Green Sauce

½ cup	Yogurt Cheese (see recipe, page 145) or drained yogurt	125 mL
2	cloves garlic, minced	2
3 tbsp	chopped fresh parsley	45 mL
2 tbsp	chopped fresh oregano	25 mL
2 tbsp	chopped fresh chives	25 mL
2 tbsp	fresh thyme leaves	25 mL
2 tsp	Dijon mustard	10 mL
1 tsp	chopped drained capers	5 mL
3 tbsp	olive oil	45 mL
2 tbsp	freshly squeezed lemon juice	25 mL

Fresh herbs are combined here for a sauce that complements fish and spring or summer vegetables.

Tip

• Store, tightly covered, in the refrigerator for up to 3 days. This sauce does not freeze well.

1. In a bowl, combine Yogurt Cheese, garlic, parsley, oregano, chives, thyme, mustard and capers. Stir to mix well.

2. In a small bowl, whisk together oil and lemon juice. Stir into yogurt mixture.

Variation

• Use ½ cup (125 mL) chopped fresh spinach in place of or in addition to the herbs.

Teriyaki Sauce

½ cup	tamari or soy sauce	125 mL
2 tbsp	freshly squeezed lemon juice	25 mL
2 to 4 tbsp	liquid honey or brown rice syrup, divided	25 to 60 mL
3	cloves garlic, minced	3
2 tsp	rice vinegar	10 mL

Vegan Friendly

This serves as a marinade for tempeh and can be used with stir-fried vegetables.

Tip

• Store, tightly covered, in the refrigerator for up to 5 days.

1. In a small bowl, combine tamari, lemon juice, 2 tbsp (25 mL) of the honey, garlic and vinegar. Stir well. Taste and add remaining 2 tbsp (25 mL) of the honey, if required.

Cheese Sauce

Our vegetarian version
of cheese sauce uses
whole wheat flour, rice
milk for cow's milk, oil
in place of the butter,
and adds some
not-so-classic but
flavorful ingredients,
such as tamari and
brewer's yeast. All the
natural ingredients make
this sauce a darker
brown color — not the
white or orange cheese
sauce we might expect.

Tip

• Increase or reduce
the milk by 3 tbsp
(45 mL) to achieve
either a thicker or a
thinner sauce.

I	clove garlic, chopped	I
2 tbsp	olive oil	25 mL
3 tbsp	whole wheat or spelt flour	45 mL
I tsp	brewer's yeast	5 mL
I cup	rice or soy milk	250 mL
¼ cup	shredded Swiss or Cheddar cheese	50 mL
2 tbsp	grated Parmesan cheese	25 mL
I tsp	tamari or soy sauce	5 mL
¼ tsp	ground nutmeg	I mL

1. In a saucepan, combine garlic and oil. Sauté over medium heat for about 3 minutes or until garlic is fragrant and soft. Add flour and yeast and stir to make a paste. Gradually whisk in milk and cook, stirring constantly, for 5 or 6 minutes or until thickened.

2. Remove from heat and stir in Swiss and Parmesan cheeses until melted. Stir in tamari and nutmeg. Serve immediately.

Mojo Sauce

Vegan Friendly

This is a great winter
sauce for tofu burgers
and grilled vegetables.

Tip

• Store, tightly covered,
in the refrigerator for
up to 3 days.

I tbsp	olive oil	15 mL
½ cup	finely chopped onion	125 mL
2	fresh jalapeño or serrano chiles, seeded and minced	2
2	cloves garlic, minced	2
I	can (19 oz/540 mL) Bartlett pear slices and juice	I
I tbsp	freshly squeezed lime juice	15 mL
¼ tsp	salt, optional	I mL
3 tbsp	chopped fresh cilantro	45 mL

1. In a saucepan, heat oil over medium heat. Sauté onion for 5 minutes or until soft. Stir in jalapeño chiles and garlic and cook, stirring, for 1 minute. Remove from heat.

2. Meanwhile, drain pears, reserving 3 tbsp (45 mL) of the juice. Stir the reserved pear juice, pears, lime juice, and salt, if using, into saucepan. Return saucepan to heat and bring mixture to a boil. Remove from heat. Set aside to cool and stir in cilantro.

Variation

- In the summer, substitute $1\frac{1}{2}$ cups (375 mL) fresh blanched fruit (pears, peaches, plums, nectarines) for the canned pears and orange or apple juice for the reserved pear juice.

Makes 2 cups (500 mL)

Vegan Friendly

This makes a fairly thick sauce that can be used as a topping for vegetables, in lasagna, or as a spread or a dip.

Tips

- To make a thinner sauce: In Step 3, with motor of food processor running, slowly add more water through opening in the lid until desired consistency is achieved.

- Store, tightly covered, in the refrigerator for up to 4 days.

Walnut Sauce

1 cup	coarsely chopped walnuts, divided	250 mL
1 cup	warm water, divided	250 mL
1	clove garlic	1
1	piece (1-inch/2.5 cm) candied ginger	1
2	slices whole-grain bread, torn into chunks	2
2 tbsp	freshly squeezed lemon juice	25 mL
2 tsp	olive oil	10 mL
2 tsp	Dijon mustard	10 mL
$\frac{1}{4}$ tsp	salt, optional	1 mL
	Freshly ground pepper	

1. In a small bowl, cover $\frac{1}{2}$ cup (125 mL) of the walnuts with $\frac{1}{2}$ cup (125 mL) of the water. Set aside for at least 30 minutes or overnight.

2. Meanwhile, chop remaining walnuts slightly more than coarse but not fine. Set aside.

3. Drain and rinse soaked walnuts and place in food processor. Add garlic and ginger and pulse to chop and combine. Add bread, lemon juice, oil, mustard, salt, if using, and pepper, to taste, and pulse to combine. With motor running, add remaining water through opening in the lid. Stop and scrape down sides of the bowl. Process until the mixture is very smooth. Taste and add more mustard, lemon juice or salt, if required.

4. Transfer purée to a small bowl and stir in reserved walnuts. Use immediately.

Cocktail Peanut Sauce

Makes ¾ cup (175 mL)

The recipe ingredients are based on using a high quality, freshly made nut butter because it contains no hydrogenated oils, sugar and preservatives. If using a commercial peanut butter, omit the rice syrup.

Tip

• Store, tightly covered, in the refrigerator for up to 3 days.

½ cup	natural peanut or cashew butter	125 mL
1	green onion, thinly sliced on the diagonal	1
1	clove garlic, minced	1
1 or 2	dried chiles, finely chopped	1 or 2
2 tbsp	brown rice syrup	25 mL
2 tbsp	soy sauce	25 mL
2 tbsp	freshly squeezed lemon juice	25 mL
2 tsp	grated fresh gingerroot	10 mL

1. In a bowl, combine peanut butter, green onion, garlic, 1 chile, rice syrup, soy sauce, lemon juice and ginger. Stir with a fork until the peanut butter is mixed in. Taste and add remaining chile, if desired. Adjust other seasonings, if required. Serve at room temperature or gently heat in a small saucepan over medium-low heat until bubbles start to form around the edge of pan.

Honey Mustard Sauce

Makes 1 cup (250 mL)

Vegan Friendly

Whole mustard seeds are dark brown or a lighter yellow color, depending on the plant variety. They are available at whole food stores.

Tip

• Store, tightly covered, in the refrigerator for up to 3 weeks.

½ cup	whole mustard seeds	125 mL
½ cup	water (approx.)	125 mL
¼ cup	liquid honey	50 mL
1	clove garlic, minced	1
3 tbsp	organic cane sugar	45 mL
1 tsp	sea salt	5 mL
1 tbsp	fresh tarragon leaves	15 mL
¼ cup	apple juice	50 mL
2 tbsp	white wine	25 mL
2 tbsp	balsamic vinegar	25 mL

1. In a food processor, combine mustard seeds and water. Process for 5 to 10 minutes or until a coarse purée is achieved. Do not remove mustard from bowl but set aside, uncovered, for at least 2 hours or as long as overnight, stirring occasionally. Add more water as necessary to keep the mixture moist.

2. Add honey, garlic, sugar, salt and tarragon to mustard purée. Process for 1 minute. With motor running, add apple juice, wine and vinegar through the opening in the lid. Process for 1 to 2 minutes or until the desired consistency is achieved. This is cracked whole seed mustard and will be somewhat grainy no matter how long it is processed.

Vegan Friendly

Flaming hot, this sauce is best used in small amounts. Handle the pepper with rubber gloves and wash utensils and surfaces thoroughly after chopping. This sauce may be doubled or tripled if necessary.

Tip

• Store, tightly covered, in the refrigerator for up to 3 weeks.

Jerk Sauce

3 tbsp	whole allspice berries	45 mL
I	whole clove	I
2 tbsp	olive oil	25 mL
¼ cup	finely chopped onion	50 mL
3	cloves garlic, minced	3
½ tsp	ground cinnamon	2 mL
¼ tsp	ground nutmeg	I mL
½ to I tsp	minced dried Scotch Bonnet pepper or hot pepper sauce	2 to 5 mL
3 tbsp	freshly squeezed lime juice	45 mL
2 tbsp	blackstrap molasses	25 mL
¼ tsp	salt	I mL

1. In a small dry saucepan, combine allspice and clove. Toast over medium heat for 1 to 2 minutes or until fragrant. Let cool. Transfer to a mortar and pestle or electric grinder and grind to a coarse or fine powder.

2. In same saucepan, heat oil over medium heat. Add onion and garlic and heat gently for 3 minutes. Stir in cinnamon and nutmeg and cook for 2 minutes. Add ½ tsp (2 mL) of the pepper, lime juice, molasses, salt and toasted allspice and clove powder. Simmer gently for another 3 minutes. Taste and add remaining pepper, if required.

Spring Green Sauce

Use this light, tangy cream sauce with any spring or summer vegetable or toss it with pasta for a lower-fat main dish.

Tip

• Store sauce, covered tightly, in the refrigerator for up to 3 days. Bring to room temperature before heating or tossing with vegetables or cooked, drained pasta.

1	leek, white and light green parts, chopped	1
1/4 cup	white wine	50 mL
1/2 cup	vegetable stock	125 mL
1 tbsp	pure maple syrup	15 mL
2 cups	fresh sorrel, torn	500 mL
2 cups	fresh spinach, torn	500 mL
1 cup	natural yogurt, drained	250 mL
1/2 tsp	ground nutmeg	2 mL
	Salt and freshly ground pepper	

1. In a saucepan, combine leek and wine. Bring to a gentle simmer over medium heat. Simmer for 10 minutes or until leek is soft. Add stock and maple syrup. Increase heat and bring to a boil. Add sorrel and spinach. Cover, reduce heat to low and cook for 3 minutes or until greens are wilted.

2. Using a slotted spoon, transfer greens to food processor or blender (reserving cooking liquids). Process greens for 10 seconds or just until chopped. Place in a bowl and let cool.

3. Stir yogurt and nutmeg into greens. Add reserved liquid, if required, for a creamy and thick sauce. Add salt and pepper, to taste.

Seasonings

Cajun Black Spice

Makes ⅓ cup (75 mL)

Vegan Friendly

Hot, black and potent, use this spice sparingly until you are familiar with its taste.

2	dried cayenne peppers	2
I tbsp	whole brown mustard seeds	15 mL
I tbsp	whole black peppercorns	15 mL
I tbsp	whole allspice berries	15 mL
I tbsp	whole fennel seeds	15 mL
I tsp	whole cloves	5 mL

1. Using scissors, cut cayenne pepper pods into small pieces. In a small spice wok or dry cast-iron skillet, combine pepper pieces and their seeds with mustard, peppercorns, allspice, fennel and cloves. Toast over medium-high heat for 2 to 3 minutes or until the seeds begin to pop and their fragrance is released. Let cool.

2. In a mortar (using pestle) or small electric grinder, pound or grind toasted spices until coarse or finely ground.

Using Whole Spices

Toasting Spices

Spice woks are tiny heavy pans shaped like Chinese woks. They are used to toast whole spices to release their fragrances. In place of a spice wok, a small heavy-bottomed skillet or copper pan may be used to toast spices.

Grinding Spices

When whole dried roots, bark, flower pods and seeds of herbs and spices are added to mixtures, they must be removed before serving. For example, whole, fragrant vanilla pods are often left whole or coarsely chopped into tisanes, custards and cream sauces while they simmer or steep, but they are always strained off.

Grinding woody plant parts means that they may be blended into the ingredients of dishes in order to lend their unique essences. For centuries, the mortar and pestle was the only tool that could render the brittle, tough texture of spices to a fine powder. Today, the electric coffee grinder offers a fast and convenient modern alternative to the traditional mortar and pestle. If using a coffee grinder, keep it exclusively for grinding spices.

Store and label spice in a small clean jar with lid in the refrigerator or cool dark place for up to 2 months.

Note: Store-bought blends are widely available and may be used to replace any of the spices here, with the exception of Ras el Hanout. Use a store-bought curry or garam masala in place of the homemade Ras el Hanout.

Yellow Curry Spice

Vegan Friendly

Curry is a blend of spices, and a very subjective interpretation by most cooks. Make your own by varying the ingredients here but always keep the fenugreek because it is the essence of a good curry.

Tip

• Store and label spice in a small clean jar with lid in the refrigerator or cool dark place for up to 2 months.

I	dried cayenne pepper	I
2 tbsp	whole fenugreek seeds	25 mL
I tbsp	whole yellow mustard seeds	15 mL
I tbsp	whole coriander seeds	15 mL
I tbsp	whole cumin seeds	15 mL
I tsp	whole allspice berries	5 mL
I tbsp	ground turmeric	15 mL
½ tsp	ground ginger	2 mL

1. Using scissors, cut cayenne pepper pod into small pieces. In a small spice wok or dry cast-iron skillet, combine pepper pieces and their seeds with fenugreek, mustard, coriander, cumin and allspice. Toast over medium-high heat for 2 to 3 minutes or until the seeds begin to pop and their fragrance is released. Let cool.

2. In a mortar (using pestle) or small electric grinder, pound or grind toasted spices until coarse or finely ground. Add turmeric and ginger to ground spices and mix well.

Red Curry Spice

Vegan Friendly

The red color is unusual for a curry and the cayenne makes it hotter than most.

Tip

• Store and label spice in a small clean jar with lid in the refrigerator or cool dark place for up to 2 months.

I	dried cayenne pepper	I
I tbsp	whole yellow or brown mustard seeds	15 mL
I tbsp	whole fenugreek seeds	15 mL
I tbsp	whole red peppercorns	15 mL
I tbsp	whole allspice berries	15 mL
I tbsp	whole fennel seeds	15 mL
2 tbsp	ground paprika	25 mL
I tbsp	ground turmeric	15 mL

1. Using scissors, cut cayenne pepper pod into small pieces. In a small spice wok or dry cast-iron skillet, combine pepper pieces and their seeds with mustard, fenugreek, peppercorns, allspice and fennel. Toast over medium-high heat for 2 to 3 minutes or until the seeds begin to pop and their fragrance is released. Let cool.

2. In a mortar (using pestle) or small electric grinder, pound or grind toasted spices until coarse or finely ground. Add paprika and turmeric to ground spices and mix well.

Ethiopian Hot Pepper Seasoning

Called *berbere* in Ethiopia, this hot and fragrant blend can be used to flavor vegetable tagines or used with legume dishes.

Tip
- Store and label spice in a small clean jar with lid in the refrigerator or cool dark place for up to 2 months.

5	dried cayenne peppers	5
1 tbsp	whole black peppercorns	15 mL
2 tsp	whole allspice berries	10 mL
1 tsp	whole cumin seeds	5 mL
1 tsp	whole cardamom seeds	5 mL
1 tsp	whole fenugreek seeds	5 mL
3	whole cloves	3
1	piece (1 inch/2.5 cm) cinnamon, broken into pieces	1

1. Using scissors, cut cayenne pepper pods into small pieces. In a small spice wok or dry cast-iron skillet, combine pepper pieces and their seeds, with peppercorns, allspice, cumin, cardamom, fenugreek, cloves and cinnamon. Toast over medium-high heat for 2 to 3 minutes or until the seeds begin to pop and their fragrance is released. Let cool.

2. In a mortar (using pestle) or small electric grinder, pound or grind toasted spices until coarse or finely ground.

Asian Five-Spice Seasoning

Chinese healers always take into account the five flavors — salty, sour, sweet, pungent and bitter. This seasoning roughly imitates these qualities.

Tip
- Store and label spice in a small clean jar with lid in the refrigerator or cool dark place for up to 2 months.

1	piece (2 inches/5 cm) cinnamon	1
10	whole cloves	10
8	whole star anise	8
2 tbsp	whole black peppercorns	25 mL
2 tbsp	whole fennel seeds	25 mL

1. Break cinnamon into small pieces. In a mortar (using pestle) or small electric grinder, pound or grind cinnamon, cloves, star anise, peppercorns and fennel until coarse or finely ground, depending on personal preference.

Makes ¼ cup (50 mL)

Garam Masala Spice Blend

Vegan Friendly

Masala is the Indian word for a blend of spices. A masala may be hot or sweetly fragrant, ground fine or crushed. It is added at different stages of the cooking process. Garam masala is the most common ground spice blend and is usually added towards the end of the cooking time. This masala is aromatic and not very hot and can be used in small amounts in sweet dishes and beverages.

Tip

• Store and label spice in a small clean jar with lid in the refrigerator or cool dark place for up to 2 months.

1	piece (2 inches/5 cm) cinnamon	1
2 tsp	whole cardamom seeds	10 mL
2 tbsp	whole coriander seeds	25 mL
1 tbsp	whole cumin seeds	15 mL
2 tsp	whole black peppercorns	10 mL
3	whole cloves	3
1	whole star anise	1
¼ tsp	ground nutmeg	1 mL

1. Break cinnamon into small pieces. In a small spice wok or dry cast-iron skillet, combine cinnamon, cardamom, coriander, cumin, peppercorns, cloves and star anise. Toast over medium-high heat for 4 to 5 minutes or until the seeds begin to pop and their fragrance is released. Let cool.

2. In a mortar (using pestle) or small electric grinder, pound or grind toasted spices until coarse or finely ground. Add nutmeg to ground spices and mix well.

Ras el Hanout

Vegan Friendly

In Morocco, every stall in the *attarine* (spice street in the market) has its own Ras el Hanout. The literal meaning is "top of the shop" and it is the very best the spice merchant has to offer. This is a secret blend of upwards of 25, sometimes 100 different spices, herbs and aphrodisiacs that people search out until they find the one they love best. A mortar and pestle works best to crush and grind the toasted spices, but if necessary, use a spice grinder or small food processor.

Tip

• Store and label spice in a small clean jar with lid in the refrigerator or cool dark place for up to 2 months.

I	piece (2 inches/5 cm) cinnamon	I
I tbsp	whole allspice berries	15 mL
I tbsp	whole coriander seeds	15 mL
I tbsp	whole fennel seeds	15 mL
2 tsp	whole cardamom seeds	10 mL
2 tsp	whole cumin seeds	10 mL
2 tsp	whole fenugreek seeds	10 mL
2 tsp	whole black peppercorns	10 mL
3	whole cloves	3
I	whole star anise	I
I tbsp	sea salt	15 mL
I tbsp	ground turmeric	15 mL
I tsp	ground ginger	5 mL

1. Break cinnamon into small pieces. In a small spice wok or dry cast-iron skillet, combine cinnamon, allspice, coriander, fennel, cardamom, cumin, fenugreek, peppercorns, cloves and star anise. Toast over medium-high heat for 4 to 5 minutes or until the seeds begin to pop and their fragrance is released. Let cool.

2. In a mortar (using pestle) or small electric grinder, pound or grind toasted spices until coarse or finely ground. Add salt, turmeric and ginger to ground spices and mix well.

Variation

• Just before adding to a dish, add 1 minced garlic clove and ¼ tsp (1 mL) finely shredded fresh gingerroot for every 1 to 2 tbsp (15 to 25 mL) Ras el Hanout blend.

Turmeric Spice Paste

Makes ⅓ cup (75 mL)

Vegan Friendly

Pastes are easy to use in cooking because they blend easily into dishes as they simmer. Make small amounts and always store spice pastes in the refrigerator. Fresh turmeric is not always available and when it is, it is usually only found in Indian spice specialty stores.

Tip

- Store and label spice in a small clean jar with lid in the refrigerator for up to 1 week or in the freezer for up to 2 months.

1	piece (1 inch/2.5 cm) cinnamon	1
1 tbsp	whole coriander seeds	15 mL
1 tbsp	whole allspice berries	15 mL
1	whole clove	1
1	piece (2 inches/5 cm) fresh turmeric root	1
1	piece (½ inch/1 cm) fresh gingerroot	1
2	cloves garlic	2
2 tbsp	olive oil (approx.)	25 mL

1. Break cinnamon into small pieces. In a small spice wok or dry cast-iron skillet, combine cinnamon, coriander, allspice and clove. Toast over medium-high heat for 3 to 4 minutes or until the seeds begin to pop and their fragrance is released. Let cool.

2. In a mortar (using pestle), pound toasted spices until finely ground. Add turmeric, ginger and garlic. Pound, stopping to add oil every few seconds until a smooth paste is formed.

Variation

- Use 2 tbsp (25 mL) ground turmeric in place of the fresh root and add in Step 2.

Za'atar

Makes ¼ cup (50 mL)

Vegan Friendly

Za'atar is a term used for a blend of spices that have an overall aroma of thyme or oregano.

Tips

- Store and label spice in a small clean jar with lid in the refrigerator or cool dark place for up to 2 months.

2 tbsp	toasted sesame seeds	25 mL
1 tbsp	dried thyme leaves	15 mL
2 tsp	ground sumac or paprika (see Caution, below)	10 mL
2 tsp	dried oregano leaves	10 mL
1 tsp	sea salt	5 mL

1. In a small jar, combine sesame seeds, thyme, sumac, oregano and salt. Cover with lid and shake to mix well.

Serving Suggestion

- Use as a rub for fish or sprinkle over oiled flat bread and toast for a tasty snack.

Caution

- Purchase sumac from specialist grocery stores selling Middle Eastern ingredients. Some members of the sumac family (found mostly in North America) have poisonous berries.

Dukkah

Vegan Friendly

This loose, dry mixture of chopped nuts and spices is crushed, not powdered or ground to a paste. In the Middle East, it is usually eaten with bread dipped in olive oil as a snack, or served at breakfast or any other time throughout the day. Each family has a slightly different version. The amounts here may be doubled or tripled.

Tip

• Store and label spice in a clean jar with lid in the refrigerator or for up to 2 weeks.

1 cup	sesame seeds	250 mL
3 tbsp	whole coriander seeds	45 mL
2 tbsp	whole cumin seeds	25 mL
1 cup	unsalted, dry roasted peanuts	250 mL
1 tsp	salt, or to taste	5 mL

1. In a small heavy skillet or saucepan, toast sesame seeds over medium heat, stirring constantly, until pale brown. Be careful not to burn the seeds. Set aside to cool.

2. In a small spice wok or dry cast-iron skillet, combine coriander and cumin. Toast over medium-high heat for 1 to 2 minutes or until the seeds begin to pop and their fragrance is released. Let cool.

3. In a food processor or using a mortar and pestle, grind or pound toasted spices until finely ground. Add sesame seeds and peanuts to food processor or mortar. Pulse or pound until chopped fine. The texture should resemble coarse sand but not a paste. Tip into a small bowl and stir in salt, adding it to taste.

Beverages

Herb Tea Blends

Drying and Storing Herbs

Herbs are often used fresh in teas but to make herb tea blends, dried herbs are best. For long-stemmed herbs (mints, yarrow, sage, thyme), gather in small bunches, tie stems and hang upside down in a warm, dry, dark place. Paper bags may be tied over the herbs to catch the falling bits as they dry and to keep the light away.

Before measuring dried herbs for tea blends, strip leaves from the stems, but try to keep the leaves whole. Store whole leaves in labeled airtight containers. Crushing or grinding the leaves just before using releases the essential oils and the medicinal components.

Making Tea Blends

Blend dried whole leaves, petals, seeds and chopped dried roots according to the following recipes. Store in a labeled airtight tin or dark-colored jar in a dark, cool place. When ready to use in teas, grind enough for 2 to 3 days (about $^1/_2$ cup/125 mL) to a fine powder. Store the powder in a dark jar and use within the week.

To Make the Perfect Pot of Tea

1. Crush a small amount of herbal tea blend or grind spices to a fine powder.
2. Bring fresh cold water to a boil over high heat. Rinse a nonreactive teapot with some of the boiling water and pour off.
3. Measure 1 tbsp (15 mL) herb blend powder for every cup (250 mL) of tea to be made. Add one extra tablespoon (15 mL) herb powder "for the pot" and toss all into the teapot.
4. Pour boiling water over, cover pot and block the spout. Steep about 5 minutes and strain into cups.
5. Sweeten with honey and add freshly squeezed lemon juice, to taste, if desired.

Vegan Friendly

All of the ingredients in this tea blend are available in whole or natural food stores.

Tip

- Store herb mixture, tightly covered, in an airtight jar or container in a cool, dry, dark cupboard for up to 4 months.

Green Tea and Summer Herb Blend

1 part	dried green tea leaves	1 part
1 part	dried calendula petals	1 part
$^1/_2$ part	dried St. John's wort petals	$^1/_2$ part
$^1/_2$ part	dried echinacea petals	$^1/_2$ part
$^1/_8$ part	dried lavender flowers	$^1/_8$ part

1. In a large bowl, combine green tea, calendula, St. John's wort, echinacea and lavender. Lightly toss to blend. Make tea following the directions above.

Digestive Tea Blend

Makes ½ cup (125 mL)

Vegan Friendly

Take this drink after meals to aid digestion.

Tip

- Store, tightly covered, in an airtight jar or container in a cool, dry, dark cupboard for up to 4 months.

2 tbsp	crushed cardamom seeds	25 mL
2 tbsp	crushed fennel seeds	25 mL
1 tbsp	crushed anise seeds	15 mL
2 tbsp	ground cinnamon	25 mL
1 tbsp	ground cloves	15 mL

1. In a large bowl, combine cardamom, fennel, anise, cinnamon and cloves. Lightly toss to blend. Make tea following the directions, left.

Stress Reducing Tea Blend

Vegan Friendly

This tea calms the muscles and nerves.

Tip

- Store, tightly covered, in an airtight jar or container in a cool, dry, dark cupboard for up to 4 months.

2 parts	dried skullcap leaves	2 parts
2 parts	dried linden flowers	2 parts
2 parts	dried lemon balm leaves	2 parts
1 part	dried lemon verbena leaves	1 part
1 part	dried passionflower	1 part
½ part	dried lavender flowers	½ part

1. In a large bowl, combine skullcap, linden, lemon balm, lemon verbena, passionflower and lavender. Lightly toss to blend. Make tea following the directions, left.

Pain and Inflammation Reducing Tea Blend

Vegan Friendly

Turmeric reduces post exercise pain. Take a cup of this tea either before or after working out.

Tip

- Store, tightly covered, in an airtight jar or container in a cool, dry, dark cupboard for up to 4 months.

1 part	dried German chamomile	1 part
1 part	dried meadowsweet flowers	1 part
1 part	crushed willow bark	1 part
⅛ part	ground nutmeg	⅛ part

1. In a large bowl, combine chamomile, meadowsweet, willow and nutmeg. Lightly toss to blend. Make tea following the directions, left.

Vegan Friendly

Powerfully antibiotic
and antiviral, this tea
fights colds and flu.
Garlic is one of the key
ingredients in this
blend, and it must be
taken fresh because the
powdered form has
little medicinal value.
For this reason, make
up in small quantities
and use as soon as cold
and flu symptoms
appear.

Cold and Flu Tea Blend

4½ cups	boiling water, divided	1.125 L
2 tsp	fresh thyme leaves or 1 tsp (5 mL) dried	10 mL
1 tsp	chopped fresh lemon balm leaves or ½ tsp (2 mL) dried	5 mL
1	clove garlic, finely chopped	1
½ tsp	finely grated fresh gingerroot	2 mL
	Honey, optional	

1. Rinse a nonreactive teapot with ½ cup (125 mL) of the boiling water and pour off. In same teapot, combine thyme, lemon balm, garlic and ginger.

2. Pour remaining boiling water over top, cover pot and block the spout. Steep for about 5 minutes and strain into cups. Add honey, if desired. Drink 1 cup (250 mL) of tea every 2 to 3 hours as soon as cold or flu symptoms appear.

Vegan Friendly

All of the ingredients in
this soothing tea blend,
including the honey,
will help to ease a sore
throat.

Tip

• Store herb mixture,
tightly covered, in
an airtight jar or
container in a cool,
dry, dark cupboard
for up to 4 months.

Throat Saver Tea Blend

1 part	dried thyme leaves	1 part
1 part	dried peppermint leaves	1 part
½ part	dried sage leaves	½ part
⅛ part	ground ginger	⅛ part
	Honey, to taste	
	Freshly squeezed lemon juice, optional	

1. In a large bowl, combine thyme, peppermint, sage and ginger. Lightly toss to blend. Make tea following the directions for making tea on page 338. Add up to 1 tbsp (15 mL) honey per cup (250 mL) and add lemon juice, if desired.

Green Barley Water

3 tbsp	bruised fresh oregano leaves	45 mL
2 cups	boiling water	500 mL
¼ cup	pot barley	50 mL
1 tbsp	honey, or to taste	15 mL
2 tbsp	freshly squeezed lemon juice, or to taste	25 mL
2 cups	noncarbonated mineral water	500 mL

Barley water has a long history of quenching thirst. Dr. Chase, writing at the end of the 19th century in his *New Receipt Book*, describes a barley water used by the men working on the New York and Brooklyn Bridges in 1876. Oregano adds an antibacterial, antifungal and antiviral quality to the drink.

Tip

• Store, tight covered, in the refrigerator for up to 3 days.

1. In a nonreactive teapot, combine oregano and boiling water. Cover tightly and steep for 5 minutes.

2. Strain off and discard oregano. Reserve and set aside 1 cup (250 mL) of the infusion. Combine the other cup (250 mL) of infusion in a saucepan with barley. Cover and bring to a boil over medium-high heat. Reduce heat and simmer gently, stirring occasionally, for 10 minutes or until barley is soft.

3. Turn heat off, stir in honey and reserved oregano infusion. Cover and let cool. Strain liquid into a glass jug and discard barley solids. Stir in lemon juice and mineral water. Taste and add more honey and lemon juice, if required. This water is meant to be taken at room temperature but may be chilled.

Spring Tonic

1	fresh dandelion root, coarsely chopped	1
1	fresh burdock root, coarsely chopped	1
1	fresh ginseng root, coarsely chopped, optional	1
2 tbsp	chopped fresh parsley	25 mL
2 tbsp	chopped fresh dandelion leaf	25 mL
1 cup	fresh maple sap or pure filtered water	250 mL

Native Americans drank fresh maple sap as a tonic drink in the spring. This tonic is a cleansing drink to be taken three or four times a day for two or three days. Make it fresh each day. Eat light, raw meals to benefit from the cleansing effects of this tonic.

Tip

• Store, tight covered, in the refrigerator for 1 day only.

1. In a saucepan, combine 2 cups (500 mL) water and dandelion, burdock and ginseng, if using. Cover and bring to a boil over medium heat. Reduce heat and simmer gently for 10 minutes. Remove from heat and stir in parsley and dandelion leaf. Let stand, covered, for 20 minutes.

2. Strain into a clean jar, pressing on solids to extract all liquid. Discard herbs and pour into a glass jar with a lid. Add maple sap, if available.

Good Health Elixir Blend

Make up this healing herbal tea blend using any measure of the dried herbs as a "part." It makes a pleasant tasting green herbal tea that may be sweetened with honey or maple syrup.

Tip

• Store, tightly covered, in an airtight jar or container in a cool, dry, dark cupboard for up to 4 months.

1 part	dried parsley leaves	1 part
1 part	dried alfalfa leaves and/or flowers	1 part
1 part	dried oregano or marjoram leaves	1 part
½ part	dried thyme leaves	½ part

1. In a large bowl, combine parsley, alfalfa, oregano and thyme. Lightly toss to blend. Make elixir following the directions for making tea on page 338.

Apple Fresh Smoothie

Serves 3

Vegan Friendly

A refreshing drink for all seasons and all times of the day.

¾ cup	apple juice	175 mL
2	apples, peeled and chopped	2
1 cup	seedless red grapes	250 mL
½	lemon, peeled and chopped	½

1. In a blender, combine apple juice, apples, grapes and lemon. Blend on low for 30 seconds. Gradually increase speed to high and blend for 30 seconds or until smooth.

Berry Blast Smoothie

Serves 2

Vegan Friendly

The goodness of summer berries is captured in this dark and delicious blend.

¾ cup	raspberry juice	175 mL
2 tbsp	freshly squeezed lemon juice	25 mL
6	frozen strawberries	6
6	frozen raspberries	6
½ cup	fresh blackberries	125 mL
½ cup	fresh blueberries	125 mL

1. In a blender, combine raspberry juice, lemon juice, strawberries, raspberries, blackberries and blueberries. Blend on low for 30 seconds. Gradually increase speed to high and blend for 30 seconds or until smooth.

Buy and use fresh apricots when in season and make this dessert-inspired cocktail.

Peach Cobbler Cocktail

1	can (14 oz/398 mL) peaches, halves or slices in juice	1
4	ice cubes	4
1/2 cup	rice or soy milk	125 mL
1/4 cup	peach-flavored yogurt	50 mL
2	fresh apricots, peeled and chopped	2
1/3 cup	peach sherbet	75 mL
Pinch	ground nutmeg	Pinch

1. In a blender, combine peaches with juice, ice, milk, yogurt, apricots, sherbet and nutmeg. Blend on low for 30 seconds. Gradually increase speed to high and blend for 30 seconds or until smooth.

Vegan Friendly

Surprisingly delicious, this drink is packed with nutrients and fiber.

Fruited Beet Smoothie

1	can (14 oz/398 mL) diced beets with liquid	1
1/4 cup	apple juice	50 mL
1 tbsp	freshly squeezed lemon juice	15 mL
1	pear, peeled and chopped	1
1	apple, peeled and chopped	1
1 tsp	chopped fresh savory	5 mL

1. Drain beets, reserving liquid. In a blender, combine beets, apple juice, lemon juice, pear, apple and savory. Blend on low for 30 seconds. Gradually increase speed to high and blend for 30 seconds or until smooth. Check for consistency. If too thick, add some of the reserved beet liquid. With motor running, slowly add liquid through opening in lid until desired consistency is achieved.

Carrot-Raisin Cooler

The raisins add extra
sweetness so this drink
becomes more than a
vegetable smoothie.

¼ cup	orange juice	50 mL
½ cup	chopped cooked carrots	125 mL
½ cup	natural yogurt	125 mL
¼ cup	raisins	50 mL
¼ tsp	ground nutmeg	1 mL
6	ice cubes	6

1. In a blender, combine orange juice, carrots, yogurt, raisins, nutmeg and ice. Blend on low for 30 seconds. Gradually increase speed to high and blend for 30 seconds or until smooth.

Tomato Juice Cocktail

The natural tomato
taste of this drink is
surprisingly milder than
commercial tomato
cocktails.

¼ cup	tomato juice	50 mL
1	can (14 oz/398 mL) diced beets with liquid	1
1	small zucchini, peeled and roughly chopped	1
2 tbsp	freshly squeezed lemon juice	25 mL
1 tbsp	chopped fresh basil	15 mL
½	clove garlic	½
⅛ tsp	ground cumin	0.5 mL
⅛ tsp	ground cayenne pepper	0.5 mL
⅛ tsp	salt, or to taste	0.5 mL
	Ice, optional	

1. In a blender, combine tomato juice, beets with liquid, zucchini, lemon juice, basil, garlic, cumin, cayenne and salt. Blend on low for 30 seconds. Gradually increase speed to high and blend for 30 seconds or until smooth. Taste and add more salt and lemon juice, if required. Serve chilled or over ice, if desired.

Desserts

Gingered Summer Fruit

Vegan Friendly

Make this easy compote when fresh fruit is plentiful and serve with frozen yogurt or toss with cooked rice for a healthy rice pudding.

Tip

• Use fresh nectarines, peaches, plums, cherries, gooseberries, elderberries, blackberries, currants or black currants.

I lb	fruit, peeled and pitted (see Tips, left)	500 g
¼ cup	brown rice syrup	50 mL
2 tsp	minced fresh gingerroot	10 mL
2 tbsp	freshly squeezed lemon juice	25 mL
I tbsp	agar flakes	15 mL

1. Cut larger fruit into quarters and smaller fruit into halves. In a nonreactive saucepan, combine fruit, syrup and ginger. Cover and cook over medium heat for 5 minutes or until juices release and fruit is slightly tender.

2. Stir in lemon juice and agar. Cook, stirring constantly, for 2 minutes. Serve warm or chilled (the mixture will thicken when cooled).

Fresh Berry Mousse

Vegan Friendly

Make this wonderful light dessert when berries are in season.

Tip

• Any fresh berries, such as strawberries, blueberries, raspberries, blackberries, black currants, elderberries, gooseberries, and cherries, work well in this dessert.

2 cups	rice or soy milk	500 mL
2 tbsp	agar flakes	25 mL
2 tbsp	chopped fresh sweet cicely	25 mL
2 cups	berries, trimmed (see Tip, left)	500 mL
I tbsp	brown rice syrup	15 mL
4	strawberries, optional	4

1. In a saucepan, bring milk to a gentle simmer over medium heat. Stir in agar and sweet cicely. Reduce heat and simmer slowly, stirring occasionally, for 5 minutes. Let cool to room temperature.

2. In a blender, combine berries, syrup and milk mixture. Process for 40 seconds or until blended and smooth. Pour into a serving bowl or individual dishes. Cover tightly and chill for 2 hours or until set. Slice strawberries and arrange on top for garnish, if desired. Serve chilled.

Variation

• Fresh basil lends a note of nutmeg. Use it in place of the sweet cicely, which is sweet and anise-flavored.

Crustless Plum Pie

In summer, use fresh fruit, such as plums, peaches and nectarines, along with berries, such as blueberries, strawberries or even cherries. This pie is dense and filling, so cut small pieces and serve ungarnished or with a dollop of light natural yogurt.

Tip

- No need to blanch and peel the stoned fruit because after baking, the skins slip off easily.

- *Preheat oven to 375°F (190°C)*
- *10-inch (25 cm) pie plate*

| 10 | fresh ripe plums (see Tip, left) | 10 |

Almond Pie Filling

1 cup	finely ground almonds	250 mL
1 cup	long shredded coconut	250 mL
¼ cup	liquid honey	50 mL
1 tbsp	grated lemon zest	15 mL
⅛ tsp	almond extract	0.5 mL
2	large eggs, beaten	2
1 cup	natural yogurt, drained, optional	250 mL

1. Cut plums in half, twist, remove and discard stone. Set aside.

2. Almond Pie Filling: In a bowl, combine almonds, coconut, honey, lemon zest and almond extract, and stir well. Stir in eggs, mix well and transfer to pie plate. Press nut mixture lightly to compact into a base.

3. Arrange plum halves, skin side up, in a decorative fashion on the top of the base. Bake in preheated oven for 20 minutes, until base is bubbly and lightly golden.

4. Let cool on a rack. Using a paring knife, gently peel the skin away from the fruit and discard. Serve while still warm or let cool to room temperature. Garnish with yogurt, if desired.

Variation

- The almonds may be doubled in order to omit the coconut.

The filling makes a light fresh springtime dessert or topping for breakfast grains. Make double or triple the filling, omit the Yogurt Cheese and freeze for later.

Strawberry-Rhubarb Crêpes

Strawberry-Rhubarb Filling

1 cup	chopped fresh or frozen rhubarb	250 mL
¼ cup	freshly squeezed orange juice	50 mL
2 tbsp	brown rice syrup	25 mL
1 cup	fresh or frozen strawberries	250 mL
⅔ cup	Yogurt Cheese (see recipe, page 145)	150 mL
8	crêpes (see recipe, page 156)	8

1. Strawberry-Rhubarb Filling: In a saucepan, combine rhubarb and orange juice. Bring to a boil over high heat. Cover, reduce heat and simmer for 7 to 10 minutes or until rhubarb is soft. Remove from heat and stir in syrup. Transfer to a bowl. Let cool and chill slightly.

2. Add strawberries and Yogurt Cheese. Cover tightly and refrigerate until ready to use. (Can be made up to 1 day in advance.) Bring to room temperature before using.

3. Spread 4 tbsp (60 mL) of the filling over the center of a crêpe, fold in half and half again to form a triangle. Repeat with remaining crêpes and filling. Serve at room temperature or warmed in the oven.

Variation

• Use 1 cup (250 mL) chopped bananas in place of the rhubarb.

Poached Pears with Apricot-Ginger Sauce

With the bounty of fall fruit, this is a wonderful way to use other fall fruit, such as apples and plums, in place of the pears.

Tip

- Use cooking apples, such as Cox's Orange Pippin, Jonathan, Gravenstein or Baldwin, and check for doneness after 6 minutes. Plums may take slightly less time to cook, so check after 5 minutes.

1 ½ cups	apple juice	375 mL
½ cup	white wine	125 mL
½	vanilla bean	½
1	piece (3 inch/7.5 cm) licorice root, optional	1
1	sprig fresh tarragon or basil leaf	1
4	pears, halved	4
⅓ cup	finely chopped dried apricots	75 mL
1 tbsp	finely chopped candied ginger	15 mL
1 cup	Sweet Almond Spread (see recipe, page 152) or Yogurt Cheese (see recipe, page 145), optional	250 mL

1. In a large deep skillet, combine apple juice, wine, vanilla, licorice, if using, and tarragon. Bring to a gentle boil over medium-high heat. Add pear halves, cut side down. Cover, reduce heat and gently simmer for 7 minutes or until pears are tender-crisp.

2. Remove pear halves from poaching liquid and set aside. Remove and discard vanilla, licorice, if using, and tarragon from poaching liquid. Add apricots and ginger and bring to a boil over high heat. Reduce heat and simmer, stirring occasionally, for 15 to 20 minutes or until liquid is reduced and syrupy.

3. Meanwhile, remove and discard core from pear halves. Arrange pears on individual plates. Spoon apricot sauce over top. Garnish with Fruit Almond Spread, if using. Serve immediately.

Peach Melba

Easy and spectacular in the fall when peaches are abundant, this recipe can be made with well drained, fancy grade canned peach halves in other seasons.

- *Preheat broiler, adjust oven rack to highest level*
- *Baking sheet, lightly oiled*

3	fresh ripe peaches, skinned, halved and stoned	3
3 tbsp	freshly squeezed lemon juice, divided	45 mL
12	coconut macaroon cookies	12
1 tbsp	butter	15 mL
1 tsp	chopped fresh sweet marjoram	5 mL
2/3 cup	raspberry or strawberry jam	150 mL
3 or 6	sprigs fresh sweet marjoram, optional	3 or 6

1. On prepared baking sheet, arrange peach halves, cut side up. Brush each with about 1 tsp (5 mL) of the lemon juice. Set aside.

2. In a food processor, combine cookies, butter and chopped marjoram. Pulse for about 30 seconds or until chopped and combined. Spoon equally into peach halves. Bake on top rack under preheated broiler for 2 to 4 minutes or until lightly browned. Let cool slightly.

3. Meanwhile, in a small saucepan, gently heat jam over medium heat until it becomes liquid. Spoon 2 tbsp (25 mL) of the jam into center of a dessert plate. Using tongs or lifter, lift 1 or 2 peach halves into center of jam on plates. Garnish with a sprig of marjoram, if using. Repeat with remaining jam, peaches and sprigs, if using. Serve immediately.

Variation

- Use 6 fresh pineapple wedges in place of the peach halves.

Fresh, frozen or even dried cranberries may be used in this autumn dish.

Tips

- If using dried cranberries, reduce the amount to ⅔ cup (150 mL).

- One 12-oz (340 g) bag of fresh whole cranberries yields 3 cups (750 mL). The remaining 2 cups (500 mL) cranberries may be sealed in a freezer bag and frozen for up to 4 months.

- Store compote, tightly covered, in the refrigerator for up to 5 days.

Apple-Cranberry Compote

1 cup	cranberries (see Tips, left)	250 mL
2	apples, peeled and sliced	2
¼ cup	dried cherries or chopped dried apricots	50 mL
¼ cup	apple juice or white wine	50 mL
2 tbsp	butter	25 mL
¼ cup	organic cane sugar	50 mL
1 tbsp	chopped fresh lemon balm or sweet cicely	15 mL

1. In a saucepan, combine cranberries, apples, cherries and apple juice. Bring to a boil over medium-high heat. Reduce heat and simmer for 7 minutes or until fruit is soft.

2. Add butter, sugar and lemon balm and simmer for 2 minutes.

Variations

- Use black currants, elderberries, gooseberries or chopped rhubarb in place of the cranberries.

- Use 1½ cups (375 mL) chopped fresh pineapple instead of the apples.

Serving Suggestions
- Use this as a dessert with whole grains or frozen yogurt, or as a condiment.

Fall Fruit en Papillotte

This simple dish makes a dramatic presentation for guests. The fruit is served in the parchment pockets so that diners open the parchment at the table. Pockets may be prepared up to 4 hours ahead of time and baked just before serving.

Vegan Version

- Omit the butter. Use 4 tsp (20 mL) of Sweet Almond Spread (see recipe, page 152) in its place. Top fruit with 1 tsp (5 mL) Sweet Almond Spread in Step 2.

- *Preheat oven to 350°F (180°C)*
- *4 sheets parchment paper, 18-by 12-inches (40 by 30 cm)*
- *Baking sheet*

1/4 cup	raisins	50 mL
1/4 cup	chopped pecans	50 mL
1/4 cup	chopped candied ginger	50 mL
4	pieces (each 1 inch/2.5 cm) cinnamon	4
4	pieces (each 1 inch/2.5 cm) licorice root, optional	4
4	pieces (each 1 inch/2.5 cm) vanilla bean	4
4	whole cloves	4
4	dried or fresh apricots, halved	4
1	pear, cut into eighths	1
1	apple, cut into eighths	1
1	peach, quartered	1
1	plum, quartered	1
1/2 cup	apple cider or apple juice	125 mL
1 tsp	butter	5 mL

1. Fold a sheet of parchment paper in half. Cut out the shape of one-half of a heart, with center fold as the center of the heart. When you open up the parchment paper, you'll have a heart-shaped piece. Repeat with remaining 3 sheets.

2. On one side of the fold line of one piece of parchment, spoon 1 tbsp (15 mL) each raisins, pecans and ginger. Add 1 piece each cinnamon, licorice, if using, vanilla bean and 1 clove. Add 2 each apricot halves, pear and apple slices. Add 1 each peach and plum quarter. Sprinkle 2 tbsp (25 mL) cider and top with 1/4 tsp (1 mL) butter.

3. Fold the other half of the parchment heart along the fold line, over fruit. Beginning at the top of the heart, roll and fold the 2 cut ends together. Work towards the bottom until the entire cut edge is sealed. Fruit is now enclosed in one half heart-shaped pocket. Repeat with remaining 3 hearts.

4. Transfer pockets to baking sheet. Bake in preheated oven for 30 to 40 minutes or until apples and pears are tender. Slide each package onto individual dessert plates. Cut an "X" on top of each package with a sharp knife. Pull back the tips of the 4 corners of the "X" to make a small opening in the parchment. Serve immediately.

Not too sweet, this dish is very good for brunch or breakfast. The Almond Pie Crust is a healthier alternative to traditional pastry.

Tip

- Make the crust and line the pan up to 2 days in advance. Cover tightly and store in the refrigerator until ready to fill and bake.

Apple and Cheddar Cheese Flan

- *Preheat oven to 400°F (200°C)*
- *9-inch (23 cm) flan or pie pan*

Almond Pie Crust

½ cup	whole almonds (unblanched)	125 mL
20	arrowroot or vanilla cookies	20
⅓ cup	butter	75 mL
2 tbsp	organic cane sugar	25 mL

Filling

6	apples, divided	6
1 cup	sour cream	250 mL
¼ cup	creamed cottage cheese	50 mL
1	large egg, beaten	1
2 cups	finely shredded Cheddar cheese	500 mL
½ cup	organic cane sugar	125 mL
1 tbsp	chopped fresh sweet cicely or mint	15 mL

1. **Almond Pie Crust:** In a food processor or blender, combine almonds and cookies. Process for 20 seconds or until medium-fine.

2. In a saucepan, melt butter over medium heat. Remove from heat, stir in almond mixture and sugar. Press crumb crust into pan. Chill until ready to fill.

3. **Filling:** Peel, core and slice 5 of the apples. In a large bowl, mix sour cream and cottage cheese together. Beat in egg. Add sliced apples, Cheddar cheese, sugar and sweet cicely and stir well.

4. Spoon cheese mixture over Almond Pie Crust, spreading to level the top. Core and thinly slice remaining apple, leaving the peel on. Arrange over top of filling. Bake in preheated oven for 1 hour or until crust is lightly brown and apples are tender. Let stand for 10 minutes before serving.

Variation

- For a savory twist, add 1 tbsp (15 mL) finely chopped onion in Step 2.

This bread pudding is perfect for brunch, a family meal dessert, and when served with fresh fruit or a fruit sauce, a warm finish to a casual dinner with company.

Tip

- Fresh peaches, apricots, mangoes, nectarines, papaya or strawberries, raspberries and cherries are exceptional in this dessert, however, drained sliced peaches and canned cherries will also work.

Serving Suggestions

- This dish is delicious on its own, but may be enlivened by serving with a sauce. Use 2 cups (500 mL) of any one of the following:

- Blueberry Sauce (page 317), Apple-Cranberry Compote (page 351), Rosemary Custard (page 361), Raspberry Coulis (page 357), Peach-Rose Sauce (page 318) or Green Tea Sauce (page 318).

Fruited Bread Pudding

- *10-cup (2.5 L) baking dish*

1 ½ cups	rice or soy milk	375 mL
½ cup	buttermilk	125 mL
6 tbsp	butter, divided	90 mL
3	large eggs	3
2 tbsp	chopped fresh lemon balm or 1 tbsp (15 mL) lemon zest	25 mL
¼ cup	orange or apple juice	50 mL
⅓ cup	organic cane sugar	75 mL
1 ⅔ cups	coarsely chopped fresh fruit (see Tip, left)	400 mL
12 to 14	slices 3-day-old bread, cut into 1-inch (2.5 cm) cubes (about 6 cups/1.5 L)	12 to 14
2 cups	sauce (see Serving Suggestions, left), optional	500 mL

1. In a saucepan, combine milk, buttermilk and 5 tbsp (75 mL) of the butter. Bring to just under a boil over medium heat, just until bubbles appear around the edge of the pan. Let cool.

2. Meanwhile, in a blender, combine eggs and lemon balm. Process for 10 seconds or until well blended. Add orange juice and sugar and process for 10 seconds. Stir into milk.

3. Grease baking dish with 1 tbsp (15 mL) of butter. Add fruit and bread cubes and toss. Pour milk mixture over top and mix thoroughly. Let pudding sit for a minimum of 30 minutes or covered, overnight in the refrigerator. Bread will absorb most of the liquid.

4. One hour before serving time, preheat oven to 350°F (180°C), bring pudding to room temperature and bring a kettle of water to a boil. Place the pudding dish in a large baking pan. Pour boiling water into the pan about halfway up sides of pudding dish. Bake, uncovered, until set. Serve with sauce, if desired.

A very comforting winter dessert that is easy to prepare. The custard is moist and floats on the top.

Tips

- If a large steamer is not available, preheat oven to 350°F (180°C). Spoon fruit into a lightly oiled 8-cup (2 L) mold or casserole dish. Pour custard over top. Cover tightly with foil. Set mold inside a deep baking pan. Pour boiling water into pan until it reaches halfway up the sides of the mold. Steam in preheated oven for 40 to 50 minutes or until custard has set.

- Remove and let stand for 10 minutes. Spoon onto dessert plates and serve immediately.

Brandied Fruit Custard

- *Four 1 cup (250 mL) ramekins, lightly oiled*
- *Large steamer*

Fruit

¾ cup	chopped peaches, plums or nectarines	175 mL
¼ cup	chopped dried apricots	50 mL
2 tbsp	chopped dates or figs	25 mL
½ tsp	ground allspice	2 mL
¼ tsp	ground nutmeg	1 mL
1 tbsp	melted butter	15 mL
2 tbsp	brandy	25 mL

Custard

1 cup	milk	250 mL
2	large eggs	2
½ tsp	vanilla	2 mL
3 tbsp	organic cane sugar	45 mL
2 tbsp	all-purpose flour	25 mL
Pinch	salt	Pinch

1. **Fruit:** In a bowl, combine peaches with apricots, dates, allspice, nutmeg, butter and brandy. Cover and marinate for 1 hour or overnight in the refrigerator. Return to room temperature before baking.

2. Spoon fruit and juices evenly into bottom of ramekins.

3. **Custard:** In a bowl, whisk milk and eggs together. Whisk in vanilla and sugar and beat until blended. Sprinkle flour and salt over and whisk until blended. Pour equally over fruit in ramekins. Cover tightly with foil.

4. Arrange ramekins in steamer on rack above boiling water. Cover steamer with lid and keep water simmering for 20 minutes or until pudding has set. Remove from heat and let stand, covered, in steamer until ready to serve, for up to 1 hour.

5. To serve, run a knife around edge to loosen and tip ramekin upside down over dessert plate. Custard will fall onto plate with fruit on top. Serve immediately.

Variation

- Replace peaches with drained, frozen berries or canned fruit.

Mixing brown rice with wild rice produces a pleasant, nutty-tasting pudding.

Lemon Cloud Rice Pudding

• *8-cup (2 L) baking dish or casserole, lightly oiled*

1 cup	mixed brown and wild rice	250 mL
1 tbsp	butter	15 mL
1 ½ cups	milk	375 mL
½ cup	organic cane sugar, divided	125 mL
½ tsp	salt	2 mL
3	large eggs, separated	3
2 tsp	finely grated lemon zest	10 mL
	Juice of 1 lemon	

1. In a saucepan, combine 2 cups (500 mL) water with rice and butter. Stir and bring to a boil over high heat. Stir again, cover, reduce heat and simmer for 30 to 40 minutes. Do not lift the lid while rice is cooking. Remove from heat, fluff with a fork and set aside.

2. Meanwhile, preheat oven to 350°F (180°C).

3. In another saucepan, heat milk over medium heat just until bubbles form around the edges of the pan. Watch carefully and do not let the milk boil. Remove from heat. Stir in 2 tbsp (25 mL) of the sugar and salt.

4. In a small bowl, whisk egg yolks. Whisk in about 2 tbsp (25 mL) of the hot milk mixture into the yolks. Keep whisking in about half of the hot milk, in small amounts, until the yolks are warmed through. Scrape yolks into remaining hot milk and stir well. Whisk in lemon zest and juice. Transfer to prepared dish.

5. In a large bowl, using an electric mixer, beat egg whites until frothy. Sprinkle 1 tbsp (15 mL) of sugar over top and beat. Keep beating whites, gradually adding all of the remaining sugar, until whites are stiff and glossy.

6. Stir rice into milk mixture in the dish. Fold in egg whites. Bake in preheated oven for 40 minutes. Serve warm or at room temperature.

Raspberry Coulis

1 cup	fresh or frozen raspberries	250 mL
2 tbsp	brown rice syrup or liquid honey	25 mL
1 tsp	finely chopped fresh lemon balm or grated lemon zest	5 mL

Fresh tasting, this thin sauce really punches up the eye-appeal of dessert dishes.

Tips

• If using fresh raspberries, you may need to add 1 to 2 tbsp (15 to 25 mL) water or fruit juice in order to purée to a smooth texture.

• Store coulis, tightly covered, in the refrigerator for up to 2 days.

1. Thaw frozen raspberries, if using. In a blender or food processor, process raspberries with juice, syrup and lemon balm until puréed. Press through a sieve to remove seeds.

Variation

• Substitute blackberries or blueberries for the raspberries.

Chocolate Pudding

Vegan Friendly

¼ cup	arrowroot	50 mL
⅓ cup	organic cane sugar, divided	75 mL
4 cups	soy or rice milk, divided	1 L
¼ cup	unsweetened cocoa powder	50 mL
2 oz	bittersweet chocolate, chopped	60 g
¼ tsp	ground nutmeg	1 mL
1 tsp	vanilla	5 mL

This vegan recipe for classic chocolate pudding relies on the arrowroot (not on the proteins in eggs or cow's milk) to thicken it.

1. In a small bowl, combine arrowroot and 2 tbsp (25 mL) of the sugar. Whisk in ½ cup (125 mL) of the milk and stir until dissolved. Set aside.

2. In a large saucepan, combine remaining ¼ cup (50 mL) of sugar and cocoa powder. Slowly whisk in the remaining 3½ cups (825 mL) of milk, stirring until there are no lumps. Bring to just under a boil over medium heat. Stir in chocolate and simmer, stirring, until chocolate is melted.

3. Reduce heat and add arrowroot mixture, a small amount at a time, stirring until all is combined. Cook, stirring, for about 7 minutes or until the pudding thickens. Remove from heat and stir in nutmeg and vanilla. Pour into dessert bowls, cover and refrigerate until cold, for up to 1 day.

Christmas Pudding

Lighter and with less fat than traditional suet Christmas puddings, this version should be made a week in advance in order to allow the full flavors to develop.

- *8-cup (2 L) pudding mold, lightly oiled*
- *Round of waxed paper, cut to fit the diameter of mold top, lightly oiled*

1½ cups	whole wheat flour	375 mL
1 cup	dry whole wheat bread crumbs	250 mL
1½ tsp	ground cinnamon	7 mL
½ tsp	ground ginger	2 mL
¼ tsp	ground allspice	1 mL
¼ tsp	ground nutmeg	1 mL
⅛ tsp	ground cloves	0.5 mL
¼ tsp	salt	1 mL
1 cup	chopped dates	250 mL
½ cup	chopped raisins	125 mL
½ cup	chopped dried apricots or figs	125 mL
¼ cup	diced mixed peel	50 mL
2	large eggs	2
¼ cup	natural cane sugar	50 mL
¼ cup	organic canola oil	50 mL
⅓ cup	blackstrap molasses	75 mL
1 cup	cooked pumpkin purée	250 mL
	Boiling water	
3 tbsp	brandy or sherry	45 mL

1. In a large mixing bowl, combine flour, bread crumbs, cinnamon, ginger, allspice, nutmeg, cloves and salt. Add dates, raisins, apricots and peel. Stir to mix well.

2. In a bowl, beat eggs. Beat in sugar, oil, molasses and pumpkin, beating after each addition. Stir pumpkin mixture into flour mixture and mix well.

3. Spoon into prepared mold. Smooth the top and cover with waxed paper round, oiled side down. Arrange a sheet of foil tightly over top and secure with string. Place pudding in a large saucepan. Pour boiling water into pan until it reaches halfway up the sides of the mold. Cover pan and bring water back to a boil over high heat. Reduce heat and simmer for 2 hours. Add more boiling water as it evaporates during cooking.

4. Remove mold from water and let cool on a wire rack. Remove and discard foil. Carefully peel back the paper round and drizzle brandy over top of pudding.

Replace round and cover tightly with plastic wrap and store in refrigerator until about 2 hours before serving or for up to 3 weeks.

5. To reheat: Bring pudding to room temperature. Replace plastic wrap with foil and secure tightly with string. Heat for 20 minutes in a boiling water bath as explained in Step 3. Serve pudding hot with a sauce (see Serving Suggestions, below), if desired.

> **Serving Suggestions**
> • Serve pudding with any of the following: Rosemary Custard (page 361), Peach-Rose Sauce (page 318), Apple-Cranberry Compote (page 351) or Sweet Almond Spread (page 152).

Lemon Custard

The light lemon flavor in this custard lends itself to most fresh fruit. Use it as a sauce for cake and fresh fruit or sweetened grain dishes. Use slightly more or less sugar as your own taste dictates.

½ cup	organic cane sugar, or to taste	125 mL
1 tbsp	grated lemon zest	15 mL
4	large eggs, at room temperature	4
2½ cups	lower-fat milk	625 mL
½ tsp	vanilla	2 mL

1. In a blender or food processor, combine sugar and zest. Process for 10 seconds to blend. With motor running, add eggs, one at a time, through opening in lid and process for 10 seconds after addition of last egg. Transfer to a small bowl. Cover and set aside.

2. In a saucepan over medium heat, gently heat milk until tiny bubbles form around the edges of the pan. Watch carefully and do not let milk boil. Remove from heat. Stir, one spoonful at a time, into reserved egg mixture to gently heat the eggs. When egg mixture is warmed, pour into remaining scalded milk in the pan.

3. Reduce heat to medium-low and return saucepan to heat. Cook, stirring constantly, for 10 to 15 minutes or until mixture has thickened and coats the back of a metal spoon. Do not let custard boil or it will curdle. Have a large bowl of cold water handy.

4. Immediately remove pan from the heat and plunge into bowl of cold water. Add vanilla and stir often, until custard is cool. Pour into dessert bowls and serve immediately or cover tightly and refrigerate until chilled.

This is not a difficult recipe, much easier in fact than if a regular pie crust were used.

Vegan Version
- Use 2 tbsp (25 mL) olive oil in place of the butter in the Ginger Crust.

Sweet Potato Pie with Ginger Crust

- *9-inch (23 cm) pie plate*

Ginger Crust

3 tbsp	brown rice syrup or honey	45 mL
2 tbsp	tahini paste	25 mL
3 tbsp	butter	45 mL
1½ cups	fine gingersnap cookie crumbs	375 mL

Sweet Potato Pie Filling

3 tbsp	kuzu or agar	45 mL
2 tbsp	finely grated orange zest	25 mL
	Juice of 1 orange	
3	medium sweet potatoes, quartered	3
1 tsp	vanilla	5 mL
½ tsp	ground cinnamon	2 mL
¼ tsp	ground ginger	1 mL
¼ tsp	salt	1 mL
⅛ tsp	ground nutmeg	0.5 mL
½ cup	pure maple syrup or brown rice syrup	125 mL

Pecan Topping

3 tbsp	pure maple syrup	45 mL
2 tbsp	freshly squeezed lemon juice	25 mL
1 tbsp	butter	15 mL
1½ cups	coarsely chopped pecans	375 mL

1. **Ginger Crust:** In a saucepan, heat syrup over medium heat until gently simmering. Remove from heat and stir in tahini and butter. Whisk until combined. Stir in cookie crumbs.

2. Turn out into pie plate and press over bottom and up the sides. Seal in a plastic bag and freeze for 30 minutes or refrigerate for a minimum of 1 hour or for up to 2 days.

3. **Sweet Potato Pie Filling:** In a small bowl, combine kuzu with orange juice. Cover and set aside.

4. In a large saucepan, cover sweet potatoes with water. Cover and bring to a boil over high heat. Reduce heat and simmer for 15 minutes or until soft. Drain and rinse under cold water. When cool, slip skins off and cut quarters in half.

5. Meanwhile, preheat oven to 350°F (180°C).

6. In a food processor, combine sweet potatoes, orange zest, vanilla, cinnamon, ginger, salt and nutmeg. Pulse until mixed. With motor running, add syrup and reserved orange juice mixture through opening in the lid. Process until well mixed. Scrape filling into crust and smooth top with a spatula.

7. Pecan Topping: In a small saucepan, combine syrup, lemon juice and butter. Bring to a boil over medium heat. Reduce heat and simmer until slightly thickened. Stir in pecans, toss to coat. Distribute topping evenly over filling. Bake in preheated oven for about 40 minutes or until hot in the center. Let cool and chill pie for at least 1 hour or for up to 1 day before slicing.

Variation
• Use vanilla wafer crumbs and 1 tsp (5 mL) ground ginger in place of the gingersnap crumbs.

Rosemary Custard

Serves 4

Vegan Friendly

Infusing the soy milk as it heats imparts not only the flavor of the herbs but their medicinal benefits as well.

Tip
• Store custard, tightly covered, in the refrigerator for 1 to 2 days.

½ cup	soy or rice milk	125 mL
1	vanilla bean, split	1
1	piece (2 inches/5 cm) licorice root or cinnamon stick	1
1	sprig rosemary	1
12 oz	firm silken-style tofu	375 g

1. In a small saucepan, combine milk, vanilla, licorice and rosemary. Cover and bring to a light simmer over medium-low heat. Remove from heat and let cool with lid on. Strain and discard vanilla, licorice and rosemary.

2. In a blender or food processor, process tofu for 30 seconds or until smooth. With motor running, add infused milk through opening in the lid. Custard should be blended and smooth.

Serving Suggestions
• Spoon over poached pears, peaches, cherries or baked apples. Pass as a sauce for gingerbread or breakfast grain dishes.

Cheese Tart with Blueberry Sauce

This is a whole food version of the favorite cream cheesecake. It is not sweet and would be exceptional with a fruit sauce such as Raspberry Coulis or Blueberry Sauce (see recipes, pages 357 and 317).

Tips

• If using store-bought granola, you may need to increase butter to 2 tbsp (25 mL) to make mixture moist enough to press together.

• *8-inch (20 cm) flan pan or springform pan, lightly oiled*

Granola Crust

I cup	Whole-Grain Granola (see recipe, page 160) or store-bought (see Tip, left)	250 mL
¼ cup	rolled oats	50 mL
I tbsp	liquid honey	15 mL
⅓ cup	unbleached all-purpose flour	75 mL
I tbsp	butter, melted	15 mL

Cheese Tart Filling

10 oz	ricotta cheese	300 g
2 tbsp	brown rice syrup or liquid honey	25 mL
I tsp	grated lemon zest	5 mL
½ tsp	vanilla	2 mL
⅓ cup	lower-fat natural yogurt, drained	75 mL
I	large egg, beaten	I
¼ cup	chopped dried apricots	50 mL
3	fresh apricots, optional	3
	Blueberry Sauce (see recipe, page 317)	

1. Granola Crust: In a food processor, combine Whole-Grain Granola and rolled oats. Process until the mixture resembles fine meal. Add honey and pulse until blended. Sprinkle flour over top and replace lid. With motor running, add butter through the feed tube and process until blended. Press into bottom and about 1-inch (2.5 cm) up sides of flan pan. Chill in the freezer for 30 minutes or in the refrigerator for at least 1 hour or up to 2 days before baking.

2. Preheat oven to 350°F (180°C).

3. Cheese Tart Filling: In a food processor or blender, combine cheese, syrup, lemon zest and vanilla. Process for 30 seconds or until blended. Transfer to a bowl. Stir in yogurt, egg and dried apricots, stirring well after each addition. You may chill until ready to fill and bake the tart, or for as long as overnight, but bring both the crust and the filling to room temperature before baking (or cooking longer). Spread evenly over chilled Granola Crust.

4. Bake in preheated oven for 25 to 30 minutes or until edges are puffed and center is almost set. Let cool and chill for several hours before serving. Slice fresh apricots, if using. Cut tart into slices and garnish with fresh apricot slices and Blueberry Sauce.

Serves 8 to 12

Children love the bright red spots in this bread and it is one snack that can be eaten without the guilt because it is relatively low in fat and high in the vitamins children need for healthy growth.

Vegetable Jewel Gingerbread

- *9-inch (2.5 L) square baking pan, lightly oiled*

1 ½ cups	whole wheat flour	375 mL
½ cup	teff	125 mL
1 tbsp	baking powder	15 mL
1 tbsp	ground cinnamon	15 mL
½ tsp	salt	2 mL
¼ tsp	each ground nutmeg, allspice and cloves	1 mL
½ cup	butter, at room temperature	125 mL
½ cup	organic cane sugar	125 mL
2	eggs	2
⅓ cup	blackstrap molasses	75 mL
½ cup	natural yogurt	125 mL
1 tsp	vanilla	5 mL
⅔ cup	grated carrot	150 mL
⅔ cup	grated parsnip	150 mL
1 cup	grated beets	250 mL
1	slice candied ginger, finely chopped	1
2 cups	Hot Spiced Applesauce (see recipe, page 317), optional	500 mL

1. In a bowl, whisk together whole wheat flour, teff, baking powder, cinnamon, salt, nutmeg, allspice and cloves.

2. In a large bowl, using a wooden spoon or electric mixer, cream butter. Beat in sugar until light and fluffy. Beat in eggs, one at a time. Beat in molasses, yogurt and vanilla. Beat flour mixture into batter, about 1 cup (250 mL) at a time, beating after each addition. Stir in carrot, parsnip, beets and ginger. Batter will be thick.

3. Scrape batter into prepared pan. Bake in preheated oven for 50 to 60 minutes or until cake springs back when gently pressed in the center. Serve with Hot Spiced Applesauce, if desired.

Date and Nut Bars

The sweetness of the dates allows for very little extra sugar in this healthy bar recipe.

Tip

• Store bars in an airtight container at room temperature for up to 3 days.

• *Preheat oven to 350°F (180°C)*
• *9-inch (2.5 L) square baking pan, lightly oiled*

2 cups	chopped dried dates	500 mL
½ cup	apple juice	125 mL
¾ cup	whole wheat flour	175 mL
¼ cup	buckwheat flour	50 mL
1 cup	Whole-Grain Granola (see recipe, page 160) or rolled oats	250 mL
2 tbsp	unsweetened cocoa powder	25 mL
½ tsp	salt	2 mL
¼ cup	chopped pecans or Brazil nuts	50 mL
6 tbsp	butter, at room temperature	90 mL
1 tbsp	organic cane sugar	15 mL
¼ cup	confectioner's (icing) sugar, optional	50 mL

1. In a saucepan, combine dates and apple juice. Bring to a boil over high heat. Cover, reduce heat and simmer for 5 minutes or until dates are soft. Let cool slightly.

2. In a bowl, whisk together whole wheat flour, buckwheat flour, granola, cocoa and salt. Stir in pecans.

3. Using a wooden spoon, beat butter and sugar into dates. Scrape the date mixture into the flour mixture and beat well.

4. Press into prepared pan. Bake in preheated oven for 20 minutes for a moist chewy bar. Bake longer (about 25 minutes) for a drier, cake-like bar. Let cool completely in pan on a rack. Cut into squares. Sift confectioner's sugar, if using, over squares.

Variation

• Use 1 cup (250 mL) chopped dates and 1 cup (250 mL) chopped figs instead of dates only.

Apricot-Apple Bars

Great to have on hand
for snacks and those
days when there is no
time for breakfast.

Tip

- Store bars in an
  airtight container at
  room temperature for
  up to 3 days.

- *Preheat oven to 350°F (180°C)*
- *9-inch (2.5 L) square baking pan, lightly oiled*

¼ cup	liquid honey	50 mL
⅓ cup	butter	75 mL
1 tsp	grated orange zest	5 mL
2 tbsp	freshly squeezed orange juice	25 mL
1 cup	whole wheat flour	250 mL
½ cup	teff or buckwheat flour	125 mL
1 cup	Whole-Grain Granola (see recipe, page 160) or rolled oats	250 mL
1	apple, peeled and grated	1
½ cup	chopped dried apricots	125 mL
½ cup	slivered almonds	125 mL
¼ cup	sesame seeds	50 mL

1. In a small saucepan, combine honey, butter, orange zest and
   orange juice. Heat over medium-low heat until butter
   is melted. Remove from heat and set aside.

2. In a large bowl, whisk together whole wheat flour, teff and
   granola. Stir in apple, apricots, almonds and sesame seeds.
   Pour honey mixture into dry ingredients and stir until well
   blended.

3. Scrape into prepared pan. Bake in preheated oven for
   35 minutes or until golden brown. Let cool completely
   in pan on a rack. Cut into squares.

Fudge Bars

With relatively little fat in them, these are the best lower-fat bars. The crunch in the teff keeps people wondering about the ingredients.

Tip

• Store bars in an airtight container at room temperature for up to 3 days.

• *Preheat oven to 350°F (180°C)*
• *8-inch (20 cm) square baking pan, lightly oiled*

¼ cup	all-purpose flour	50 mL
3 tbsp	teff	45 mL
2 tbsp	buckwheat flour	25 mL
⅓ cup	unsweetened cocoa powder	75 mL
¼ tsp	salt	1 mL
¼ tsp	ground cinnamon	1 mL
⅛ tsp	baking soda	0.5 mL
½ cup	lower-fat natural yogurt	125 mL
3 tbsp	organic canola oil	45 mL
3 tbsp	organic cane sugar	45 mL
1 tbsp	brown rice syrup	15 mL
1 tsp	vanilla	5 mL
2 oz	semisweet or bittersweet chocolate, melted	60 g
2	egg whites, at room temperature	2

1. In a large bowl, whisk together all-purpose flour, teff, buckwheat flour, cocoa, salt, cinnamon and baking soda.

2. In another bowl, whisk together yogurt, oil, sugar, syrup, vanilla and chocolate until blended and smooth.

3. In another bowl, using an electric mixture, beat egg whites until soft peaks form.

4. Stir yogurt mixture into the dry ingredients. Stir until blended and smooth. Fold egg whites into the batter.

5. Pour into prepared pan. Bake in preheated oven for 25 minutes, until a tester inserted in the center has moist crumbs clinging to it, for a soft, fudge-like consistency. Bake longer (about 35 minutes) until a tester inserted in the center comes out clean, for a drier, cake-like bar. Let cool completely in pan on a rack. Cut into squares.

Glossary

Adaptogen: A substance that builds resistance to stress by balancing the functions of the glands and immune response, thus strengthening the immune system, nervous system and glandular system. Adaptogens promote overall vitality. *Examples: astragalus and ginseng.*

Alterative: A substance that gradually changes a condition by restoring health.

Analgesic: A substance that relieves pain by acting as a nervine, antiseptic or counterirritant. *Examples: German chamomile, meadowsweet and nutmeg.*

Anodyne: A substance that relieves pain. *Example: Clove.*

Anthocyanins: See Phenolic compounds, page 369.

Antibiotic: Meaning "against life," an antibiotic is a substance that kills infectious agents, including bacteria and fungi, without endangering health. *Examples: garlic, green tea, lavender, sage and thyme.*

Antihistamine: A substance that relieves the physical effects of histamines.

Anti-inflammatory: A substance that controls or reduces swelling, redness, pain and heat, which are normal bodily reactions to injury or infection. *Examples: German chamomile and St. John's wort.*

Antimicrobial: A substance that destroys or inhibits the growth of disease-causing bacteria or other microorganisms.

Antioxidant: A compound that protects cells by preventing polyunsaturated fatty acids (PUFAs) in cell membranes from oxidizing, or breaking down. Antioxidants do this by neutralizing free radicals (see Free radical, page 368). Vitamins C and E and beta-carotene are antioxidant nutrients, and foods high in them have antioxidant properties. *Examples: alfalfa, beet greens, dandelion leaf, garlic, parsley, thyme and watercress.*

Antipyretic: A substance that reduces fever. *Examples: German chamomile, sage and yarrow.*

Antiseptic: A substance used to prevent or reduce the growth of disease germs in order to prevent infection. *Examples: cabbage, calendula, clove, garlic, German chamomile, honey, nutmeg, onions, parsley, peppermint, rosemary, salt, thyme, turmeric and vinegar.*

Antispasmodic: A substance that relieves muscle spasms or cramps, including colic. *Examples: German chamomile, ginger, licorice and peppermint.*

Astringent: A drying and contracting substance that reduces secretions from the skin. *Examples: cinnamon, lemons, sage and thyme.*

Beta-carotene: The natural coloring agent (carotenoid) that gives fruits and vegetables (such as carrots) their deep orange color. It converts in the body to vitamin A. Eating foods high in beta-carotene helps prevent cancer, lowers the risk of heart disease, increases immunity, lowers the risk of cataracts and improves mental function. Beta-carotene is high in squash, carrots, yams, sweet potatoes, pumpkins and red peppers.

Betaine: A phytochemical that nourishes and strengthens the liver and gallbladder. It is found in high concentrations in beets.

Boron: A trace mineral that boosts the estrogen level in the blood, boron is also thought to help prevent calcium loss that leads to osteoporosis and to affect the brain's electrical activity. It is found in legumes, leafy greens and nuts.

Carbohydrates: An important group of plant foods that are composed of carbon, hydrogen and oxygen. A carbohydrate can be a single simple sugar or a combination of simple sugars. The chief sources of carbohydrates in a whole-food diet are grains, vegetables and fruits. Other sources include sugars, natural sweeteners and syrups.

Carcinogen: A cancer-causing substance.

Carminative: A substance that relaxes the stomach muscles and is taken to relieve gas and gripe. *Examples: clove, dill, fennel, garlic, ginger, parsley, peppermint, sage and thyme.*

Carotenoid: See Beta-carotene, above.

Cathartic: A substance that has a laxative effect. See also Purgative, page 370. *Examples: dandelion, licorice and parsley.*

Chlorophyll: Found only in plants, chlorophyll has a unique structure that allows it to enhance the body's ability to produce hemoglobin, which, in turn, enhances the delivery of oxygen to cells.

Cholagogue: Promotes the secretion of bile, assisting digestion and bowel elimination. *Examples: dandelion root, licorice and yellow dock.*

Choline: A phytochemical that researchers believe improves mental function, and is therefore helpful for people with Alzheimer's disease. Good sources of lecithin (which contains choline) are dandelion, fenugreek, ginkgo, sage and stinging nettle.

Cruciferous vegetables: The name given to the *Brassica* genus of vegetables, which includes broccoli, Brussels sprouts, cabbage, cauliflower, collard greens, kale, bok choy, rutabagas, turnips and mustard greens. The plants in this family were named *Cruciferae* because their flower petals grow in a cross shape.

Decoction: A solution made by boiling the woody parts of plants (roots, seeds and bark) in water for 10 to 20 minutes.

Demulcent: A soothing substance taken internally to protect damaged tissue. *Examples: barley, cucumbers, fenugreek, figs, honey and marshmallow.*

Depurative: Herbs taken to cleanse the blood. *Examples: burdock, dandelion root, garlic, onion, stinging nettles and yellow dock.*

Diaphoretic: A substance that induces sweating. *Examples: cayenne, cinnamon, German chamomile and ginger.*

Digestive: A substance that aids digestion. (See also Digestive System, page 18.)

Diuretic: A substance that increases the flow of urine. These are meant to be used in the short term only. *Examples: Cucumbers, burdock (root and leaf), dandelion (leaf and root), fennel seeds, lemons, linden, parsley and pumpkin seeds.*

Dysmenorrhea: Menstruation accompanied by cramping pains that may be incapacitating in their intensity.

Elixir: A tonic that invigorates or strengthens the body by stimulating or restoring health.

Ellagic acid: A natural plant phenol (see Phenolic compounds, page 369) thought to have powerful anticancer and antiaging properties. It is found in cherries, grapes, strawberries, and other red, orange or yellow fruits; nuts; seeds; garlic; and onions.

Emetic: A substance taken in large doses to induce vomiting to expel poisons. Small quantities of some emetics, such as salt, nutmeg and mustard, are used often in cooking with no ill effects.

Emmenagogue: A substance that promotes healthy menstruation. *Examples: calendula and German chamomile.*

Enzymes: The elements found in food that act as the catalysts for chemical reactions within the body, allowing efficient digestion and absorption of food and enabling the metabolic processes that support tissue growth, support high energy levels and promote good health. Enzymes are destroyed by heat, but using fruits and vegetables raw in smoothies leaves enzymes intact and readily absorbable.

Essential fatty acids (EFAs): Fat is an essential part of a healthy diet — about 20 fatty acids are used by the human body to maintain normal function. Fats are necessary to maintain healthy skin and hair, transport the fat-soluble vitamins (A, D, E and K) and signal the feeling of fullness after meals. The three fatty acids considered the most important, or essential, are omega-6 linoleic, omega-3 linolenic and gamma linolenic acids. Evidence suggests that increasing the proportion of these fatty acids in the diet may increase immunity and reduce the risks of heart disease, high

blood pressure and arthritis. The best vegetable source of omega-3 EFAs in the diet is flaxseeds. Other sources of EFAs are hemp (seeds and nuts), nuts, seeds, olives, avocados and oily fish.

Expectorant: A substance that relieves mucus congestion caused by colds and flu. *Examples: elder, garlic, ginger, hyssop and thyme.*

Febrigue: Herbs that help reduce fever. *Examples: German chamomile, sage and yarrow.*

Fiber: An indigestible carbohydrate. Fiber protects against intestinal problems and bowel disorders. The best sources are raw fruits and vegetables, seeds and whole grains.

Types of fiber include *pectin*, which reduces the risk of heart disease (by lowering cholesterol) and helps eliminate toxins. It is found mainly in fruits, such as apples, berries and citrus fruits; vegetables; and dried legumes. *Cellulose* prevents varicose veins, constipation and colitis and plays a role in deflecting colon cancer. Because cellulose is found in the outermost layers of fruits and vegetables, it is important to buy only organic produce and leave the peels on. The *hemicellulose* in fruits, vegetables and grains aids in weight loss, prevents constipation, lowers the risk of colon cancer and helps remove cancer-forming toxins from the intestinal tract. *Lignin*, a fiber known to lower cholesterol, prevent gallstone formation and help people with diabetes, is found only in fruits, vegetables and Brazil nuts.

When raw fresh whole fruits or vegetables are used in smoothies, the pulp, or fiber, is still present in the drink and provides all the health benefits listed above.

Flavonoids: These phytochemicals (e.g., genistein and quercetin) are antioxidants that have been shown to inhibit cholesterol production. They are found in cruciferous vegetables (see Cruciferous vegetables, page 367), onions and garlic.

Food Combining: See page 24.

Free radical: A highly unstable compound that attacks cell membranes and causes cell breakdown, aging and a predisposition to some diseases. Free radicals come from the environment as a result of exposure to radiation, ultraviolet (UV) light, smoke, ozone and certain medications. Free radicals are also formed in the body by enzymes and during the conversion of food to energy. See also Antioxidant, page 367.

Gluten: A protein found in wheat that is responsible for keeping bread dough from collapsing during baking. It may cause allergic reactions in some people. Winter hard wheat (used for bread flour blends) contains more gluten than summer soft wheat (used for cake and pastry flours).

Hemicellulose: See Fiber, above.

Hepatic: Herbs that strengthen, tone and stimulate secretive functions of the liver. *Examples: dandelion, lemon balm, milk thistle, rosemary and turmeric.*

Hypotensive: A substance that lowers blood pressure. *Examples: garlic, hawthorn, linden flower and yarrow.*

Immunostimulant: A substance that assists the immune system.

Indole: A phytochemical found in cruciferous vegetables (see Cruciferous vegetables, page 367) that may help prevent cancer by detoxifying carcinogens.

Isoflavone: A phytoestrogen, or the plant version of the human hormone estrogen, that is found in nuts, soybeans and legumes. Isoflavones help prevent several types of cancer — including pancreatic, colon, breast and prostate cancers — by preserving vitamin C in the body and acting as antioxidants.

Lactose intolerance: Deficiency of the enzyme lactase, which breaks down lactose, the sugar in both cow's and human milk. If you don't have sufficient lactase, milk sugar will ferment in the large intestine, causing bloating, diarrhea, abdominal pain and gas.

Laxative: A substance that stimulates bowel movements. Laxatives are meant to be used in the short term only. *Examples: dandelion root, licorice root, prunes, rhubarb and yellow dock.*

Lignin: See Fiber, page 368.

Limonene: A type of Limonoid (see Terpene) thought to assist in detoxifying the liver and prevent cancer. *Examples: grapefruit, lemons, limes and tangerines.*

Limonoid: A subclass of terpenes (see Terpene, page 370) found in citrus fruit rinds.

Lutein: A carotenoid (see Beta-Carotene, page 367) found in beet greens; collard greens; mustard greens; and other red, orange and yellow vegetables.

Lycopene: An antioxidant carotenoid (see Beta-carotene, page 367) that's relatively rare in food. High levels are found, however, in tomatoes, pink grapefruit and watermelon. Lycopene is thought to reduce the effects of aging by maintaining physical and mental function and to reduce the risk of some forms of cancer.

Lysine: An amino acid that controls protein absorption in the body. Lysine is higher in amaranth than any other complex carbohydrate.

Macrobiotic diet: Eating whole food that is seasonal and produced locally. Whole grains, vegetables, fruits (except tropical fruits), legumes, small amounts of fish or organic meat, sea herbs, nuts and seeds are appropriate foods for North Americans who eat macrobiotically.

Metabolism: The rate at which the body produces energy (or burns calories). It is measured by the amount of heat produced by the body, at rest or engaged in various activities, while maintaining its normal temperature.

Milk allergy: Many individuals, especially babies and young children, have allergic reactions to the protein in cow's milk, which causes wheezing, eczema, rashes, mucus buildup and asthma-like symptoms.

Mucilage: A thick, sticky, glue-like substance found in high concentrations in some herbs, which contains and helps spread the active ingredients of those herbs while soothing inflamed surfaces. *Examples: marshmallow and slippery elm.*

Mucopolysaccharides: Carbohydrates that aid in blood clotting and stimulate the body's immune system to increase resistance to infection. *Example: spelt.*

Nervine: A substance that eases anxiety and stress and nourishes the nerves by strengthening nerve fibers. *Examples: German chamomile, lemon balm, oats, skullcap, St. John's wort, thyme and valerian.*

Nonreactive cooking utensils: The acids in foods can react with certain materials and promote the oxidation of some nutrients, as well as discolor the materials themselves. Nonreactive materials suitable for brewing teas are glass, enameled cast iron or enameled stainless steel. While cast-iron pans are recommended for cooking (a meal cooked in unglazed cast iron can provide 20% of the recommended daily intake of iron), and stainless steel is a nonreactive cooking material, neither is recommended for brewing or steeping teas.

Omega-3 Fatty Acids: Polyunsaturated fatty acids found in oily fish and some vegetables, important for heart health. The body doesn't manufacture them. (See also Essential Fatty Acids, page 368.)

Organosulfides: Compounds that have been shown to reduce blood pressure, lower cholesterol levels and reduce blood clotting. *Examples: garlic and onions.*

Pectin: A type of fiber that helps to lower both cholesterol and colon cancer. Apples are high in pectin.

Phenolic compounds: Found in red wine, phenolic compounds, including catechins, anthocyanins, ellagic acid and tannins, can prevent the oxidation of "bad" low-density lipoprotein (LDL) cholesterol, thus reducing the risk of heart disease.

Phytochemicals: Chemicals that come from plants. *Phyto,* from the Greek, means "to bring forth" and is used as a prefix to mean "from a plant."

Proanthocyanidins: Phytonutrients that may contribute to the maintenance of urinary tract and heart health. *Examples: apples and cranberries.*

Protein: The building block of body tissues. Protein is necessary for healthy growth, cell repair, reproduction and protection against infection. Protein consists of 22 parts called amino acids. Eight of the 22 amino acids in protein are especially important because they can not be manufactured by the body. Those eight are called essential amino acids.

A food that contains all eight essential amino acids is said to be a complete protein. Protein from animal products — meat, fish, poultry and dairy products — is complete. The only accepted plant sources of complete protein are soybeans and soy products, but research is establishing new theories that the protein content of legumes may be complete enough to replace animal protein.

A food that contains some, but not all, eight essential amino acids is called an incomplete protein. Nuts, seeds, legumes, cereals and grains are plant products that provide incomplete proteins. If your meals include foods from two complementary incomplete protein sources, your body will combine the incomplete proteins in the right proportions to make a complete protein. For example, many cultures have a tradition of using legumes and whole grains together in dishes. Scientifically, this combination provides a good amino-acid (complete protein) balance in the diet, because legumes are low in methionine but high in lysine, and whole grains are high in methionine but low in lysine. When eaten together, the body combines them to make complete proteins. Nuts and seeds must be paired with dairy or soy proteins in order to provide complete proteins.

Purgative: A substance that promotes bowel movements and increased intestinal peristalsis. *Example: Yellow dock.*

Quercetin: See Flavonoid, page 368.

Resveratrol: A fungicide that occurs naturally in grapes and has been linked to the prevention of clogged arteries by lowering blood cholesterol levels. Resveratrol is found in red wine and, to a lesser extent, in purple grape juice.

Rhizome: An underground stem that is usually thick and fleshy. *Examples: ginger and turmeric.*

Rubefacient: A substance that, when applied to the skin, stimulates circulation in that area, bringing a good supply of blood to the skin and increasing heat in the tissue. *Examples: cayenne, garlic, ginger, mustard seeds; and oils of peppermint, rosemary and thyme.*

Sedative: A substance that has a powerful quieting effect on the nervous system that relieves tension and induces sleep. *Examples: German chamomile, lettuce, linden, lavender and valerian.*

Stimulant: A substance that focuses the mind and increases activity. *Examples: basil, cayenne, cinnamon, peppermint and rosemary.*

Styptic: Herbs causing capillaries to contract and thereby stop superficial hemorrhage bleeding. *Examples: calendula and cayenne.*

Tannin: A chemical constituent in herbs that causes astringency (see Astringent, page 367) and helps stanch internal bleeding. See also Phenolic compounds, page 369. *Examples: coffee, tea and witch hazel.*

Tea: Strictly speaking, "tea" refers to a solution made by pouring boiling water on the fermented leaves and stems of a plant which have been allowed to dry after fermentation (green or black tea). The term is often used when referring to a solution made by pouring boiling water on any plant's leaves, petals or stems. (See also Tea, page 120.)

Terpene: A class of phytochemicals found in a wide variety of fruits, vegetables and herbs that are potent antioxidants. Ginkgo biloba is a good source of some terpenes. Limonoids (see Limonoid, page 369), which are found in citrus fruit rinds, are a subclass of terpenes.

Therapeutic dose: Amount recommended by herbalist for healing certain ailments, usually higher and for longer periods of time than herbs used in cooking (which maintain health). Standardized amounts of specific herbs are used.

Tincture: A liquid herbal extract made by soaking an herb in alcohol and pure water to extract the plant's active components. Some herbalists maintain that tinctures are the most effective way to take herbs, because they contain a wide range of the plant's chemical constituents and are easily absorbed.

Tisane: The "official" term used for a solution made by steeping fresh or dried herbs in boiling water. The term is interchangeable with the word *tea* when herbs are used.

Tonic: An infusion of herbs that tones or strengthens the system. Often tonics act as alteratives (see Alterative, page 367). Taken either hot or cold, tonics purify the blood and are nutritive. Tonic herbs support the body's systems in maintaining health. *Examples: alfalfa, astragalus, dandelion (root and leaf) and ginseng.*

Vasodilator: A substance that relaxes blood vessels, increasing circulation to the arms, hands, legs, feet and brain. *Examples: peppermint and sage.*

Volatile oil: Essential component found in the aerial parts of an herb. Often extracted to make essential oils, volatile oils are antiseptic and very effective at stimulating the body parts to which they are applied.

Vulnerary: An herbal remedy that helps to heal external wounds and reduce inflammation. *Examples: aloe vera, calendula, comfrey, marshmallow root and slippery elm bark powder.*

Whole foods: The most nutrient-rich form of foods. They are as close to their natural state as possible. (See also Whole Foods, page 57.)

Wildcrafting: The practice of gathering herbs from the wild. Many plants today are endangered because of excessive wildcrafting. To avoid contributing to this problem, buy herbs that are organically cultivated.

Sources

Herb and Organic Associations, Organizations, Agencies

Canadian Organic Growers (COG)
Box 6408, Station J
Ottawa, ON
Canada, K2A 3Y6
Tel (613) 231 9047
www.cog.ca
Canada's national information network for organic farmers, gardeners and consumers.

Herb Society of America (HSA)
9019 Chardon Road
Kirtland, OH 44094 USA
Tel (440) 256 0514
Fax (440) 256 0541
www.herbsociety.org
A well-organized group of herb enthusiasts with 6 Districts and many active local units.

International Herb Association (IHA)
910 Charles Street
Fredericksburg, VA 22401 USA
Tel (540) 368 0590
Fax (540) 370 0015
www.iherb.org
A professional organization of herb growers and business owners.

Organic Trade Association (OTA)
P.O. Box 547
Greenfield, MA 01302-0547 USA
Tel (413) 774 7511
Fax (413) 774 6432
www.ota.com
Promotes awareness and understanding of organic production, as well as providing a unified voice for the industry.

Herb Farms and Herb Mail-Order Sources

Frontier Natural Brands
3021 78th Street
PO Box 299
Norway, IA 52318
Tel (319) 227-7996
Fax (319) 227-7966
www.frontiercoop.com
Supplier of bulk herbs.

Jekka's Herb Farm
Rose Cottage
Shellards Lane
Alveston,
Bristol BS35 3SY, UK
Tel 01454 418 878
Fax 01454 411 988
www.jekkasherbfarm.com
Supplier of organic plants and seeds.

Laurel Farm Herbs
Main Road, Kelsale
Saxmundham
Suffolk IP17 2RG, UK
Tel 01728 668 223
Fax 01728 668 468
www.theherbfarm.co.uk
Wide range of herb plants for shipping.

Mountain Rose Herbs
85472 Dilley Lane
Eugene, OR 97405 USA
Tel (800) 879 3337
Fax (510) 217 4012
www.mountainroseherbs.com
Bulk organic herbs, oils, butters, clays, teas (mail order).

Narina Farms
RR#2 S59C10 Smithers BC
Canada, V0J 2N0
Fax (205) 847-3698
www.narniafarms.bc.ca
Organic seasonings, vinegars, mustard, honey, jellies, syrups.

Richters Herbs
357 Highway 47
Goodwood, ON
Canada, L0C 1A0
Tel (905) 640 6677
Fax (905) 640 6641
www.richters.com
Herb specialists with over 800 varieties, selling herbs since 1969. Mail order seeds, plants, books. Free color catalogue, seminars and herbal events.

Related Consumer Websites

www.biodynamics.com
Information about biodynamic gardening and farming.

www.cog.ca
Canadian Organic Growers, a national membership-based organization representing farmers, gardeners and consumers in all provinces. Click on "Where to Buy Organics" for lists of Canadian organic growers and retailers.

www.davidsuzuki.org
A site dedicated to helping people choose solutions that will benefit the planet.

www.demeter.net
The biodynamic certifying body, Demeter.

www.ewg.org
Environmental Working Group (US based).

www.localharvest.org
Lists organic growers and producers with a map and locator to find what's grown closest to you. Use the website to find local farmers' markets and family farms in your area and other sources of food grown by sustainable methods.

www.mcspotlight.org/media/reports/surgen_rep.html
Gives extracts of the Surgeon General's Report on Nutrition and Health.

www.ocia.org
Organic Crop Improvement Association – one of the organic food international certification bodies.

www.ofrf.org
Organic Farming Research Foundation – sponsors research related to organic farming practices.

www.OrganicConsumers.org
Activist organization with information and action strategies for organic, genetically modified foods, irradiation, mad cow and other issues.

www.rodaleinstitute.org
In the mid 1900s, J. J. Rodale developed an emphasis on health and organic gardening through his publications and the Rodale family institute.

www.seedsofchange.com
Provides seeds, information and tools for organic gardening as well as organic grains, sauces and other foods.

www.thinkvegetables.co.uk
A very good source of information about vegetables with a nutrient search and recipes for each vegetable.

www.whfoods.com
The "world's healthiest foods" site is provided by the George Mateljan Foundation, a non-profit organization that lists the nutrients and scientific information on whole foods. Recipes, tips and other non-biased information are available here.

Bibliography

Ameye, L.G., et al. *Osteoarthritis and Nutrition. From neutraceuticals to functional foods: a systemic review of the scientific evidence.* Arthritis Research and Therapy 2006 July 19;8(4): R127.

Applegate, L. *101 Miracle Foods That Heal Your Heart.* Paramus, NJ: Prentice Hall Press, 2000.

Balch, P., Balch J. *Prescription for Dietary Wellness.* Greenfield, IN: PAB Books, 1993.

Baumel, S. *Dealing with Depression Naturally.* New Canaan, CN: Keats Publishing, Inc, 1995.

Berkson, D.L. *Healthy Digestion the Natural Way.* New York, NY; John Wiley & Sons, Inc., 2000.

Boik, J. *Cancer & Natural Medicine (A Textbook of Basic Science and Research).* Princeton MN: Oregon Medical Press, 1995.

Carper, Jean. *Food your Miracle Medicine.* New York NY: Harper Collins Publishers Inc, 1993.

Challem, J., et al. *The Complete Nutritional Program to Prevent and Reverse Insulin Resistance Syndrome X.* New York, NY: John Wiley & Sons Inc, 2000.

Crocker, Pat. *Oregano.* Neustadt ON: Riversong Studios, 2005.

_____ *Tastes of the Kasbah.* Neustadt ON: Riversong Studios, 2005.

_____ *The Smoothies Bible.* Toronto ON: Robert Rose, 2003.

_____ *The Juicing Bible.* Toronto ON: Robert Rose, 2000.

Dalais F.S., et al. *Effects of a diet rich in phytoestrogens on prostate-specific antigen and sex hormones in men diagnosed with prostate cancer.* Urology. 2004 Sept; 64(3): 510-5.

Davis, Holly. *Nourish.* Toronto ON: Ten Speed Press, 1999.

DeBaggio, Thomas and Arthur O. Tucker, Ph.D. *The Big Book of Herbs.* Emmaus, PA: Rodale Press, 1997.

Dikasso D., et al. *Investigation on the antibacterial properties of garlic (Allium sativum) on pneumonia causing bacteria.* Ethiopian Medical Journal 2002 July; 40(3): 241-9.

Duke, James, Ph.D. *The Green Pharmacy.* Loveland, CO: Interweave Press, 2000.

Elkins, Rita. *Depression and Natural Medicine.* Pleasant Grove, UT: Woodland, Publishing Inc., 1995.

Estruch R., et al. *Effects of a Mediterranean-Style Diet on Cardiovascular Risk Factors.* Annals of Internal Medicine. 2006; 145: 1-11.

Fang, N., et al. *Inhibition of growth and induction of apoptosis in human cancer cell lines by an ethyl acetate fraction from shiitake mushrooms.* Journal of Alternative and Complementary Medicine 2006 Mar; 12(2):125-32.

Foster, Steven. *Herbal Renaissance: Growing, Using and Understanding Herbs in the Modern World.* Layton, Utah: Gibbs Smith, 1992.

Foster, Steven and Rebecca Johnson. *National Geographic Desk Reference to Nature's Medicine.* Washington, D.C.: National Geographic, 2006.

Fulghum, Bruce D. and M. Grossan. *The Sinus Cure.* New York, NY: Ballantine Books, 2001.

Gerras, Charles, Editor. *Rodale's Basic Natural Foods Cookbook.* Emmaus, PA: Rodale Press, 1978.

Goldberg, B. *Alternative Medicine Guide to Heart Disease, Stroke and High Blood Pressure.* Tiburon, CA: Future Medicine Publishing, 1998.

Halvorsen, B.L., et al. *Content of redox-active compounds (ie, antioxidants) in foods consumed in the United States.* American Journal of Clinical Nutrition 2006 Jul; 84(1): 95-135.

Hoffman, D. *Healthy Heart Strengthen your Cardiovascular System Naturally.* Pownal, VT: Storey Books, 2000.

Hoffmann, D. *Holistic Herbal.* Boston, MA: Element Books Limited, 1996.

Hudson et al. *Characterization of potentially chemoprotective phenols in extracts of brown rice that inhibit the growth of human breast and colon cancer cells.* Cancer Epidemiology Biomarkers and Prevention 2000 Nov; 9(11): 1163-70.

Hudson, T. *Women's Encyclopedia of Natural Medicine.* Los Angeles, CA: Keats Publishing, 1999.

Ivker, R.S., Nelson, T. *Asthma Survival.* New York, NY: Tarcher/Putman, 2001.

James, M.J., et al. *Dietary polyunsaturated fatty acids and inflammatory mediator production.* American Journal of Clinical Nutrition 2000 Jan; 71(1 Suppl): 343S-8S. Review.

Joseph, James A., Ph.D., Daniel A. Nadeau, M.D., and Anne Underwood. *The Color Code. A Revolutionary Eating Plan for Optimum Health.* New York, NY: Hyperion, 2002.

Judd, J.T., et al. *Dietary trans fatty acids: effect on plasma lipids and lipoproteins of healthy men and women.* American Journal of Clinical Nutrition, April 1994; 59:861-868.

Kaur, S.D. *The Complete Natural Medicine Guide to Breast Cancer.* Toronto, ON: Robert Rose Inc, 2003.

Kendall-Reed, P. and S. Reed. *Healing Arthritis.* Toronto, ON: CCNM Press, 2004.

Kumar, N.B., et al. *The specific role of isoflavones in reducing prostate cancer risk.* Prostate. 2004 May 1; 59(2): 141-7.

Kumar, P., et al. *Effect of quercetin supplementation on lung antioxidants after experimental influenza virus infection.* Experimental Lung Research 2005 June; 31(5): 449-59.

Lininger, S., Wright, J., Austin, S., Brown, D., Gaby, A. *The Natural Pharmacy.* Rocklin, CA: Prima Health Division of Publishing, 1998.

Logan, A. *Neurobehavioral Aspects of Omega-3 fatty acids: possible mechanisms and Therapeutic Value in Major Depression.* Alternative Medicine Review 2003;8(4): 410-425.

Lycopene. Alternative Medicine Review 2003; 8(3): 336-342.

Makabe, H., et al. *Anti-inflammatory sesquiterpenes from Curcuma zedoaria.* Journal of Asian Natural Products Research 2006 June; 20(7): 680-5.

Mickleborough, T.D., et al. *Protective effect of fish oil supplementation on exercise-induced bronchoconstriction in asthma.* Chest. 2006 Jan; 129(1): 39-49.

Miller, A.L., et al. *Homocysteine Metabolism: Nutritional Modulation and Impact on Health and Disease.* Alternative Medicine Review 1997; 2(4): 234-254.

Mozaffarian, D., et al. *Fish Consumption and Stroke Risk in Elderly Individuals: The Cardiovascular Health Study.* Archives of Internal Medicine 2005; 165(2): 200-206.

Murray, M. *Diabetes and Hypoglycemia.* Rocklin, CA: Prima Health, 1994.

_____*Natural Alternatives to Prozac.* New York, NY: Quill, 1996.

_____Pizzorno J. *Encyclopedia of Natural Medicine 2nd Edition.* Rocklin, CA: Prima Health Division of Publishing, 1998.

Nez Heatherley, Ana. *Healing Plants, A Medicinal Guide to Native North American Plants and Herbs.* Toronto ON: Harper Collins Publishers Ltd., 1998.

O'Connor, D.J. *Understanding Osteoporosis and Clinical Strategies to Assess, Arrest and Restore Bone Loss.* Alternative Medicine Review 1997; 2(1): 36-47.

Ody, Penelope. *The Complete Medicinal Herbal.* Toronto, ON: Key Porter Books, 1993.

_____with A. Lyon and D. Vilinac. *The Chinese Herbal Cookbook. Healing Foods for Inner Balance.* Trumbull, CT: Weatherhill Inc., 2001.

Penny, M., Etherton, K. *Evidence that the antioxidant flavonoids in tea and cocoa are beneficial for cardiovascular health.* Current Opinion in Lipidology. Feb 2002; 13(1): 41-49.

Physicians Committee for Responsible Medicine, Melina V. *Healthy Eating for Life to Prevent and Treat Cancer.* New York, NY: John Wiley & Sons Inc., 2002.

Pitchford, Paul. *Healing with Whole Foods: Oriental Traditions and Modern Nutrition.* Berkeley CA: North Atlantic Books, 1993.

Prousky, J. *Anxiety Orthomolecular Diagnosis and Treatment.* Toronto, ON: CCNM Press, 2003.

Quercitin, Alternative Medicine Review 1998; 3(2): 140-143.

Robertson, Robin and Jon Robertson. *The Sacred Kitchen. Higher Consciousness Cooking for Health and Wholeness.* Novato, CA: New World Library, 1999.

Schroder, F.H., et al. *Randomized, double-blind, placebo-controlled crossover study in men with prostate cancer and rising PSA: effectiveness of a dietary supplement.* European Urology 2005 Dec; 48(6):922-30.

Sinclair, S. Male Infertility: *Nutritional and Environmental Considerations.* Alternative Medicine Review 2000; 5(1):28-38.

Sussman, Vic. *The Vegetarian Alternative.* Emmaus PA: Rodale Press, 1978.

Turner, Lisa. *Meals That Heal.* Rochester VT: Healing Arts Press, 1998.

Vanderhaeghe, L.R. and K. Karst. *Healthy Fats for Life Preventing and Treating Common Health Problems with Essential Fatty Acids.* Kingston, ON: Quarry Health Books, 2003.

_____Bouic, P.J.D. *The Immune System Cure.* Toronto, ON: Prentice Hall Canada, 1999.

_____*Healthy Immunity Scientifically Proven Natural Treatments for conditions A-Z,* Toronto. ON: Macmillan, 2001.

Whitaker, J. *The Memory Solution.* Garden City Park, NY: Avery Publishing Group, 1999.

Zampieron, E., E. Kamhi and B. Goldman. *Alternative Medicine Guide to Arthritis.* Tiburon, CA: AlternativeMedicine.com Books, 1999.

Library and Archives Canada Cataloguing in Publication

Crocker, Pat
   The vegetarian cook's bible / Pat Crocker.

Includes index.
ISBN-13: 978-0-7788-0153-5
ISBN-10: 0-7788-0153-5

1. Vegetarian cookery. 2. Vegetarianism. I. Title.

TX837.C75 2007   641.5'636   C2006-905909-8

Index